CAMBRIDGE LIBRARY COLLECTION

Books of enduring scholarly value

Printing and Publishing History

The interface between authors and their readers is a fascinating subject in its own right, revealing a great deal about social attitudes, technological progress, aesthetic values, fashionable interests, political positions, economic constraints, and individual personalities. This part of the Cambridge Library Collection reissues classic studies in the area of printing and publishing history that shed light on developments in typography and book design, printing and binding, the rise and fall of publishing houses and periodicals, and the roles of authors and illustrators. It documents the ebb and flow of the book trade supplying a wide range of customers with products from almanacs to novels, bibles to erotica, and poetry to statistics.

White Knights Library

The dispersal of the library amassed by George Spencer-Churchill (1766–1840), Marquess of Blandford and later fifth Duke of Malborough, is most commonly cited today as a preservative against folly. The collection contained some of the most sought-after incunabula of a period defined by the high prices paid for early printed books. It included a fine selection of Caxtons, spectacular botanical and emblem books, and the iconic Valdarfer Boccaccio – the first edition of the *Decameron*, purchased by Blandford in 1812 for the unprecedented sum of £2,260. The Boccaccio was symptomatic of the profligate expenditure of its buyer. By 1819 his spendthrift ways had ruined him, leading to the sale of his opulent estate at Whiteknights, near Reading, and the dispersal of one of the key libraries in the era of bibliomania. Reissued here together are the two parts of the auction catalogue, both annotated by an auction attendee who recorded details of the purchasers and the prices paid. Ed Potten, Head of Rare Books at Cambridge University Library, has provided a new introduction that places the catalogue in its wider context.

Cambridge University Press has long been a pioneer in the reissuing of out-of-print titles from its own backlist, producing digital reprints of books that are still sought after by scholars and students but could not be reprinted economically using traditional technology. The Cambridge Library Collection extends this activity to a wider range of books which are still of importance to researchers and professionals, either for the source material they contain, or as landmarks in the history of their academic discipline.

Drawing from the world-renowned collections in the Cambridge University Library and other partner libraries, and guided by the advice of experts in each subject area, Cambridge University Press is using state-of-the-art scanning machines in its own Printing House to capture the content of each book selected for inclusion. The files are processed to give a consistently clear, crisp image, and the books finished to the high quality standard for which the Press is recognised around the world. The latest print-on-demand technology ensures that the books will remain available indefinitely, and that orders for single or multiple copies can quickly be supplied.

The Cambridge Library Collection brings back to life books of enduring scholarly value (including out-of-copyright works originally issued by other publishers) across a wide range of disciplines in the humanities and social sciences and in science and technology.

White Knights Library

Catalogue of that Distinguished and Celebrated Library Which Will Be Sold by Auction

Robert Harding Evans

CAMBRIDGE
UNIVERSITY PRESS

University Printing House, Cambridge, CB2 8BS, United Kingdom

Published in the United States of America by Cambridge University Press, New York

Cambridge University Press is part of the University of Cambridge.
It furthers the University's mission by disseminating knowledge in the pursuit of education, learning and research at the highest international levels of excellence.

www.cambridge.org
Information on this title: www.cambridge.org/9781108065986

This edition first published 1819
This digitally printed version 2014

ISBN 978-1-108-06598-6 Paperback

Selected books of related interest, also reissued in the CAMBRIDGE LIBRARY COLLECTION

Anonymous: *Catalogue of the Valuable Library of the Late Rev. Henry Richards Luard* (1891) [ISBN 9781108057295]

Baker and Leigh: *Bibliotheca Askeviana* (1774–84) [ISBN 9781108065849]

Bodleian Library: *A Catalogue of the Books Relating to British Topography, and Saxon and Northern Literature* (1814) [ISBN 9781108057318]

Christie, James: *Bibliotheca Ratcliffiana* (1776) [ISBN 9781108065825]

Clark, John Willis: *The Care of Books* (1902) [ISBN 9781108005081]

Curwen, Henry: *A History of Booksellers* (1874) [ISBN 9781108021432]

Dee, John, edited by James Orchard Halliwell, James Crossley, John Eglington Bailey and M.R. James: *John Dee's Diary, Catalogue of Manuscripts and Selected Letters* (1842, 1851, 1880, 1921) [ISBN 9781108050562]

Dibdin, Thomas Frognall: *Bibliomania* (1811) [ISBN 9781108015806]

Dibdin, Thomas Frognall: *Bibliophobia* (1832) [ISBN 9781108015592]

Dibdin, Thomas Frognall: *Bibliotheca Spenceriana* (4 vols., 1814–15) [ISBN 9781108051118]

Dibdin, Thomas Frognall: *Reminiscences of a Literary Life* (2 vols., 1836) [ISBN 9781108009355]

Duff, E. Gordon: *A Century of the English Book Trade* (1905) [ISBN 9781108026765]

Duff, E. Gordon: *Early Printed Books* (1893) [ISBN 9781108026741]

Edwards, Edward: *Free Town Libraries, their Formation, Management, and History* (1869) [ISBN 9781108009362]

Edwards, Edward: *Libraries and Founders of Libraries* (1864) [ISBN 9781108010528]

Edwards, Edward: *Memoirs of Libraries* (3 vols., 1859) [ISBN 9781108010566]

Evans, Robert Harding: *A Catalogue of the Library of the Late John, Duke of Roxburghe* (1812) [ISBN 9781108065832]

Evans, Robert Harding: *White Knights Library* (1819) [ISBN 9781108065986]

Fagan, Louis: *The Life of Sir Anthony Panizzi, K.C.B.* (2 vols., 1880) [ISBN 9781108044912]

King, Thomas: *Bibliotheca Farmeriana* (1798) [ISBN 9781108065993]

Oates, J.C.T.: *Catalogue of the Fifteenth-Century Printed Books in the University Library, Cambridge* (2 vols., 1954) [ISBN 9781108008488]

Sayle, C.E.: *Early English Printed Books in the University Library, Cambridge* (4 vols., 1900–7) [ISBN 9781108007818]

Wheatley, Henry Benjamin: *How to Form a Library* (1886) [ISBN 9781108021494]

Wheatley, Henry Benjamin: *How to Catalogue a Library* (1889) [ISBN 9781108021487]

For a complete list of titles in the Cambridge Library Collection please visit:
www.cambridge.org/features/CambridgeLibraryCollection/books.htm

Introduction

Ed Potten, Head of Rare Books,
Cambridge University Library

The library amassed by George Spencer-Churchill (1766–1840), Marquess of Blandford and later fifth Duke of Marlborough, is one of the behemoths of the bibliomania, but is now primarily remembered as an example of the folly of noble collectors. Blandford's activities at the 1812 sale of the library of John Ker, third Duke of Roxburghe, gained him a notoriety which has lasted centuries. The Roxburghe sale broke all records. For the first time at a British auction, books changed hands for more than £1,000, but the crowning glory of the sale was the epic contest between Blandford and George John, second Earl Spencer (1758–1834), for the iconic Valdarfer Boccaccio, the *editio princeps* of the *Decameron*. Blandford was the victor, paying the unheard-of sum of £2,260 for the then unique *Decameron*. The event was national news, and was immediately eulogised, hyperbolised and mythologised by Thomas Frognall Dibdin:

> LORENZO: I can anticipate the *important article* in the favourite class of collection to which you bring us. The DECAMERON of BOCCACCIO!?
>
> LISARDO: 'Tis bravely conjectured, my Lorenzo: yes ... when the hammer fell at *Two Thousand Two Hundred and Sixty Pounds* upon the VALDARFER BOCCACCIO of 1471, the spectators stood aghast! – and the sound of Mr. Evans's prostrate sceptre of dominion reached, and resounded from, the utmost shores of Italy. The echo of that fallen hammer was heard in the libraries of Rome, of Milan, and St. Mark. Boccaccio himself startled from his slumber of some five hundred years.[1]

The price paid by Blandford caused outrage in some circles. *The Times* concluded:

> We can only say that it is a lamentably erroneous way of indicating the love of learning, to give immense prices for rare or old editions, which do not even possess equal means of infusing knowledge with the modern or common ones. It would be a better testimony of a correct taste, to study useful, than to purchase scarce books.

Francis Douce, meanwhile, branded Blandford 'a mad collector of books who never reads them'.[2]

Blandford's extravagance in acquiring the Valdarfer Boccaccio was not an isolated event. His name appears frequently in the auction records of the period – often using his agent Triphook to bid to secure a rarity 'not known to Ames'[3] – and his library contained some of the most sought-after incunabula of a period defined by the high

1 T.F. Dibdin, *Bibliographical Decameron* (London: 1817) vol. 3, pp.62–5.

2 K. Jensen, *Revolution and the Antiquarian Book* (Cambridge: 2012) p.129.

3 Not in J. Ames, *Typographical Antiquities: Being an Historical Account of Printing in England* (London: 1749). Ames' work was greatly supplemented by William Herbert and reissued in 1785–90.

prices paid for pre-1501 books. He amassed a fine collection of Caxtons and other early English books, which included copies of the 1476 *Propositio ad Carolum ducem Burgundiae* (today recorded in only two copies), the 1490 *Art and Craft to Know Well to Die*, the 1483 *Pylgremage of the Sowle*, and the 1474 *Play of Chess*. The library also contained some impressive and significant manuscripts: a ninth-century *Evangelia*, two manuscripts of the tenth century, a Wycliffite Revelation and, perhaps its crowning glory, the Bedford Hours, secured by Blandford in 1815 from the library of James Edwards for £687 15s.[4]

The *Bibliotheca Blandfordiensis* was not Blandford's only extravagance; he was equally profligate in other spheres of life. In 1798 he purchased the estate of White-knights, Berkshire, from William Byam Martin, and over the ensuing twenty years poured money into redesigning the house, grounds and gardens. The mid-eighteenth-century house was redecorated and populated with paintings by Old Masters, Titian, Guido, Carracci, Tintoretto, Caravaggio, Rembrandt and Holbein, alongside the best and most fashionable British art by such figures as Gainsborough, Reynolds and Romney. The Grecian Room was typical:

> admirably painted to represent verde antique columns of the Ionic order, upon a ground of Sienna marble. The chimney-piece, of white marble, is handsomely wrought ... The curtains, Ottomans, chaises longues, and chairs, are covered with a gold and silver Indian chintz. An upright piano forte, and a beautiful cabinet of the finest French China, correspond on each side of the first door, together with various stands, on which are placed noble jars of gilt Dresden China, silver filigree ornaments ... and most beautiful urns of alabaster, with bronze masks.[5]

The picturesque grounds, landscaped by Sir Henry Englefield in the 1780s, were transformed at huge cost to create a flower garden, a botanic garden, a Japanese garden and a 'Chantilly' garden, an imitation of that at Château de Chantilly. Blandford created an arboretum, a rosery, a vineyard and numerous woodland walks, turning the gardens at Whiteknights into 'the most renowned in Southern England'.[6] Nor was Blandford shy of publicising his extravagance. Between 1812 and 1814 he paid for the production of a privately printed catalogue of his library,[7] and in 1816 he commissioned the landscape painter Thomas Christopher Hofland (1777–1843) to paint Whiteknights. The paintings were engraved by T. Medland and L. Byrne and published in 1819 under the title *A Descriptive Account of the Mansion and Gardens of White-Knights*, the text provided by Hofland's wife.

The publication of *A Descriptive Account* in 1819 is a monument to folly – a poignant example of Blandford's decadent approach to expenditure and his inability to

4 Now British Library Add. MS 18850.

5 B. Hofland & T.C. Hofland, *A Descriptive Account of the Mansion and Gardens of White-Knights* (London: [1819]) pp.33–4.

6 W. Page & P.H. Ditchfield, *The Victoria History of the County of Berkshire*, vol. 3 (London: 1923) pp.210–11.

7 *Catalogus librorum qui in Bibliothecâ Blandfordiensi* ([London: 1812, supplement 1814]).

acknowledge pending disaster. The lavish folio volume describes an estate moulded to the tastes of 'its noble possessor', yet on the cusp of dissolution. By the time it was published, Blandford's finances were in ruins. T.C. Hofland was never paid for his work: 'his only recompense being the profits from the sale of the twenty-three engravings, a fact which still rankled nearly ten years later, after the marquess had succeeded to the title of Duke of Marlborough'.[8] By the end of 1819 the house and many of its contents were on the market.

The sale of the *Bibliotheca Blandfordiensis* is as mythologised as the Roxburghe sale of 1812, but for rather different reasons. If the 1812 purchase of the Valdarfer Boccaccio was seized upon as a defining moment in the bibliomania, its sale from Whiteknights in 1819 marked the beginning of the end of this perceived 'golden' era. Although the 1819 auction was 'brilliantly attended',[9] with Spencer, Richard Heber (1773–1833), and Thomas Grenville (1755–1846) buying heavily, the result is said to have been disappointing. Earl Spencer may have been the underbidder for the Boccaccio in 1812, but he was to have the last laugh, securing it in 1819 for the relative bargain price of £918 15s. Other books acquired by Blandford at the Roxburghe sale failed to make back their purchase price, or barely scraped a profit: lot 1116, a two-volume bind-up of an assortment of Thomas Churchyard's works, several 'not mentioned by Ames or Herbert', was purchased at the Roxburghe sale for £96 and sold in 1819 for £85 1s; lot 1726, *This Mater Treateth of a Merchauntes Wyfe that Afterwarde Went Like a Man and Was Called Frederyke of Jennen* ([Antwerp: 1518])[10] was purchased for £65 2s, yet sold for only £44 12s 6d. The end result certainly appears disappointing, particularly when compared to the Roxburghe sale: the Whiteknights sale raised £14,383 36s, compared to £23,341 from the sale of the Roxburghe books.

The disappointing result, however, may be not quite as it appears. There is no doubt that Blandford was a financial numbskull and paid heavily over the odds for many of the books he owned, but not everything in the Whiteknights sale sold at a loss. Lot 3752, Blandford's unique copy of John Russell's *Propositio clarissimi oratoris* was purchased by him for £52 10s[11] and sold in 1819 for £126, while lot 3799, the highly illuminated manuscript *Recueil des Romans des chevaliere de la Table Ronde* was acquired for £78 15s, then sold for £100. It is worth noting too that comparisons between sales are more complicated than they appear. The Roxburghe sale took place in an atmosphere of fevered excitement, and the final figure raised owes much to the purchase of a handful of items – the Boccaccio and the fifteen Caxtons. The Roxburghe dispersal was also considerably larger than that from Whiteknights – 10,120 items over two sales, compared with only 4,703 from Blandford's library. A rough calculation of the

---

8 T. Wilcox, 'Hofland, Thomas Christopher (1777–1843)', *Oxford Dictionary of National Biography* (Oxford: 2004) [http://www.oxforddnb.com/view/article/13458, accessed 3 April 2013].

9 S. de Ricci, *English Collectors of Books & Manuscripts, 1530–1930, and their Marks of Ownership* (Cambridge: 1930) p.78.

10 ESTC S125703, recorded today in only two copies.

11 Purchased from Triphook – see manuscript note on p.175 of the copy of the Whiteknights auction catalogue reissued in the Cambridge Library Collection.

average price raised per item is enlightening and indicates that a more detailed analysis is needed: Roxburghe's sale averaged out at approximately £2 per book, Blandford's at £3.

What do we know about the library itself? A detailed study of the 1812–14 library catalogue, alongside the 1819 sale catalogue, has yet to be undertaken, but even a cursory glance is informative. The library certainly did contain much which conforms to our idea of the model bibliophilic library. There are copies of all four Shakespeare folios, with twelve of the quartos, alongside some spectacular early printed treasures. There is no denying too that the collection was extremely strong in early English typography, that staple of the early nineteenth-century bibliophile. There are twenty-six English incunabula, including seventeen Caxtons, and a further 360 sixteenth-century English books, many of which are to this day the sole surviving copies.

Looking beyond these stereotypes, however, aspects of the collection appear which are distinctly atypical, or at least unexpected. Yes, there is the Boccaccio, and there are Caxtons, but this is, surprisingly, not a collection strong in fifteenth-century printing, the commodity which most characterises collecting of the period. In 1814 there were around 100 incunabula in the library, a figure which had risen to only 136 by 1819 – hardly a spectacular array when compared with Spencer's contemporary collection of 2,000, and representing only 2.8 per cent of the items sold in 1819. The chronological sweep of the collection overall is telling. One might expect the bulk of the library to be made up of early books, yet on analysis only 30 per cent of the collection comes from the fifteenth and sixteenth centuries, with some 60 per cent printed in the seventeenth and eighteenth centuries. The tally of Aldines is equally telling. From the publication in 1803 of Antoine Augustin Renouard's *Annales de l'imprimerie des Alde,* the collecting of Aldines was a bibliophilic staple. Blandford had a copy of Renouard, but amassed only around forty examples from the press.

With the exception of the English printing, there is little evidence that Blandford collected the monuments of typography – there is no Gutenberg Bible, indeed no printed bibles at all from the incunable period, and relatively few continental incunabula from presses key to the spread and development of printing. Indeed, many of Blandford's continental incunabula appear to have been purchased to fit clear existing subject strengths in the broader collection, rather than as typographic exemplars. When you analyse the books more closely, what appears is not random trophy buying, but rather focussed collecting in a few specific areas.

The collection of emblem books at Whiteknights was justly famous and is as remarkable as one might expect, encompassing not just key antiquarian books, but also contemporary editions and studies. The collection of botanical books and drawings is equally impressive. Blandford had been a keen botanist from the 1790s, corresponding with Joseph Banks, among others, and publishing on the lotus plant. Both the grounds and the library at Whiteknights reflect that this was more than a passing fad. A rapid count identifies more than 200 botanical publications from across Europe, including many, like Blandford's copy of the Schoeffer herbal of 1484, which are decidedly bibliomaniacal. Alongside the treasures, however, lies a well-formed and sophisticated library of contemporary flora, books on agriculture and garden design, plant catalogues, the works of Linnaeus and the other pioneers of classification and morphology, and scientific studies. There is evidence too of a strong interest in Hispanic studies, with around 150 Spanish books, ranging from incunabula to later Spanish literature and romances of all periods, seventeenth- and eighteenth-century Spanish and Portuguese histories, chronicles and travel books, and contemporary dictionaries and grammars for the Spanish language. There is also evidence of a somewhat more learned approach to bibliography than one might have expected from Douce's characterisation, in a small but rich collection of bibliographical books, marked-up auction catalogues and typographic histories.

What of the man? It would be a grave mistake to make the assumption that owning scholarly botanical or bibliographical books necessarily equates to reading them; and from Douce onwards, Blandford has been the epitome of the idle nobleman, reducing his books to objects of luxury. Is this a fair appraisal? Kristian Jensen has noted that Douce's original attack on Blandford was somewhat unjust, pointing out that Douce's own correspondence contains letters from Blandford which display a much more sophisticated interaction between owner and book,[12] while in 1804 Douce himself co-authored a botanical and antiquarian note for *The Botanist's Repository* with Blandford, so at that stage he clearly had no objection to being linked to the mad collector. There is some evidence that Blandford amassed a second library after the Whiteknights sale, albeit on a rather more modest level, indicating that the love of books did not die on 7 June 1819.[13] There is a single book in Oxford which came from this sale and which is perhaps indicative: a copy of Caxton's 1489/90 *The Dictes or Sayengis of the Philosophres*.[14] At present, however, beyond these few hints, we simply do not know whether the appraisal is fair or not; the answer lies in the Blenheim papers.

Beyond the study of the Blandford himself, the marked-up copy of the Whiteknights sale offers interesting insights into the world of collecting and the mechanics of the trade. It is a more detailed document than many of its predecessors, the detail redolent of the tastes of the time. Features designed to catch the eye of the discerning buyer are highlighted in capitals ('LARGE PAPER', 'EXCESSIVELY RARE', 'UNIQUE', 'UNCUT'), much is made of noble or significant provenances ('from the Roxburghe Library', 'from the Merley Library', 'G. Steevens's copy'), binding descriptions are given for many items ('by Derome', 'Roger Payne', 'large paper, elegantly bound in green morocco'), as are suitably tempting bibliographical notes ('this book is printed on the first paper manufactured in England'). There are occasional hints of newly

12 K. Jensen, *Revolution and the Antiquarian Book* (Cambridge: 2012) p.251, note 97.

13 T.A. Birrell has suggested that a sale which took place in Oxford on 28 May 1840 of 'a valuable and extensive collection of books removed from Blenheim' is likely to be Blandford's second library, pointing out that the Sunderland Library at Blenheim at that date was still entailed. See A. Coates, K. Jensen et al., *A Catalogue of Books Printed in the Fifteenth Century Now in the Bodleian Library* (Oxford: 2005) vol. 6, p.2919.

14 Ibid., vol. 3, D-109.

developing tastes and trends in book collecting. It is interesting that in a period characterised by the desire for tall, clean copies in contemporary gilded crushed morocco bindings, early or original bindings are occasionally cited as a selling point. Lot 578, the 1541 Lutheran Bible, for example, is described as 'in the original oak binding, covered with purple velvet, with richly gilt clasps and arms', while lot 2826, a sixteenth-century manuscript *Officium*, is in a 'very rich old morocco binding, in compartments with clasps, in the finest preservation'.

The analysis of the buyers at the 1819 sale confirms de Ricci's observation that it was 'brilliantly attended'. Richard Heber bought particularly heavily, as did Spencer and Thomas Grenville. The activity of agents, particularly Longman, Triphook, Clarke and Payne, is apparent and occasionally offers insights into the complex and interrelated worlds of agents, collectors, friends and employees. Earl Spencer, for example, is represented formally by Longman & Co., his favoured agent, when bidding for the Boccaccio, but by his pet bibliographer Dibdin when bidding for the Russell cited above, and by George Appleyard (d.1855), his secretary and librarian at Althorp and at Spencer House, when bidding for the Edinburgh printing of Boece's *Hystory and Croniklis of Scotland*.[15]

The reissue by Cambridge University Press of a marked-up copy of the Whiteknights auction catalogue offers opportunities to explore in depth one of the key collections of the period, but more important are the opportunities to study the use, trade, movement, distribution and collection of books during a much-maligned and little-studied period in book history – that of the bibliomania.

15 Lots 765, 3752 and 4012 respectively.

WHITE KNIGHTS LIBRARY.

CATALOGUE

OF

THAT DISTINGUISHED AND CELEBRATED

LIBRARY,

CONTAINING

Numerous very fine and rare Specimens from the Presses of

CAXTON, PYNSON, AND WYNKYN DE WORDE, &c.

AN UNRIVALLED COLLECTION OF ITALIAN, SPANISH AND FRENCH ROMANCES OF CHIVALRY, POETRY, AND FACETIÆ.

AN UNIQUE ASSEMBLAGE OF BOOKS OF EMBLEMS, AND BOOKS ORNAMENTED WITH WOOD CUTS.

VERY FINE BOTANICAL WORKS WITH ORIGINAL DRAWINGS.

AND A SELECTION OF RARE, CURIOUS, AND SPLENDID ARTICLES IN EVERY DEPARTMENT OF LITERATURE.

PART I.

WHICH WILL BE

SOLD BY AUCTION,

BY MR. EVANS,

AT HIS HOUSE, No. 26, PALL-MALL,

On Monday, June 7, and Eleven following Days, Sunday excepted.

Catalogues, Price Two Shillings, may be had at the Place of Sale, where the Books may be viewed Four Days prior to the Auction.

1819.

Printed by W. Bulmer and Co.
Cleveland-row, St. James's.

CONDITIONS OF SALE.

I. The highest Bidder to be the Buyer; and if any Dispute arises between two or more Bidders, the Lot so disputed, shall be immediately put up again and re-sold.

II. No Person to advance less than 1*s.*; above Five Pounds 2*s.* 6*d.* and so in Proportion.

III. The Purchasers to give in their Names and Places of Abode, and to pay down 5*s.* in the Pound in Part Payment of the Purchase-money; in Default of which the Lot or Lots so purchased to be immediately put up again and re-sold.

IV. The Lots to be taken away, at the Buyer's Expence, within Three Days after the Conclusion of the Sale; and the remainder of the Purchase-money to be absolutely paid on or before Delivery.

V. The Books are presumed to be perfect, unless otherwise expressed; but if, upon collating, AT THE PLACE OF SALE, any should prove defective, the Purchasers will be at Liberty to take or reject them.

VI. Upon failure of complying with the above Conditions the Money deposited in Part of Payment shall be forfeited, and all Lots uncleared within the Time aforesaid, shall be re-sold by public or private Sale, and the Deficiency (if any) attending such Re-sale, shall be made good by the Defaulters at this Sale.

☞ No Books will be delivered during the time of Sale.

Gentlemen who cannot attend the Sale may have their Commissions faithfully executed by their humble Servant,

R. H. EVANS,

26, *Pall-Mall.*

PART I.

INDEX TO THE DAYS OF SALE.

1st.	Day,— Monday,—	June 7.	471	19	6
2nd.	Day,— Tuesday,—	June 8.	567	15	"
3rd.	Day,— Wednesday,—	June 9.	673	14	6
4th.	Day,— Thursday,—	June 10.	405	6	6
5th.	Day,— Friday,—	June 11.	666	8	6
6th.	Day,— Saturday,—	June 12.	734	5	6
7th.	Day,— Monday,—	June 14.	443	19	"
8th.	Day,— Tuesday,—	June 15.	534	16	"
9th.	Day,— Wednesday,—	June 16.	424	12	6
10th.	Day,— Thursday,—	June 17.	1550	15	6
11th.	Day,— Friday,—	June 18.	420	12	"
12th.	Day,— Saturday,—	June 19.	512	17	"

A

CATALOGUE

OF A

RARE AND SPLENDID LIBRARY.

FIRST DAY'S SALE.

Each Day's Sale will commence PRECISELY AT HALF PAST TWELVE.

Octavo et Infra.

1 Abælardi et Heloissæ Epistolæ, cura Rawlinson, *large paper, russia* - - - - 1718

2 Abraham Von St. Clara, Dutch Emblems of Manufactures, &c. 2 vols. *red morocco* - - *Amst.* 1717

3 Abus des Nuditez de Gorge, *blue morocco* *Bruxelles.* 1675

4 Academie Universelle des Jeux, 3 vols. *Amst.* 1786

5 Academie Galante des Diverses Histoires très Curieuses, 2 vols. in 1 - - - *Amst.* 1732

6 Academy of Compliments, with a Collection of the choicest Songs, *blue morocco* - - 1713

7 Academy of Compliments - - *no date*

8 Achilles Tatius de Clitophontis et Leucippes Amoribus, Salmasii, *red morocco* - *Lugd. Bat.* 1640

9 Achilles Tatius, Gr. et Lat. ex Recensione Boden, *fine paper, yellow morocco* - - *Lipsiæ.* 1776

10 Addison's Miscellaneous Works, and Tour in Italy, 4 vols. 1777

11 Adele de Senange, ou Lettres de Lord Sydenham, 2 vols. *Hambourg.* 1797

12 Adrian le Jeune, les Emblemes de, *Anvers, Plantin.* 1568

13 Adriene, 2 vols. - - *Milan.* 1716

14 Advis Fidelle aux Veritables Hollandois, *scarce, red morocco* 1673

15 Ænigmas, or Riddles, a Collection of - 1725

16 Æsopi Fabulæ, Gr. et Lat. cum Figuris, *green morocco* *Lugduni.* 1609

17 Æsopi Fabulæ, Gr. et Lat. Neveleti, *cuts, blue morocco* *Francof.* 1610

18 Æsopi Fabulæ, Gr. et Lat, *cuts* - *Amst.* 1726

19 Æsopicarum Fabularum Delectus, Gr. et Lat. ab Alsop, large paper, *red morocco*, by ROGER PAYNE *Oxon.* 1698

20 Æsopicarum Fabularum Collectio, Gr. et Lat. Hudsoni, *large paper, red morocco, with joints* *Oxon.* 1718

21 Esopo, Fabule Historiate, Lat. et Ital. à Zucho, *wood cuts, red morocco, with red morocco inside,* RARE *Venetiis per Simonem de Prello.* 1533

22 Esopo Vita e Favole, da Làndi, *wood cuts, yellow morocco* *Venet.* 1575

23 Esopo Vida y Fabulas Exemplares, traducidas en Rimas Castellanas, por Antonio de Arfe, *wood cuts, morocco* *Sevilla.* 1682

24 Esope's, Aryan's, Alfonce's, and Poge's Fables, in Englishe, *black letter* - *London, by H. Wykes*

25 Æsop's Fables and Life, 2 vols. *plates, green morocco, with joints* - - - - 1793

26 Esop, select Fables of - - - - 1761

27 Esope, Fables de, en Prose et en Vers, 2 vols. *cuts* *Bruss.* 1700

28 Agrippa de la Noblesse et Pre-excellence du Sexe Femenin *Par. sans date.*

29 Aikin's (Miss) Poems - - 1777

30 Aikin's Poems, *red morocco* - - 1791

31 Alamanni, Opere Toscane de, *red morocco* *Lugd. Gryphius.* 1532

32 Albertini Emblemata, a Melitano - *Coloniæ.* 1647

33 Alciati Emblemata, Lat. et Germanicè, per Wolphgangum Hungerum, - - - *Par.* 1542

34 ——————— *blue morocco, with joints* *Par. Wechel.* 1544

35 ——————— - - *Venet. Aldus.* 1546

36 ——————— *Lugd. Rovillio,* 1551. Sambuci Emblemata cum aliquot Nummis Antiqui Operis, *Ant. Plantin.* 1564. 2 vols. in 1, *blue morocco, joints, fine impressions of the plates,*

37 ——————— - *Lugd. Rovillio.* 1564

37* ——————— - - *Ib.* 1564

38 ——————— cura Stockameri, *red morocco, joints* *Ant. Plantin.* 1565

39 ——————— ab Autore postremo recognita, *blue morocco, joints* - - *Francof.* 1583

40 ——————— et Vita per Cl. Minoem, *blue morocco, with joints* - - *Ant. Plantin.* 1584

40* ——————— ———————

41 ——————— per Cl. Minoem, *Lugd. Bat.* 1591. Hadriani Junii Emblemata, *Plantin.* 1596. Sambuci Emblemata, *Plantin.* 1599. 3 vols. in 1

42 ——————— cum Append. nusquam antea Editis per Cl. Minoem, *russia, gilt leaves* - *Par.* 1602

43 Alciati Emblemata - - Par. 1608

44 ———— cum Comment. Minois, *russia, gilt leaves* - - - Plantin. 1608

45 ———— - - Patavii. 1618

46 ———— et Vita per Minoem, *blue morocco, with joints* - - Ant. Plantin. 1648

47 Alciato, Embleme di, Lat. et Ital. *russia* Padova. 1626

48 Alciat, Livret des Emblemes de, Lettres Gothiques, *red morocco* - - Par. Wechel. 1536

49 Alciato Diverse Imprese accommodate a diverse Moralità, *blue morocco* - - Lionc. 1551

50 Alcibiade Fanciullo a Scola, *red morocco, gilt leaves* Oranges. 1652

51 Alcoranus Arabicè, MS. on paper, with Illuminations ——

52 Alcoran des Cordeliers, 2 vols. *plates by Picart, red morocco* Amst. 1734

53 Alen's (Edmond) Catechisme, that is to say, a Christen Instruccion of the Principall Pointes of Christes Religion, *black letter, blue morocco* London, Edw. Whitchurche. 1551

54 Alexis, ou la Maisonnette dans les Bois, 2 vols. Gren. 1789

55 Aleyn's Battailes of Crescey and Poictiers - 1633

56 ——— Historie of Henry the Seventh, in Verse 1638

57 Alfarache, Guzman de, The Spanish Rogue ——

58 Alfieri, Tragedie di, 6 vols. *vellum paper, red morocco* Parigi, Didot. 1787

59 Allacci Poeti Antichi raccolti della Biblioteca Vaticana e Barberina, *red morocco,* - Napoli, 1661

60 Allen's Killing no Murder - - 1689

61 Allot's England's Parnassus, or the Choysest Flowers of our Moderne Poets, *red morocco,* 1600

62 Almanack but for one Day. The Devil's Almanack, Lond. 1745

63 Almanach des Gourmands, 7 vols. - Par. 1804

64 Alphonse Histoire Portugaise - Ib. 1798

65 Alvarez Historia de las Cosas de Etiopia, traduzido de Portugues en Castellano por Thomas de Padilla, *morocco gilt leaves* - - - Anv. 1557

66 Amadis de Gaule, les Vingt quatre Livres de, traduites par Nicholas de Herbery et autres, avec le Tresor, 23 vols. 12mo. and 3 vols. 8vo. and Duplicates of vols. 4, 15, 16, 19, and 20, together 31 vols. *red morocco,* Par. 1577-1615.

67 Amadis de Gaule, 15 vols. 8vo. and 9 vols. 12mo. 24 vols. Par. 1550, &c.

68 Amand, la Rome Ridicule, Caprice, *blue morocco* 1649

69 Ambrosii Officiorum Libri tres, *Par.* 1583. Epictetus et Cebes, Gr. et Lat. *Plantin,* 1585. Boethius, *Plantin,* 1599. Vives Exercitationes Animi, *Gryphius,* 1556, in 1 vol. ruled, *beautiful copy in rich old morocco binding.*

70 America, or an exact Description of the West Indies 1675

71 Amoretti Lettera sull' Anno Natalizio d'Aldo Pio Manuzio ed alcuni Stampi Manuziani, PRINTED UPON VELLUM, *red morocco* - - - *Roma*, 1804

72 Amori - - - - - *Bodoni*, 1795

73 Amoris Divini et Humani Antipathia, Lat. et Gallicè, *plates, fine impressions, blue morocco, gilt leaves* *Par.* 1628

74 Amoris Effigies, or the Picture of Love - 1682

75 Amour a la Mode, Satyre Historique, *red morocco* *Ib.* 1698

76 Amour, Almanach Perpetuel d', *red morocco* - 1681

77 Amours, le Cinquante deuxiesme Arrest d', *red morocco* *Par.* 1528

78 Amours, Plaidoyers et Arrests d', *green morocco* *Rouen*, 1727

79 Amour, Dictionnaire d' - - *Haye*, 1741

80 Amour Divisé, Discours Academique - *Par.* 1651

81 Amour Divin et Humain, les Emblemes d', *plates fine impressions, red morocco* - *Par. Messager*, 1631

82 Amour, le Judgment d', auquel est racontee l'Histoire de Ysabel, fille du Roy d'Escosse, *black letter*, VERY RARE, *red morocco* - - *Par. par Denis, sans date*

83 Amour, le Jardin d' - - - - *Par.* ——

84 Amour, Labyrinthe d' - - *Rouen*, 1615

85 Amour, Carcel d', Espagnol et Fr. - *Lyon*, 1583

86 Amour, Recreations, Devises et Mignardises que les Amoreux font - - - *Lyon*, 1592

87 Amour, Lettres d', d'une Religieuse Portugaise ——

88 Amour, les Ruses d' - - - - 1681

89 Amour, le Secret d', compose par Michel d'Amboyse, tant en Rithme qu'en Prose, *scarce, yellow morocco* *Par.* 1542

90 Amour, le Tresor d' - - *Ib.* 1597

91 Amour, le Tuteur d', *ruled morocco* - *Ib.* 1553

92 Amour, des Declamations, Procedures et Arrestz d' *Ib.* 1545

93 Amour, Voyage de l'Isle d' - - *Ib.* 1713

94 Amour, l'Art de faire, sans parler, sans ecrire et sans se voir, avec un Dictionnaire du Langage Muet, *morocco* *Amst.* ——

95 Amour, les Moyens de se guerir de l', *red morocco* *Par.* 1681

96 Amours d'Anne d'Autriche, Epouse de Louis XIII. *green morocco* - - - - - - *Cologne*, 1693

97 Amours de Gregoire VII. de Richelieu, &c. *morocco* *Cologne*, 1700

98 Amant Mal Traicté de sa Mie, *wood cuts* - *sans date*

99 Amans, les Affections de Divers, *red morocco* - 1743

100 Amant Malheureux, Drame - - *Haye*, 1774

101 Amoureux Repos de Guillaume des Autelz, Gentilhomme Charrolois, *portraits, morocco* *Lyon*, 1553

102 Amorous Gallants Tip'd with Golden Expressions 1717

103 Ana, ou Choix de Bons Mots, Contes et Anecdotes des Hommes Célébres, 10 vols. - - *Amst.* ——

104 Anabaptistes, Histoire des, *plates, fine impressions, scarce, red morocco* - - *Par.* 1615

105 Anacreontis Carmina, Gr. et Lat. a Barnes, 3 *portraits* *Cantab.* 1721

106 Anacreon, Gr. *red morcoco* - - *Glasg.* 1751

107 Anacreon et Sappho, Gr. - - - 1754

108 Anacreontis Carmina Litteris Capitalibus Impressa, *blue morocco* - - *Parma, Bodoni,* 1791

109 Anacreontis Odaria, Gr. a Forster, *large paper, red morocco, gilt leaves* - - - *Londini,* 1802

110 Anacreon, with the Greek translated, by Addison - 1735

111 Anacreon, translated by Moore, 2 vols. - 1802

112 Anacreon Vengé, ou Lettre au sujet d'une Pretendue Traduction d'Anacreon, *red morocco* - *Par.* 1757

113 Anderson's Genealogical History of the House of Yvery, 2 vols, *very fine copy, red morocco* - 1742

114 André, Confusion de la Sexte de Muhamed, *green morocco* *Par.* 1574

115 Andreas' (Bartimeus) certaine verie Worthie and Profitable Sermons, *black letter,* RARE, *blue morocco* *London, by R. Valdegrave,* 1583

116 Angling, the true Art of, *red morocco* ———

117 Anne, Lives of the Nobility and Ministers of the Court of Queen, Lives of the Nobility, &c. of Scotland, MS.

118 Angot les Nouveaux Satires et Exercices Gaillardes de ce Temps, *red morocco* - - *Rouen.* 1637

119 Anselme, Disputation de l'Asne contre, Faicte en la Cité de Tuniez l'An 1417 - *Lyons, sans date*

120 Antenor, Voyage en Grece et en Asie, 3 vols. *plates* *Par.* 1796

121 Anthologia, seu Florilegium Diversorum Epigrammatum, *blue morocco* - - *Aldus.* 1503

122 Anthologie Francoise, ou Chansons Choisies, 3 vols. 1765

123 Antichrist, a short Description of, unto the Nobility of England, &c. *black letter,* RARE, *blue morocco* *no date*

124 Anti-Huguenot, 1599. La Science de l'Histoire, 1665. in one vol.

Quarto.

125 Abulcacim Historia Verdadera del Rey Don Rodrigo, traduzida por Luna, *Valen.* 1606. Segunda Parte de la Historico de la Perdida de Espana traduzida por Luna, *Valen.* 1606, 2 vols. *blue morocco.* See MS. Note in Vol. I.

126 Account of the Popish Plots, Conspiracies, &c. 1679

* 117 - With a fine drawing of Hobbes.

197 Acuna Nuevo Descubrimento del Gran Rio de las Amazonas, EXCESSIVELY RARE, *red morocco, from Colonel Stanley's Collection* - - *Mad.* 1641

"Acuna, a Missionary Jesuit, was dispatched by the Spanish Government to obtain circumstantial information respecting the River of the Amazons, and the best means of rendering its navigation easy and advantageous. On his return he presented the following Work, which was printed at the expense of the King. The impression was scarcely completed when the Spanish Court heard of the Portuguese Revolution, the loss of the Brazils and the Colony of Para, on the mouth of the Amazon; fearing, therefore, that this Work, no longer useful to themselves, might afford important information to the enemy, it was suppressed, and the utmost diligence employed to regain and destroy the few copies which had gone forth. This accounts for its *unusual rarity*."

128 Advis Fidelle aux Veritables Hollandois, par Wicquefort, *plates by Romain de Hooge, blue morocco, very fine copy* 1673

129 Æsopi Fabulæ, Græcè et Latinè *Regii per Dionysium Bertochum.* 1497

130 Æsopus per Laurentium Vallensem traductus, *scarce, green morocco* - *Daventriæ per Jac. de Breda. s. anno*

131 Agrippa Camillo Trattato di Scientia d'Arme, *many plates, russia* - - *Roma Blado.* 1553

132 Ainsworth's Latin and English Dictionary, 2 vols. 1796

133 Alberti Baptistæ Opus Præclarum in Amoris Remedio, *fine copy, blue morocco* - - 1471

134 Alberti Magni Liber Secretorum de Virtutibus Herbarum *per me Wilh. de Mechlinia impressus in opulentissima civitate Londiniarum juxta pontem qui vulgariter dicitur Flete brigge, fine copy, morocco, formerly Herbert's* *sine anno*

Mr. Dibdin says it is "the most elegant specimen of Mechlinia's press with which he is acquainted."

135 Alcazar Battell of, with the Death of three Kings and Capt. Stukely, *scarce* - - 1594

136 Alciati Emblemata, cum Commentariis Variorum *Patavii.* 1621

137 Alciat, Emblemes de, *green morocco* *Lyon. Roville.* 1549

138 Alexander's (John) Love one another, a Tub Lecture *no date*

139 Allen's Killing no Murder - - 1689

140 Alpini de Plantis Ægypti Liber, cum Notis Veslingii, *russia* *Patavii.* 1640

141 Ames's Typographical Antiquities of England, by Herbert. 3 vol. - - - - 1785

£ s. d.	Lot	Description	Buyer
13 13 -	142	Ames's Typographical Antiquities of England, a new Edition, enlarged by the Rev. T. F. Dibdin, 2 vols. *large paper* - - - - - 1812	Booth
1 8 -	143	Ammon Figuren der Evangelien, Latinè et Germanicè, *many plates, blue morocco* - *Francof.* 1579	Triphook
2 7 -	144	——————— Latinè et Germanicè, *plates of Hunting, &c. blue morocco* - - *Ib.* 1592	Heber
10 6	145	Ammonii Imitatio Crameriana sive Exercitatium Pietatis Domesticum, *fine impressions, blue morocco* *Norib.* 1647	Triphook
3 17 -	146	Amani Theatrum Mulierum Omnium per Europam, *plates, red morocco, with joints* - *Francof.* 1586	Arch
2 1 -	147	The same Book in German, *blue morocco* *Ib.* 1586	Triphook
1 19 -	148	Aman's Book of Arts, Sciences, Heraldry, &c. in German, *plates, blue morocco* - - *Ib.* 1599	Do.
1 1 -	149	Amour, les Emblemes de, en Latin, François, et Hollandois, *fine plates, green morocco, with joints* *Amst.* 1611	Do.
2 2 -	150	Amour, le Centre de l', decouvert sous Divers Emblesmes Galans et Facetieux, *blue morocco* - *Par.* 1698	Do.
9 -	151	Amour Emblemes d', illustrez d'une Explication en Prose *sans date*	Clarke
3 -	152	Amorum Aresta, cum Benedicti Curtii Explanatione, *Venetian morocco* - *Lugdun. ap Gryphium.* 1533	Heber
19 -	153	Amsinck's Tunbridge Wells, *plates, boards* - 1812	Alexander
5 10 -	154	Andreini l'Adamo Sacra Rapresentatione, *portrait and plates, Venetian morocco, by Roger Payne* *Milano.* 1617 *This Mystery is supposed to have suggested to Milton his idea of Paradise Lost.*	Longman
6 -	155	Andrelini Poetæ Laureati Epistolæ Proverbiales *Argent.* 1510	Heber
20 9 6	156	Andrews's Botanist's Repository, 8 vols. *coloured plates, half-bound, uncut* - - - - 1797	Clarke
1 4 -	157	Annalia Dubrensia upon the yeerely Celebration of Mr. Dover's Olympick Games upon Cotswold Hills, by Drayton, Ben Jonson, &c. *frontispiece, blue morocco* 1636	Rodd
8 -	158	Angling, the Art of, with many rare Secrets very necessary to be knowne - - - - - 1653	Anderdon
2 -	159	Anti-Jacobin Review - - - - - - 1797	Perring
19 -	160	Antonii a Burgundia Mundi Lapis Lydius, sive Vanitas per Veritatem Falsi accusata, *plates, yellow morocco* *Antv.* 1639	Triphook
15 -	161	——————— Mundi Lapis Lydius, *plates, blue morocro* *Ib.* 1665	Do.
2 - -	162	Ape—Gentle-woman, or the Character of an Exchange Wench - - - - 1675	Lepard
5 - -	163	Apolonius—Histoire du Roy Apolonius Prince de Thir en Afrique, *black letter, wood cuts* *Par. I. Bonfons, sans date*	Hibbert
passed	164	Aprentice's Advice to the XII Bishops - 1642	—
2 18 -	165	Apuleius, his Eleven Bookes of the Golden Asse, *black letter, rusaia* - - - - - - - - 1596	Triphook
2 11 -	166	——————— translated by Adlington, *black letter, red morocco* - - - 1639	Rodd

167 Apuleius l'Amour de Cupido et Psiche, Mere de Volupté, *32 plates, by Gaultier, fine impressions, red morocco*

168 Apulee, la Fable de Psyche, Figures de Raphael, *vellum paper, blue morocco* - - - *Par. Didot*, 1802

169 Arabian Nights, translated by Forster, with plates by Smirke, 5 vols. *large paper, blue morocco* - - 1802

170 L'Arbre des Batailles (par Honorat Bonnor) *black letter* *Lyon par Arnoullet*,

171 Archy's Dream, sometimes Jester to His Majestie, but exiled the Court by Canterburies Malice, VERY RARE 1641

172 Ariosto, Orlando Furioso, con molta diligentia *da lui corretto*, 4to. *a very fine copy, beautifully bound in morocco by R. Payne* - - *Ferrara*, 1528

"Few books are rarer than this edition of Ariosto. I cannot find it mentioned by any Bibliographer. It certainly was not known to Quadrio, Fontanini, Apostolo Zeno, Haym, De Bure, nor to Orlandini, who prefixed a critical catalogue of editions of Ariosto to his own edition of 1730, in folio. No copy has occurred in the sales of the best Italian collections that I can discover. It was not in the libraries of Capponi, Floncel, Crevenna, La Valliere, Gaignat, Crofts, Pinelli, or Dr. Monro, which sufficiently attests its extreme rarity. But its rarity is by no means its only recommendation to the collector of curious books. I consider it as a very valuable literary curiosity for the following reasons.— In 1516 the first edition of Ariosto's Orlando Furioso was published in forty cantos. This is so scarce, that I believe Lord Spencer's copy is the only one in the kingdom. Notwithstanding the great merit of the poem, it was not reprinted till 1521, when it was republished, but incorrectly to a scandalous degree, omitting a whole stanza in one place, and yet from this incorrect and mutilated text, the two editions of 1524 and that of 1527 were printed. At length appeared this valuable and rare edition, exactly copied from the text of the first edition, and corrected by the author himself. All subsequent editions vary from this, as Ariosto re-wrote a considerable portion of his poem after the publication of this edition, and enlarged it into 46 Cantos. THIS EDITION THEREFORE IS THE ONLY ONE WHICH FAITHFULLY REPRESENTS THE TEXT OF THE FIRST EDITION, and is absolutely necessary to elucidate some passages in the text as it is now printed; for when Ariosto re-wrote his poem he omitted some incidents, and not adverting to the circumstance, refers to them as being in his poem." Stanley Catalogue,

173 Ariosto, Orlando Furioso di nuovo ristampato et historiato, *wood cuts, red morocco,* VERY RARE *Venet. per Dom. Zio et Fratelli,* 1539

No mention is made of this edition of the Orlando Furioso, either by Haym or Fontanini. see M. S. note.

174 Ariosto, Orlando Furioso di nuove Figure adornato, *beautiful copy in old red morocco, in compartments* *Venet. Valgrisi,* 1562

175 Ariosto, Orlando Furioso da Porcacchi, *cuts* *Venet.* 1575

176 Aristotelis de Moribus, Græcè, *russia* *Florent. apud Juntas,* 1560

177 Aristotelis in Libros Œconomicorum, Leon. Aretini Comment. *russia* - - - - *sine ulla nota*

178 Aristotle's Rhetorick, translated into English, M. S. ——

Folio.

179 Abitatori del Cielo e del Inferno, Poema, *ornamented binding* *Venet.* 1771

180 Abraham, a S. Clara, Hun! und Pfun! Lat. et Germanicè, *plates* - - - - - - *Wurtzb.* 1707

181 Acosta Trattato della Historia, Natura et Virtu delle Droghe Medicinali, con figure, *russia* - *Venet.* 1585

182 Æneas Silvius. Historiæ Bohemicæ Libri quinque ad Alphonsem Areigonum Regem.—Dialogus de Somnio, *manuscript upon vellum at the end of the* 15*th century, with illuminated capitals, red morocco*

183 Æsopi, Avieni, Remicii et Aliorum Fabulæ Latinis Versibus, cum Commento, *wood cuts, green morocco,* EXTREMELY RARE *sine ulla nota sed circa* (1480)

See Laire Catalogue de Brienne, vol. 1, *p.* 76.

184 Æsopi Vita et Fabulæ Rimicii cum Fabulis Aviani, Alfonsii, Poggii, et Aliorum, cum Commento, *wood cuts, russia,* VERY RARE - *Antverpii, per Gerardum Leeu,* 1486

185 Æsop's Fables paraphrased in Verse, by John Ogilby, *portrait by Lombart, and plates by Hollar, first impressions, very fine copy, red morocco* - - 1665

186 Æsop's Fables, with his Life, translated by Barlow, *plates, fine copy* - - - - 1687

187 Agricolæ de Re Metallica Libri XII. *plates, red morocco, Basil Froben,* 1556

188 AMADIS. Los quatro Libros de Amadis de Gaula, neuvamente impressos y hystoriados, *wood cuts, fine Copy from Col. Stanley's Collection, blue morocco,* EXTREMELY RARE, *Venetia por Antonio de Sabia,* 1533

189 Amours—Livre d'Amours ouquel est relatee, La Grant amour et facon par laquelle PAMPHILA peut jouyr de

GALATHEE—Et le moyen quen fist la Maquerelle. A BEAUTIFUL COPY OF A VERY SCARCE EDITION *Par, par Verard,* 1494

190 André-Michaux Histoire des Chênes de l'Amerique, *vellum paper, elegantly bound in russia* - *Par.* 1801

191 Andrews's Coloured Engravings of Heaths, the Drawings taken from Living Plants only, 3 vols. *elegantly bound in green morocco,* DEDICATION COPY - - 1802-9

192 Anthologia, seu Florilegium Diversorum Epigrammatum Grœcorum, *red morocco, with joints* - *H. Steph.* 1566

193 Apostolen, Derheilengen der XII. *wood cuts, coloured, blue morocco* - - - *Wittemb.* 1570

194 Apuleijo del Asno de Oro en Neustra Lengua quotidiana. *Edition extremement rare et inconnue des Bibliographes Santander vol. 2, No. 3238, russia* - *Medina,* 1543

195 Aquino Sacra Exequialia in Funere Jacobi II. Britanniæ Regis, *plates* - - - - - - *Romæ,* 1702

196 Architecture, Peinture et Sculpture de la Maison de Ville d'Amsterdam, *plates, elegantly bound in russia* *Amst.* 1719

197 Ariosto Orlando Furioso, 8 vols. in 4, *with plates and engraved borders, russia* - - *Venet. Zatta,* 1772

198 Arnolde's Chronicle, or the Customes of London, with the Ballad of the "Notte Broune Mayde," *first edition, russia,* VERY RARE *Supposed to be printed at Antw. about* 1502

End of the First Day's Sale.

SECOND DAY'S SALE.

Octavo et Infra.

199 Anti-Jacobin Review, 4 vols. *plates* - 1799

200 Antiquarian and Topographical Cabinet, 10 vols. Ancient Reliques, 2 vols. 12 vols. *large paper, proof impressions of the plates* - - - - - 1807-1812

201 Antonii a Burgundia Linguæ Vitia et Remedia, *plates, green morocco* - - - *Antv.* 1631

202 Alia Editio, *blue morocco, with joints* - *Antv.* 1652

203 Antonini Itinerarium, cum Comment. Suritæ, *red morocco* *Colon. Agrip.* 1600

204 Apocalypse, an Old English Manuscript on vellum, from the Dering Collection

205 Apollonii Rhodii Argonauticon, Gr. et Lat. ab Hoelzlino, *russia* - - - - *Elzevir,* 1641

206 Apologie Catholique contre les Libelles, Declarations, &c. par les Liguez, *green morocco* - - 1585

207 Apologie ou Defense de Guillaume Prince d'Orange *Delft,* 1581

208 Apologie de l'Ecriture Sainte, *Amst.* 1698—Confirmation de la Discipline Ecclesiastique, *Stephani,* 1566—Abrégé de la Vie de Monsieur Daille, 1673, 3 vols in 1

209 Apologie, or Answere in Defence of the Churche of Englande, *black letter* - *Lond. R. Wolfe,* 1564

210 Apotheose du Beau Sexe - - *Lond.* 1741

211 Apuleio dell' Asino d'Oro tradotto da Fiorenzuola, *wood cuts, green morocco* - - *Venet, s. a.*

212 Apulegio tradotta da Boiardo, *wood cuts* - *Venet.* 1520

213 Apuleo Volgare tradotto da Boiardo, *wood cuts* *Vineg.* 1537

214 ——— tradotto da Firenzuola - *Firenz. Giolito.* 1550

215 Apuleio tradotto dal Pompeo, *wood cuts* - *Ceneda,* 1715

216 Apulee, les Metamorphoses ou l'Asne D'Or, *plates, yellow morocco* - - - - *Par.* 1631

217 ——— l'Amour de Cupido & Psyche, Mere de Volupté, *cuts* - - - - - - - *Ib.* 1546

218 Arcan et de Belize, les Amours et les Aventures d' *Leyde,* 1714

219 Archer's every Man his own Doctor - - 1673

220 Aretino Ragionamenti Capricciosi e Piacevoli, con la Puttana Errante, *fine copy, in vellum* - *Elzevir,* 1660

221 ——— Quattro Comedie, *red morocco* - 1588

222 ——— Tre primi Canti di Marfisa, *red morocco* *Venet.* 1545

223 ——— Dubbii Amorosi - - - *s. a.*

224 ——— Coloquio de las Damas traduzido por Fernan Xuares, *red morocco* - - - - 1607

225 Aretin, Dialogues sur les Courtisanes de Rome, *red morocco, gilt leaves* - - - *s. a.*

226 ——— les Mirroirs des Courtisanes, *red morocco* *Lyon,* 1580

227 Aretine's Historie of the Warres betweene the Imperialles and the Gothes for the Possession of Italie, translated by Arthur Goldyng, *black letter, red morocco* *Lond. R. Hall,* 1563

228 Argelati, il Decamerone di, 2 vols. - *Bologna,* 1751

229 Ariosto Orlando Furioso, *wood cuts* - *Vineg. Giolito,* 1547

230 ——————— *blue morocco* *Lione Rovillio,* 1569

231 ——————— con figure, 2 vols. - *Venet.* 1600

232 ——————— *elegantly bound in blue morocco by* R. PAYNE - - - *Venet.* 1630

233 Arioste, Roland Furieux, 4 vols. *large paper, plates, red morocco* - - - - - *Haye,* 1741

234 Ariosto, Rime, *blue morocco* - *Vineg. Giolito,* 1557

235 ——— Comedie, *green morocco* - - *Ib.* 1562

236 Aristeus's History of the Septuagint, English'd by John Done - - - - - 1685

9 - 237 Aristofane Comedie, tradutte per Rositini, *red morocco, ruled* - - - *Vineg.* 1545 Osborne
12 - 238 Aristotelis de Poetica Liber, Gr. et Lat. a Tyrwhitt, *large paper, yellow morocco* - - - 1806 Christie
10 - 239 Arnauld des Vrayes et Fausses Idées de l'Auteur de la Recherche de la Verite, *Cologne*, 1683. Trois Lettres de Malebranche sur la Defense de M. Arnauld, *Rott.* 1685. Reponse de Malebranche a la Troisieme Lettre de M. Arnauld, *Amst.* 1704, 3 vols. *red moracco* Osborne
2 - 240 Arnaudi Joci - - *Avenioni*, 1605 Triphook
13 - 241 Arnisæi Doctrina Politica, *red morocco* - *Elzevir*, 1643 Payne
11 - 242 Arrests d'Amours, Lat. et Fr. *yellow morocco Rouen*, 1587 Christie
5 - 243 Arrets d'Amours par Martial d'Auvergne, 2 vols. *Par.* 1731 Osborne
17 - 244 Art de Desopiler la Rate ——— Triphook
11 - 245 ——— Plumer la Poule sans crier - *Cologne*, 1710 D°
7 - 246 ——— rendre les Femmes Fideles - *Par.* 1803 Dulau
4 - 247 Art of Secret Information, without a Key - 1685 Lewis
7 - 248 ——— Ingeniously Tormenting - - - 1804 Durant
5 2 6 249 Ashmole's Antiquities of Berkshire, 3 vols. *red morocco* 1719 Payne
4 6 - 250 Another copy, 3 vols. *russia*. L. P. without portraits 1723 Rodd
19 - 251 Askham Lytel Herball of the Properties of Herbes, *black letter, russia* - - - *Lond Powell.* 1550 D°
10 6 252 Another copy, *black letter* - *Lond. J. Kyng* Triphook
5 10 - 253 Astræa's Teares, an Elegy on the Death of that learned and honest Judge, Sir Richard Hutton, and Panaretee's Triumph, or Hymen's Heavenly Hymne, *frontispiece, fine copy, red morocco* - - *Lond.* 1641 D°
6 - 254 Atila Flagellum Dei Vulgar, *blue morocco Vinez. Sessa*, 1521 D°
3 - 255 Aubespin le Fouet des Apostats, *yellow morocco Lyon*, 1601 D°
17 17 - 256 Auctores Classici Editore Maittaire, scilicet Lucretius, Virgilius, Horatius, Ovidius, Catullus, Tibullus, et Propertius, C. Nepos, Florus, Cæsar, Quintus Curtius, Juvenal, et Persius, Paterculus, Lucanus, Martial, et Novum Testamentum Græcè, 15 vols. LARGE PAPER, *morocco* wants Justin only - *Lond.* 1713-19 Boswell
5 - 257 Augurelli Carmina, *blue morocco* - *Aldus*, 1505 Heber
1 6 - 258 Augustini Confessiones, *red morocco* - *Elzevir*, 1675 Payne
9 - 259 Aulicus Inculpatus, traductus a Pastorio, *red morocco Elzevir*, 1649 D°
3 - 260 Auli Gellii Noctes Atticæ - - *Aldus*, 1515 Money
2 - 261 Aulus Gellius - - *Elzevir*, 1651 Christie
10 - 262 Aurelio et Isabella Historia, Ital. et Fr. *red morocco* 1553 Dulau
10 - 263 ——— e Isabella, Fr. Ital. Espag. et Ang. *blue morocco Anv.* 1556 Clarke
6 - 264 Ausonii Carmina, *red morocco* - *Aldus*, 1517 Triphook
5 - 265 Avanturier Hollandois, avec figures - *Amst.* 1729 Heber
9 - 266 Avantures de Pomponius, Chevalier Romain, *red morocco Rome*, 1728 Triphook
6 - 267 Ayres's Emblems of Love, in four languages, *russia no date* D°

268 Ayres's Emblems of Love - - 1683

269 Ayton's Hortus Kewensis, 3 vols. - 1789

270 Bacchi et Veneris Facetiæ - - 1617

271 Baconi Historia Ventorum, *red morocco* *Lugd. Bat.* 1638

272 ——— Sylva Sylvarum, a Grutero, *blue morocco* *Elzev.* 1648

273 Baif Euvres en Rime, de Jan Antoine de *Par.* 1573

274 Baif, les Passetems de - - *Ib.* 1573

275 Baif, les Jeux de - - - *Ib.* 1573

276 Baillard Discours du Tabac - - *Ib.* 1668

277 Bale's Acts of Englyshe Votaryes, collected out of their owne Legendes and Chronycles, *printed at Wesel*, 1546.—Bale's Second Part of the Englyshe Votaryes, *London*, 1551, *black letter*, 2 vols. *russia*

278 Bale's Actes of the Englyshe Votaryes, 2 parts *in one*, *black letter, russia* - - *London, J. Tysdale*, 1560

279 Bale's Image of bothe Churches, after the moste wonderfull and Heavenly Revelacion of St. John, 3 parts in 1 vol. *black letter, russia* - *London, J. Daye, no date*

280 Bale's Mysterye of Inyquyte dysclosed and confuted, *black letter, russia* - - *Geneva, M. Woode*, 1545

281 Bale's Brefe Chronycle of Sir John Oldecastell, *black letter, very scarce, russia* - - *no date*

282 Bale's Examination of Anne Askewe, *both parts, black letter, scarce, russia* - *Marpurg, in the lande of Hessen*, 1547

283 Bale's first Examination of Anne Askew, *black letter, blue morocco* - - - *no date*

284 Balinghem, Apres Dinees et Propos de Table contre l'Excez au Boire et au Manger, *red morocco*, *Lille.* 1615

285 Ballads, Collection of Old, 3 vols, *plates, scarce* 1723

286 Ballard, Nouvelles, Parodies, Bachiques, &c. 3 vols. *Par.* 1700

287 Balzac, Œuvres Diverses de, *green morocco, fine copy* *Elzev.* 1658

288 Balzac Aristippe ou de la Cour, *red morocco* *Ib.* 1658

289 Bancks's Miscellaneous Works, in Verse and Prose, 2 vols. *russia* - - - - 1738

290 Barbauld's Poems - - - 1792

291 Barbier's famous Game of Chesse Play - 1618

292 Another Copy, *red morocco* - - 1672

293 Barclaii Argenis, cum Clave, *red morocco* *Elzev.* 1630

294 Barclaii Satyricon, *red morocco* - *Ib.* 1637

295 ——————— *yellow morocco* - *Ib.* 1655

296 Barlandi Jocorum Centuriæ Duæ - *Lovanii.* 1524

297 ——— Joci, *Coloniæ*, 1529. Symphosii Poetæ Veteris Ænigmata, *Par. Kerver*, 1537, in 1 vol.

298 Barlowe's (Bishop of Bathe) Dialogue describing the originall Ground of these Lutheran Faccions and many of their Abuses, *black letter, blue morocco* *London, J. Cawood, no date*

299 Barnabee's (Drunken) Journall under the Names of Mirtilus and Faustulus, *first edition, blue morocco, rare* *no date*

300 Barnaby's Four Journeys, *second edition, blue morocco* 1716

301 ———————— *third edition, with plates* 1723

302 ———————— *fourth edition* - 1778

303 ———————— - - - 1805

304 Baron's Cyprian Academy, *frontispiece by Marshall* 1648

305 Barron's Pocula Castalia, *scarce, portrait by Marshall, red morocco* - - - 1650

306 Barrouso le Jardin Amoureulz avec toutes les reigles d'Amours, *black letter, scarce, red morocco* *Par. Al. Lotrian, sans date*

307 Barthelemy Apologie du Banquet Sanctifie de la Veille des Rois, *green morocco* - - *Par.* 1665

308 ———— Carite et Polydore - - 1799

309 Basilii Magni et Greg. Nazanzeni Epistolæ Græcæ nunc primum editæ, *blue morocco, with morocco lining* *Haganoæ.* 1528

310 Bassompiere Memoires du Marechal de, 2 vols. *red morocco* *Cologne*, 1665

311 ———— Ambassade en Suisse, 2 vols. *red morocco* *Ib.* 1668

312 Bastard's Chrestoleros. Seven Books of Epigrames, EXTREMELY RARE, *green morocco. London, R. Bradocke*, 1598

313 Batailles et Victoires du Chevalier Celeste contre le Chevalier Terrestre, *red morocco* - *Par.* 1560

314 Battely Antiquitates Rutupinæ - *Oxon.* 1711

315 Baudii Amores, edente Scriverio - *Lugd. Bat.* 1638

316 Baudoin Recueil d'Emblemes Divers, 2 vols., vol. 1 *wants title* - - - *Par.* 1639

317 Baudwin's Treatice of Morall Philosophy, by Paulfreyman, *black letter, red morocco* - - 1579

318 Baxteri Glossarium Antiquitatum Britannicarum, *large paper, russia* - - *Lond.* 1719

319 Bayfius de Vasculis et de Re Vestiaria - *Par.* 1536

320 Beatino le Rime Volgari et Latine, *rare, blue morocco* *Vinetia Giolito* 1551

321 Beaulieu la Solitude Amoureuse, *fine portrait by Crispin de Passe, green morocco, with joints* *s. a.*

322 Beaulxamis Enqueste et Griefz sur le Sac et Pieces contre le Pape de Rome, *red morocco* *Par. Marnef.* 1562

323 Beaumont l'Enciclopedie Perruquiere a l'Usage de toutes sortes de Tetes, enrichi de Figures, *blue morocco* *Par.* 1757

324 Beaumont's Bosworth Field, with a Taste of the Variety of other Poems, *red morocco* - - 1629

325 ———————— 1629. Sandys's Christ's Passion, a Tragedy, 1643, in 1 vol.

326 Beaumont's (F.) Poems - - 1653

Quarto.

327 Arthur. The most Ancient and Famous History of the Renowned Prince Arthur and his Knights of the Round Table, *very fine copy, bound in russia by Walther, from the Stanley Collection* - - 1634

328 Arthur, and the Knights of the Round Table. History of Parismus, Prince of Bohemia. Guy, Earl of Warwick. The Shoe-maker's Glory, or the History of Gentle Craft. The pleasant History of Thomas of Reading, and other Worthy Clothiers of the West and North of England. Fryar Bacon. Life of Dr. Faustus. The History of Mother Shipton. Doctor Merry-Man, or Nothing but Mirth; being a Posie of pleasant Poems. 10 Tracts in 1 Vol. - - *Newcastle.*

329 Articles. In this Boke is conteyned the Articles of oure Fayth. The X Commaundementes; the VII Works of Mercy; the VII Dedely Synnes, &c. *black letter, containing only four leaves, blue morocco,* EXTREMELY RARE, *unknown to Herbert.*
Impressum per Me Ricardum Pynson, sine anno (circa 1500)

330 Articles Ministred by His Majestie's Commissioners for Causes Ecclesiasticall - 1641

331 Arusiens. Here begyneth a litil Boke, the whiche traytied and reherced many gode thinges necessarie for the infirmitie and grete sekeness called Pestilence, made by the most expert Doctour in Phisike, Bishop of Arusiens, *russia* *Printed by Macklinia, without date*

For a Fac-simile of the Type and Description of this *exceedingly rare* Tract, see the New Edition of Ames. Mr. Dibdin's account is taken from this copy.

332 Ascham's Toxophilus, a Schoole of Shooting. Ascham's Schoolemaster. Ascham's Discourse on the State of Germany, 3 vols. in 1 - *London, Daye,* 1571

333 ——— English Works, by Bennet - 1767

334 Astle on the Origin and Progress of Writing 1784

335 Atkyns's Original and Growth of Printing, *frontispiece, blue morocco* - - *Lond.* 1664

336 Atlas d'Angleterre, divisé en 52 Comtés, &c *Par.* 1767

337 —— Minimus Universalis, *coloured* - 1798

338 Augustini et Crisostomi Tractatus Varii, ab Ulrico Zel de Hanau impressi, scilicet, Augustinus De Vita Christiana. De Singularitate Clericorum, *per me Olricum Han.* 1467, *very rare.* Sermo super Orationem Dominicam, &c. Augustini Enchiridion. Crisostomi Sermones Duæ super "Miserere Mei." *5 Tracts in very fine preservation, with rubricated Capitals. At the commencement of the Volume is the following Note:—Hunc Librum Magister Olricus Pressor Librorum dedit Fratribus domus Sanctæ Barbaræ in Colonia pro Memoria sui-*

339 Augustini Confessiones, *russia* *Mediolani Joh. Bonus.* 1475

340 Ausonii Carmina in Usum Delphini, *red morocco* *Par.* 1730

341 Bacon's Letters and Memoirs, published by Stephens 1736

342 Bacon, The famous History of Friar, *blue morocco* *no date*

343 Badii Stultiferæ Naviculæ, seu Scaphæ Fatuarum Mulierum, *wood cuts, red morocco* *J. Prusz. Argent.* 1502

344 Balei Illustres Scriptores, Britanniæ, Angliæ, et Cambriæ, *russia, wants title* - - *Lond.* 1543

345 Baldwin's Mirroure for Magistrates, *first edition, blue morocco, page* 100 *omitted in the printing* *Marshe,* 1559

346 ——————————— *fine copy, red morocco, from the Roxburghe Collection* - - 1563

347 Baldwin Tre Opere Drammatiche prese nelle Visioni di Dafni, *red morocco, with joints, privately printed* *Lond.* 1811

348 Bancroft's Daungerous Positions and Proceedings under pretence of Reformation - *London, Wolfe.* 1595

349 Bandello Novelle, Tre Parti, 3 vols. *Lucca.* 1554. La Quarta Parte, 8vo. *Lione.* 1573. 4 vols. *original edition, fine copy, green morocco, from the Roxburghe Library*

350 Banks's Dormant and Extinct Baronage of England, 3 vols. 1807

351 Barberino Documenti d'Amore, *plates, by Bloemaert, yellow morocco* - - - *Roma* 1640

352 Baretti's Spanish and English Dictionary, *russia* 1800

353 ———- Italian and English Dictionary, 2 vols. in 1, *russia* 1790

354 Bargagli Imprese di Scipione, *Venetia,* 1589. Cento Imprese de gl' Illustri Signori, &c. *Bologna,* 1591. *in one vol. blue morocco*

355 Bargagli Dialogo de Giuochi che nella Vegghie Sanesi si usano di Fare, - - - - - *Siena,* 1572

356 Bartholomio Formulario de Epistole Vulgare, *fine copy, blue morocco, wood cut* *Bologna per mi Ugo di Rugerii Stampadore,* 1485

357 Batchelar's Banquet, or a Banquet for Batchelars *(by Dekker)* - - - - - 1603

358 Bate's Mysteries of Nature and Art, in four parts - 1654

359 Baudouyn Conte de Flandres, l'Histoire et Chronique du, *black letter, wood cuts, yellow morocco,* RARE *Mich. le Noir, s. d.*

360 Bayard, les Gestes et la Vie du Chevalier, *black letter, wood cuts, portrait of Bayard by Mariette inserted.*—Compendiosa Illustrissimi Bayardi Vita Campegii, in 1 vol, *green morocco* - - - ———

361 Beattie's Minstrel, and other Poems - *Edinb.* 1803

362 Beauchasteau (le Petit) la Lyre du Jeune Apollon, *numerous portraits* - - - *Par.* 1657

363 Beaujoyeulx Balet Comique de la Royne aux Noces de Monsieur le Duc de Joyeuse - *Ib.* 1582

364 Beaver's African Memoranda, *map and plates* - 1805

365 Bebeliana Opuscula Nova et Florulenta, *blue morocco, ruled* *Par.* 1516

366 Bedwell's Description of the Towne of Tottenham High Crosse in Middlesex, *red morocco, with joints* - 1631

367 Belman of London bringing to Light the most Notorious Villainies that are now practised in the Kingdome, by Decker, VERY RARE, *russia* - - 1608

368 Belial Der Teutsch, Belial de Latino in Vulgarem Stilum mirifice translatus, *a rare edition, with wood cuts, printed at Augspurg, at the end of the fifteenth century*

369 Bellianis of Greece, Famous and Delectable History of 1703

370 Bellora and Fidelio, The Tragicall History of, a Paire of Turtle Doves, *black letter*, SCARCE - *F. Burton*, 1606

371 Belon Observations sur plusieurs singularitez et choses memorables trouvees en Grece, Asie, &c. *red morocco, cuts* - - - - *Par.* 1553

372 Belon Portraits d'Oyseaux, Animaux, Serpens, &c. *numerous plates* - - - *Ib.* 1557

373 Bembo gli Asolani, *first edition, with the dedication to Lucretia Borgia, red morocco* - *Venet. Aldo*, 1505

374 Bembo Istoria Viniziana pubblicata da J. Morelli, 2 vols. *printed on blue paper* - *Vinegia*, 1790

375 Benavidii Loculati Opusculi Libri Quinque, *portrait and plates, red morocco* - *Patavii*, 1580

376 Berinus, l'Hystoire du Noble Chevalier, *black letter, wood cuts* - - *Par. Jehan Trepperel, sans date*

377 Beuves de Hantoune, l'Histoire du Noble très Preuz et Vaillant Chevalier, *black letter, scarce* *Par. Bonfons, sans date*

Folio.

378 Athenæi Deipnosophistarum Libri XV. Gr. et Lat. Casauboni, *best edition* - - *Lugd.* 1657

379 Atlas General, par Bleau et autres, 4 vols.

380 Audibert Histoire Naturelle des Singes et des Makis, COLOURED PLATES, VELLUM PAPER, *elegantly bound in russia* *Par.* 1800

381 Augustini Commentarii in Psalmos, MS. of the 14th century, ON VELLUM, *russia*

382 Augustinus de Arte Predicandi, *first edition, red morocco, gilt leaves* - *Moguntiæ typis Johannis Fust. circa.* 1466

383 Augustino della Citta di Dio, *red morocco* - *senza nota*

384 Baccius de Naturali Vinorum Historia, *in rich old morocco binding, by De Seuil* - - *Romæ*, 1597

385 Balthazar, les Genealogies et Anciennes Descentes des Forestiers et Comtes de Flandres, *many plates, blue morocco* *Anv.* 1598

386 Barclay's Ship of Fooles, *black letter, wood cuts, fine copy, russia, with joints* - John Cawood, 1570

387 Bazin Recueil d'Estampes de Devotion, *fine impressions* Par. sans date

388 Baudoyn Conte de Flandres, le Livre de, *first Book printed at Chambery, wood cuts, very rare* Chambery Ant. Neyret, 1485

389 Baurn Iconographia, complectens Passionem, Miracula et Vitam Christi, &c. - *August. Vindel.* 1670

390 Bayly's Wall Flower, a History partly true, partly romantick - - - - 1679

391 Beaumont and Fletcher's Works - 1679

392 Beaumont's Travels through the Rhætian Alps, *plates, large paper* - - - - 1792

393 Bedæ Historia Ecclesiastica, *blue morocco* - *Cantab.* 1643

394 BERNERS— The Bokys of Haukyng and Huntyng, with other plesuris dyverse, and also Cootarmuris by Juliana Berners, *a tall fine copy, but made perfect by Manuscript, red morocco, from the Roxburghe Collection* - *Seynt Albons*, 1486

"A volume of the most uncommon rarity, and held in prodigious estimation by the curious in ancient English lore." Spencer Cat. vol. 4, page 373

395 Berners (Juliana) Treatyses of Hawkynge, Huntynge, Cot-Armours, Fisshynge, and Blasynge of Armys, *fine copy, Venetian morocco,* EXTREMELY RARE *Enprynted at Westmestre by W. de Worde*, 1496

396 Bertrand de Guesclin, Chevalier jadis Connestable de France et Seigneur de Longueville, *black letter, wood cuts, remarkably fine copy of one of the scarcest French Romances, red morocco* *sans date*

End of the Second Day's Sale.

THIRD DAY'S SALE.

Octavo et Infra.

399 Beaux Jours de la Haie, *green morocco* - *Lond.* 1709

400 Bebelii, Pogii, Erasmi et Aliorum Facetiæ, *blue morocco, with joints* - - *Francof.* 1590

401 Beck's Universal Character and Grammatical Directions for all Nations, *frontispiece, russia* - 1657

402 Becket, Life of St. Thomas, Archbishop of Canterbury, *blue morocco, portrait inserted* - *Colloniæ*, 1639

403 Beckford's Caliph Vathek, *large paper* - 1786

404 Beckmann's History of Inventions and Discoveries, by Johnson, 3 vols. - - - 1792

405 Becon's Pomaunder of Prayer, *black letter* - *I. Day*, 1565

406 Bee Hive of the Romish Church, translated by George Gilpin, *black letter, blue morocco* - 1623

407 Believer's Dowry, a Poem - - 1733

408 Bellendeni de Statu Libri Tres - 1787

409 Bellingen Explication des Proverbes François *Haye*, 1656

410 Bellonii, de Aquatilibus Libri Duo, cum Iconibus, *oblong, green morocco, with joints* - *Par. Steph.* 1553

411 Beloe's Anecdotes of Literature, 6 vols. *the two first bound* 1807

412 Belon's Treasure of a Christian Soule, translated by Chanterell, *black letter* - - - 1601

413 Bembo Rime di, *red morocco* *Vinegia Giolito*, 1557

414 Benjaminis Itinerarium, *blue morocco* - *Elzev.* 1633

415 Benese (Syr Richard) of the Maner of measuryng of all maner of Lande, as well of Woodlande as of Plowelande, *black letter, russia, with joints*
Imprynted by R. Wyer. no date

416 Bentivoglio della Guerra di Fiandra—Memorie ove Diario del—Relationi del, 5 vol. *red morocco, Coloniæ.* 1635-48

417 Berlue, (la) - - - *Lond.* 1759

418 Bernard de Bluet d'Arberes, Comte de Permission, &c. Recueil des Œuvres de, qui ne scait n'y lire, n'y escrire 1600

These brochures, which were distributed in the streets for charity by the Comte de Permission, are very rarely collected together. The present copy is deficient from the 2nd to the 6th Book inclusive, and from the 99th to the 103rd, and also wants several single leaves. See De Bure Bibliographie, vol. 4. p. 230.

419 Bernard, Pourtraits Divers, par le Petit Bernard, *very fine copy* - *A Lyon, par Jan de Tournes.* 1556

420 Bernardi Opuscula, *red morocco* - *Venetiis.* 1495

421 Bernia Tutte le Opere—Rime di Casa—Rime del Mauro, *in 1 vol. red morocco* - *Venezia.* 1538

422 Bernier, Voyages de, dans les Etats du Grand Mogol, 2 vols. in 1, *plates* - - *Amst.* 1699

423 Autre Edition, 2 vols. - - - - *Ib.* 1724

424 Bernier's Mogul Empire, 4 vols. *plates* - 1676

425 Beroalde, le Moyen de Parvenir, *blue morocco,* *sans date.*

426 ——— de Verville le Cabinet de Minerve, *yellow morocco* - - - *Par.* 1596

427 Berquin, les Idylles de, 2 vols. *plates, large paper, sans date.*

Price	Lot	Description	Buyer
2 -	428	Berthod les Emblesmes Sacrez expliquez, en Vers François - - - *Par.* 1665	Triphook
19 -	429	Bertrami Britannicarum Gentium Historiæ Antiquæ Scriptores Tres, *privately printed* *Hafniæ.* 1757	Payne
9 -	430	Berwick's Lives of Marcus Corvinus, and Titus Atticus, *Venetian morocco* - - *Edin.* 1813	Triphook
- -	431	Beze les Vrais Portraits des Hommes illustres, avec Quarante quatre Emblemes - *Lyon,* 1581	Passed
2 -	432	Betes (la derniere Guerre des) pour l'Histoire du XVIII Siecle, 2 parts in 1 - - *Lond.* 1758	Davenport
8 -	433	Betty Land, the Present State of, - 1684	Warden
7 -	434	Beughem Incunabula Typographiæ, *red morocco* *Amst.* 1688	Clarke
1 -	435	Beurhusii Erotematum Musicæ Libri Duo *Norimb.* 1580	Heber
4 -	436	Beuter Cronica Generale d'Hispagna et del Regno di Valenza, tradotta dal Ulloa - *Venegia, Giolito,* 1556	Triphook
9 -	437	Bezæ Poemata, Varia et Bezæ Abrahamus Sacrificans, Tragœdia, &c. in 1 vol. *russia* - 1599	D°
1 -	438	Bibiena le Petit Toutou - - *Amst.* 1775	Rodd
3 -	439	Biblia Picturis Illustrata - - *Par.* 1540	D°
4 -	440	Biblia Sacra Latina ex Versione Bezæ, accesserunt Libri Apocryphi ex versione Junii, *red morocco* *Amst.* 1627	Hayes
12 -	441	Biblia Sacra Vulgatæ Editionis jussu Cardinalis de Richelieu edita, *red morocco* - *Par. Martin,* 1656	Payne
2 - -	442	Biblia Sacra Vulgatæ Editionis, 6 vols. *red morocco* *Coloniæ.* 1679	Clarke
7 -	443	La Bible, - - - *Amst.* 1635	D°
15 -	444	——— *red morocco* *Charenton par Cellier.* 1652	D°
1 13 -	445	The Holy Bible, 2 vols. *ruled, red morocco, with silver clasps and corners* - - *Lond. Field.* 1653	Christie
4 -	446	——— vol. 1, *plates inserted* - 1658	Triphook
2 8 -	447	——— *ruled, blue morocco.* See MS. Note at the beginning and the Psalm at the end, said to be written by Buckinger, a German, who had neither hands nor feet - - - *Field.* 1660	D°
17 -	448	——— *morocco, with silver corners* *Edin. Watson.* 1716	Hancock
1 5 -	449	——— *blue morocco* - *Lond. Pasham.* 1776	Christie
1 1 -	450	——— 2 vols. *blue morocco* *Lond. Corrall.* 1800	D°
2 -	451	Holy Bible - - - *Bristol.* 1803	Evans
9 -	452	——— and the Psalms, in Short-Hand, *fine copy, blue morocco* - - - 1650	Clarke
5 5 -	453	Bible, The true and lyvely Historyke Purtreatures of the Woll Bible, by Peter Derendel, *wood cuts, fine copy, blue morocco, gilt leaves* - *Lyons, by Tourner.* 1553	Triphook
8 -	454	——— Quadrins Historiques de la Bible, *wood cuts, blue morocco* - - - *Lion.* 1555	D°
2 -	455	——— the Historie of the, *black letter, wood cuts, blue morocco, imperfect*	D°

456 Bibel, Historien, *plates, blue morocco* *Augsburg.* 1739

457 Bibliander. A Godly Consultation unto the Brethren and Companyons of the Christen Religyon. By what meanes the cruel power of the Turkes bothe may and ought for to be repelled of the Christen People, *black letter, blue morocco* - *Basill, by R. Bonifante.* 1542

458 Bibliotheque Universelle des Romans, 112 vols. et la Nouvelle Bibliotheque des Romans, 16 vols. in 8, together 120 vols. *uniform* - *Par.* 1775-1790

459 Bigarrures du Seigneur des Accordz, *yellow morocco* *Par. Richer.* 1583

460 ——— et Touches du Seigneur des Accords, avec les Apophtegmes du Sieur Gaulard et les Escraignes Dijonnoises, 2 vols. *red morocco* - *Rouen.* 1640

461 Bigarure (la) ou Melange curieux, Instructif et Amusant de Nouvelles, &c. 5 vols. - *A la Haye.* 1749

462 Bijoux (les) Indiscrets, 3 vols. *cuts* - 1753

463 Biochimo's Royall Game of Chesse Play, illustrated with almost an hundred Gamblets. Portrait of Charles I. by *Stent, blue morocco* - - 1656

464 Biographical Dictionary, 15 vols. *russia* - 1798

465 Bird Fancyer's Delight, or Observations on Teaching all sorts of Singing Birds

466 Birinthea, a Romance - - 1664

467 Blackmore's Prince Arthur, *russia* - *Tonson.* 1714

468 Blake's Account of the Dreadful Fire at Blandford Forum, on June 4, 1731 - - - 1735

469 Blasons Anatomiques du Corps Femenin, ensemble les contreblasons de nouveau composez et additionez, avec les figures, *morocco, with joints* *Pour Charles Langelier.* 1543

470 Blenheim, new Description of, - - 1789

471 Blessebois, le Rut ou la Pudeur Eteinte *Leyde.* 1676

472 Blome's Description of Jamaica, *with maps* - 1672

473 Blosuis's Mirrour for Monkes, *frontispiece and plates, blue morocco* - - *Par.* 1676

474 Blount's Jocular Tenures - - 1679

475 Boccaccio il Decameron, *fine copy, green morocco* *Amst. Elzevir.* 1665

476 Boccaccio il Decamerone, 5 vols. with two sets of plates *red morocco, very fine copy* - *Lond.* 1757

477 Bocace, le Decameron traduit par Maçon, *red morocco, gilt leaves* - - - *Par.* 1572

478 ——— Contes et Nouvelles de, avec figures, par *Romain de Hooge,* 2 vols. *blue morocco* - *Amst.* 1799

479 Autre exemplaire, 2 vols. *blue morocco* *Cologne.* 1732

480 Bocace, Contes de, *plates by Gravelot inserted,* 10 vols. *Lond.* 1779

481 Boccace's Decameron, *red morocco* - 1741

482 Boccaccio Il Filocopo - - *Venet.* 1575

483 ——— l'Amoroso Fiammetta, *Venet.* 1589.—Ameto Comedia delle Ninfe Fiorentine, *Venet.* 1592.—Dialogo d'Amore, *Venet.* 1592, in one volume, *green moroçço*

484 ——— l'Amorosa Fiammetta - *Vineg.* 1575

485 ———, Ameto, *red morocco* *Firenze Giunta*, 1529

486 Boccaccio la Theseide in Prosa per Granucci di Lucca, *blue morocco* - - *Lucca*, 1579

487 ———, Urbano di, Historia molto Dilettevole, *red morocco, scarce* - *Vineg. Sabbio*, 1526

488 Bocace Treize Elegantes demandes d'Amours, *black letter, blue morocco* - *Par. sans date*

489 ———, Le Nimphal Flossolan, traduit par Guercin du Crest - - - *Lyon*, 1556

490 Boccalini Pietra del Paragone Politico, *cuts, green morocco* *Cosmopoli*, 1652

491 ——— altro esemplare, *red morocco* *Ib.* 1664

492 Bodrugen's Epitome of the Title that the Kynges Majestie of Englande hath to the Sovereignetie of Scotlande, *black letter, very fine copy,* RARE. *Lond. Richardi Graftoni*, 1548

493 Boethius de Consolatione Philosophiæ, *red morocco* *Amst.* 1625

494 ———, *red morocco* *Amst.* 1640

495 Bohemian Persecution, History of the, - 1650

496 Bohorizh Arcticæ Horulæ Succisivæ, de Latino—Carniolana Literatura ad Latinæ Linguæ Analogiam accommodata, &c. *russia, scarce* - - *Witebergæ*, 1584

497 Boileau, Œuvres de, avec Figures par Picart, 4 vols. *red morocco, gilt leaves* - *a la Haye*, 1722

498 Bolingbroke's Letters on the Study and Use of History 1752

499 Bolswert, Le Pelerinage de deux Soeurs Colombelle et Volontairette, vers leur Bien Aimé dans la Cité de Jerusalem, *cuts* - - - *Liege sans date.*

500 Boniface et le Pedant, Comedie en Prose imitee de l'Italien de Bruno Nolano - - *Par.* 1633

501 Bonarelli Filli di Sciro, *cuts* - *Parigi*, 1678

502 Bonavanture des Periers, Les Contes ou les nouvelles Recreations et joyeux Devis de, 2 vols. *green morocco* *Amst.* 1735

503 Bonaventure des Periers Cymbalum Mundi, ou Dialogues Satyriques sur differens sujets, *plates* *Amst.* 1711

504 Bonnefons, Imitations du Latin de, avec autres gayetez Amoureuses, *yellow morocco* - *Leyden*, 1659

505 Bonne, Atlas maritime de France - *Par.* 1778

506 Bonneval, Memoires de Mademoiselle de *a la Haye*, 1738

507 Boordes Compendyous Regimente or Dyetary of Health made in Mount Pyllor, *black letter, title MS. blue morocco, Lond. W. Myddylton*, 1564

508 Borri, La Chiave del Gabinetto del Cavagliere, G. F. *Colonia*, 1681. Borri Instruzioni Politiche. *Colonia*, 1681. 2 vols. in 1, *morocco*

509 Borromeo Notizia de' Novellieri Italiani *Bassano*, 1794

510 Boscan, las Obras de, y algunas de Garcilasso dela Vega *fine copy, yellow morocco, ruled,* RARE *Leon*, 1549

511 Boscobel, or the History of the Preservation of Charles II. after the Battle of Worcester, *portrait* - 1748

512 Bosman's Description of the Coast of Guinea 1721

513 Boswell's Life of Johnson, 4 vols. - 1804

514 Bouchet les Triumphes de la Noble Dame Amoureuse *Lovain*, 1563

515 Bouchet, les Serees de Guillaume Bouchet, Sieur de Brocourt, 3 vols. *yellow morocco* - *Lyon*, 1618

516 Boufon de la Cour ou Remede preservatif contre la Melancolie - - - *Par.* 1690

517 Bouquet (le) Printanier ou Recueil des plus belles fleurs de ce temps, *wood cuts, green morocco* *Autun*, 1662

518 Bourdon Histoire des Rats pour servir à l'Histoire Universelle - - - *Ratopolis*, 1738

519 Bourgeize, (la Petite), Poeme, *scarce* *Rouen*, 1610

520 Bourgoys Mysteres de la Vie, Passion et Mort de Jesus Christ, enrichies de figures par Bolswert *Anv.* 1622

Quarto.

521 Beze, les Vrais Pourtraits des Hommes Illustres, et Quarante quatre Emblemes, *numerous plates* *Lyon*, 1581

522 Biblia Sacra Latina, 2 vols. *manuscript, upon vellum, of the fourteenth century*

523 Bible, the Holy, translated by the English College of Doway, 2 vols. *Doway*, 1635

524 Bible, the Holy, *ruled, red morocco* - *Lond.* 1649

525 Bible, the Holy, *blue morocco* *Cambridge Field*, 1663

526 Biblische Figuren des Alten and Newen Testaments, *wood cuts* - - - *Francof*, 1560

527 Billaut, Adam, Menuisier de Nevers les Chevilles de, *yellow morocco, portrait* - - *Par.* 1644

528 Binet Abregé des Vies des Fondateurs des Religions de l'Eglise, *fine impressions of the portraits, blue morocco, ruled* - - - *Anv.* 1634

529 Biringoccio Pirotechnia, *plates* *Vinegia*, 1559

530 Bishop's Potion, the, or a Dialogue betweene the Bishop of Canterburie and his Physitian - 1641

531 Biveri Sacrum Sanctuarium Crucis et Patientiæ Crucifixorum et Cruciferorum Emblematicis Imaginibus ornatum, *many plates, fine impressions* - *Ant. Plantin*, 1634

532 Biveri Sacrum Oratorium Piarum Imaginum Immaculatæ Mariæ, *very fine impressions, blue morocco* *Ant. Plantin,* 1634

533 Black Box, Relation of the Contents of the, 1680

534 Bligh's Narrative of his Voyage, and of the Mutiny in the Bounty - - - - 1792

535 Blith's English Improver Improved, or the Survey of Husbandry - - - - - 1652

536 Bloomfield's Farmer's Boy, and other Poems 1800

537 Bloomfield, Illustrations of, with Life, by Brayley 1806

538 Blundeville's Art of Riding - *Lond.* 1597

539 Boccaccio il Decamerone con tre Novelle aggiunte, *blue morocco* - *Firenze Phil. de Giunta,* 1516

540 ——— il Decamerone, a most beautiful copy from Count Hoym's and Col. Stanley's Collection, the initials *painted with gold* *Vineg. per Gregorio de Gregori,* 1516

541 ——— il Decamerone nuovamente corretto, e con diligentia stampato, ORIGINAL EDITION, *red morocco, from the Roxburghe Library* - *Firenza Giunta,* 1527

542 Boccacio il Decamerone, con nuove Figure, da Crucioli, *russia* - *Venetia Jolito di Ferrarii,* 1542

543 ——— il Decamerone, *wood cuts, russia, ruled* *Venet Jolito,* 1546

544 ———, il Decamerone, per Rolli, LARGE PAPER, *a most beautiful copy, splendidly bound, (out of sheets) by Hering, in red morocco, from Colonel Stanley's Collection* *Lond.* 1725

545 Boccaccio il Libro di Fiameta, *russia* *Venet.* 1481

546 ——— Laberinto de Amor agora nuevamente traduzido en Lengua Castellana *Sevilla en Casa de Andres de Burgos,* 1546

547 Bocchii Symbolicæ Quæstiones, *first edition, cuts, by Bonasoni* - - - *Bonon.* 1555

548 Bocchii alia Editio, *plates, red morocco, with joints* *Bonon.* 1574

549 Bocconis Icones et Descriptiones Rariorum Plantarum Siciliæ, Melitæ, &c. *russia* - - *Oxon.* 1674

550 Boccus and Sydracke.—The History of Kyng Boccus and Sydracke, how he confoundyd his lerned men, and in the syght of them dronke stronge Venym in the name of the Trinite and dyd hjm no hurt, *black letter,* EXTREMELY RARE, *from the Roxburghe Collection* *Lond. T. Godfrey, for R. Saltwood, of Canterbury*

551 Bockii Veræ Imagines ad Vivum expressæ Herbarum, Fruticum, et Arborum - *Strasburg,* 1553

552 Boetius, the Boke of, called the Comforte of Philosophye, *black letter, russia* - - 1556

553 Boiardo Orlando Inamorato, con molte Stanze aggiunte de proprio Autore quale gli mancavano, *wood cuts, red morocco,* RARE - *Vinegia Aristot. de Ferrara,* 1533

554 Boiardo, Orlando Inamorato (coi tre Libri aggiunti da Niccolo degli Agostini) *a very rare edition, fine copy, russia,* *Mediol.* 1539

From Colonel Stanley's Collection. This edition is not mentioned by any Bibliographer. It is not the same as that printed at Venice by Niccolini da Sabio the same year.

555 ——— Orlando Innamorato rifatto da Berni, *green morocco* - - - *Milano,* 1542

556 ——— Orlando Innamorato rifatto da Berni, *yellow morocco, Count Hoym's copy* - *Venet. Giunta,* 1545

557 Boissardi Emblemata, Latin et François *Metis,* 1588

558 ——— Theatrum Vitæ Humanæ, *plates by De Bry* *Franc.* 1638

559 Boissard, les Emblemes de, planches par Theodore de Bry *Metz.* 1595

560 ——— Schawspiel Menschliches Lebens, *plates, blue morocco* - - - *Franc.* 1597

561 Boissart Mascarades recueillies et mises en taille douce, avec celles de Jacob de Geyn, *fine impressions, blue morocco* - - - - 1597

562 Bol (Hans.) Emblemata Evangelica ad XII Signa Cœlestia sive totidem Anni Menses accommodata, *remarkably fine impressions of the plates, by Sadeler, together with the beautiful* ORIGINAL DRAWINGS, BY HANS BOL. *Inlaid on fine drawing paper, and splendidly bound in red morocco* 1585

563 Bolton's Elements of Armories, *red morocco* *Lond.* 1610

564 Bonanni Ordinum Religiosorum in Ecclesia Militanti Catalogus, eorumque Indumenta in Iconibus expressa et oblata, Latinè et Italicè, 3 vols. *fine impressions of the plates, blue morocco, with joints* - *Roma,* 1706-10

565 ——— Ordinum Equestrium et Militarium Catalogus in Imaginibus, Latinè et Italicè, *fine impressions, blue morocco* *Roma,* 1711

566 ——— Gabinetto Armonico pieno d'Istromenti Sonori, *plates, fine impressions, blue morocco* *Roma,* 1722

567 Bonarelli Il Solimano Tragedia, *plates by Callot, yellow morocco* - - - *Bologna,* 1649

568 Boord's Breviary of Helthe, for all maner of Syckenesses and Diseases, *black letter, russia* *Myddelton, no date*

569 Boria Emblemata Moralia, *blue morocco,* *Berolini,* 1697

570 Bornitii Emblemata Ethico-Politica, *green morocco* *Mogunt.* 1669

571 Boschini l'Arcipelago, con tutte le Isole, Scogli, Secche, e Bassi Fondi, &c. *plates* - *Venet.* 1658

572 Bossewell's Workes of Armorie, *with plates, blue morocco* *Rich. Totel*, 1572

573 Another copy - - *H. Ballard*, 1597

Folio.

574 Besleri Hortus Eystettensis, sive Plantarum &c. quæ in viridariis arcem episcopal. cingentibus conspiciuntur, Repræsentatio, 2 vols. *plates, first edition, russia* *Norimbergæ*, 1613

575 Biblia Sacra Latina, cum Concordantiis, *wood cuts, russia, with joints* - - *Lugduni Koburger*, 1521

576 ————————, *ruled* - *Par. R. Stephani*, 1540

577 ——— Vulgare, con figure in legno *Venet. Rusconi*, 1517

578 Biblia Germanica, ex recensione et cum notis Martini Lutheri, 2 vols. - *Wittemberg*, 1541

The first edition of Luther's translation of the Bible after his final revision. A magnificent copy, printed upon the finest vellum, with the wood cuts coloured in a superior manner; in the original oak binding, covered with purple velvet, with richly gilt clasps and arms. Presumed to be the only copy printed upon vellum.

579 The Holy Bible, *fine copy, ruled* *Lond. Barker*, 1595

580 ———————— *Cambridge, Buck*, 1629

581 Biblia Pauperum, an accurate fac-simile, in Manuscript, of the first edition, by Leclabart, *red morocco.*

582 La Bible Moralizée, a Manuscript of the 15th century, upon vellum, with about 20 miniatures tastefully executed, and the capitals illuminated, *blue morocco, ruled.*

583 Bible. Figures des Histoires de la Sainte Bible accompagnees de briefs discours, *wood cuts* - *Par.* 1681

584 ——, Prints to illustrate the, by various Masters ———

585 ——, Figures representans les Evenemens les plus memobles de la, gravées par Picart, et autres, &c. 3 vols. *fine impressions* - - - *Amst.* 1720

586 Bleda Coronica de los Moros de Espana, *russia, with joints, by* Roger Payne, *fine copy, from the Stanley Collection* *Valencia*, 1618

587 Blondi Flavii Italiæ Illustratæ Libri VII. first edition, *red morocco* - *Romæ Ph. de Lignamine*, 1474

End of the Third Day's Sale.

FOURTH DAY'S SALE.

Octavo et Infra.

588 Bovii Rhetoricæ Suburbani, Partes Tres, *cuts* *Romæ*, 1676

589 Bovilli Samarobrini Proverbiorum Vulgarium libri tres *excudebat Petrus Vidovæus*, 1531

590 Bowles's Sonnets and other Poems, 2 vols. *green morocco* 1802

591 Bowlker's Art of Angling - - *Worcester*, ——

592 Bowyer's Origin of Printing - - 1786

593 Boxhornii Emblemata Politica - *Amst.* 1651

594 Bradley's Riches of a Hop Garden explained - 1729

595 Brandt Stultifera Navis Mortalium, *wood cuts, russia* *Basil.* 1572

596 Brantome, Œuvres de, 15 vols. - *a la Haye*, 1740

597 Brathwayte's Strappado for the Divell, Epigrams and Satyres alluding to the time, and Love's Labyrinth, or the True Lover's Knot - - 1615

598 Brathwait's Arcadian Princesse, or the Triumph of Justice, *with frontispiece, by Marshall* - 1635

599 Bremond (St.) The Triumph of Love over Fortune, *red morocco* - - - 1678

600 ———— le Double-Cocu, Histoire du Tems *Par.* 1678

601 Brescia, Cronichetta Breve e delettevole, nela quale si narra il principio di questa Cita de Brescia, *blue morocco*, RARE *Brescia per Ludovico da Sabio*, 1554

602 Brigentio Patavino, Villa Burghesia vulgo Princiana, Poeticè descripta - - - *Romæ*, 1716

603 Brightwell's Pistle to the Christen Reader—The Revelation of Anti-Christ—Antithesis, wherein are compared togeder Christes Actes and oure holye Father the Pope, *black letter, russia*, RARE *at Malborow, in the lunde of Hesse*, 1529

604 Brittain (Great) Description of, in Dutch, *plates, blue morocco, with joints* - - - *Middelburgh*, 1666

605 British Chronologist, 3 vols. - - 1789

606 British Garden, 2 vols. - - *Bath*, 1799

607 British Essayists, with Prefaces, Historical and Biographical, by A. Chalmers, 45 vols. *yellow morocco* - 1803

608 British Poets, collated with the best Editions, by Park, 42 vols. *fine paper, plates, yellow morocco* - 1805

10 10 -	609	British Theatre, with Biographical and Critical Remarks, by Mrs. Inchbald, 25 vols. *fine paper* - 1808	Risdon
7 7 -	610	British Drama, 5 vols. *fine paper, red morocco* - 1804	Do
18 -	611	Brome's Songs and other Poems, *portrait, morocco* 1661	Triphook
5 -	612	——————— - - 1664	Money
6 -	613	Brookes's Art of Angling, *cuts* - - 1766	King
5 -	614	——————— - - 1774	Triphook
2 -	615	Brown's Nature's Cabinet Unlock'd - - 1657	Heber
1 -	616	——— (Hawkins) Pipe of Tobacco in Imitatation of Six several Authors - - - 1736	Do
3 -	617	——— Collection of Miscellany Poems, Letters, &c. 1699	Money
		Pendragon, or the Carpet Knight, his Kalendar - 1698	Do
19 -	618	Browne's Britannia's Pastorals, 2 parts *Lond. Haviland*, 1625	Rodd
10 - -	619	Brumoy Theatre des Grecs, 13 vols. *Papier Velin, gravures avant la lettre, red morocco, by Derome* - *Par.* 1785	Payne
14 -	620	Brunet Manuel du Libraire, 3 vols. - *Ib.* 1810	Triphook
7 -	621	Bruni Epistole Heroiche, Poesie, *cuts, blue morocco* *Roma*, 1634	Singer
2 4 -	622	Bruno Nolano de gl'Heroici Furori al molto illustre et eccellente Cavilliero, Signor Philippo Sidneo, *red morocco* *Parigi*, 1585	Triphook
4 -	623	Brunt's Voyage to Cacklogallinia, *frontispicce* - 1727	Burn
5 -	624	Bruscambille, les Œuvres de, - *Lyon*, 1634	Triphook
12 -	625	——————— Fantasies de, - *Par.* 1668	Do
16 -	626	Brusoni Nuova Scelta di Sentenze, Motti e Burle d'Huomini illustri, *green morocco* - - *Venet.* 1657	Calkin
5 -	627	Bryant's Observations upon Rowley's Poems - 1781	Osborne
5 -	628	——— Vindication of Josephus, 1780. Bryant's Address to Dr. Priestley - - - 1780	Ward
6 -	629	Bryant on the Authenticity of the Scriptures - 1792	Triphook
1 5 -	630	Bryant's Observations upon the Plagues inflicted upon the Egyptians, *red morocco* - - 1794	Do
6 -	631	——— Sentiments of Philo-Judæus concerning the Λογος, or Word of God - - *Camb.* 1797	Do
9 -	632	Buchanani Poemata, *red morocco* - *Elzev.* 1628	Ward
11 -	633	——————— *red morcoco* - *Amst.* 1687	Clarke
2 -	634	Bulwer's Chirologia, or the Naturall Language of the Hand 1644	Triphook
4 -	635	Buonaparte, la Vedova, Commedia Facetissima *Par.* 1803	Do
15 15 -	636	Burnet's History of his own Time, 4 vols. LARGE PAPER, *elegantly bound in green morocco* - 1809	Ld. Yarmouth
16 -	637	Burney's Cecilia, 5 vols. - - 1783	Money
13 -	638	——————— traduite de l'Anglais, 6 vols. *morocco* *Geneve*, 1784	Heber
17 -	639	——— Camilla, 5 vols. - - 1796	Money
11 -	640	Burgi de Bello Suecico Commentarii, cum figuris, *red morocco* - - - - - *Leodii*, 1643	Triphook
9 -	641	Burton's Epitome of all the Lives of the Kings of France, *cuts*, - - - - 1639	Do
10 -	642	——— Anatomy of Melancholy, 2 vols. - 1800	Lewis

643 Busbequii Epistolæ ad Rudolphum II. - *Brux.* 1631

644 ——— Omnia quæ extant, *blue morocco* - *Elzev.* 1633

645 Aliud exemplar - - - 1660

646 Busbequii Omnia quæ extant, quibus accessit Epitome de Moribus Turcarum, *green morocco* - *Lond.* 1660

647 Busbequius's Epistles concerning his Embassy into Turkey 1694

648 ——— Travels into Turkey - - 1744

650 Busenello's Prospective of the Naval Triumph of the Venetians over the Turk - - 1658

651 Butcher's Survey and Antiquity of the Town of Stamford, and Bedwell's Tottenham High Cross, *large paper, russia* 1717

652 Butler's Hudibras, the first part - - 1663

653 ——— with cuts, *green morocco* - 1710

654 ——— Posthumous Works, in Prose and Verse, *green morocco* - - - 1715

655 Butler's Analogy of Religion, natural and revealed 1785

656 Bysshe's Art of English Poetry - - 1708

657 ——— 2 vols. - 1762

658 Cabinet des Fées ou Collection Choisie des Contes des Fées, et autres Contes Merveilleux, 41 vols. *Amst.* 1785-9

659 ——— du Roy de France, dans lequel il y a trois Perles d'inestimable Valeur, *red morocco* - 1581

660 ——— Satyrique des Vers Piquants et Gaillards, *Par.* 1621

661 Le Meme, 2 vols. *green morocco* - *sans date.*

662 Cælii Secundi Curionis Christianæ Religionis Institutio, *red morocco* - - - 1549

663 Cæsaris Commentarii de Bello Gallico, *genuine edition, red morocco* - - - *Elzev.* 1635

664 ——— 2 vols. *blue morocco* *Lond.* 1744

665 Caillieres la Logique des Amans, *red morocco* *Par.* 1669

666 Calisto y Melibea Tragicomedia, en la quel se contienen de mas de su agradable y dulce estilo, &c. *letras goticas,* RARE, *blue morocco, with blue morocco lining, wood cuts,* - *Sevilla.* 1523

667 Calisto y Melibea - - *Anvers.* 1599

668 Callcott's Musical Grammar - - 1806

669 Callot Salvatoris, Beatæ M. Virginis, Sanctorum Apostolorum Icones, *first impressions* - *Par.* 1631

670 —— Nouveau Testament, *green morocco, plates* *Ib.* 1632

671 —— Martyrium Apostolorum, *green morocco* *sine anno*

672 —— la Vie de l'Enfant Prodigue, *green morocco* *Ib.* 1635

673 —— la Petite Passion, 17 *plates, first impressions,*— Les Vices Humains, 8 *plates,* in 1 vol. *yellow morocco*

674 Callot Vita et Historia B. M. Virginis, *first impressions, red morocco*

675 —— Misere de la Guerre, *with two sets of the plates, one before the letter, red morocco* - *Par.* 1636

676 Callot Mysteres de Notre Seigneur, 20 *oval plates, yellow morocco*

677 —— Varie Figure Gobbi, *green morocco* - 1616

678 Altro esemplare - - - 1616

679 Callot Bailli de Sfessania, *first impressions, yellow morocco*

680 Les Faintaisies de Noble Callot. Les Exercices Militaires, in 1 vol. *green morocco*

681 Green's Catalogue of Callot's Works - 1804

682 Calmo le Bizzarre Faconde Rime Pescatorie, et altre Opere, *yellow morocco* - *Vinegia.* 1553

683 Altro esemplare, *blue morocco, cuts* - *Ib.* 1556

684 Calvin Advertissement sur les Reliques qui sont tant en Italie qu'en France, Allemaigne, &c. *red morocco* 1588

685 —— Declaration pour maintenir la vraye Foy contre les Erreurs detestables de Servet, *red morocco* *Geneve.* 1554

686 Camerarii Emblemata Amatoria, *red morocco* *Venet.* 1627

687 Camillo Scaglieri, la Nobilissima Anzi Asinissima Compagnia delli Briganti della Bastina, *blue morocco* *Milan.* 1598

688 Camoens, os Lusiadas de Luis, *blue morocco* *Lisboa.* 1644

689 Camus's Triumphs of Love - - 1720

690 Canceller's Alphabet of Prayers, very fruitefull to be exercised and used of everye Christian Man, *black letter, blue morocco* - *Lond. Denham.* 1565

691 Candia, Description of, in its Ancient and Modern State 1670

692 Canisii Catechismus Catholicus, *blue morocco* *Augustæ.* 1613

693 Cardani Arcana Politica, *red morocco* *Elzevir.* 1635

694 Carew's Poems, Songs, and Sonnets - 1670

695 Carlisle's Relation of three Embassies from Charles II. 1669

696 Carmina apposita ad Pasquillum, Anno 1522, *Romæ.* 1522

697 Carmina Quadragesimalia ab Ædis Christi Alumnis Composita, 2 vols. *green morocco* - *Oxon.* 1723

698 Carneval van Roomen of de Vastenavonds Vermaaklykheden, *cuts* - - - *Haarlem,* 1718

699 Carnavale Italiano Mascherato, *curious Masquerade prints, yellow morocco* - - - 1642

700 Caro (Annibale) gli Straccioni, Comedia, *red morocco* *Venet. Aldo,* 1582

701 Carter's true Relation of that as Honourable as Unfortunate Expedition of Kent, Essex, and Colchester, *russia* 1650

702 ——— Analysis of Honour and Armoury, *plates,* - 1660

703 ——— Views of Ancient Buildings in England, 3 vols. *red morocco* - - - - - 1786

704 ——— Admonition to Parliament, *black letter, wants title*

705 Cartwright's Comedies, Tragi-Comedies, and other Poems, *portrait by Lombart* - - 1651

706 Casa Rime et Prose di, *blue morocco* *Fiorenza Giunta,* 1554

707 Case, le Galatee en Francois, Latin, Allemand et Espagnol, *printed in cursive types, blue morocco* - *Lyon*, 1609

708 Cases of Divorce for several Causes - 1715

709 ——— Conscience concerning Astrologie - 1659

710 Cantique des Cantiques de Solomon, par Pierre de Courcelles - - - *Par.* 1564

711 Capella l'Anthropologia, *yellow morocco* *Venet. Aldi*, 1533

712 Capellæ Satyricon cum Notis Grotii, *portrait of the Prince of Condé, and of Grotius* - *Lugd. Bat.* 1599

713 Capicius de Principiis Rerum, *red morocco* *Venet. Aldi*. 1546

714 Capitoli Burleschi d'Incerto Autore - IXIC

715 Capper's Topographical Dictionary of the United Kingdom, *coloured maps* - - - - - 1808

716 Caprices Romanesques, 2 parts in 1 - *Amst.* 1745

717 Caquets de l'Accouchée, Recueil General de, et l'Anti-Caquet, *red morocco* - *Troyes, sans date*

718 ——————————— des Caquets de l'Accouchée, ou Discours facecieux ou se voit les moeurs, actions, et facons de faire des grands et petits de ce siecle, 3 vols. *red morocco*, a more complete set than has occurred on sale for many years - *Par.* 1555, 1633, &c.

Quarto.

719 Botero Agiunta alla Quarta Parte dell'Indie, di Mostri et Usanze di quelle Parti, &c. *curious wood cuts, Venet.* 1623. Botero, I Capitani del, *Venet.* 1622, in 1 vol.

720 Bouchet le Labirynth de Fortune et Sejour de trois Nobles Dames, *black letter, fine copy, blue morocco* *Par. par Marnef.* ——

721 ——— le Jugement Poetic de l'Honneur Feminin, et Sejour des Claires et Honnestes Dames, *black letter, wood cuts* - - *Poitiers Marnef*. 1538

722 ——— le Panegyrique du Chevalier sans Reproche en prose et en vers, *black letter, red morocco* *Poitiers*, 1527

723 Boullaye le Gouz les Voyages et Observations du Sieur, *many plates, red morocco* - *Par.* 1653

724 Boussueti de Natura Aquitalium Carmina, *plates*, *Lugd.* 1558

725 Brandeburgh, Memoires pour servir à l'Histoire de la Maison de - - - *Berlin*, 1751

726 Brandi Cronologia de Sommi Pontefici con le Effigii, Nomi, &c. - - - *Roma*, 1627

727 Brant Stultifera Navis, *first edition, wood cuts, red morocco* *Basil, Bergman de Olpe*, 1497

728 —— Navis Stultifera a Badio illustrata, *wood cuts, red morocco, with joints* *per Nicol, Lamperter*, 1406 (sic)

729 Brant Stultifera Navis, *wood cuts, red morocco* *Parisiis, sine anno*

730 —— la Grand Nef des Fols du Monde, *wood cuts, fine copy, red morocco* - *Lyon d'Ogerolles*, 1579

731 ———————— Folles, *wood cuts, blue morocco, fine copy* - - - *Ib.* 1583

732 Brant Carmina in Memorabiles Evangelistarum Figuras, *red morocco* - - - 1502

733 Bread, The Assize of, with Ordinances for Bakers, Brewers, &c. - - - - - 1671

734 Breynii Prodromi Fasciculi Rariorum Plantarum, *plates, russia, with joints* - - *Gedani*, 1739

735 Britannia Nova, offring most excellent Fruites by Planting in Virginia, *green morocco* - - 1602

736 Britannie, The Historie of Great, to the Raigne of Egbert, *russia* - - - 1606

737 Brouerius le tres Beau Water-Graefs decrit par, *numerous plates*

738 Browne's Fiftie yeares practise of Snaffle-riding - 1624

739 Brown's Travels through a great Part of Germany, *plates*, 1677

740 Bruck Emblemata Moralia et Bellica, *Argent.* 1615. Les Emblemes Moraulx et Militaires de Bruck, *Strasb.* 1616 *in 1 vol. yellow morocco*

741 Bruck Emblemata Politica *Argent. Hogenberg*, 1618

742 Brunelli Vigelli Speculum Stultorum, *wood cuts, blue morocco* - - - *Coloniæ*, 1499

743 Brunes Emblemata of Sinne-Werck, *very fine impressions, red morocco, with joints* - *Amst.* 1661

744 Bryant's New System of Ancient Mythology, 3 vols, *fine impressions, with the plate of Cupid and Psyche, by Bartolozzi, and a duplicate inserted by Sherwin, red morocco, with joints* - - - - - 1775

745 ———— Dissertation concerning the War of Troy ——

746 ———— Expostulation addressed to the British Critic 1799

747 Bucaniers of America, 3 parts, *plates, russia* - 1684

748 Bucoliche Composte da Bernardo Pulci et da altri, *first edition, red morocco* - *Firenza Mischomini*, 1494

749 Burke's Works, 4 vols. - - 1792

750 Burmanni Thesaurus Zeylanicus, exhibens Plantas in Insula Zeylana nascentes - *Amst.* 1737

751 ———— Rariorum Africanarum Plantarum Decades Decem, *plates, russia, with joints* - *Ib.* 1738

752 Burns' Views in North Britain to illustrate, by Storer and Greig - - - - 1805

753 Burney's Eight Sermons on Charles II. *fine portrait of Charles, blue morocco, with joints* - *no date*

754 Butler's History of Bees, *blue morocco* - *Oxf.* 1634

755 ———— Principles of Musick - - 1636

£ s. d.	Lot	Description	Buyer
7 -	756	Calendrier et Compost des Bergers, composé par le Berger de la grande Montagne, *wood cuts* - Troyes, ——	Payne
1 1 -	757	Callimachus cum scholiis nunc primum editis, *green morocco* - - *Basil Froben*, 1532	Triphook
2 13 -	758	Callot, Nobles et Gueux, 36 *plates, fine impressions* ——	D°
1 4 -	759	Callot Emblemes sur la Vie de la Mere de Dieu, *blue morocco*	D°
2 12 6	760	Callot, les Miseres et les Malheurs de la Guerre, gravées par Israel, *fine copy* - - *Par.* 1633	Johnstone
2 9 -	761	Callot, a Collection of 109 Prints from various Works, by Callot ——	D°
1 18 -	762	Callot's 25 Prints of Beggars ——	D°
1 12 -	763	Calvine's Commentaries upon the Prophet Daniel, translated into English - - *Lond.* 1570	Hancock
1 6 -	764	Camerarii Symbolorum et Emblematum centuria una collecta, *red morocco* - 1605	Payne

Folio.

£ s. d.	Lot	Description	Buyer
918 15	765	BOCCACCIO IL DECAMERONE, (VENEZIA) PER CHRISTOFAL VALDARFER DI RATISPONA, M:CCCC:LXXI.	Bought by Longman & Co. for Earl Spencer

Sold on the 17th Inst. for £918..15..-

Notwithstanding the publicity of the extraordinary sum which this Book produced at the Roxburghe Sale, all researches throughout Europe to procure another copy have proved entirely fruitless. This Volume still continues to be THE ONLY KNOWN PERFECT COPY OF THIS EDITION, and is, in all probability, the only copy which will ever be offered for public sale. Its unparalleled rarity, however, is not its only recommendation, as it contains many important Readings which have not been followed in any subsequent Edition.

The sale of this Book will be postponed till the 17th of June, the anniversary of its former sale in 1812. It will be the last Article in that Day's Sale.

£ s. d.	Lot	Description	Buyer
3 7 -	766	Boccace, le Decameron traduit par Maçon, *in rich old binding, in compartments, ruled* *Par.* 1545	Triphook
1 10 -	767	Boccaccio's Decameron, *with wood cuts, russia* 1620	D°
1 15 -	768	Boccaccius de Mulieribus Claris, *wood cuts, first edition, red morocco, imperfect. Ulmæ, Zeiner de Reutlingen.* 1473	D°
2 2 -	769	———— *with wood cuts, coloured, very rare, Lovanii per Egidium Vander Heerstraten,* 1487. Caoursin Rhodiæ Obsidionis Descriptio, *sine anno,* in 1 vol. *russia*	D°
3 - -	770	Boccase de la Louange et Vertu de Nobles et Clairs Dames, *black letter, wood cuts, blue morocco* *Par. Verard.* 1493	Booth
4 1 -	771	Boccaccius de Montibus, Sylvis, &c *first edition, fine copy, red morocco, with joints. Venet. Vindelin de Spira.* 1473	Payne
3 3 -	772	Bocatius's Falle of Princes and Princesses, translated by Lydgate, *black letter, wood cuts* *Lond. R. Tottel.* 1554	Rodd

1 2 - 773 Boetii de Consolatione Philosophiæ Libri V., *a rare edition, Supposed to be printed by Biel and Wensler, at Bazil, about* 1474 } Heber

22 11 6 774 BOETIUS. The Boke of Consolation of Philosophie. Atte requeste of a singular frend and gossib of myne, I, WILLIAM CAXTON, HAVE DONE MY DEBUOIR AND PAYNE TENPRYNTE IT. *Imperfect, bound in russia, without date* } Triphook
four leaves wanting

1 19 - 775 Boileau, Œuvres de, 2 vols. *plates by Picart, red morocco, gilt leaves* - - - *Amst.* 1718 } Heber

2 - - 776 Boke of Distyllacyon of the Water of all maner of Herbes, with the Fygures of the Styllatoryes, *black letter, wood cuts* - - *Lond. L. Andrewe,* 1527 } Payne

16 - 777 Bordone Isolario di tutti l'Isole del Mondo, *plates, russia* *Veneg. Torresano,* 1547 Booth

6 16 6 778 Bradford's Sketches of the Country, Character and Costume of Portugal and Spain, *coloured plates* 1810 } Hollingworth

7 - - 779 Braun Civitates Orbis Terrarum, 2 vols. *plates, vellum* —— Booth

4 14 6 780 Bretaigne, les Grandes Croniques de, *black letter* *Paris, Galliot du Pré,* 1514 } D°

27 10 - 781 Brusonii Facetiarum Libri Septem. ORIGINAL AND ONLY COMPLETE EDITION, all others being castrated, *blue morocco* - *Romæ, per Mazochium,* 1518 } Longman

2 16 - 782 Burgher's Leonora, translated by Spencer, with plates after the Designs of Lady Diana Beauclerk, *large paper, proofs, black morocco, with joints* - - 1796 } Naghton

3 3 - 783 Burnet's History of his own Time, 2 vols. *russia* 1724 Jefferies

4 16 - 784 Burton's Anatomy of Melancholy, *with a plate representing Melancholy, by Albert Durer, and a copy from it inserted, fine copy* - - - *Oxford.* 1632 } Jarvis

1 16 - 785 Burton's Description of Leicestershire, *with portrait and frontispiece by Delaram, russia* - - 1622 } Booth

3 15 - 786 Byrne's Twenty Views of Scottish Scenery, *russia, with joints* - - - - - 1807 } Dorrant

End of the Fourth Day's Sale.

FIFTH DAY'S SALE.

Octavo et Infra.

2 - 787 Casimer, King of Poland; or, the Amorous Prince 1681 Jacob

- 788 Cassette Verte, la - - *Haye,* 1779 sold with Lot 789

789 Castaneda Historia del Descubrimiento y Conquista de la India por los Portugueses traduzida en Romance Castellano, *russia* - - - *Anvers.* 1554

790 Castiglione il Libro del Cortegiano *Vineg. Giolito,* 1559

791 ———— le Courtisan de, - *Par.* 1538

792 Castlehaven's (Earl of) Trial for a Rape and Sodomy, *portrait* - - - - 1631

793 Cat may look upon a King - *Amst.* 1714

794 Catalogue of the Nobility of England, Scotland, and Ireland, *blue morocco* - - 1642

795 Cats Spiegel vanden Oudenende Nieuwentijt, *plates* *Dordrecht.* 1636

796 ———————— Nieuwen Tydt, *plates* *Ghedruckt.* 1652

797 Catherine Quene of Englande's Prayers or Meditacions, wherein the mind is stirred paciently to suffre all afflictions here, &c. *black letter, first edition, red morocco* *T. Berthelette.* 1545

798 Catón les Mots Dorez, en Latin et François, *red morocco* *Par.* 1577

799 Catullus, Tibullus, Propertius, *vellum* - *Amst.* 1640

800 Catullus's Poems, with Notes, 2 vols. - 1795

801 Cavallo on Electricity - - 1782

802 Caylus Nouveaux Contes Orientaux, 2 vols. *plates* *Amst.* 1780

803 Caylus Féeries Nouvelles, 2 vols. *red morocco* *Haye,* 1741

803* Cebes, la Table de l'Ancien Philosophe Cebes, avec trente Dialogues de Lucien, Auteur jadis Grec. *blue morocco* *Paris, J. Petit.* 1529

804 Celsus de Medecina, *green morocco* - *Elzev.* 1657

805 Censorinus de Die Natali, Havercampi *Lugd. Bat.* 1743

806 Cent Nouvelles Nouvelles, 2 vols. *figures detachées, blue morocco* - - - *Cologne,* 1701

807 Cerises (les) et la Double Meprise, Contes en Vers, *red morocco* - - - *Haye,* 1769

808 Cervantes. Vida y Hechos del Don Quixote de la Mancha, 4 vols. *plates by Folkema, blue morocco* *Haya,* 1744

809 ———————— con Notas de Don Juan Antonio Pellicer, 9 vols. *plates, blue morocco* *Madrid,* 1798

810 Cervantes Histoire de Don Quichotte, 6 vols. Nouvelles de Cervantes, 2 vols. 8 vols. *plates* - *Amst.* 1768

811 ———————— traduite par Florian, 6 vols. *vellum paper, plates, blue morocco* *Par.* 1799

812 Cervantes' Don Quixote, translated by Jarvis, 4 vols. *plates, russia* - - - - - 1801

813 Cervantes, les Nouvelles de, traduites par Rosset, &c. 2 vols. *blue morocco* - - *Par.* 1618

814 ———— Novelas Exemplares, 2 vols. *plates, red morocco* *Haya,* 1739

1 15 - 815 Chalkill's Thealma and Clearchus, a Pastoral History, in smooth and easie Verse, *rare, morocco* - 1683 } Triphook

2 18 - 816 Chamberlayne's Pharonnida, a Heroick Poem, *russia, scarce* - - - - 1659 } D°

5 - 817 Chandler's Vindication of the Miracles, 2 vols. 1729 Rodd

2 12 6 818 Chaos del Tri per Uno (da Teofilo Folengi) *vellum* *Vinegia, Sabio.* 1527 Payne

1 15 - 819 Chapelain La Pucelle, ou la France Delivrée, Poeme Heroique, *Venetian morocco. with joints, &c. by Roger Payne* *Par.* 1656 } Heber

18 - 820 Chapuis les Facetieuses Journees en Cent Nouvelles, *red morocco* - - - *Par.* 1584 } Triphook

passed 821 Charles V. Vie et Actions de l'Empereur, *plates* *Brussellès,* 1700 (Vol. 2. only)

7 - 822 Charles Stuart Roy d'Angleterre, Histoire du Procez de, *red morocco, ruled* - - *Lond.* 1650 } Ld. Aylesbury

1 - - 823 Charles II. Account of the Preservation of, after the Battle of Worcester, *red morocco, with joints* - 1766 } D°

1 11 6 824 Charron, Trois Livres de la Sagesse par, *red morocco* *Elseviers,* 1646 Payne

1 4 - 825 Autre Exemplaire, *red morocco, by De Rome* *Elzev. s. date* Sir J. Copley

17 - 826 ——————, *red morocco* - *Elzevir.* 1662 Lepard

1 1 - 827 Chartier les Œuvres d'Alain, *ruled* *Par. Galliot du Pré,* 1529 Clarke

1 1 - 828 Cheeke (Sir John) The Hurt of Sedition, how grievous it is to a Common-Welth, *black letter, red morocco* *Lond. Seres,* 1569 } Rodd

5 - 829 Cheitomæi Græco Barbara Novi Testamenti, *blue morocco* *Elzev.* 1649 } Triphook

5 - 830 Chetardye Instructions pour un Jeune Seigneur *Par.* 1683 Warner

2 - 831 Childrey's Natural Rarities of England, Scotland, and Wales - - - 1661 } Triphook

9 - 832 Choiseul, Memoires de M. le Duc de, 2 vols. *Par.* 1790 Hibbert

1 16 - 833 Cholieres les Apres Disnees du Seigneur de, *red morocco* *Par.* 1587 } Lepard

1 10 - 834 —— les Neuf Matinees du Seigneur de *Ib.* 1585 D°

1 5 - 835 Chompre, Dictionnaire Portatif de la Fable, revue par Meon, 2 vols. in 1, *vellum paper* - *Par.* 1801 } Warner

2 10 - 836 Christoferson's Exhortation to all Menne to take hede and beware of Rebellion, *black letter* *Lond. Cawood,* 1554 } Rodd

8 - 837 Chudleigh's Poems on several Occasions, *blue morocco* 1713 Triphook

18 - 838 Ciacconius de Triclinio, sive de modo convivandi apud priscos Romanos, *plates, blue morocco* - *Amst.* 1664 } Hibbert

6 - - 839 Ciceronis Opera Omnia, 10 vols. *very fine copy, red morocco* *Elzevir,* 1642 } Lepard

3 10 - 840 ——————, ex recensione Ernesti, 8 vols. *Halæ Sax.* 1774 } Hayes

17 - 841 —— Epistolæ ad Atticum, *blue morocco, scarce* *Aldus,* 1513 } Heber

842 Ciceronis de Philosophia, Pars Prima, LARGE PAPER, *russia*, RARE - - - *Aldus*, 1541

843 ——— Tusculanæ Disputationes, Davisii et Bentleii *Oxon.* 1805

844 ——— de Officiis Libri Tres, *red morocco* *ex off. Plantiniana*, 1603

845 Cicero de Officiis, *red morocco* *Lutet. Barbou.* 1773

846 Ciceronis Cata Major, *red morocco* *Lutet. Barbou.* 1758

847 Ciceroe's thre Bookes of Duties turned out of Latine into English, by Nicolas Grimalde, whereunto the Latine is adjoyned, *black letter*, *russia* *Lond. by R. Tottil*, 1558

848 Another edition, *russia* - *Ib. R. Tottell*, 1583

849 Cicero's Prince, the Reasons and Counsels for Settlement and good Government of a Kingdom, collected out of Cicero's Works, by Bellendenus, *blue morocco* 1668

850 Cieco. Mambriano Istoriato, composto per Francisco Cieco Ferrarese qual ne la Lingua volgare obtene il primo loco, *wood cuts*, *scarce* - - *Milano*, 1517

851 Ciel (Le) Réformé, Essai de Traduction de partie du livre Italien, Spaccio della Bestia Trionfante, *morocco* 1750

852 Cinthio, Le Fiamme di Giovanni Battista Giraldi, *green morocco* - - *Vineg. Giolito*, 1548

853 Cities (The) great Concern in this Case or Question of Honour and Arms, whether Apprenticeship extinguisheth Gentry? Portrait of Lord Fittswater - 1674

854 Clarendon's History of the Rebellion and Civil Wars of England, 6 vols. LARGE PAPER, *elegantly bound in blue morocco, with joints* - *Oxford*, 1807

855 Claudiani Opera, *blue morocco* - *Aldus*, 1523

856 Claudianus, *green morocco, morocco inside* *Amst.* 1620

857 ————, *red morocco* - - *Ib.* 1628

858 ———— Heinsii, *red morocco* *Lugd. Bat. Elzevir.* 1650

859 Cleavland's Poems, *portrait* - - 1659

860 Cleaveland Revived; Poems, Orations, Epistles, and other of his genuine incomparable Pieces, *portrait* 1660

861 Cloppenburgii Sacrificiorum Patriarchalium Schola Sacra, *red morocco* - *Lug. Bat. Elzevir.* 1637

862 Clusii Rariorum aliquot stirpium per Hispanias observatarum Historia, *russia* - *Ant. Plantin*, 1576

863 Cluverii Introductio in Geographiam, *maps*, *red morocco* *Elzevir.* 1651

864 Alia editio, *red morocco* - - 1661

865 Cocaii (Merlini) (Theophili Folengi) Opus Macaronicorum, totum in pristinam formam per me Magistrum Aquariam Lodolam optime redactum, *scarce* *Tusculani apud Lacum Benacensem*, 1521

866 Cocaii (Merlini) Macaronicorum Poemata, *red morocco* *Venet.* 1554

Price	Lot	Description	Buyer
1 9 -	867	Cocaii (Merlini) Opus Macaronicorum, *red morocco, ruled, Amst.* 1692	Clarke
12 -	868	Cocles (Barthelemy) Enseignemens de Physionomie et Chiromancie, monstrans par le regard du visage, signes de la face et lignes de la main, les mœurs et complexions des Hommes, *wood cuts, blue morocco* *Paris*, 1638	Barker
9 -	869	Cocus, Sermon pour la Consolation des *Amboise*, 1751	Triphook
7 -	870	Cocuage, les Privileges du - *a Vicon.* 1722	D°
7 -	871	Codicille d'Or, ou petit recueil tiré de l'Institution du Prince Chrestien, composée par Erasme, *red morocco* 1665	Clarke
3 -	872	Coffee, Tea and Chocolate, The Manner of Making 1685	Hibbert
1 -	873	Coigny (Marechal Duc de) Campagne en Allemagne, 3 vols. *Amst.* 1761	Warner
16 -	874	Coins of the World, *wants title* *Typis Ægidii Radæi* 1575	Arch
2 9 -	875	Cokain's (Aston) Small Poems of divers sorts, *scarce, red morocco* - - - 1658	Hibbert
2 -	876	Coles's Art of Simpling - - 1656	Warner
12 -	877	Colet Histoire Palladienne traitant des Gestes et genereux faits d'armes et d'Amours de plusieurs grands Princes et Seigneurs, specialement de Palladien, *red morocco* *Paris*, 1573	Rodd
7 -	878	Colletet, les Diversemens du Sieur, *blue morocco* *Ib.* 1633	Triphook
5 -	879	Collier, Journal du Voyage de, resident à la Porte *Paris*, 1672	D°
5 -	880	Collier, Contes et Poesies, 2 vols. - *Saverne*, 1792	Warner
17 -	881	Colligny, La Vie de Messire Gaspar de, *yellow morocco* *Elzevier*, 1642	Payne
10 -	882	Colligni, La Tragedie de, par François de Chantelouve *morocco*, (Reprint) - - 1575	Hibbert
4 -	883	Collins's Poetical Works, *red morocco* - 1805	Triphook
10 -	884	Collop's Poesis Rediviva, or Poesie Reviv'd - 1666	Rodd
1 9 -	885	Colloque Amoureux ou Dialogues familiers, ou est remarqué l'astuce et finesse des garçons, et la fragilité des filles, *scarce* - - - *Cologne*, 1670	Triphook
passed	886	Collyer's History of England, 14 vols. - 1775	—
6 -	887	Colombina, il Bomprovifaccia per Sani et Amalati, *green morocco* - - *Padova*, 1621	Hibbert
9 -	888	Colvil's Whiggs Supplication, or the Scotch-Hudibras 1710	Johnstone
2 -	889	Combatz (Les) du fidelle Papiste Pelerin Romain contre l'Apostat Antipapiste, tirant a la Synagogue de Geneve, *green morocco. gilt leaves* - *Rouen*, 1551	Hibbert
17 -	890	Autre exemplaire, *blue morocco* - *Lyon*, 1551	Heber
6 -	891	Comarrieu, Elise Dumesnil, par Marie de, 5 vols. 1800	Eaton
2 -	892	Comedies—La Coifeuse a la Mode, *Paris*, 1649.—Le Chevalier a la Mode par Dancourt, *Haye*, 1616.—La Tapisserie Vivante, 1696	Warner
3 -	893	Comedies en Proverbes *sans date*	Triphook
4 -	894	Comenii Janua Aurea Reserata quatuor Linguarum, 2 vols. *green morocco* - *Ludg. Bat. Elzevir*, 1640	D°

895 Comenii Latinæ Linguæ Janua, Lat. and Eng. Portrait by Cross - - - 1656

896 Comenii Orbis Sensualium Picta, hoc est, omnium principalium in mundo rerum et in vita actionum, Pictura et Nomenclatura, 2 vols. *wood cuts* - *Noribergæ,* 1746

897 Commines, les Memoires de Messire Philippe de, *red morocco* - - *Leide, Elzeviers,* 1648

898 Compan, le Palais de la Frivolité - *Amst.* 1773

899 Compere (le) Mathieu, ou les Bigarrures de l'Esprit Humain, 3 vols. *red morocco* - *Lond.* 1772

900 Complements, The Mirrour of, with addition of Witty Songs, &c. - - - - 1650

901 Comte de Gabalis ou Entretiens sur les Sciences secretes, *yellow morocco* - - *Par.* 1670

902 Comtes (les) du Monde Adventureux - *Ib.* 1560

903 Conciones et Orationes ex Historicis Latinis excerptæ, *blue morocco* - - *Amst. Elzev.* 1652

904 Alia editio, *green morocco, with joints,* UNCUT *Ib.* 1662

905 Alia editio, *blue morocco, with joints,* UNCUT *Ib.* 1672

906 Confession of the true and Christian Fayth, according to God's Word and Actes of Parliament, holden at Edenburghe, the 28th of Januarie, 1581, being the 14th yere of the King's (James VI.) reigne, *black letter, blue morocco,* RARE - *Lond. by R. Waldegrave,* ——

907 Confidence Philosophique - *Lond.* 1771

908 Confutation of that Treatise which one John Standish made against the protestacion of D. Barnes in the yeare 1540, wherein the holy scriptures (perverted and wrested in his sayd treatise) are restored to their owne true understonding agayne, by Myles Coverdale, *black letter, blue morocco,* RARE - - - *no date*

909 Consolatorium timorate Conscientie Johannis Nyder *sine anno aut loco*

910 Constantini, la Vie de Scaramouche *Brusselles,* 1696

Quarto.

911 Camilli, Imprese Illustri di diversi coi Discorci di Camillo Camillo et con le figure intagliate da Porro *Venet.* 1586

912 Campo, Cremona Fedelissima Citta rappresentata in Disegno, et illustrata d'una breve Historia, *plates* *Milano,* 1645

913 Capaccio Trattato delle Imprese, *white morocco, plates, gilt leaves* - - - *Napoli,* 1592

914 Capelloni Vita del Prencipe Andre d'Oria *Venét. Giolito,* 1569

915 Cappello Rime de Bernardo, *fine copy, green morocco* *Venet.* 1560

916 Carew's Survey of Cornwall, *morocco, with joints* - 1602

917 Carion, The thre Bokes of Cronicles, whyche John Carion (a man syngularly well sene in the Mathematycall Sciences) gathered with great diligence, with an Appendix, by John Funcke, from 1532 to 1550, *black letter, fine copy* - - *Lond. Gwalter Lynne* 1550

918 Caritone Racconti Amorosi di Cherea e di Callirroe 1752

919 Carleton's Thankfull Remembrance of God's Mercy, *plates, blue morocco, with joints* - - 1627

920 Carlyle's Specimens of Arabian Poetry, *russia* *Camb.* 1796

921 Caroso da Sermoneta il Ballarino, ornato di molte Figure, *ruled* - - - *Venet.* 1581

922 Cartari, le Imagini de i Dei de gli Antichi, *plates, ruled* *Venet Valgrisi,* 1571

923 Altro esemplare, *blue morocco, with joints* - *Lione,* 1581

924 Cary's Map of England and Wales, *coloured* - 1794

925 Casa, Rime e Prose di Giovanni della Casa, *russia* *Vineg. Bevilacque,* 1558

926 Casas, Brevissima Relacion de la Destruycion de las Indias: colegida por el Obispo don Fray Bartolome de las Casas, o Casaus, de la Orden de Santo Domingo, 1552. Treynta Proposiciones muy Juridicas, 1552. Una Disputa entre el Obispo, Bartolome de las Casas y el Dotor Gines de Sepulveda, 1552, *fine copy, russia, rare*

927 A Catalogue of the Five Conquerors of this Island and theire Armes, viz. The Britaynes, the Romaines, the Saxons, the Danes, and lastly, the Normans, and of theire Succession. MANUSCRIPT ON VELLUM, with 14 Emblazoned Coats of Arms, *red morocco, with Waller the Poet's Autograph*

928 Catalogue of the most vendible Books in England. 1658

929 Catechisme, That is to say, ane commone and catholick instructioun of the Christin people in materis of our catholick faith and Religioun: set furth by John, Aschbischop of Sanct Androus, at Edinburgh, the 26 Day of Januarie, the zeir of our Lord, 1551, *black letter, fine copy, blue morocco,* RARE *Prentit at sanct Androus,* 1553

930 Catherina da Siena Dialogo dela Divina Providentia, *blue morocco* *Venet. per Mathio di Codeca da Parma,* 1483

931 Catherinæ Senensis Vita ac Miracula selectiora formis Æneis expressa, *very fine impressions* *Antv. apud Philippum Gallum,* 1603

932 Cato cum Commentario, *red morocco, with joints* *sine anno*

933 Catzii Emblemata varia, *blue morocco* - *Rott.* 1627

934 Cavallerino, Ino, Tragedia - *Modona,* 1583

935 Cavallero Teterminado, Traduzido de Lengua Francesa en Castellana por Don Hernando de Acuna, *plates* *Anv.* 1591

936 Cavendish's Life of Cardinal Wolsey, *portrait, morocco, with joints* - - - 1641

937 **Caylus Recueil d'Antiquités Egyptiennes, Etrusques, Grecques, et Romaines, 7 vols.** *very fine copy, red morocco* Par. 1752

938 Ceccheregli delle Attioni et Sentenze del Alessandro de' Medici primo Duca di Fiorenza *Vineg. Giolito,* 1565

939 Cellini, Vita di Benvenuto, da lui Medesimo scritta *Colonia, senz. anno*

940 Centeno, Historia de Cosas del Oriente, *russia, scarce* *Cordova,* 1595

941 Cervantes' Don Quixote, by Jarvis, 2 vols. *with very fine impressions of Hogarth's, Vandergutch's, Hayman's, Coypell's, and the plates from the Madrid edition inserted, green morocco, with joints* - 1742

942 Chambers' Jesuits' Practice of Perspective - 1726

943 Character of a London Diurnall, with severall select Poems 1647

944 Caracaturas by Leonardo da Vinci, from Drawings by Hollar, out of the Portland Museum - 1786

945 Charles VII. Traité de Paix, *black letter,* - *sans date*

946 ——— I. His Tryal, *half bound, morocco* - 1649

947 ——— The manner of the Deposition of, - 1649

948 ——— His Speech made upon the Scaffold, immediately before his Execution - - 1649

949 Charles, Prince of great Brittaine, his Joyfull returne from the Court of Spaine, *scarce* - 1623

950 Charlemaigne. Chronique de Charlemaigne des douze Pairs de France et de Fierabras, *black letter, wood cuts,* VERY RARE, *imperfect at the beginning* - *Lyon,* 1486

951 Charlemaigne, la Conqueste du Grant roy Charlemaigne des Espaignes. Et les vaillances des douze pers de France. Et aussi celles de Fierabras, *black letter, wood cuts* - - - *Lyon,* 1501

952 Charleton's Chorea Gigantium, vulgarly called Stone-Heng, restored to the Danes, *green morocco, gilt leaves* 1663

953 Chasteau (le) de Labour, *black letter, fine copy, red morocco,* RARE - *Rouen par Jacques le Forestier,* 1500

954 Chaucer's Canterbury Tales, with Notes and a Glossary, by Tyrwhitt, 2 vols. *large paper, with Mortimer's plates inserted, russia* - - *Oxf* 1798

955 ——— Plough-man's Tale, with a short exposition of the words and matters - *Lond. by Macham,* 1606

956 Chauchard's Description of Germany, Holland, &c by Stockdale, with the map in folio - 1800

957 Chertablon, la Maniere de se bien preparer à la Mort par des considerations sur la Cene, la Passion et la Mort de Jesus Christ, avec de tres-belles Estampes Emblematiques, *very fine impressions, black morocco. Anvers.* 1700

958 **Chesse Play, with certain briefe instructions thereunto belonging, with a prety Poeme of a whole Game played at Chesse, written by G. B.,** *scarce* **Lond. Jackson. 1597**

5 – 959 Chesse. The Game at Chesse, a metaphorical Discourse, shewing the present Estate of this Kingdome 1643 *Hollingworth*

9 – 960 Cheval, Description du, selon ses Poils principaux et leur diverses Divisions, sa Complexion et les qualites qui en resultent, *coloured plates, by Ridinger, red morocco* *Rodd*

3 4 – 961 Chinois, les Punitions des, représentés en vingt-deux gravures, avec des Explications en Anglais et en Français, *coloured plates, green morocco* - 1801 *Triphook*

15 – 962 Choisy, Histoire de la Vie de David, enrichie de figures *Par. sans date* *Hollingworth*

Folio.

3 6 – 963 Callot, les Images de tous les Saints et Saintes de l'Année *Par.* 1636 *Triphook*

3 10 – 964 Cantarini Varii Disegni Istoriati, fifty-two very spirited Drawings in Crayons *Do.*

1 2 – 965 Carrachi, le Arte di Bologna, designate di, ed intagliate da Cimone Guiline, *russia* - *Roma,* 1776 *Johnston*

22 1 – 966 Cathon. The Booke called Cathon, translated oute of Frensshe in to Englysshe, by William Caxton, *wanting signature* e, *russia* - Caxton. 1483 *Triphook*

17 – 967 Caylus, Histoire de Joseph, par Figures, *blue morocco* *Amst.* 1757 *Do.*

9 9 – 968 Cent Nouvelles Nouvelles, *wood cuts, black letter, red morocco* - - *Paris, A. Verard, sans date* *Do.*

1 10 – 969 Chartier, (Alain) les Faits de Maitre, *black letter, damaged* *Paris, Carron.* 1489 *Dibden*

32 11 – 970 Chastysing of Goddes Chyldren. The Prouffytable Boke for mannes soule, and right comfortable to the body, and specyally in aduersitee and tribulacyon, Caxton, *without date.* The Tretyse of the Love of Jhesu Christ, Wynken de Worde, *without date,* 2 vols. in 1, *fine copies of two books of* very great rarity *Ld. Aylesbury*

3 3 – 971 Chaucer's Works, by Speght, *black letter, russia* 1602 *Cattley*

162 15 – 972 Chaucer's Troylus and Creside, *fine copy, russia, wants one leaf, signature* p. I. from the Towneley Collection, very rare - - *explicit per Caxton, sine anno* *Triphook*

26 5 – 973 Chauncy's Historical Antiquities of Hertfordshire, *fine copy, red morocco, with all the plates* - 1700 *Rodd*

Imperfect Sold first time for £42.0.0 36 15 – 974 Chesse. The Game and Playe of the Chesse, translated oute of the Frenche, and emprynted by Caxton 1474 *Triphook*

This is one of the rarest productions of Caxton's Press, and reputed to be *the first book printed in England. Fine copy, Venetian morocco,* but the last leaf is supplied by MS. and the leaf of the table wanting

1 13 – 975 Chifletii Lilium Francicum Veritate Illustratum, *plates* *Antv. Plantin.* 1658 *Clarke*

20 - - 976 Chronica del muy esclariscido Principe y Rey don Alfonso el Onzeno, *very rare, blue morocco* *Valladolid,* 1551 } Arch

13 5 - 977 Chronica del Famosa Cavallero Cid Ruy Diez Campidor, *very scarce* - *Burgos, P. de Junta.* 1593 } D°

3 10 - 978 Chronica dos Reys de Portugal - *Lisboa,* 1677 D°

3 13 6 979 Coronica del Serenissimo Rey Don Pedro, *scarce* *Pampluna,* 1591 } D°

4 - - 980 Cronicas del Rey Don Joam e dos Reys de Portugal *Lisboa,* 1643 } D°

1 15 - 981 Cronycle of Englondes with the fruyte of Tymes, *wants the first leaf* - - *Wynken de Worde,* 1502 } Longman

End of the Fifth Day's Sale.

SIXTH DAY'S SALE.

Octavo et Infra.

17 - 982 Contes Nouveaux, Fables et Œuvres Melées de M. G * *, *green morocco* - - - *Amst.* 1745 } Warner

7 - 983 ——— Chinois, ornées de Figures, 2 vols. *Par.* 1723 D°

1 7 - 984 ——— Persans, les Mille et un Jour, traduits par De la Croix, 5 vols. - - *Par.* 1729 } Triphook

17 - 985 ——— Tartares, les Mille et un Quart-d'Heure, 3 vols. *Par.* 1753 D°

2 6 - 986 Contes (Nouveaux) à Rire, et Avantures Plaisantes ou Recreations Françoises, 2 vols. *plates, red morocco* *Cologne.* 1722 } Wellesley

1 19 - 987 Contes et Nouvelles, en Vers, par Grecourt, et autres, 4 vols. *red morocco* - - *Londres,* 1778 } Dulau

7 - 988 Conti (Giusto de) la Bellamano ristorato per Corbinelli, *yellow morocco* - - *Parigi,* 1595 } Heber

3 3 - 989 Contreditz du Prince des Sotz Autrement dit Songecreux, par Gringore, *black letter* *Paris, N. Coutou, pour Galliot du Pré.* 1530 } Triphook

18 - 990 Autre Edition, *la table et la souscription manquent, black letter* - - *Paris, Jehan Longis,* 1532 } Lang

991 Contreras (Hierosme de) Histoire des Amours extremes d'un Chevalier de Sevile dit Luzman, a l'endroit d'une belle Demoiselle appellée Arbolea, traduite de l'Espagnol par G. Chappuys - - *Lyon.* 1580

992 Controverses des Sexes Masculin et Femenin, en trois livres, par Gratian du Pont, *wood cuts, red morocco* 1538

993 Cooke's Reprehension of naked Breasts and Shoulders 1678

994 Cookerie, a Booke of, and the Order of Meates to bee served to the Table, both for Flesh and Fish Days, *black letter, russia* - - - 1620

995 Copywell's Shrubs of Parnassus, *russia* - 1760

996 Coquillart, les Œuvres de, *red morocco, ruled* *Paris, Galiot du Pré,* 1532

997 Corbett's Poetica Stromata, or a Collection of sundry Pieces in Poetry, *blue morocco* - 1648

998 ——— Poems, more copious than the preceding 1672

999 Cornazano Opera nova in Terza Rima, *wood cuts, red morocco, scarce* *Venetia per Zorzi di Rusconi.* 1517

1000 Corneille, les Chef-d'œuvres de, *with a portrait inserted, large paper, blue morocco* - *Oxford,* 1746

1001 Corneille, a Collection of Plates to illustrate, &c. *red morocco, gilt leaves, fine impressions*

1002 Cornelianum Dolium Comœdia lepidissima, *with frontispiece* - - - *Londini,* 1638

1003 Cornelius Nepos, *morocco* - *Brindley,* 1744

1004 Corne-waley's (Sir William) Essayes - 1600

1005 Coronelli's Account of the Morea, Negropont, &c. *plates* 1687

1006 Corrozet, Hecatongraphie, c'est a dire la Description de cent Figures et Hystoires, *wood cuts, blue morocco* *Par.* 1541

1007 Autre edition, *yellow morocco* - *Ib.* 1543

1008 ——— *red morocco* - - - 1548

1009 Corrozet, le Parnasse des Poetes François modernes, contenant leurs plus riches et graves Sentences, Discours, &c. *red morocco* - - *Par.* 1571

1010 Corrozet et Champier, le Caithalogue des Villes et Citez Assises et Troys Gaulles, avec ung traicté des fleuves et fontaines, illustré de nouvelles figures, *red morocco* *Par.* 1539

1011 Corrozet les Antiquitez Chroniques et Singularitez de Paris, avec le Second Livre par J. Rabel, *plates* *Par.* 1586. 1588

1012 Costalii (Petri) Pegma, cum Narrationibus Philosophicis, *wood cuts, very fine copy, blue morocco, gilt leaves* *Lugduni,* 1555

1013 Costo, il Fuggilozio, diviso in otto giornate *Venet.* 1600

1014 Cotton's Poetical Works - - 1765

1015 **Country-Man's Commonwealth, containing divers Golden Sentences** - - - 1634

1016 Courval-Sonnet, les Satyres de, *portrait, first edition, blue morocco* - - - *Par.* 1621

1017 ———— Satyre Menippe sur les poignantes traverses du Mariage, *blue morocco* - *Par.* 1621

1018 Cousin de Mahomet, 2 vols. *cuts* - 1781

1019 Coustau, le Pegme, avec les Narrations Philosophiques, par Lanteaume, *wood cuts* - *Lyon.* 1560

1020 Coverdale (Myles) The Olde Fayth, an evydent probation out of the Holy Scripture, that the Christen Fayth (which is the right true olde and unfounded faith) hath endured sens the begynnynge of the worlde, *black letter, very fine copy, blue morocco,* RARE - 1541

1021 Coxe's Sketches of the State of Swisserland 1779

1022 Coyer, Bagatelles Morales - - 1769

1023 Cramerii Octoginta Emblemata Moralia nova *Francof.* 1630

1024 Cranmer's Catechismus, that is to say, a short Instruction into Christian Religion, for the synguler commoditie and profyte of children and yong people, *black letter, fine copy, portrait inserted, blue morocco,* RARE *Gualterus Lynne excudebat.* 1548

1025 Crashaw's Steps to the Temple, Sacred Poems; with the Delights of the Muses, *frontispiece, blue morocco* 1648

1026 Crashawi Poemata et Epigrammata, Latina et Græca *Cantab.* 1670

1027 Craven (Miladi) Voyage en Crimée et à Constantinople, *maps* - - - - - 1789

1028 Cremonne (Baptiste Platine de) de l'Honneste Volupte, *red morocco* - - *Lyon,* 1571

1029 Cremoninus de Calido Innato et Semine, *morocco* *Elzev.* 1634

1030 Crescimbeni Commentarii della Poesia Italiana, riduplicati da Mathias, 3 vols. - - *Lond.* 1803

1031 Crescimbeni Storia dell' Accademia degli Arcadi istituita in Roma l'Anno 1690, *plates* - *Lond.* 1804

1032 Cretin, les Poesies de, *morocco* - *Par.* 1723

1033 Croce, Opere Varie di Giulio Cesare della Croce, raccolte in quattro Volume, con Indice di tutti gli Oposculi, 4 vols. *green morocco, from Croft's Collection* *Bologna,* 1611-29

1034 Croft's Catalogue, with the Prices - - 1783

1035 Cromer's notable Example of God's Vengeance upon a murdering King, *black letter. Lond. by John Daye.* ——

1036 Cromwell, Court and Kitchen of Elizabeth, commonly called Joan Cromwell, *portrait, blue morocco* 1664

1037 Cronel, Histoire de Mademoiselle, dite Fretillon *a la Haye,* 1740

1038 Crosilles, l'Heresie suspecte a la Monarchie, *red morocco* *Par.* 1624

1039 Cronicle of Yeres from the Begynnynge of the Worlde, wherin ye shale fynd the Names of al the Kynges of Englande, of the Mayers and Shyreffes of the Cyte of London, and bryefly of many notable acts done in and syth the reygne of Kyng Henry the Fourthe, *black letter* *Lond. by Thomas Petyt,* 1543

1040 Crowley's Confutation of 13 Articles wherunto Nicholas Sharton, late Bishop of Salysburye subscribed and caused to be set forth in print in the yere 1546, when he recanted in Smithfield at the burning of Anne Askue, which is lively set forthe in the figure followynge, *black letter, blue morocco,* RARE - - *Lond. John Daye,* ——

1041 Cruttwell's Universal Gazetteer, 3 vols. and Atlas, 4to. 1798

1042 Cumberland (The Duke of) and Lady Grosvenor, complete History of - - - 1770

1043 Cupidon dans le Bain, ou les Avantures Amoureuses des Personnes de Qualité, *red morocco* *a la Haye,* 1698

1044 Curtis's Botanical Magazine, 18 vols. in 6 - 1787

1045 Cutts's Poetical Exercises - - 1687

1046 Cynthien, Cent Excellentes Nouvelles de J. B. Giraldy Cynthien, traduites par Chappuys, 2 vols. *green morocco* *Par.* 1584

1047 Cytherée a Madame la Duchesse de Lorraine, 4 vols. *Par.* 1642

1048 Cynthia, with the tragical Account of the unfortunate Loves of Almerin and Desdemona *no date*

1049 D'Ageno, Prose e Rime - - 1790

1050 Daillbiere, les Entretiens Curieux de Tartuffe et de Rabelais sur les Femmes, *blue morocco* *Middelbourg,* 1688

1051 D'Alquie, la Defence du Cœur contre les Attaques d'Amour, *morocco* - - *Amst.* 1688

1052 ——— la Science et l'Ecole des Amans, *red morocco* *Amst.* 1679

1053 Dalrymple's Collection of English Songs - 1796

1054 D'Amboise, Discours ou Traicté des Devises, *Par.* 1726; Devises Royales par Adrien d'Amboise *Par.* 1721

1055 Damvilliers, Les Imaginaires ou Lettres sur l'Heresie Imaginaire, *red morocco* - - *Liege,* 1667

1056 Dance (la) aux Aveugles et autres Poesies du XV. Siecle, *Lille,* 1748

1057 D'Ancourt, les Œuvres de Théatre de, 12 vols. *yellow morocco* - - - *Par.* 1760

1058 Daniell, The Worthy Tract of Paulus Jovius, contayning a discourse of rare inventions, both militarie and amourous, called Imprese, *green morocco* *Lond. by Simon Waterson,* 1585

1059 Daniell's certaine small Works, *yellow morocco, scarce* *Lond. for S. Waterson*, 1611

1060 ——— Poetical Works, to which is prefix'd Memoirs of his Life and Writings, 2 vols. - - 1718

1061 Dante, le Terze Rime, *russia* - *Venet. Aldus.* 1502

1062 ——, Commedia di, con uno Dialogo circa el Sito, Forma e Misure dello Inferno, *fine copy, blue morrocco* *Firenze Giunta*, 1516

1063 ——— con Nuove et Utili Ispositioni, *red morocco, ruled* *Lione, Rovillio*, 1571

1064 D'Anville, Proposition d'une Mesure de la Terre *Par.* 1735

1065 ————, Mesure Conjecturale de la Terre sur l'Equateur *Par.* 1736

1066 ———— Reponse au Memoire envoyé à l'Academie Royale des Sciences contre le Mesure Conjecturale, 1738

1067 ———— Lettre au Castel au sujet de Pays de Kamtchatka et de Jeço, et Reponse du Castel 1737

1068 D'Anville Eclaircissemens Geographiques sur l'ancienne Gaule - - - *Par.* 1741

1069 ———— Traité des Mesures Itineraires *Ib.* 1769

1070 ———— Geographie Ancienne, abrégée, 3 vols. *maps* *Par.* 1768

1071 D'Anville l'Empire de Russie son Origine et ses Accroissemens - - - *Par.* 1772

1072 ———— l'Empire Turc considéré dans son Etablissement et dans ses Accroissemens successifs *Par.* 1772

1073 Autre exemplaire - - - 1772

1074 D'Anville Memoire sur la Chine - *Ib.* 1776

1075 ———— Considerations sur l'Etude et les Connoissances que demande la Composition des Ouvrages de Geographie *Par.* 1777

1076 Da Ponte, Saggi Poetici di - - 1801

1077 D'Aranda Diverses Histoires Morales et Divertissants, *red morocco* - - - *Leyde*, 1671

1078 D'Arnaud Œuvres completes, 4 vols. - *Amst.* 1775

1079 ———— Epreuves du Sentiment, 6 vols. *Par.* 1781

1080 ———— Lorezzo, Nouvelle, *blue morocco, silk lining* *Par.* 1781

1081 D'Assigny's Art of Memory - - 1697

1082 Dassy Dialogue tres elegant, intitule le Pelegrin, traduit de l'Italien, *red morocco* - *Par.* 1535

1083 Autre edition, *yellow morocco, with joints* *Ib.* 1540

1084 Daudiguier Histoire des Amours de Lysandre et de Caliste, *avec figures* - - *Amst.* 1679

1085 D'Aulnoi's Queen Mab, a select Collection of the Tales of the Fairies - - - 1799

1086 Davenant's Madagascar, with other Poems, *blue morocco* 1638

1087 Davenant, certain Verses written by severall of the Author's Friends, to be reprinted with the Second Edition of Gondibert, 1653. The Loves of Hero and Leander, a Mock Poem - - - 1653

1088 Davies's Life of Garrick, 2 vols. - - 1780

1089 Daygue (Estienne) Singulier Traité, contenant la proprieté des Tortues, Escargots, Brenoilles et Artichaults, *black letter, blue morocco* - - *a Lyon.* ——

1090 Deageant, Memoires de M., envoyez a M. le Cardinal de Richelieu, *red morocco* - - *Grenoble,* 1668

1091 De Baif, Les Mimes, Enseignemens et Proverbes de Jan Antoine de Baif, *red morocco* - *Par.* 1581

1092 Debellacyon of Salem and Bizance, *black letter, fine copy, see Dibdin's Ames, vol.* iii. *page* 378, *russia. Rastell,* 1533

1093 De Belley, les Evenemens Singuliers de, 2 vols. *Rouen,* 1659

1094 Debes' Description of the Islands and Inhabitants of Foeroe, enlished by J. Sterpin, *maps* - 1676

1095 De Bure Bibliographie Instructive, avec le Catalogue de Gaignat, 9 vols. - - - *Par.* 1763

1096 ——— Catalogue des Livres de la Bibliotheque de l'Heritier de Brutelle - - *Par.* 1802

1097 Declaration of the Power of God's Worde concerning the Holy Supper of the Lord, &c. *black letter, blue morocco Lond. T. Raynald,* 1548

1098 Defoe's History of the Plague in London, in 1665 1754

1099 De la Chambre, l'Art de Connoistre les Hommes, *blue morocco* - - - *Amst.* 1660

1100 De la Grace, la Chasse du Renard Pasquin *Villefranche,* 1602

1101 De la Croix, Relation Universelle de l'Afrique, 4 vols. *plates* - - - - *Lyon,* 1688

1102 De la Herissaye, les Contes et Discours d'Eutrapel, *red morocco* - - - *Reimes,* 1598

1103 De Lamarck et Decandolle, Flore Française ou Descriptions succinctes de toutes les Plantes qui croissent naturellement en France, 4 vols. - *Par.* 1805

1104 ——————— Synopsis Plantarum in Flora Gallica Descriptarum - - *Par.* 1806

1105 De la Monnoye, Poesies de, - *a la Haye,* 1716

Quarto.

1106 CHRISTI VITA, The Lyfe of our Lord Jhesu Chryste after Bonaventure, *black letter, wood cuts, blue morocco, very rare* *Wynkyn de Worde,* 1517

1107 CHRIST, La Vie de Notre Seigneur Jesus Christ, suivie de plusieurs Prieres, MANUSCRIT SUR VELIN du commencement de quinzieme Siecle, avec vingt-cinq miniatures tres curieuses.

1108 Christi Passio ab Alberto Durer Nurembergensi Effigiata, 36 plates by Albert Durer, *blue morocco*

1109 ——————————————, *coloured plates*, with Manuscript Descriptions in French Verse.

1110 Christo, La Passione di N. S. Giesu Christo, d'Alberto Durero, sposta in ottava rima da Moro, *wood cuts, blue morocco* - - - *Venet.* 1612

1111 Christi Passio Neo-cœlatis iconibus expressa, a Weigel, *plates* - - - - *Wien.* 1693

1112 ——— Symbolica Vitæ Christi Meditatio, *plates, wants title*

1113 Christie's Inquiry into the Ancient Greek Game, supposed to have been invented by Palamedes, &c. 1801

1114 Christofol, Varios Versos per Honrrar de Sant Christofol, *containing a series of Prize Poems in praise of Saint Christopher in the Valencian Dialect*, VERY RARE *Valencia per Peretringer*, 1498

1115 Christoval Suarez de Figueroa, Hechos de Don Garcia Hurtado de Mendoza - *Madrid*, 1613

1116 CHURCHYARDE'S (THOMAS) WORKS, collected in two volumes, *morocco*, OF UNCOMMON RARITY, from the Roxburghe Collection

Vol. I. contains

1 Churchyard's Challenge *Lond. John Wolfe*, 1593

2 ———— Chippes, contayninge twelve severall Labours - - *Thomas Marshe*, 1578

3 ————, The Worthines of Wales *G. Robinson*, 1587

Vol. II. contains

1 A lamentable and pitifull Description of the Wofull Warres in Flaunders - *R Newberrie*, 1578

2 A Discourse of the Queene's Majestie's Entertainement in Suffolk and Nortfolk.—A Matter touching the Journey of Sir Humfrey Gilbarte, Knight.—A Welcome-home to Master Martin Frobisher *H. Bynneman, no date.*

3 A light Bondell of lively Discourses, called Churchyarde's Charge - - *J. Kyngston*, 1580

4 The Contention betwyte Churchyeard and Camell, upon David Dycers Dreame *Owen Rogers*, 1560

The three last Pieces in the Second Volume have not been mentioned by Ames or Herbert

1117 Ciceronis Opera omnia, Oliveti, 9 vols. *Genevæ*, 1758

1118 Ciceronis Opera, cum Indicibus et variis Lectionibus, 10 vols. *Oxon.* 1783

£	s.	d.	Lot	Description	Buyer
14	14		1119	Ciento Novelle Antike, (Le) *original edition, very fine copy, green morocco,* RARE, from the Roxburghe Collection *Bologna Girol. Benedetti,* 1525	Triphook
	17	-	1120	——————— da Carlo Gualteruzzi, di nuovo ricorrette, con agguinta di quattro altre nel fine, *blue morocco* - *Fiorenza Guinta,* 1572	do
	10	6	1121	Cinthio. Hecatommithi overo Cento Novelle di Giraldi Cinthio - - - *Venetia,* 1608	Warder
4	2	-	1122	Clamades. Listoire et cronique du noble et vaillant Clamades filz du roy despaigne, Et de la belle Clèrimonde fille du roy Carnuant, *black letter, wood cuts* *Paris, Michel le Noir, sans date*	Heber
1	8	-	1123	Clarke's Tomb of Alexander, *plates* *Cambridge,* 1805	Dorant
12	12	-	1124	Clarke's Travels in various Parts of Europe, Asia, and Africa, 3 vols. LARGE PAPER, *boards* - 1810, &c.	Arch
	3	-	1125	Claytoni Flora Virginica, cura Gronovii. *Lugd. Bat.* 1762	Haworth
1	4	-	1126	Clement Bibliotheque Curieuse Historique, et Critique, 8 vols. in 4 - - *Gottingen,* 1750	Triphook
	6	-	1127	Clergie. A Reasonable Motion in behalfe of such of the Clergie as are now questioned in Parliament for their places. With the Conference betwixt the Archbishop of Canterbury and the Earle of Strafford - 1641	Longman
4	14	6	1128	Cleriadus. La Cronique de Messire Cleriadus filz au conte Desture, et de Meliadice fille au Roy Dangleterre, *black letter,* RARE - *Lyon, Olivier Arnoullet,* 1529	Arch
	5	-	1129	Clerke's Triall of Bastardie - *A. Islip.* 1594	Triphook
1	5	-	1130	Coates's History and Antiquities of Reading, *large paper, plates* - - - - - 1802	Higgs
8	8	-	1131	Cockes and Cock-fighting, The Commendation of, wherein is shewed, that Cocke-fighting was before the comming of Christ, by George Wilson, *black letter, russia, rare* *K. Tomes,* 1607	Longman
	2	-	1132	Cocker's Morals or the Muses Spring-Garden - 1675	Rodd
	2	-	1133	Cogan's Haven of Health, *black letter, russia* *M. Bradwood,* 1612	Triphook
1	-	-	1134	Cole Oratio de Ridiculo, *blue morocco, not published* *Londini,* 1811	Arch
1	10	-	1135	Collius de Sanguine Christi, *blue morocco* *Mediolani* 1617	Hunter
	2	-	1136	Conference betweene the two great Monarchs of France and Spaine - - - - 1641	Longman
	15	-	1137	Confucius, Abrégé de la Vie de, orné de 24 Estampes par Helman - - - *Par. sans date*	Hollingworth
1	9	-	1138	Contile, Comedie, La Pescara—Rea Gonzaga, La Trinozzia *Milano,* 1550	Hibbert
	15	-	1139	Contile, La Nice; brevemente comentata da Vendramini *Milano,* 1551	Hare
3	16	-	1140	Cook and King's Voyage to the Pacific Ocean, 3 vols. and Atlas, folio - - - - 1784	Arch
4	-	-	1141	Cooper's Chronicle, *black letter, fine copy, red morocco* 1565	Booth

1142 Coornhert's Emblems with descriptions in Dutch and German verse, *fine copy, blue morocco* *Amst.* 1620

1143 Cope's Historie of Two the most noble Capitaines of the Worlde, Anniball and Scipio, *black letter, very fine copy, russia,* RARE - *Berthelet,* 1548 (1568)

1144 Cope's (Sir Anthony) Godly Meditacion upon twenty select and chosen Psalmes of the Prophet David, *black letter, blue morocco, scarce* *Lond. by John Daye,* 1548

1145 Copland's Hye Way to the Spyttel Hous, in verse, *black letter, morocco,* EXTREMELY RARE *Lond. R. Copland, no date*

1146 Cornazani (Antonii), quod de proverbiorum origine inscribitur: opus nunquam alias impressum, &c. *fine copy, bound in russia, by Roger Payne,* VERY RARE *Mediolani,* 1503

1147 Corneille, Rodogune Princesse des Parthes, *red morocco* 1760

1148 Corsini, Descrizioni delle Feste fatte in Firenze per la Canonizzazione di St. Andrea Corsini, *plates, Venetian morocco, with joints* - *Fiorenza,* 1632

1149 Coryat's Crudities hastily gobled up in five moneths travells in France, Italy, &c. *with the frontispiece; the plate of the Clock at Strasbourg wanting, blue morocco* - 1611

1150 Coriat's Odcombian Banquet served up by a number of Noble Wits in prayse of his Crudities *and* Crambe *too, russia* - - - - 1611

1151 Coryat's Crambe, or his Colwort twise sodden, *very fine copy, red morocco* - - - 1611

1152 Coriate, Traveller for the English Wits, Greeting. From the Court of the Great Mogul, (reprint) 1616

1153 Coriat (Mr. Thomas) to his Friends in England sendeth greeting from Agra, the Capitall of the Great Mogul, *red morocco* - - 1618

1154 Costume of the Russian Empire, illustrated by a Series of Seventy-three Coloured Engravings, with Descriptions in French and English, *red morocco* 1803

1155 ——— of the Russian Army, and Russian Cries, 2 vols. in 1, COLOURED PLATES, *red morocco* 1807-1809

1156 ——— of Turkey, illustrated by a Series of Coloured Engravings, with Descriptions in French and English, *red morocco* - 1802

1157 Countryman's Recreation, or the Art of Planting, Graffing, and Gardening, *green morocco* - 1654

1158 Cowper Illustrated by a Series of Views in or near the Park of Weston-Underwood, *green morocco* - 1803

1159 Coxe's Travels into Poland, Russia, Sweden, and Denmark, 2 vols. - - - - 1784

1160 Cracovia (Matthæi de) tractatus Rationis et Conscientiæ de sumpcione pabuli Corporis N. Jesu Christi, a very early edition, in characters resembling those of the

£	s	d	Lot	Description	Buyer
				Catholicon of 1460, attributed to Guttemberg, *a beautiful copy,* UNCUT, *elegantly bound in Venetian morocco, by* ROGER PAYNE, VERY RARE.	Longman

Folio.

£	s	d	Lot	Description	Buyer
56	14	-	1161	Chronycles of Englonde, with the Description of Britain, *black letter, red morocco, from the Roxburghe Collection,* VERY RARE. - *Lond. Julian Notary,* 1513	Higgs
87	3	-	1162	CICERO. THE BOKE OF TULLE OF OLD AGE AND FRIENDSHIP, *russia* EMPRINTED BY ME, SYMPLE PERSONE, WILLIAM CAXTON, 1481. A remarkably beautiful copy of one of the best specimens of Caxton's Press. From the Merly Library.	Triphook
2	-	-	1163	Ciceronis Officia in Lingua Germanica, *with wood cuts, coloured, splendidly bound in green morocco, with joints* *Augspurg,* 1531	Longman
1	2	-	1164	Cipriani Epistolæ, Manuscript on vellum, of the fourteenth century, *russia*	Triphook
1	14	-	1165	Cipriani's Collection of Drawings, engraved by Earlom 1789	Johnston
33	12	-	1166	Cirongilio. Los quatro libros del Valeroso Cavallero Don Cirangilio de Tracia, por Bernardo de Vargas, *very fine copy, red morocco,* EXTREMELY RARE, from Col. Stanley's Library - - *Sevilla,* 1545	Triphook
2	5	-	1167	Clusii Rariorum Plantarum Historia, cum figuris, 3 vols. in 1, *red morocco* - *Antv. Plantin.* 1601	Do
	15	-	1168	Comines, las Memorias de, traducidas por Don Juan Vitrian, 2 vols. - - *Amberes,* 1643	Do
5	5	-	1169	Compost et Kalendrier des Bergiers, *wood cuts, black letter,* *Par. Guy Marchant,* 1500	Hibbert
7	-	-	1170	Corregio, Pitture di, Esistenti in Parma nel Monistero di San Paolo, *thirty-five plates, with Descriptions in Latin, French, and Italian, elegantly bound in russia* - 1800	Clarke
	5	-	1171	Crome's Fiddle new Model'd, with Music *Lond.* ——	Knell
2	14	-	1172	Dalboquerque, (Commentarios de Grande) Capitam Geral que foy das Indias Orientaes, *russia* - *Lisboa,* 1576	Heber
68	5	-	1173	Daniell's Oriental Scenery, containing ONE HUNDRED AND THIRTY-TWO MOST EXQUISITELY BEAUTIFUL COLOURED VIEWS, on a grand scale, faithfully representing the Edifices, Antiquities, Ruins, Mausolea, Hill Forts, Landscapes, &c. of Hindostan, and the Hindoo Excavations at Ellora, in 6 vols. Atlas folio - 1795, &c. THIS IS THE FINEST WORK EVER PUBLISHED UPON INDIA. The views are all coloured, so as to resemble the finest Drawings. This copy wants the twelve first Plates of the Second Series.	Arch

1174 Daniell's Views of London and of the Docks, IN TWELVE BEAUTIFULLY COLOURED PLATES - 1805

1175 Daniell's Picturesque Voyage to India by the Way of China, in a Series of COLOURED PLATES - 1810

1176 D'Anville's Modern Atlas - *Lond.* 1788

1177 Decandolle Astragalogia, nempe Astragali, Biserrulæ et Oxytripodis, &c. Historia, with 50 plates by Redouté, LARGE VELLUM PAPER, *splendidly bound in russia, with joints* - - - *Par.* 1802

1178 D'Eisenberg l'Art de monter à Cheval, *plates* *Haye*, 1733

1179 Della Bella, et Callot. A volume containing SIX HUNDRED AND TWENTY Engravings from the Works of these Masters.

1180 De Lobel (Matthia) Plantarum Historiæ Physicæ, *plates*, *Lond.* 1605

1181 Des Marests, Delices de l'Esprit - *Par.* 1659

1182 Denon, Voyage dans la Basse et la Haute Egypte, 2 vols. *plates, splendidly bound in blue morocco, with joints* *Par.* 1802

1183 De Solis Historia de la Conquista de Mexico, *plates, russia* *Amberes*, 1704

1184 Dioscoridis Opera Lat. cum Commentis Matthioli, *ruled, gilt leaves* - - *Venet.* 1554

1185 Dodoens Niewe Herball, translated by Lyte, *plates, russia* 1578

1186 D'Ohsson (Mouradja) Tableau général de l'Empire Othoman, 2 vols. *plates, elegantly bound in russia*, *Par.* 1787-90

End of the Sixth Day's Sale.

SEVENTH DAY'S SALE.

Octavo et Infra.

1187 De la Noue, la Coquette Corrigée, Comedie, *morocco* *Par.* 1757

1188 De la Place, Oronoko ou le Prince Negre - *Lond.* 1769

1189 De la Rue, Idyllia, *large paper, blue morocco* - *Par.* 1672

£	s.	d.	Lot	Description	Buyer
	3	-	1190	De Laune's Present State of London, *cuts* - 1681	Hollingworth
9	.	.	1191	Delices de la Grande Bretagne et de l'Irlande par Beeverell, 8 vols. *plates, first edition* *Leide*, 1707	Warner
			1192	Delices de l'Espagne et du Portugal, par Colmenar, 5 vols. *plates* - - - *Leide*, 1707	
			1193	Delices de l'Italie, par de Rogissart, 3 vols. *plates*, *Ib.* 1706	
			1194	——— des Pais-Bas, 4 vols. *plates* *Brusselle*, 1743	
			1195	——— de la Suisse, par Kypseler de Munster, 4 vols. *plates*, *Leide*, 1714	
	15	-	1196	Delie object de plus haulte vertu, par Maurice Sceve, *cuts, blue morocco, rare* - - *Lyon*, 1544	Triphook
	17	-	1197	Delights for Ladies to adorne their Persons, Tables, Closets, and Distillatories, with Beauties, Banquets, Perfumes, and Waters; with a Closet for Ladies, *blue morocco, scarce* - - - 1617	Hollingworth
	12	.	1198	De Lille's Gardens, a Poem, by Montolieu, *plates by Bartolozzi, red morocco* - - 1805	Do
	8	.	1199	De Lussan, les Veillées de Thessalie, 2 vols. *red morocco* *Par.* 1741	Triphook
	6	.	1200	Demetrius Phalerius de Elocutione, Gr. *russia* *Florent. Juntas*, 1552	Heber
	11	.	1201	Demosthene Cinque Orationi, et una di Eschine, *hog skin, gilt leaves* - - *Venet. Aldus*, 1557	Do
	14	.	1202	Demosthenes, translated by Leland, 3 vols. 1770	Christie
	2	.	1203	Denham's Poems - - - 1769	Warner
	2	.	1204	Des Barres, Histoire de Madame la Comtesse *Bruxelles*, 1736	Triphook
1	2	.	1205	Des Camps, la Vie des Peintres Flamands, Allemands, et Hollandois, avec des Portraits—Voyage Pittoresque de la Flandre et du Brabant, 5 vols. - *Par.* 1753	Evans
	6	.	1206	Deshoulieres, Œuvres de Madame et Mademoiselle, 2 vols. *Par.* 1747	Johnston
	2	.	1207	Deslyons, Discours Ecclesiastiques contre le Paganisme des Roys de la Feve et du Roy-Boit, *green morocco*, *Par.* 1664	Triphook
	3		1208	Desordres de la Bassette, nouvelle Galante - *Ib.* 1682	Dulau
	2	.	1209	Des Periers (Bonaventures) Recueil de ses Œuvres *Lyon*, 1544	Triphook
	3	.	1210	Des Portes, les Premieres Œuvres de Philippes des Portes *Par.* 1587	Warner
	2	.	1213	Autre edition - *Anv.* 1590	Johnston
	10	-	1214	D'Esternod l'Espadon Satyrique, *edition la plus recherchée, red morocco* - - *Cologne*, 1680	Dulau
2	12	6	1215	Destouches, Œuvres de, 5 vols *plates, green morocco* *Amst.* 1755	Johnston
	14	-	1216	De Vaines Dictionnaire Raisonné de Diplomatique, 2 vols. *Par.* 1774	Payne
	1	-	1217	Deverell's Miscellanies, in Prose and Verse, 2 vols 1781	Christie
	10	-	1218	Dialogo dove si ragiona della bella Creanza della Donne, *blue morocco* *Venet.* 1574	Money

£	s.	d.	Lot	Description	Buyer
1	11	6	1219	Dialogue or Familiar talke betwene two neighbours concernyng the chyefest ceremonyes that were by the mighti power of God's most holie pure Worde, suppressed in Englande, and now for our unworthines, set up agayne by the Bishoppes the impes of Antichrist, *blue morocco, rare* *From Roane, by Michael Wodde,* 1554	Rodd
	7		1220	Dialogues in Englyshe bytwene a Doctour of Dyvynyte and a Student in the Lawes of Englande, *black letter* *Lond. W Myddylton,* 1543	Triphook
	9	-	1221	Dialogue entre St. Pierre et Jules II. à la Porte de Paris, la Doctrine Catholique touchant l'Autorité des Papes, *morocco* 1727	Longman
	6	-	1222	Dichos Lindos y Galanes italianos y Hespanoles para las Famosas y mas Senaladas Damas y Senoras de Francia, *old morocco binding, scarce* - *senz. anno*	Triphook
	9	-	1223	Dictionnaire Historique, 9 vols. - *Caen,* 1789	Do.
	3		1224	Dictys Cretensis et Dares Phrygius, *green morocco* *R. Steph.* 1618	Heber
	2	-	1225	Diderot, Œuvres de Théâtre, 2 vols. - *Amst.* 1772	Jones
1	-	-	1226	Dionysii Carthusiani de quatuor hominis novissimis liber, *beautifully bound in old French morocco, ruled, Lugd.* 1591	Clarke
	2	-	1227	Discours en forme de Dialogue, touchant la vraye et parfaicte Amitié, *red morocco* *Lyon,* 1577	Heber
1	10	-	1228	Discovery (The) of a New World, or a Description of the South Indies, hetherto unknowne, by an English Mercury, *blue morocco, scarce* - *no date*	Triphook
	13	-	1229	D'Israeli's Curiosities of Literature, 2 vols. - 1793	Do.
	4	-	1230	——— Miscellanies, or Literary Recreations - 1796	Anderdon
	2	-	1231	Ditz Moraulx et belles Sentences de plusieurs grands Philosophes, *red morocco* *Lyon,* 1552	Triphook
	1	-	1232	D'Ivernois Tableau Historique et Politique de Geneve, 2 vols 1789	Rodd
	8	-	1233	Divertissemens Agreables, contenant divers Contes et Fables choisies de Bocace, Douville, et autres *Par.* 1669	Triphook
	9	-	1234	Divertissemens Comiques, Noveau Recueil, *blue morocco* *Par.* 1670	Dulau
	12	-	1235	Doddridge's (Sir John) Historical Account of Wales, Cornwall, and Chester, *red morocco* 1714	Triphook
	14	-	1236	Dodsley's Collection of Poems, 6 vols. - 1775	Christie
1	-	-	1237	——— Fugitive Pieces, on various Subjects, 2 vols. 1771	Payne
	4	-	1238	Dolce, Giocaste, Tragedia - *Vineg. Aldi. filii.* 1549	Warner
	12	-	1239	Domenichi. Facetie, Motti et Burle, di diversi, raccolte per Domenichi - - *Venet.* 1574	Triphook
	12	-	1240	Doni la Zucca, *green morocco, with joints* *Vineg. Marcolini,* 1551-2	Do.
	2	-	1241	Doni, les Mondes Celestes, Terrestres et Infernaux, par Gabriel Chappuis - - *Lyon,* 1583	Do.
1	1	-	1242	Donne's Poems, with Elegies on his Death, *portrait by Marshall, blue morocco* 1635	Do.

£	s	d	Lot	Description	Buyer
	13		1243	Donne's Poems, with Elegies on his Death, *with portrait, red morocco* - - - 1635	Triphook
	10	6	1244	Donne's Poems, *blue morocco, with joints.* *Tonson,* 1719	Rodd
4	10	-	1245	Another copy, *with portrait by Marshall inserted,* UNCUT, *red morocco, with joints* - *Tonson,* 1719	Do
3	8	-	1246	Dorat, Œuvres de, 9 vols. *plates* *a la Haye,* 1773	Heber
1	4	-	1247	Douce's Illustrations of Shakspeare, and of Ancient Manners, 2 vols. - - - 1807	Payne
	2	-	1248	Doujat, Eloges de Personnes Illustres de l'Ancien Testament, *coloured plates, red morocco* *Par.* 1688	Warner
	10	-	1249	Dove (London); or, a Memoriall of the Life and Death of Maister Robert Dove, Citizen and Merchant-Taylor of London, *black letter, red morocco* - - 1612	Christie
	2	-	1250	D'Oyly's History of the Life and Death of our Blessed Saviour - - *Southampton,* 1794	Lewis
	4	-	1251	Drake. The English Hero; or, Sir Fran. Drake reviv'd 1698	Hollingworth
	11	-	1252	Dramatic Poets, a complete List of all the English; and of all the Plays - - - 1748	Money
	13	-	1253	Drayton's (Michael) Poems, *russia, with joints* *Lond. Stansby, no date.*	Triphook
	9	-	1254	Drexelii Infernus Damnatorum Carcer et Rogus Æternitatis, *blue morocco, with joints* - *Antv.* 1631	Do.
	10	-	1255	——— Orbis Phæton, hoc est de Universis Vitiis Linguæ, *yellow morocco* - - *Col.* 1631	Clarke
	17	-	1256	Aliud exemplar, *green morocco* - *Ib.* 1634	Hare
1	9	-	1257	Drexelii Zodiacus Christianus locupletatus, *red morocco* *Col. Agrip.* 1632	Clarke
	4	-	1258	———, The Christian's Zodiake - 1647	Cochrane
	4	-	1259	———, Gymnasium Patientiæ, *blue morocco* 1632	Penning
	4	-	1260	Drixelius, Tribunal Christi, *blue morocco* - 1635	Triphook
1	11	6	1261	———'s Forerunner of Eternity, or Messenger of Death, *blue morocco* - - - 1642	Clarke
	4	-	1262	Drudonis, Practica Ars Amandi - *Francof.* 1625	Triphook
3	3	-	1263	Drummond of Hawthornden's Poems. This copy has both the title pages, *with portrait by Gaywood, bound in russia by* ROGER PAYNE, RARE - - 1656	Jewis
	7	-	1264	Drurei Alured sive Alfredus, Tragi Comœdia, *blue morocco* *Duaci,* 1620	Hare
	19	-	1265	Du Bartas' Second Weeke, or Childhood of the World, translated by Sylvester, *scarce* - - 1598	Rodd
	7	-	1266	Du Bellay, les Œuvres Françoises, 3 vols. *red morocco* *Rouen,* 1592	Triphook
	5	-	1267	Du Boccage, la Columbiade, ou la Foi portée au Nouveau Monde, *plates, blue morocco* *Lond.* 1758	Warner
	4	-	1268	Du Bourg, la Vraie Histoire, contenant l'inique judgment et fausse procedure faite contre le fidele serviteur de Dieu Anne du Bourg, *green morocco* 1561	Triphook
	6	-	1269	Duck (Stephen) the Wiltshire Poet, a full Account of, 1731	Warner

£	s.	d.	Lot	Description	Buyer
	1	-	1270	Du Fresnoy l'Histoire justifiée contre les Romans *Amst.* 1735	Rodd
	6	-	1271	Dunton's Bull Baiting, or Sacheverell dress'd up in Fire-Works - - - - 1709	Triphook
1	11	6	1272	Du Moulin Anatomie de la Messe, *blue morocco* *Elsevier,* 1638	Payne
	4	-	1273	———, The Capucin Treated; or, the Lives of the Capucins, *frontispiece* - - 1665	Triphook
	11	-	1274	Durand, Les Petits Soupers de l'Esté, ou Avantures Galants, *blue morocco* - - *Amst.* 1734	D°
2	10	-	1275	D'Urfey's Wit and Mirth, or Pills to purge Melancholy, 5 vols. - - - - 1719	D°
	12	-	1276	Dutch (the) drawn to the Life, *frontispiece, russia* 1664	Hollingworth
	4	-	1277	Duten's Memoires d'un Voyageur qui se repose, 3 vols. 1806	Chamier
	10	-	1278	——— des Pierres precieuses et des Pierres fines, *red morocco* - - - - - *Paris,* 1776	Hollingworth
	5	-	1279	——— Itineraire des Routes de l'Europe - 1793	Ld Yarmouth
	11	-	1280	Ebriosorum de Generibus et de Ebrietate Vitanda, *blue morocco* - - - - 1565	Clarke
	6	-	1281	Echecs, le Jeu des - - *Amst.* 1792	Lepard
	11	-	1282	———, les Stratagemes des, *blue morocco* *Par.* 1802	Triphook
	19	-	1283	Ederi Methodus Catechismi Catholici, *in very rich old binding in morocco* - - *Lugduni,* 1579	Heber
3	6	-	1284	Edinburgh Review, from 1806 to 1811, inclusive, 10 vols. 1807	Triphook
	5	-	1285	Edmund of the Forest, 4 vols. - - 1797	D°
	2	-	1286	Egaremens du Cœur, 2 vols. - - 1782	Jones
	13	-	1287	Egede's Description of Greenland, *plates, red morocco* 1745	Ponton
1	3	-	1288	Eicon Basalice, The Pourtraicture of his Sacred Majesty in his Solitudes, *frontispiece by Marshall, blue morocco, with the royal cipher on the sides* - - 1649	Seymour
6	16	6	1289	Elder, John. Copie of a Letter sent into Scotlande, of the Arrivall, and Landynge, and Marryage of the Prince of Spain to Quene Mary, *black letter, rare* *J. Wayland,* (1555)	Triphook
	1	-	1290	Eldad, Darius Hebræus Historicus de Judæis Clausis, Latinè - - - *Morel.* 1563	Heber
3	18	-	1291	Elegant Extracts, in Prose, Verse, and Epistles, 6 vols. *russia* - - - - - 1797	Clarke, P.
	7	-	1292	Elizabeth and James, Historical Memoirs of the Reigns of, *portrait of Elizabeth* - - - 1658	Hollingworth
1	1	-	1293	Elizabeth and the Earl of Essex, Secret History of, *red morocco* - - - - - 1725	Anderdon
	6	-	1294	———, Letter of the Entertainment of her Majesty at Killingwoorth Castle in Warwick Sheer *Warwick,* 1784	Triphook
	14	-	1295	———, Novels of, with the History of Anne Bullen 1680	Anderdon

1	13	-	1296	Ellis's Specimens of the Early English Poets, 3 vols. 1801	Seymour
2	-	-	1297	Ellison's Description of Benwel Village, in Verse 1725	Hare
	5	-	1298	Eloge de l'Enfer, 2 vols. - - *Haye*, 1759	Warner
	10	-	1299	Elyot's Castell of Helth, *black letter* - - 1541	Anderdon
5	15	6	1300	Emblemes Divers, Recueil de, 100 *Emblems painted upon vellum with great spirit and delicacy of execution, bound in red morocco*	Payne
	15	-	1301	Emblemes ou Devises Chretiennes *Utrecht*, 1697	Do
2	19	-	1302	Emblemata Amores Moresque spectantia, Hollandicè, Gallicè, et Anglicè, 52 *plates* - - *sine nota*	Clarke
1	2	-	1303	Emblems for the Entertainment and Improvement of Youth, with Explanations, *on* 62 *Copper-plates, fine impressions, blue morocco, with joints*	Johnston
	9	-	1304	Emblems Divine and Moral, Ancient and Modern 1732	Payne
1	-	-	1305	Emblems of Mortality, *with a set of Hollar's plates* 1789	Do
	5	-	1306	Emillianne's History of Monastical Orders 1693	Triphook
	5	-	1307	Empereurs Chroniques des, avec les pourtraicts et effigies d'iceux - - - *sans date*	Loveday
	1	-	1308	Emperour and Empire Betray'd by Whom and How, 1681	Hollingworth
	13	-	1309	Enchanted Plants, Fables in Verse, *blue morocco* 1801	Do

Quarto.

10	15	-	1310	Cramer, Papillons Exotiques des trois Parties du Monde, l'Asie, l'Afrique, et l'Amérique, dessinés sur les Originaux, gravés et enluminés, sous sa direction, 4 vols. 400 COLOURED PLATES, *elegantly bound* *Amst.* 1779, &c.	Hollingworth
	2	-	1311	Crashaw's Mittimus to the Jubilee at Rome, or the Rates of the Pope's Custome House - 1625	Warner
2	19	-	1312	Crastoni Vocabularium, in Epitome redactum ab Accursio Pisano, cum ejus Epistola, VERY RARE *Regii per D. de Bertochis*, 1497	Heber
	5	-	1313	Crescentiensis de Agricultura, *russia* *Basiliæ*, 1538	Rodd
1	11	6	1314	Crevenna, Catalogue de Livres de la Bibliothèque de, 6 vols. *large paper* - - *Amst.* 1789	Triphook
	9	-	1315	Crisostomi (Sancti Johannis) Liber Dialogorum et Sanctus Basilius de Dignitate Sacerdocii, *editio antiqua* *sine ulla nota*	Heber
	6	-	1316	Cromwell (Craftie) or Oliver ordering our New State, a Tragi-Comedie - - 1648	Lepard
3	-	-	1317	Cromwell. Irenodia Gratulatoria Oliveri Cromwelli, dedicatum Domino Præsidi Bradshawo, cæterisque Concilii-Statu-Consultis, &c. a Payne Fisher. Two Portraits of Cromwell, one on horseback, by Faithorne, the other, a Page putting on his sash, by Trevillian. With an Account of the Family of Cromwell in MS. by Richard Verney, *blue morocco*, RARE - *Londini*, 1652	Do
	2	-	1318	Cromwelli Panegyricus - - 1654	Hollingworth
	6	-	1319	Cromwell. The World's Mistake in Oliver Cromwell 1668	Anderdon

£	s.	d.	Lot	Description	Buyer
	2	-	1320	Crosnier l'Année Burlesque ou Recueil de Pieces que le Mercure a faites pendant l'Anné 1682 *Amst.* 1683	Triphook
	7	-	1321	Cusacke's Briefe Discourse, instanceing the Manner of finding Lunatiques, manuscript - ——	Do
	16	-	1322	Custodis (Raphaelis) Emblemata Amoris *August.* 1622	Payne
	18	-	1323	Dale's History and Antiquities of Harwich and Dover-court, *plates* - - - 1730	Newland
5	15	6	1324	Damascenus. Liber Gestarum Barlaam et Josaphat servorum Dei, greco sermone editus a Johanne Damasceno. *editio antiqua, red morocco* - *sine ulla nota* This celebrated Romance was a great favourite during the middle ages. Boccacio borrowed from it several of his Tales, and it was the Model of the Romances of Spiritual Fiction among the French.	Triphook
	1	-	1325	Danby, Articles of Impeachment for High Treason against Thomas Earl of,	Hollingworth
	5	-	1326	Danfrie, Declaration de l'Usage du Graphometre, *plates* *Par.* 1597	Payne
8	18	6	1327	Daniell's Rural Sports, 3 vols. LARGE PAPER, COLOURED PLATES, *elegantly bound in red morocco, with joints* 1805	Knell
1	3	-	1328	D'Anville Analyse Geographique de l'Italie, *gilt leaves* *Par.* 1744	Newland
1	2	-	1329	——— Notice de l'Ancienne Gaule *Ib.* 1760	Do
1	3	-	1330	——— Etats formés en Europe après la Chute de l'Empire Romain en Occident - *Par.* 1771	Do
1	3	-	1331	D'Anville, Antiquité Geographique de l'Inde, &c. *Ib.* 1775	Do
1	14	-	1332	——— l'Euphrate et le Tigre - *Ib.* 1779	Payne
1	10	-	1333	Dares Phrygius de Origine Troianorum. A very early Edition, in the Roman Character resembling that used at Venice about 1472, *russia,* RARE *sine ulla nota*	Triphook
2	2	-	1334	Dares Phrygius de Excidio Troje, *cum figuris, russia* *Parisiis,* 1527	Hibbert
18	7	6	1335	Daryus. A pretie new Enterlude, both Pithie and Pleasaunt, of the Storye of King Daryus, *black letter, red morocco,* VERY RARE *London, by T. Colwell,* 1565	Jewis
	11	-	1336	David, Occasio Arrepta, Neglecta, hujus Commoda, illius Incommoda, *plates, russia* *Antverpiæ,* 1605	Triphook
1	3	-	1337	David, Veridicus Christianus, *plates, gilt leaves* *Ib.* 1606	Hollingworth
3	16	-	1338	——— Virtutis Exercitatissimæ probatum Deo Spectaculum, cum figuris Fratrum De Bry, *blue morocco, with joints* - - - *Francof.* 1597	Clarke
19	8	6	1339	De Bry (Theodori) Emblemata Nobilitati et vulgo scitu Digna-Singulis Historiis Symbola adscripta et elegantes versus Historiam explicantes, 2 vols. *fine impressions, red morocco* - - *Francof.* 1593	Payne
39	18		1340	DECOR PUELLARUM. Questa sie una Opera la quale si chiama Decor Puellarum: Zoe honore delle Donzelle. *Jenson,* 1461 (sic). LUCTUS CHRISTIANORUM. Questa e una opera la quale se chiama, Luctus Christianorum ex	Appleyard

passione Christi, &c. *Jenson*, 1471. PALMA VIRTUTUM zioe Triumpho de Virtude, *Jenson*, 1471. GLORIA MULIERUM. Qui comenza el proemio del ben viver de le done Maridade, *Jenson*, (circa 1471). PAROLE DEVOTE DE L'ANIMA INAMORATA IN MISSER JESU, *Jenson*, 1471. Five Tracts of the GREATEST RARITY. In very fine condition, bound in one volume in russia.

1341 Dei, le Nozze dei, Favola, del Coppola, *plates by Della Bella, and portrait by Hollar* - *Firenze*, 1637

1342 Delectable Demaundes, and pleasaunt Questions, with their severall Aunswers in Matters of Love, Naturall Causes with Morall and Politique Devises, *black letter* *John Cawood*, 1566

1343 Delille, les Jardins, Poeme, *blue morocco* *Londres*, 1801

1344 ——— the Gardens, a Poem, *red morocco* - 1798

1345 Della Bella, Recueil de divers Griffonemens, Tetes, Animaux, &c. gravés par, *fine copy, green morocco, Par.* ———

1346 Des Fontaines, Flora Atlantica sive Historia Plantarum quæ in Atlante, Agro Tunetano et Algeriensi crescunt, 4 vols. *Papier Velin, plates, elegantly bound in russia, with joints* - - - *Parisiis*, 1800

1347 Des Maret's l'Ariane, enrichie de plusieurs figures, *red morocco, with joints* - - *Par.* 1639

1348 Dethicke's Gardener's Labyrinth, 2 parts in one vol. *black letter, wood cuts, red morocco* *H. Bynneman*, 1577

1349 Devises et Emblemes curieux Anciennes et Modernes, tirées de plus célébres Auteurs *Augsbourg*, 1703

1350 ——— de la Fleur du Soleil, ou Veritables Emblemes de l'Homme par rapport a cette Fleur, par I. Du Busc, *drawn in pen and ink* - - 1699

1351 Dialoges of Creatures Moralysed, of late translated out of Latyn into our Englisshe tonge, *wood cuts, black letter, red morocco*, RARE.
They be to sell upon Powly's Churche Yarde, *no date.*

1352 Dialogue between Sacke and Six 1641

1353 Dictionnaire de l'Académie Françoise, 2 vols. *Par.* 1802

1354 Didier (Henry de Sainct) Traitté contenant les secrets du premier Livre sur l'Espée seule, *cuts, red morocco* *Par.* 1573

1355 Dighy (Sir Kenelm) on the Nature of Bodies and the Nature of Man's Soule, *with portrait* - 1645

1356 Dinet Cinq Livres des Hieroglyphiques où sont contenus les plus rares secrets de la Nature, *blue morocco, with joints* - - - - *Par.* 1613

1357 Diogenes Laertius de Vita et Moribus Philosophorum, Latinè - - - *Venet.* 1490

1358 Dixon's Canidia, or the Witches, in five parts 1683

1359 Doddridge's History of Wales, Cornwall, and Chester 1630

1360 Dolce, Il Palmerino, *fine copy, red morocco* *Venet. Sesso*, 1561

£	s.	d.	Lot	Description	Buyer
1	-	-	1361	Dolce, Vita di Carlo Quinto, *russia* *Vineg. Giolito*, 1567	Triphook
	15	-	1362	——, le Trasformationi tratte da Ovidio, *con figure in legno, russia* - - *Venet. Sansovino*, 1568	Cicognane
2	10	-	1363	——, l'Achille et l'Enea, in ottava Rima, *con figure, yellow morocco* - - *Vineg. Giolito*, 1572	Clarke
1	19	-	1364	——, le Prime Imprese del Conte Orlando, *con figure, red morocco* - - *Vineg. Giolito*, 1572	Hare
1	18	-	1365	Dolce, l'Imprese et Tornamenti di Primaleone Figliuolo del Palmerino, ridotti in ottava Rima, *red morocco* *Vineg.* 1597	D°
3	15	-	1366	—— Imprese di Diversi Prencipi et d'Altri Personaggi Illustri, *plates, red morocco, with joints* *Venet. Porro*, 1578	Hibbert
	5	-	1367	Dolet, l'Avant Naissance de Claude, tradicte en Langue Francoyse - - *Lyon, E. Dolet*, 1539	Heber
	1	-	1368	Donati trattato de Semplici, Pietri et Pesci Marini *Venet.* 1631	Triphook

Folio.

£	s.	d.	Lot	Description	Buyer
5	10	-	1369	Doomsday Book, 2 vols. *russia.* - - - - - - - - -	Newland
	9	-	1370	Douglas's Description of the Guernsey Lilly 1737	Calkin
3	4	-	1371	Drayton's Poly-Olbion, *frontispiece and portrait of Prince Henry, by Hole, and maps, fine copy* - 1613	Christie
2	12	6	1372	Drummond of Hauthornden's History of Scotland, *with portraits, by Gaywood, russia* - - 1655	Hibbert
14	3	6	1373	Dugdale's Antiquities of Warwickshire, enlarged by Thomas, 2 vols. *plates* - - 1730	Priestley
	2	-	1374	Durante Herbario Novo, *cuts* - *Venet.* 1602	Heber
3	19	-	1375	Durerus (Albertus) De Geometria et Symmetria, *cuts, Thuanus's Copy, in yellow morocco* - *Par.* 1535	Payne
1	6	-	1376	—— (A.) De Urbibus, Arcibus, Castellisque condendis, Paris, 1533. Vegetius de Re Militari, *Lutetiæ*, 1532. 2 vols. in 1, *plates, russia, with joints.*	Heber
sold for 5	2	6	1377	Dyalogus Creaturarum optime Moralizatus Jocundis Fabulis plenus, *wood cuts, first edition, very fine copy, red morocco*. Imperfect. *Goudæ per Gerardum Leeu*, 1480 (sold first time for £10.0.0)	Triphook
5	2	6	1378	Emblesmes et Devises Chrestiennes et Morales, consisting of thirty Drawings in pen and ink, with M.S. explanations in French, *blue morocco.*	Payne
11	11	-	1379	Esplandian, Las Sergas de Esplandian Hijo Legitimo de Amadis de Gaula, *yellow morocco,* VERY RARE *Alcala*, 1588	Arch

> " Esplandian was written by Ordonez de Montalvo, the original editor of the four first books of Amadis of Gaul, in Spanish, and intended to form the fifth book of that celebrated romance. Esplandian was in Don Quixote's Library."—*Stanley Cat.*

£	s.	d.	Lot	Description	Buyer
	6	-	1380	Etymologium Magnum, Gr. - *Venet.* 1710	Newland

£	s.	d.	Lot	Description	Buyer
7	7		1381	Evangelia Quatuor Latinè. A manuscript upon vellum, which appears by the initial letters, &c. to have been written about the 10th century. The figures intended to represent the four Evangelists are drawn in the most grotesque and ludicrous stile imaginable, and are evidently of very great antiquity. From the Monastery of Como, bound in purple velvet.	Booth
85	1		1382	EVERDINGEN'S ORIGINAL SPIRITED DRAWINGS for the History of REYNARD THE FOX, WITH A PROOF SET OF THE ETCHINGS, carefully mounted on drawing paper, and bound in 2 vols. in russia.	Hibbert
	13	-	1383	Fabris, la Scienza d'Arme, *plates* - 1606	Anderdon
	13	-	1384	Fasciculus Temporum *Conradus De Hoenborch,* 1476	Newland
3	16	-	1385	Faxardo Corona Gothica, Castellana y Austriaca con los Retratos de los Reyes Godos, 4 vols. in 2, *red morocco* *Ambares,* 1708	Payne

End of the Seventh Day's Sale.

EIGHTH DAY'S SALE.

Octavo et Infra.

£	s.	d.	Lot	Description	Buyer
	4	-	1386	Enchiridion Piarum Precationum cum Passionali et Calendario, *wood cuts* - - *Wittembergæ,* 1543	Heber
	3	-	1387	Encomia Admiranda Rerum Admirabilium *Noviom. Bat.* 1666	Sedgwick
	1	-	1388	Enea Silvio, Epistole de dui Amanti Eurialo et Lucretia, *Vinegia, Sessa,* 1531	Wilbraham
	2	-	1389	Enfant Gaté, ou le Debauche de la Haye, 2 parts in 1, *red morocco, plates* - - *Delft,* 1682	Triphook
	2	-	1390	Enfant sans Soucy - *Ville Franche,* 1682	D^o.
	14	-	1391	Enfer (L') de la Mere Cardine, traitant de la cruelle et horrible Bataille qui fut aux enfers, *yellow morocco* *Par.* 1793	Heber
	13	-	1392	Enfer (L') Burlesque - *Cologne,* 1677	Lepard
	10	-	1393	Engelgrave Lux Evangelica sub Velum Sacrorum Emblematum recondita, *plates, blue morocco,* *Coloniæ,* 1655	Payne
	9	-	1394	England's Witty and Ingenious Jester - - *no date*	Perry
6	17	6	1395	English Rogue, the, 4 vols. in 2, *portrait and plates, fine copy, russia, scarce* - - 1672	Triphook

£	s.	d.	Lot	Description	Buyer
	4	-	1396	English Hermit, the, - - 1768	Triphook
	12	-	1397	——— Theatre, the, 8 vols. - - 1762	Pybus
	8	-	1398	Enigmes de ce Temps, Recueil de, - 1646	Triphook
	2	-	1399	Ennui, Ressource contre l', 2 vols. - *Haye*, 1766	Do
	2	-	1400	Epicteti Enchiridion, Grecè - *Glasguæ*, 1751	Heber
	2	-	1401	——————— made English by Walker 1695	Christie
	2	-	1402	Epictete, Manuel d', en Grec, avec une Traduction par Villebrune, *red morocco* - *Par.* 1783	Triphook
	3	-	1403	Epigrammata Græca selecta ex Anthologia, cum Interpr. Latina, *vellum* - - *Par.* 1570	Clark.. P.
	18	-	1404	——————— et Poematia Vetera, *blue morocco*, *Ib.* 1590	Heber
	8	-	1405	Epigrams, Collection of, - - 1727	Triphook
	19	-	1406	Epiphanii (S. Patris) Physiologus de Ferarum ac Volucrum Natura, *plates, blue morocco* *Antverp.* 1588	Clarke
	11	-	1407	Epistolæ Principum et Illustrium Virorum, *green morocco* *Elzev.* 1644	Payne
2	12	-	1408	Epitaphs, Elogys, &c. select Collection, in MS. with an Index, by J. Brand - - - - - - - - - 1764	Clarke
	8	-	1409	——— Collection of, with Dr. Johnson's Essay, 2 vols. 1806	Clark. P.
	10	-	1410	Epulum Parasiticum, *vellum* - *Norimb.* 1665	Heber
	5	-	1411	Equicola de la Nature d'Amour, trad. par Chappuis, *red morocco* - - - *Lyon.* 1598	Triphook
	18	-	1412	Erasmi Adagiorum Epitome, *red morocco* *Elzevir*, 1650	Payne
1	17	-	1413	——— Proverbes or Adagies gathered oute of the Chiliades of Erasmus, by R. Taverner, *black letter* 1552	Rodd
	15	-	1414	Erasmi Colloquia, *green morocco* *Amst. Elzevir.* 1636	Christie
	7	-	1415	——————— *red morocco* - *Ib.* 1677	Triphook
	2	-	1416	Erasmus de Conscribendis Epistolis - *Basil*, 1526	Heber
	10	-	1417	Erasmo Enquiridio o Manual traduzido en Castellano por Don Alonso Manrrique Arcobispo de Sevilla, *green morocco, scarce* - - *Alcala*, 1527	Triphook
2	8	-	1418	Erasmus's Enchiridion Militis Christiani, which may be called in Englysshe the hansom Weapon of a Christen Knyght, *first edition, black letter, blue morocco* *London, J. Byddell*, 1534	Heber
	12	-	1419	Another copy, *black letter, Rob. Toy, without date*—Hooper's Sermons, *black letter, wants title*, in 1 vol. *red morocco*	Triphook
	4	-	1420	Erasmus's Exposition or Declaration of the Commune Crede, *reprint of an edition by Redman*	Cochrane
1	-	-	1421	——— Epicurus, translated by Gerrard, *black letter, wants title, not mentioned in Mr. Dibdin's Ames* *R. Grafton*, 1545	Rodd
	7	-	1422	Erasmi Moriæ Encomium, *ruled* *Basil. Frobenii.* 1551	Heber
1	15	-	1423	——————— Figuris Holbenianis adornata, UNCUT, *blue morocco* - - *Basil.* 1676	Payne
	3	-	1424	Erasmo la Moria in Volgare tradotta, *red morocco* *Venet.* 1545	Heber

	8	-	1425	Erasme Eloge de la Folie, traduit par le Veaux, *fine paper, plates* - - - *Basle,* 1780	Christie
	1	-	1426	———————, traduite par Gueudeville *Leide,* 1713	Payne
	17	-	1427	Erasmus's Panegyrick upon Folly, with fifty cuts by Hans Holbein - - - 1709	Miller
	14	-	1428	Ercole in Tebe, Festa Teatrale per le Nozze di Cosimo Terzo e Margherita Aloisa, *plates, blue morocco* *Fiorenza,* 1661	Payne
1	-	-	1429	Erdeswicke's Survey of Staffordshire, and Congreve's Proposal for a Navigable Communication between the Trent and Severn, *russia* - - 1717	Jervis
	7	-	1430	Erondell's French Garden, for the Knowledge of the French Tongue - - - 1621	Rodd
	1	-	1431	Eromena, or the Noble Stranger - 1683	John
2	12	6	1432	Erreurs Amoureuses, en Vers, *very scarce, blue morocco* *Lyon, Jan de Tournes,* 1555	Rice
	3	-	1433	Escole de l'Interest et l'Université d'Amour, *red morocco* *Par.* 1662	Triphook
	18	-	1434	Espagne, Memoires de la Cour d', 2 vols. *red morocco* *Par.* 1690	Clark, P.
2	-	-	1435	——— et Portugal, Abrégé Chronologique de l'Histoire d', 2 vols. *red morocco* - *Par.* 1765	Clarke
	16	-	1436	Estienne. Les Censures des Theologiens de Paris pour condamner les Bibles, imprimées par R. Estienne, avec sa reponse, *red morocco* - - 1552	Triphook
	4	-	1437	Estienne, Introduction au Traité de la Conformité des Merveilles Anciennes avec les Modernes, *first edition* 1566	Hayes
	7	-	1438	Autre edition - - *Lyon,* 1592	Triphook
	12	-	1439	Estienne Project du Livre, intitulé de la precellence du Langage François, *blue morocco* - *Par.* 1579	Heber
	8	-	1440	Etrennes de la St. Jean, *large paper, red morocco* *Troyes,* 1742	Triphook
	15	-	1441	Euler's Letters to a German Princess, translated by Hunter, 2 vols. - - - 1795	Egerton
	2	-	1442	Eunuchism Displayed - - 1718	Triphook
4	14	6	1443	Euripidis Tragœdiæ Septemdecim, *first edition, red morocco* - - *Venet. Aldi,* 1503	Lepard
	10	-	1444	Eustathe, les Amours d'Ismene et d'Ismenias, traduit par de Beauchamps, *plates, red morocco* *Amst.* 1729	Cicognara
	6	-	1445	Evangelia Quatuor Latinè, *red morocco, ruled* *Par. Colin.* 1523	Heber
	18	-	1446	Evelyn's Sculptura, or the History of Chalcography 1662	Payne
	3	-	1447	Everartus de Herba Panacea Tabaci *Antverp.* 1587	Heber
	5	-	1448	Faber's Dissertation on the Prophecies, 2 vols. *boards* 1810	Payne
1	1	-	1449	Fabliaux et Contes des Poetes François, des XII. XIII. XIV. et XVes. Siècles, 3 vols. *blue morocco* *Par.* 1766	Christie

£	s.	d.	Lot	Description	Buyer
1	18	-	1450	Fabliaux et Contes, &c. avec des Notes par Le Grand, 4 vols. - - - *Par.* 1779	Triphook
5	5	-	1451	Fabliaux et Contes, &c. Nouvelle Edition, par Meon, 4 vols. GRAND PAPIER DE HOLLANDE, *proof plates, russia, gilt leaves* - - - *Par.* 1808	Warder
	16	-	1452	Fabliaux (Choix de) mis en Vers. 2 vols. *blue morocco* *Geneve,* 1788	Triphook
	7	-	1453	Fabri, le Grant et vray Art de pleine Rethorique, *black letter, green morocco* - *Par.* 1532	D°
	6	-	1454	Fabricii Bibliotheca Latina, 3 vols. *Hamburgi,* 1721	Dunbar
	11	-	1455	———————— Mediæ et Infimæ Ætatis, 6 vols. - - - *Hamb.* 1734	D°
	9	-	1456	Fabricii Codex Apocryphus Novi Testamenti, 2 vols. *Hamb.* 1703	Cochran
	11	-	1457	Fabulæ Centum ex Antiquis Scriptoribus acceptæ, explicatæ a Fabio Paulino, *wood cuts, blue morocco* *Venet.* 1587	Clarke
1	9	-	1458	Facecies et Motz Subtilz, d'aucuns excellens espritz et tres nobles Seigneurs, en Fr. et Ital. *yellow morocco* *Lyon.* 1582	Triphook
	7	-	1459	Facetiæ Facetiarum hoc est Joco-Seriorum Fasciculus *Francof.* 1615	Heber
	14	-	1460	Alia editio, *blue morocco* *Pathopoli,* 1645	Clarke
	8	-	1461	Facecieux (Le) Reveille Matin des Esprits Melancoliques *Par.* 1645	Triphook
	6	-	1462	Autre edition *Rouen,* 1660	D°
	9	-	1463	———————— - - *Utrecht,* 1662	D°
	14	-	1464	Faerni Centum Fabulæ ex Antiquis Auctoribus delectæ, *wood cuts, red morocco* *ex Off. Plantiniana,* 1600	Heber
1	1	-	1465	Faerni Centum Fabulæ, &c. *wood cuts, green morocco, uncut* - - - - - *Bruxellis,* 1682	Triphook
	5	-	1466	Faerno's Fables, in English and French Verse, *with one hundred plates* - - - - 1741	Christie
	2	-	1467	Fagel, Catalogue of the Library of the Greffier, 2 vols. 1802	Triphook
	6	-	1468	Fair (the) Extravagant, or, the Humorous Bride 1682	Warder
1	1	-	1469	Faithorne's Art of Graveing and Etching, *plates, fine copy, blue morocco* - - - 1662	Triphook
	3	-	1470	Falconer's Shipwreck, *morocco* - - 1805	Knell
	12	-	1471	Falkland. The Returnes of Spiritual Comfort and Grief in a Devout Soul, exemplified in the Life and Death of Vi-Countess Falkland, *portrait by Marshall, blue morocco, with joints* - - - 1648	Cochran
	12	-	1472	Falle's Account of Jersey, *plates* - - 1734	Christie
	2	-	1473	Famosissima (della) Compagnia della Lesina *Venet.* 1547	Triphook
4	16	-	1474	Fardle (the) of Facions, conteining the Aunciente Maners, Customes, and Lawes of the Peoples of Affrike and Asie, *black letter, scarce* *London, J. Kingstone,* 1555	D°

1475 Farinaste diverses Figures a l'eau forte de Petits Amours, Anges Vollants, &c. - - *Par.* 1644

1476 Farlæi Kalendarium Humanæ Vitæ, the Kalendar of Man's Life, *wood cuts, title MS. scarce* *Lond.* 1638

1477 Farlæi Lychnocausia, sive Moralia Facum Emblemata, Light Morall Emblems, *wood cuts, blue morocco, rare* 1638

1478 Farmer's Essay on the Learning of Shakspeare *Camb.* 1767

1479 ——— History of Waltham Abbey, *plates, russia, with joints* - - - - - 1735

1480 Farrago, containing Essays, Moral, Philosophical, &c. 2 vols. *boards* - - - 1792

1481 Faulconstein Forest, a Romantic Tale - 1810

1482 Fauquel, Epitaphe de la Ville de Calais, plus une Chanson sur la prinse du dict Calais, *red morocco* *Par.* 1558

1483 Faut-Mourir et les Excuses inutiles que l'on apporte a cette necessité - - *Rouen,* 1675

1484 Favoral, les Plaisantes Journees de St. *yellow morocco* *Par.* 1626

1485 Favourites (The) Chronicle *Printed according to the French Copie,* 1621

1486 Faxardo's Royal Politician represented in one hundred Emblems, translated by Astry, 2 vols. 1700

1487 Female Perfection, a President of, - 1656

1488 Femmes, Tableau Historique des Ruses et Subtilitez des Femmes, *yellow morocco* - - *Par.* 1623

1489 Femmes les Triomphes des, *blue morocco* *Anv.* 1700

1490 ——— les Avantages du Sexe, ou le Triomphe des Femmes - - - - *Anv.* 1698

1491 Femme, la Jolie, 2 vols. - *Lyon,* 1769

1492 ——— les Confidences d'une Jolie Femme, 2 vols. *Amst.* 1775

1493 ——— la Jolie, ou la Femme du Jour, 2 vols. *Toulouse,* 1778

1494 Fenelon, les Aventures de Telemaque, 2 vols. *fine paper, plates* - - - *Par.* 1799

1495 Fernandez de Ondatigui Historia Tragica de Leonora y Rosaura, *blue morocco* - *Madrid,* 1736

1496 Ferrand, les Pieces Libres de, *red morocco,* *Lond.* 1744

1497 Fêtes (les) Roulantes et les Regrets des Petites Rues, *green morocco* - - - - 1747

1498 Feynes, Voyage faict par Terre depuis Paris jusqu'a la Chine, *frontispiece* - - *Par.* 1630

1499 Fierville Caco-Gynie ou Mechanceté des Femmes, *yellow morocco* - - - - *Caen,* 1617

1500 Fiesque, la Conjuration du Comte de, *red morocco, with joints* - - - - - 1665

£	s.	d.	Lot	Description	Buyer
	1	-	1501	Filles de Joye de Paris, la Deroute et l'Adieu des, *Par.* 1667	Triphook
	9	-	1502	Fina Oraison Funebre sur la Mort de la Reine Marie II. Reine d'Angleterre, d'Ecosse, &c. - 1695	Hollingworth
	5	-	1503	Fine, la Theorique des Cieulx et Sept Planetes, *plates, yellow morocco, with joints* - *Par.* 1558	Triphook
	1	-	1504	Firenzuola, le Rime di, - *Fiorenza,* 1549	Rodd
2	8	-	1505	Fitzherbarde's Boke of Husbandry, *black letter, green morocco* - - *Berthelet, no date*	Milner
	6	-	1506	Flaminii Paraphrasis in Triginta Psalmos, versibus conscripta - - *Lutet. C. Steph.* 1552	Heber

Quarto.

£	s.	d.	Lot	Description	Buyer
1	14	-	1507	Don Juan Lamberto, or a Comical History of the late times - - - - 1661	Triphook
4	4	-	1508	Donovan's Epitome of the Natural History of the Insects of China, COLOURED PLATES, *green morocco* - 1798	Alexander
2	11	-	1509	Drake. The World encompassed by Sir Francis Drake, collected out of the Notes of Francis Fletcher, *map* 1628	Milner
10	15	-	1510	Dramatick Satires. A New Play called Canterburie his Change of Diot, 1641. Canterburie's Amazement, 1641. The Devill and the Parliament, 1648. Mrs. Parliament her Invitation to Mrs. London, 1648. Mrs. Parliament brought to bed of a monstrous Childe of Reformation, 1648. Mrs. Parliament presented in her Bed after the Birth of the Childe of Deformation, 1648. Crafty Cromwell, 1648. New Market Fayre, 1649. A Phanatick Play, 1660. Lambert's Last Game plaid, 1660, *morocco, rare,* from the Roxburghe collection -	Heber
4	4	-	1511	Drawings (Twenty) by Old Masters, *bound in velvet.* - -	Jefferies
	3	-	1512	Drayton's Owle, *imperfect.*	Triphook
4	14	6	1513	Drury's Illustrations of Natural History, 3 vols. *coloured plates, red morocco* - - 1770	Knell
3	5	-	1514	Dubravius's New Booke of good Husbandry, translated by Churchey, *black letter, blue morocco* *Lond. White,* 1599	Milner
5	5	-	1515	Duhamel du Monceau Traité des Arbres Fruitiers, 2 vols. *plates, green morocco, by Derome* - *Par.* 1768	Johnston
	12	-	1516	Dunton's True Journall of the Sally Fleet - 1637	Triphook
	10	6	1517	Dygbeius de Arte Natandi, *plates* *Lond. Dawson,* 1587	Do.
34	13	-	1518	Dysputacyon, or Complaint of the Herte thorughe perced with the lokynge of the eye, *fine copy, morocco,* VERY RARE. INPRYNTED AT LONDON BY WYNKYN DE WORDE, *without date*	Knell
	10	-	1519	Eagle, Trusser's Elogie on the Loss of Gustavus Adolphus, by G. T. - - - 1660	Rodd

£	s.	d.	Lot	Description	Buyer
13	13	-	1520	Edward. The Lyfe of Saynt Edwarde Confessour and Kynge of Englande, *black letter, splendidly bound in red morocco, with joints,* EXTREMELY RARE *Wynkyn de Worde,* 1533	Triphook
2	7	-	1521	Edward VI. Certayne Sermons or Homilies appointed by the Kinge's Majestie to be declared and redde every Sonday, *black letter, red morocco, scarce* *Lond Whitchurche,* 1547	Cochran
22	1	-	1522	Edyth. XII. Merry Jests of the Wyddow Edyth, in Verse, *black letter,* VERY RARE *Rich. Johnes,* 1573	Triphook
10	5	-	1523	Egeria. The Adventures of Lady Egeria, her miserable Banishment by Duke Lampanus her Husbande, &c. by W. C. *scarce* *Lond. R. Walde-grave,* ——	Heber
1	17	-	1524	Elegantiarum Viginti Præcepta ad perpulchras conficiendas Epistolas, *black letter* *R. Pynson, sine anno*	Rodd
1	1	-	1525	Elizabeth's (Queen) Letter to Lord Treasurer Burghley, to dispense with Subjects or others that shall bringe in Wines in Strange Bottoms, dated 21st Dec. 1572, *in a morocco case* - - -	Longman
	10	-	1526	Elizabeth. True Report of sundry Horrible Conspiracies to take away the Life of the Queene's most excellent Majestie - - *Yetsweirt,* 1594	Anderdon
	10	-	1527	Elizabeth's (Queen) Closet of Physical Secrets 1656	Hollingworth
2	-	-	1528	Elucidarius Carminum et Historiarum, item Vocabula et Interpretationes Grecorum et Hebraicorum, *splendidly bound in red morocco, with joints,* RARE *Hagenau, per Henr. Grau.* ——	Longman
1	-	-	1529	Emblematische Gedancken Muster, *numerous cuts* ——	Payne
7	7	-	1530	Emblematum Philomelæ Thiloniæ Epidigma, Verses and Emblems on the Family of Thilo, *with an engraved title, and very fine impressions of the plates, green morocco, with joints* - *Typis Ligiis Sartorianis,* 1603	D^o^
1	4	-	1531	Emblemata Sacra dat is Eenighe Geestelicke Sinnebeelden, *green morocco* - *Ghedruckt,* 1631	Triphook
1	16	-	1532	——————, S. Steph. Caelii Montis Intercolumniis affixa, *blue morocco, joints* - - 1589	Heber
	10	-	1533	Emblemata Anniversaria Academiæ Altorfinæ *Norimb.* 1597	Clarke
1	-	-	1534	Emblems of the Nobility of the Court of Lewis XIV. ——	Hollingworth
1	10	-	1535	Emblemata pro Toga et Sago, *yellow morocco* *Norimb. s. anno*	Triphook
1	12	-	1536	Emblematicus Apparatus Sacræ Celebritatis Francisci Borgiæ, *numerous plates* - *Viennæ,* 1671	Clarke
1	4	-	1537	Emblematum Elegantissimorum Corpusculum, Latinè et Belgicè, *yellow morocco, with joints* *Ludg. Bat.* 1696	Heber
1	19	-	1538	Emblemata Selectiora, Typis Elegantissimis expressa, *blue morocco, with joints* - - *Amst.* 1704	Payne
1	1	-	1539	English Rogue, the Life and Death of the 1679	Triphook

£	s.	d.	Lot	Description	Buyer
9	15	-	1540	Englyasshe and Frensshe. Here begynneth a lytell Treatyse for to lerne Englysshe and Frensshe, *black letter*, VERY RARE AND CURIOUS *Wynkyn de Worde, n. date*	Rodd
13	-	-	1541	Royal Entertainments. A Letter of the Entertainment untoo the Queen's Majesty at Killingworth Castle in Warwick-Sheer, in 1575, *black letter, original edition, extremely rare, inlaid and bound in red morocco*	Freeling
1	3		1542	——— of Queen Elizabeth, when she marched through London, 1558, *wants title, red morcoco* *Rich. Tottill,* ——	Longman
5	10	-	1543	——— of the Queene's Majestie into hir Highnesse Citie of Norwich, *red morocco, rare* *Bynneman*, 1578	Do
3	15	-	1544	——— of the Landgrave of Hessen to her Majesties Embassadour, *red morocco* *R. Robinson*, 1596	Heber
4	8	-	1545	Entertainment. Ben Jonson, his Part of King James, his Royall and Magnificent Entertainment through his Honourable Cittie of London, *red morocco* *Edw. Blount*, 1604	Clarke
3	6	-	1546	——— given to King James, Queen Anne, and Prince Frederick, with the Speeches and Songs, by Dekker, *red morocco* - - 1604	Longman
5	5	-	1547	——— of the Queen and Prince, their Highnesse to Althrope, at the Rt. Hon. the Lord Spencer's, *red morocco* - - - - 1603	Clarke
1	1	-	1548	Entertainment of Prince Frederick Count Palatine, and Elizabeth Daughter of James I. in Germany, *red morocco* 1613	Triphook
1	2	-	1549	——— by Lord Knowles to Queene Anne, in 1613, by Thos. Campion, *red morocco* - 1613	Heber
4	4	-	1550	Entertainement by Water at Chelsey and White-Hall, at the Receiving of Charles Prince of Wales, *red morocco* 1616	Clarke
	5	-	1551	Episcopus Puerorum, an ancient Custom at Sarum, making an Anniversary Bishop among the Choristers 1671	Hollingworth
4	-	-	1552	Epistles and Gospells, with a brief Postil upon the same from after Easter till Advent, *black letter, blue morocco*, VERY RARE - - *Richarde Bankes*, 1540	Cochran
	16	-	1553	Erasmi Moriæ Encomium, *first edition, with a date, red morocco* - - *Argent*. 1511	Heber
	9	-	1554	———, cum aliis Opusculis, *russia* *Basil*, 1521	Triphook
5	12	6	1555	Erasme les Louenges de Folie, *black letter, wood cuts, very fine copy, yellow morocco. Paris, Galliot du Pré*, 1520	Hibbert
1	10	-	1556	——— l'Eloge de la Folie, traduit par Gucudeville, *large paper, plates by Eisen, yellow morocco, with joints* *Par.* 1751	Perry
1	13	-	1557	Erasmus's Praise of Folly, englished by Sir Thom. Chaloner, *black letter, yellow morocco, with joints.* *Berthelet*, 1569	Triphook

£	s.	d.	Lot	Description	Buyer
	9	-	1558	Erizzo, le Sei Giornate, publicate da Dolce. *Venetia,* 1567	Triphook
1	6	-	1559	Erondelle's Nova Francia and Virginia, *map, russia* 1609	Heber
	1	-	1560	Essex, Robert Earl of, his Ghost sent from Elizian, 2 Parts - - - - - 1624	Hollingworth
1	1	-	1561	Essex, Procession of the Funeral of the Rt. Hon. the Earle of, *portrait by Marshall* . - - 1646	Clarke
	5	-	1562	Essex's Innocency and Honour vindicated by R. Braddon 1690	Hollingworth
5	5	-	1563	Espee, Icy commenche ung tres beau Livre, contenant la Chevalereuse Science des Joueurs d'Espee, *black letter, numerous very curious wood cuts, blue morocco,* EXCESSIVELY RARE. *Anvers, par Guillaume Vorsterman,* 1538	Payne
	14	-	1564	Estienne's Art of making Devises, translated by T. Blount, *plates by Marshall, blue morocco, with joints, fine copy* 1650	Triphook
1	14	-	1565	Euriale et la Belle Lucresse, *black letter, wood cuts, wanting the last leaf, red morocco*	Do
8	-	-	1566	Exhornatorium Curatorum for the Cure of Soules, *black letter, consisting of* 16 *leaves, not mentioned in the last edition of Ames, red morocco, very rare* *Julian Notary,* 1519	Longman
3	4	-	1567	Evangeliorum Quatuor Harmonia, à White, *blue morocco, with joints* - - - *Oxon.* 1805	Barclay
7	-	-	1568	Evelyn's Silva; or, Discourse on Forest Trees, with Notes by Hunter, 2 vols. in 1, *plates, russia* *York,* 1776	Blunt

Folio.

£	s.	d.	Lot	Description	Buyer
44	2	-	1569	FAYTTES OF ARMES. Here begynneth the Book of Fayttes of Armes, and of Chyvalrie, *splendidly bound in Venetian morocco, with morocco lining.* PER CAXTON, (1489) — wants Title — A very fine specimen from Caxton's press.	Longman
2	6	-	1570	Ferrarii Hesperides, sive de Malorum Aureorum cultura et usu, *yellow morocco, ruled* - *Romæ,* 1646	Triphook
1	11	6	1571	Ferrerio Palazzi di Roma, de piu celebri Architetti disignati, 2 vols.—Li Giardini di Roma disignati da Falda, 3 vols. in 1, *plates*	Johnson
1	1	-	1572	Ferro, Teatro d'Imprese di, 2 Parts in 1 vol. *numerous plates* - - - *Venetia,* 1623	Triphook
29	18	6	1573	FIER A BRAS. Le Roman de Fier a Bras, le Geant, FIRST EDITION, *fine copy, morocco,* from the Roxburghe Collection, EXTREMELY RARE - - *Geneve,* 1478	Do.
24	13	6	1574	Le Même, *fine copy, with curious woods cuts, blue morocco,* VERY RARE - *Lyon, par Guill. le Roy,* 1486	Lang
1	10	-	1575	Fiestas de la Santa Iglesia de Sevilla al nuovo culto del Reys Fernando, *plates, russia* *Sevilla,* 1671	Longman

£	s.	d.	Lot	Description	Buyer
4	16	-	1576	Fitler's Scotia Depicta, *large paper, plates, russia, with joints* - - - 1804	Cochran
3	3	-	1577	Flaxman's Designs for Homer's Iliad and Odyssey, *russia, with joints* - - - 1805	Triphook
	10	-	1578	Florilegium Renovatum et Auctum, plates by Merian, *russia, with joints* - - *Franc.* 1641	Do.
26	15	6	1579	Florando. La Coronica del Valiente y Efforcado Principe Don Florando d'Inglatierra hijo del Principe Paladiano, *wood cuts, blue morocco, very fine copy,* EXTREMELY RARE *Lisbona,* 1545	Do.
13	2	6	1580	Fontaine, les Fables de la, avec figures par Oudry, 4 vols. *large paper, red morocco, borders of gold* *Par.* 1755-59	Knell
7	-	-	1581	France. Collection des Portraits des Personnages célébres dans la Revolution Française, 60 *plates, bound in hog-skin.*	Clarke P.
5	10	-	1582	Froissart Chronique de France, &c. 4 vols. in 2, *best edition, russia, with joints* - *Lyon,* 1559	Longman
34	2	6	1583	Froissart's Cronycles of Englande, Fraunce, &c. translated by John Bouchier Lord Berners, 2 vols. in 1, VERY FINE COPY, *in blue morocco, by* ROGER PAYNE *Lond. Myddelton and Pynson,* 1525	Clarke

End of the Eighth Day's Sale.

NINTH DAY'S SALE.

Octavo et Infra.

£	s.	d.	Lot	Description	Buyer
	6	.	1584	Fleckno's Diarium, or Journall, divided into 12 Jornadas in Burlesque Rhime, or Drolling Verse 1658	Triphook
	1	-	1585	Fleming's Stemma Sacrum, the Royal Progeny delineated 1660	Do.
	10	.	1586	Fleurs (Les) du Bien dire, recueillies es Cabinets des plus rares Esprits de ce temps, 3 vols. - *Par.* 1603	Payne
1	1	.	1587	Flitneri Nebulo Nebulonum hoc est jocoseria modernæ nequitiæ censura, *plates, fine copy, yellow morocco* *Franc.* 1620	Clarke
	7	-	1588	Fleury, Discours sur l'Histoire Ecclesiastique, *red morocco* *Par.* 1747	Triphook

£	s.	d.	Lot	Description	Buyer
	11		1589	Flores de Grece, Histoire du tres-vaillant et redouté Dom Flores de Grece, surnomme le Chevalier des Cignes, en François par Nicolas de Herberay, *red morocco* *Par.* 1573	Triphook
	7		1590	Florist, the Compleat, *coloured plates* 1747	Forsyth
	10	-	1591	Florus et Ampelius, *yellow morocco* *Lugd. Bat. Elzevir,* 1638	Clarke
	19	-	1592	Force (Mademoiselle de la) Histoire Secrete de Bourgogne 3 vols. *gilt leaves* - - *Par.* 1782	Dulau
1	16	-	1593	———— Histoire de Marguerite de Valois, 6 vols. - - - *Par.* 1783	Do
2	12	6	1594	Fontaine (De la) Contes et Nouvelles en Vers, 2 vols. plates by R. de Hooge, *red morocco* *Amst.* 1685	Wellesley
4	4	-	1595	———— Contes et Nouvelles, (Edition des fermiers généraux) 2 vols. *fine impressions of the plates, red morocco* *Amst.* 1762	Clarke
	19	-	1596	———— Contes et Nouvelles, 2 vols. *with Romain de Hooge's plates inserted, green morocco* *Par.* 1800	Warner
1	11	6	1597	Fontaine (De la) Fables Choisies, mises en Vers, 5 vols. *plates* - - - - *Par.* 1673	Dulau
3	4	-	1598	———— Fables Choisies, avec figures par Simon de Coigny, 6 vols. *thick paper, red morocco* *Par.* 1787	Triphook
1	3	-	1599	———— Fables, imprimé pour l'Education du Dauphin - - - *Ib.* 1789	Do
	8	-	1600	Fontaine (De la) Les Amours de Psyche et de Cupidon, *red morocco, ruled* - - - *Ib.* 1669	Jones
1	11	6	1601	———— Les Amours de Cupidon et de Psyche avec figures par Moreau le Jeune, 2 vols. *vellum paper, red morocco* - - - - *Par.* 1797	Clarke
	5	-	1602	Fontaines Relation du Pays de Jansenie - *Ib.* 1660	Triphook
	10	-	1603	Fontenelle, Eloge du Czar Pierre I. - *Ib.* 1727	Cattley
			1604	Foreign Tales, Witty and Merry Sayings, Repartees, &c. French and English - - - 1719	
1		-	1605	Forest (Le) de Conscience contenant la chasse des princes spirituelle, *black letter, wood cuts, blue morocco* *Par. Michel le Noir,* 1520	Triphook
	10	-	1606	Autre exemplaire, *blue morocco* - 1520	Do
	14	-	1607	Forest of Montalbano, 4 vols. *extra bound* - 1810	Do
	13	-	1608	Formulaire fort recreatif de tous Contracts, Donations, &c. fait par Bredin le Cocu, *red morocco* *Lyon,* 1605	Do
	1	-	1609	Forsyth's Botanical Nomenclator - 1794	John
	14	-	1610	Fortresse (The) of Fathers ernestlie defending the puritie of Religion and Ceremonies, by the trew exposition of certaine places of Scripture, translated out of Latine by J. B. *red morocco* - - - 1566	Hollingworth
	17	-	1611	Fortunatus, les Riches Entretiens des Aventures et Voyages de, traduits de l'Espagnol - *Par.* 1637	Clarke
	13	-	1612	————, the Tragical History of, *cuts* 1682	Triphook
	2		1613	Foster on the Christian Revelation - 1734	Hollingworth

£	s.	d.	Lot	Description	Buyer
1	-	-	1614	Fouet (Le) des Paillards, ou juste punition des voluptueux et charnels, *yellow morocco* - *Rouen*, 1623	Clarke
	7	-	1615	Foulies (Las) dau Sage de Mounpelie (en vers) 1650	Rodd
	2	-	1616	Frambotto, Anti-Gastorello, overo Astrologia Giudiciaria, *russia* - - - *Padova*, 1659	Triphook
	4	-	1617	Framery Memoires de M. le Marquis de S. Forlaix, 2 vols. *Par.* 1770	D°
	19	-	1618	France. Le Faux Visage descouvert du Fin Renard de la France, 1589. Les Sorceleries de Henry de Valois et les oblations qu'il faisoit au diable dans le bois de Vincennes 1589. Les Regretz Complaintes et Confusion de Jean Vallette, dit de Nogaret, 1579, in one volume, *green morocco.*	Clarke
	2	-	1619	France, Traitté de la Politique de - *Utrecht*, 1670	Triphook
1	15	-	1620	———, De l'Etat Reel de la, 2 vols. *Hambourg*, 1796	Lepard
			1621	———, Voyages en, ornées de gravures, 4 vols. *green morocco* - - - *Par.* 1796	
	3	-	1622	——— (la) Galante, ou Histoires Amoureuses de la Cour, *cuts* - - - *Cologne*, 1695	Triphook
	3	-	1623	Autre edition - - - 1709	Money
	10	-	1624	Franqueville, le Miroir de l'Art et de la Nature, *plates* *Par.* 1691	Triphook
	10	-	1625	Franzini Palatia, Templa, et Icones Statuarum Antiquarum Urbis Romæ, 3 vols. *plates* - *Romæ*, 1599	D°
	1	-	1626	Frederic II Roi de Prusse, sa Vie, 4 vols. *Strasbourg*, 1788	Rodd
	3	-	1627	Frederic, 3 vols - - *Par.* 1799	Dulau
1	6	-	1628	Fredro Scriptorum seu Togæ et Belli Natationum Fragmenta, *plates, green morocco* - *Dantisci.* 1660	Triphook
	5	-	1629	French (the) Convert - - 1706	Rodd
			1630	——— Rogue, or the Life of M. Ragoue de Versailles 1716	
	6	-	1631	Frezier, Voyage de la Mer du Sud, 2 vols. *plates* *Amst.* 1717	Dulau
	14	-	1632	Frischlini et aliorum Facetiæ, *yellow morocco* *Ib.* 1651	Clarke
1	3	-	1633	——— Bebelii et Poggii Facetiæ, *blue morocco, with joints* - - - *Amst.* 1660	D°
1	3	-	1634	Frith's (John) Disputacion of Purgatorie.—An other Boke against Rastel, named the Subsedye, or bulwark to his fyrst Boke, by J. Frythe, presonner in the Tower, 2 vols. in 1, *black letter, fine copies,* RARE - *no date*	Rodd
1	3	-	1635	——- Answer to More's Lettur which he wrote agenst Frith's Treatyse concerninge the Sacramente of the Body and Bloude of Christ, unto which are added the Articles of his Examination; for which J. F. was condemned and burnet in Smithfelde, *printed at Monster*, 1533, *fine copy, blue morocco,* RARE.	D°
	2	-	1636	Froelich de Gentiana Libellus - *Erlangæ*, 1796	Heber
	2	-	1637	Froideur (De) Lettre a M. Barrillon Damoncourt, contenant la Relation des Travaux qui se font en Languedoc pour la Communication des Deux Mers, *russia,* RARE *Toulouse*, 1672	Triphook

£	s.	d.	Lot	Description	Buyer
	2	-	1638	Frontinus's Stratagems of War - 1686	Triphook
	10	6	1639	Frossardi Historia, *blue morocco* - *Amst.* 1656	Rodd
	3	-	1640	Fuchsii Historia Plantarum, *wants title, russia.* ———	K
	18	-	1641	Fuchsio Historia de y ervas, y plantas, en Espanol, *green morocco, with joints* - - *Anv.* 1557	Rodd
	16		1642	Fulke's Defense of the Translations of the Holie Scriptures into the English Tong, *blue morocco* *Lond. Bynneman,* 1583	Hollingworth
	3	-	1643	Fuller's (W.) Plain Proof of the True Father and Mother of the Pretended Prince of Wales - 1700	Triphook
	3	-	1644	Gage, les Voyages de, dans la Nouvelle Espagne, 2 vols. *plates* - - - *Amst.* 1699	Rodd
1	3	-	1645	Galardi la Tyrannie Heureuse, ou Cromwell Politique *Leide,* 1671	Hollingworth
	1	-	1646	Galenus de Motu Musculorum, Latinè *Par. Colin,* 1528	Heber
	1	-	1647	——— de Semine, Latinè - *Ib.* 1533	D^o.
	2	-	1647*	Galimatias d'un Gascon et d'un Provençal - *Par.* 1619	Rodd
3	3	-	1648	Gallæi Icones Illustrium Feminarum Veteris et Novi Testamenti et Prophetarum Veteris Testamenti, *blue morocco* - - - - 1594	Clarke
	1	-	1648*	Galtruchii Mathematicæ Totius Institutio - 1668	John
1	18	-	1649	Gambini Commentario, della Origine de Turchi, *Vineg.* 1541. Guazzo Historie di Mahometto, *Ib.* 1545. Il Viazo del Contarini Ambasciator di Venetia al Signor Uxuncassen Re de Persia in 1473, *Venet.* 1543, in one vol. *russia*	Heber
	9	-	1650	Garcia's Sonne of the Rogue, or the Politicke Theefe 1638	Warder
1	7	-	1651	Gardiner's (Bishop of Winchester) Declaration of suche true Articles as George Joye hath gone about to confute as false, *black letter,* VERY RARE *Lond. Johannes Herforde,* 1546	Cochran
	2	-	1652	Gardening, Observations on Modern - 1777	Warder
	4	-	1653	——— The City Gardener, by Fairchild, 1722. Bradley's Gentleman and Gardener's Kalendar, 1718. Bradley's New Improvements of Planting and Gardening. 1720. Turner's Proposal for raising Timber, 1757, in one vol.	Triphook
	10	-	1654	Garguille Nouvelles Chansons de Gaultier, *yellow morocco* *Par.* 1636	Rodd
	13	-	1655	Garon, le Chasse Ennuy - - *Ib.* 1641	Triphook
	11	-	1656	Garzoni, l'Hospital des Fols Incurables, traduit par Clarier, *red morocco* - - *Par.* 1620	D^o.
	2	-	1657	Gay's Fables - - - 1775	Butler
	18	-	1658	Gaya Ceremonies Nuptiales de Toutes les Nations, *morocco* - - - *Par.* 1681	Payne
	3	-	1659	Gelli, la Circe di Giovan Batista, *morocco* *Firenza,* 1549	Triphook
	8	-	1660	——— les Discours Fantastiques de Tonnelier *Par.* 1575	Heber
	14	-	1661	Geneva, The Lawes and Statutes of, translated by Robert Fills, *black letter* - - *R. Hall,* 1562	Triphook

£	s.	d.	Lot	Description	Buyer
	8	-	1662	Genlis les Vœux Temeraires, 2 vols. - *Hamb.* 1798	Heber
	5	-	1663	Genlis Theatre of Education, 4 vols. - 1781	Triphook
	15	-	1664	Gent's Compendious History of England and of Rome, 2 vols. - - - 1741	Do
	9	-	1665	Gent's History of the famous City of York, *uncut* 1730	Do
	17	-	1666	———— of Rippon, *plates* - 1733	Bentham
	11	-	1667	———— of Kingston upon Hull, *plates* - 1735	Warner
2	13	-	1668	———— of the Ancient Militia in Yorkshire 1760	Bentham
	18	-	1669	———— of the Great Eastern Window of York, *plates* - - - - 1762	Archer
	10	-	1670	Gentilericcio della Filosofia di Amore, *extra bound* *Venet* 1618	Triphook
	1	-	1671	Gentilis de diversis Temporum Appellationibus *Hanov.* 1607	Do
	4	-	1672	Gentilis's Chiefe Events of the Monarchie of Spain, *blue morocco* - - - 1647	Warner
2	8	-	1673	Geraldini Itinerarium ad Regiones sub Æquinoctiali Plaga Constitutas, *blue morocco* {with Walker's English Poem} *Romæ*, 1631	Payne
	4	-	1674	Gerardo, Vita et Gesti d'Ezzelino Terzo da Romano *Vineg.* 1552	Triphook
	2	-	1675	Gerard, le Charactere de l'Honneste Homme, *red morocco, ruled* - - *Par.* 1682	Warner
	8	-	1676	Gerileon d'Angleterre, la Plaisante et Delectable Histoire de, *blue morocco* - - *Lyon*, 1602	Triphook
3	3	-	1677	Germany. The Lamentations of Germany, composed by Dr. Vincent. The Teares of Germany, The Warnings and Prodigies of Germany. The Invasions of Germany, with the Pictures of the chiefe Commanders, 4 vols. *red morocco, numerous plates,* VERY RARE - 1638	Clarke
4	17	-	1678	Gessner Œuvres de, 4 vols. *plates by Moreau, red morocco* *Par.* 1799	Payne
1	19	-	1679	Gesta Romanorum cum Applicationibus moralizatis ac misticis, *green morocco* - *Par. Regnault*, 1508	Knell
1	5	-	1680	Gesta Romanorum - - *Par.* 1517	Triphook
1	1	-	1681	———— *green morocco* - *Lugd.* 1540	Do
5	7	6	1682	———— or Record of Ancient Histories, *black letter, blue morocco* - *Stansby, n. d.*	Do
	14	-	1683	Gesta Romanorum or Forty-five Histories - 1703	Hodgson
1	1	-	1684	Gibeciere (la) de Mome, ou la Thresor du Ridicule, *red morocco* - - - *Par.* 1644	Triphook
	13	-	1685	Gifford's Baviad and Mæviad - 1797	Money
1	15	-	1686	Gigantea, la, et la Nanea, insieme con la Guerra de Mostri (di Ant. Grazzini) *red morocco, scarce* *Firenza*, 1612	Triphook
	4	-	1687	Gil Poetici Conatus - - *Lond.* 1632	Do
	1	-	1688	Gilbert's Florist's Vade Mecum - 1693	Do
2	7	-	1689	Gildas, The Epistle of Gildas, The most Ancient British Author, *portrait by Marshall, blue morocco* - 1638	Clarke
	10	-	1690	Gillii Descriptio Nova Elephanti, *red morocco* *Hamb.* 1614	Do

£	s.	d.	Lot	Description	Buyer
	6	-	1691	Gil Polo la Diana Enamorado, *yellow morocco* *Brusselas*, 1613	Triphook
	12	-	1692	Giovanni Fiorentino il Pecorone - *Milano*, 1554	Do.
	4	-	1693	Giovio le Vite di dodici Visconti Prencipi di Milano, *green morocco* - - *Venet. Giolito*, 1549	Do.
	10	-	1694	Giovio Dialogo dell' Imprese Militari et Amorose, *plates, red morocco* - *Lyone Rovillio*, 1574	Calkin
	8	-	1695	Girard, les Synonymes François, 2 vols. *Lyon*, 1801	Hollingworth
	8	-	1696	Glanville's Poetical Prolusions, *russia* - 1800	Heber
4	4	-	1697	Glasse of the Truthe (on the Divorce of Henry the Eighth from Catherine of Arragon) *Berthelet, without date.* Articles devised by the holle consent of the Kynges counsayle, *Berthelet*, 1533, in one vol. *fine copies, scarce, blue morocco.*	Payne
	3	-	1698	Glorious Lover, the, a Divine Poem - 1679	Triphook
	17	-	1699	Glossographia Anglicana Nova, or Dictionary of Hard Words - - - 1707	Calkin
	12	-	1700	Godeau, Poesies Chrestiennes et Morales de, 3 vols. *blue morocco* - - - *Par.* 1560	Triphook
	10	-	1701	Godeau les Tableaux de la Penitence, *plates, blue morocco* *Par.* 1675	Do.
	1	-	1702	Godofredi Proverbiorum Liber - *Steph.* 1555	Do.
	8	-	1703	Goes, Damiani a, Fides, Religio, &c. Æthiopum sub Imperio Presbyteri Joannis, *blue morocco* *Par. Wechel.* 1541	Do.
	6	-	1704	Goldsmith's Poems, *red morocco* . wants plates · 1800	Cattley
	4	-	1705	——————— by Aikin - 1804	Do.

Quarto.

£	s.	d.	Lot	Description	Buyer
1	1	-	1706	Fabricii Allusioni, Imprese et Emblemi sopra la Vita di Gregorio XIII. *numerous plates* - *Roma*, 1588	Clarke
	19	-	1707	Faerni Fabulæ Centum, cum Figuris, *red morocco* *Romæ*, 1565	Heber
	5	-	1708	Faerni Fabulæ, Latinè et Gallicè par Perrault, *plates* *Lond.* 1743	Butler
1	7	-	1709	Fauchet l'Origine de la Langue et Poesie Françoise *Par.* 1581	Heber
1	10	-	1710	Fauchet les Antiquitez et Histoires Gauloyses, *red morocco* *Geneve*, 1611	Triphook
3	12	-	1711	Fenton's Certaine Tragicall Discourses, *black letter, green morocco* - - *T. Marsh*, 1579	Warder
	9	-	1712	Ferrarii Senensis de Florum Cultura Libri IV. *plates* *Romæ*, 1633	Cattley
1	11	6	1713	Feuille (de la) Devises et Emblemes Anciennes et Modernes, *blue morocco, with joints, fine copy*, *Amst.* 1693	Clarke
	5	-	1714	Feuille (de la) Essay d'un Dictionnaire contenant la Connoissance du Monde, des Sciences Universelles, &c. *cuts*, *Amst.* 1700	Triphook

1715 Figures Emblematiques, *Manuscript upon vellum, containing* 81 *very spirited Emblematical Drawings, with the Moral of each in French Verse, morocco.*

1716 Fiore di Virtu - *Venez. Jeronimo,* 1486

1717 Fletcher's Purple Island and Piscatorie Eclogs *Camb.* 1633

1718 Flores Chronicorum sive Cathalogus Pontificum Romanorum, 2 vols. *Manuscript of the fourteenth century, upon vellum.*

1719 Flores of Greece, excellent History of, *russia* 1664

1720 FLOUDON FELDE. Hereafter ensue the trewe encountre, or Batayle lately don betwene Englande and Scotland. In which Batayle the Scottisshe Kynge was slayne, *black letter, consisting of four leaves, a tract, of* EXTRAORDINARY RARITY, *green morocco,* &c.
Emprynted by me, Richarde Faques, no date

1721 Fortescue's Forest, or Collection of Historyes, *black letter, russia* - - - 1576

1722 Fox's History of James II. *largest paper, splendidly bound in russia, with joints* - - 1808

1723 Frampton's Joyfull Newes out of the Newe Founde Worlde, *blue morocco* - - 1577

1724 Franeau Jardin d'Hyver, ou Cabinet des Fleurs en XXIV Elegies, *plates, arms of Thuanus* - *Douay,* 1616

1725 Fraunce, Commentaries of the Civill Warres of, translated by Thomas Timure - - 1574

1726 FREDERYKE OF JENNEN. This mater treateth of a merchauntes Wyfe that afterwarde went like a man, and becam a great Lorde, and was called Frederyke of Jennen afterwarde, *black letter, with singular wood cuts,* a Book of the greatest rarity, from the Roxburghe Library.
Imprynted in Anwarpe, by me, John Dusborowghe, 1518

1727 Freheri Paradoxa, Emblemata, Ænigmata, Hieroglyphica, A Manuscript, evidently prepared for Publication. The Mathematical Figures are drawn with very great accuracy, and are accompanied with Explanations in Latin and English. There is also a Portrait of Freherus, by Leuchter, *yellow morocco, with joints.*

1728 Freitagii Mythologia Ethica, *numerous plates* *Antv.* 1579

1729 French Politician found out - - 1680

1730 Fruits and Flowers, Book of, *plates* - 1653

1731 Fueslin Insectes de la Suisse, *plates, beautifully coloured, green morocco* - - *Zurich,* 1781

1732 Fureri Itinerarium Ægypti, Arabiæ, Palæstinæ, &c. *plates, russia* - - - *Norimb.* 1621

1733 Fyssher's (Bishop of Rochester) Treatyse concernynge the Fruytfull Sayenges of David, in seven Sermons, made at the exortacyon of Margarete, mother to Kynge Henry the Seventh, *black letter, fine copy. blue morocco,* VERY RARE - *Wynkyn de Worde,* 1525

£	s	d	Lot	Description	Buyer
8	10	6	1734	Fyssher's Sermon on the moost famouse Prynce Kynge Henry the VII. *black letter, very rare, blue morocco* *Wynkyn de Worde,* 1509	Triphook
8	10	6	1735	Fysser's Mornynge Remembraunce for Margarette, Mother unto Kynge Henry the VII. *black letter, blue morocco, very rare* - *Wynkyn de Worde,* 1509	D^o
1	10		1736	Gærtner de Fructibus de Seminibus Plantarum, 2 vols. *plates* - - - *Stutgardiæ,* 1788	Cattley
3	18	-	1737	Galien Rethore Noble et puissant Chevalier filz du Conte Olivier de Vienne Per de France, *wood cuts, black letter, red morocco,* RARE *Paris, Denis Janot, sans date*	Triphook
1	13	-	1738	Galien. Histoire des Nobles Prouesses et Vaillances de Galien Restauré, *wood cuts, blue morocco* *Troyes,* 1606	Heber
2	1	-	1739	Galtheri Alexandreidos libri decem, *litteris cursivis excusi, blue morocco* Persian Types.- *Lugduni,* 1558	D^o
5	10	-	1740	Gardiner's England's Grievance Discovered, in relation to the Coal Trade, *with portraits of the Kings and Queens of England, and other plates, russia, scarce* *Lond.* 1665	Longman
3	5	-	1741	Garrarde's Arte of Warre. Beeing the onely rare Booke of Myllitarie Profession, corrected and finished by Captaine Hichcock, *plates, black letter, with joints* *R. Warde,* 1591	Booth
9	-	-	1742	Gascoigne (George). Flowers. Dan Bartholomew of Bath. The Reporter. Comedie, called Supposes. Jocasta. Herbes. The Fruites of Warre. The Fable of Ferdinando Jeronimi. The Steele Glasse; and Phylomene, *black letter, russia, wants title and some leaves of text.*	D^o
1	1	-	1743	Gasparini Pergamensis Epistolæ, *blue morocco* *Par.* 1498	Heber
2	2	-	1744	Geddes's Booke of sundry Draughtes, principally serving for Glasiers, with the Manner how to Anniel in Glas, *plates, green morocco, with joints* *London, printed in Shoolane,* 1615	Triphook
7	-	-	1745	Geoffroy. Sensuyt les faitz et gestes des nobles coquestes de Geoffroy a la Grant Dent seigneur de Lusignen et siziesme filx de Raymondin Conte du dict lieu et de Melusine, *black letter, green morocco, the last leaf supplied by M.S.* A VERY RARE ROMANCE - *sans date*	D^o
5	-		1746	Gerard. L'Histoire de tres noble et chevaleureux Prince Gerard Conte de Nevers et de Rethel, et de la tres vertueuse et tres chaste Princesse Euriant de Savoye sa mye, *black letter, wood cuts,* RARE *Paris, pour Philippe le Noir,* 1526	D^o
6	16	6	1747	Gerardo di Vera Tre Navigationi fatti dagli Olandesi e Zelandesi al Settentrione, *Venet.* 1599. Diarium Gulielmi C. Schoutenii, *Amst.* 1662. 2 vols. in 1, *plates, russia.*	Hibbert
	3	-	1748	Germanie. The Estate of the Germaine Empire, with the Description of Germanie *Ralphe Blower,* 1595	Rodd

£	s.	d.	Lot	Description	Buyer
11	15	-	1749	Gerson. A Treatyse of the Imytacion and Folowynge the blessed Lyfe of oure moste Mercyfull Savyoure Criste, compyled in Latin by John Gerson, and translate into Englysshe, the yere of oure Lorde, 1502, by Maister Willyam Atkynson, Doctor of Divinite, R. Pynson, 1503. The fourthe Boke of the folowinge Jesu Chrjst, and of the contempninge the World, R. Pynson, 1504, *in* 1 *volume*, RARE	Heber
	8	-	1750	Gesnerus's Newe Jewell of Health, by George Baker, *black letter, wood cuts* - *H. Denham*, 1576	Booth
2	4	-	1751	Gessner. Contes Moraux et Nouvelles Idylles, (traduits de l'Allemagne) 2 vols. avec figures dessinées et gravées par Gessner lui-même, *red morocco, gilt leaves* *Zurich, chez l'Auteur*, 1773	Payne
4	5	-	1752	Gesta Romanorum cum quibusdam aliis historiis eisdem annexis de vitiis virtutibusque cum applicationibus moralisatis et misticis, *fine copy, russia,* VERY RARE *Impressit Johannes de Westphalia alma in Universitate Lovaniensi* - - *sine anno*	Triphook
	4	-	1753	Gesta Grayorum, or the History of Henry Prince of Purpoole, &c. - - - 1688	Rhodes
1	16	-	1754	Geyn (Jaques de) Maniement d'Armes d'Arquebuses, Mousqeto et Picques. Fr. Allmand, et Anglais, *wood cuts* - - - *a Zutphen*, 1619	Heber
1	5	-	1755	Giardæ (Christ.) Icones Symbolicæ Elogiis Illustratæ, *plates* - - *Apud Bidellium.* 1628	Clarke
2	2	-	1756	Gibsoni Chronicon Saxonicum, *russia, with joints* *Oxon.* 1692	Cochran
6	10	-	1757	Giglan. L'Hystoire de Giglan filz de Messire Gauvain qui fut Roy de Galles. Et de Geoffroy de Maiënce son Compaignon, *black letter, wood cuts, yellow morocco,* RARE *Lyon, Huguetan*, 1539	Laing
	2	-	1758	Gioachino, Profetie di, *cuts* - *Padova*, 1625	Butter
	12	-	1759	Girard Traité des Armes, orné de Figures en Taille Douce, *russia* - - *a la Haye*, 1740	King
4	-	-	1760	Gmelin Flora Sibirica, sive Historia Plantarum Sibiriæ, 4 vols. in 3, *plates, russia, with joints* *Petropoli*, 1747	Cattley
18	18	-	1761	Godeffroy. Les Faitz et Gestes du preux Godeffroy de Boulion, et de ses freres Baudouin et Eustache, *black letter, wood cuts, fine copy, from the Roxburghe Collection,* VERY RARE - *Paris, par Jehan Bouffon, sans date*	Longman
4	10	-	1762	Godefroy. Les Passages de oultre mer du Noble Godefroy de Bouillon qui fut Roy de Hierusalem, *black letter* *Paris, Fr. Regnault*, ——	Triphook
	14	-	1763	Goes (Damiani a) aliquot Opuscula *Lovanii*, 1544	Heber

Folio.

£	s.	d.	Lot	Description	Buyer
1	17	-	1764	Fuchsii Historia Plantarum cum Commentariis, *plates, russia, with joints* - - *Basiliæ,* 1542	Cattley
	19	-	1765	Fousch Histoire des Plantes, *plates, red morocco, ruled* *Paris, Gazeáu,* 1549	Johnstone
	6	-	1766	Autre edition, *plates* - - *Lyon,* 1575	Cattley
	10	-	1767	Garidel Histoire des Plantes de Provence, *plates Par.* 1719	Do
3	4	-	1768	Gaultier. A Collection of eighty-five Plates from the New Testament, engraved by T. Gaultier.	Triphook
3	9	-	1769	Gazettes from May to October 1706, (Campaign of the Duke of Marlborough)	Hay (Major)
4	14	6	1770	Genii in Nuptiali Solennitate Philippi Wilhelmi Comitis Palatini et Annæ Catharinæ Sigismundi III. Filiæ, *plates by Loffler, fine impressions, splendidly bound in red morocco, with joints* - - *Coloniæ,* 1642	Clarke
1	6	-	1771	Gerarde's Herball, by Johnson, *russia* 1633	Longman
	17	-	1772	German Atlas, in ninety-six Maps. ——	Woodfall
	15	-	1773	Gerundensis Paralipomenon Hispaniæ Libri decem —— *apud Granatam,* 1545	Longman
4	1	-	1774	Gesta Romanorum cum Applicationibus Moralizatis ac Mysticis, *russia, with joints* - - 1493	Triphook
1	13	-	1775	Gesta Dei per Francos Bongarsii, 2 vols. in 1, *Hanov.* 1611	Dibdin
1	18	-	1776	Geyn Wapenhandelinghe van Roers Musquetten ende Spiessen, *fine impressions of the plates, russia, Amst.* 1608	Hollingworth
1	16	-	1777	Gille Corona Gratulatoria Universitatis Salisburgensis, *many plates, red morocco* - *Salisburg,* 1681	Triphook
53	11	-	1778	Glanvilla, Bartholomeus, de Proprietatibus Rerum, translated into English, *fine copy,* WYNKEN DE WORDE, *no date* This Book is printed on the first paper manufactured in England.	Do
8	5	-	1779	Good Lyvyng and good Deying, the Traytte of, et the paynys of Hel et the paynys of Purgatoyr, &c. *wood cuts,* VERY RARE, imperfect at the beginning *Paris, A. Verard, without date.*	Longman

End of the Ninth Day's Sale.

TENTH DAY'S SALE.

Octavo et Infra.

1780 Golnitz Compendium Geographicum, *blue morocco* *Amst. Elzev.* 1643

1781 Idem, *yellow morocco* - - *Elzev.* 1649

1782 Golnitz Ulysses Belgico-Gallicus, *red morocco* *Ib.* 1631

1783 Aliud exemplar, *red morocco.* *Lugd. Bat. Hackii,* 1655

1784 Gomara Historia de Mexico con el Descubrimiento de la Nueva Espana - - *Anv.* 1554

1785 Gombauld's Endimion, by Hurst, *cuts* - 1639

1786 Gomersall's Poems, *frontispiece* - 1633

1787 Gomez, les Journées Amusantes de, 8 vols. *Amst.* 1744

1788 Gomgam, ou l'Homme Prodigieux transporté dans l'Air, 2 vols. in 1, *plates, russia* - - *Amst.* 1713

1789 Gonin, les Tours de Maître, 2 vols. *plates* *Anv.* 1714

1790 Gonon, la Chasteté Recompensée, ou l'Histoire de sept Pucelles Doctes et Savantes - *Bourg.* 1643

1791 Gonsalvii S. Inquisitionis Hispaniæ Artes detectæ, *red morocco* - - - *Heidelb.* 1567

1792 Gostelow, Charles Stuart and Oliver Cromwell united 1655

1793 Gostling's Walk about Canterbury, *plates.* *Canterb.* 1777

1794 Gouan Flora Monsepeliaca ad sua Genera relata *Lugduni,* 1765

1795 Goulburn's Blueviad, a Satyrical Poem 1805

1796 Gouvernement (le) Present, ou Eloge de son Eminence, Satyre, *red morocco* *sans date*

1797 Gozanne, la Retraite de la Marquise de, 2 vols. in 1 *Amst.* 1735

1798 Graaf, Voyages aux Indes Orientales, *plates* *Ib.* 1719

1799 Grafigny, Lettres d'une Peruvienne, 2 vols. *red morocco* *Par.* 1752

1800 ———————————, 2 vols. *vellum paper* *Par.* 1797

1801 Les même Lettres, avec une Traduction Italienne par Deodati, *large paper, proofs, and a set of etchings* *Par.* 1796

1802 Grafton's Abridgement of the Chronicles of Englande, *black letter, russia, scarce* - - *Tottell,* 1572

£	s.	d.	Lot	Title	Date	Buyer
2		-	1803	Grammatical Drollery, in Poems and Songs	1682	Rodd
1	15	-	1804	Granada, Historia de las Guerras Civiles de, *russia, with joints, by* ROGER PAYNE - - *Par.*	1660	Payne
	13	-	1805	Lo Mesmo, *russia, with joints* - *Sevilla,*	1692	Triphook
	14	-	1806	Grande Confrarie des Soulx d'ouvrer et enragez de rien faire - - - - - *Par.*	1537	Heber
2	2	-	1807	Granger's Biographical History of England, 4 vols.	1804	Triphook
	8	-	1808	——— Letters, by Malcolm, *portrait* -	1805	Do
	10	-	1809	Grant's Letters from the Mountains, 3 vols.	1806	Heber
	7	-	1810	Granucci, la Piacevol Notte e Lieto Giorno di, *russia* *Venet.*	1573	Drury
2	10	-	1811	Gravelot Iconologie par Figures, ou Traité complet des Allegories, Emblemes, &c. 4 vols. *large paper, yellow morocco, with joints, &c.* - - *Par. s. d.*		Triphook
	8	-	1812	Gravina Region Poetica, par Mathias, *green morocco.*	1806	Drury
	7	-	1813	Gray's Memoria Technica - - -	1730	Clarke
	18	-	1814	——-- Poems, with Life by Mason, 4 vols.	1778	Triphook
	7	-	1815	——-- Poetical Works, *red morocco* -	1805	Do
	7	-	1816	Grazzini, La Seconda Cena, *uncut* *Stambul.*	——	Clarke
2	6	-	1817	Grelot Voyage de Constantinople, *plates, yellow morocco* *Par.*	1681	Do
	1	-	1818	Green's Annals of George the Third, 2 vols.	1808	Triphook
	15	-	1819	——— Survey of the City of Worcester, *plates*	1764	Do
	6	-	1820	Greenwood's Virgin Muse, a Collection of English Poems,	1717	Arch
1	7	-	1821	Gresset, Œuvres de, 2 vols. *red morocco* *Lond.*	1748	Rogers
	6	-	1822	————————- Choisies de - - *Par.*	1804	J. Boswell
	5	-	1823	Grew Anatomie des Plantes, *morrocco, ruled* *Ib.*	1675	Drury
	5	-	1824	Grigi Histoire Veritable, 2 Parts in 1	59749	Triphook
	17	-	1825	Groenland, Relation de, *plates* - *Par.*	1647	Clarke
	8	-	1826	Grose's Essays, Dialogues, &c. - -	1792	Drury
	12	-	1827	Grotii Argumenta Theologica, Juridica, Politica, *red morocco* - - - *Elzev.*	1652	Payne
	6	-	1828	Grotii Epistolæ ad Gallos, *green morocco* *Ib.*	1650	Drury
	14	-	1829	Grotius de Veritate Religionis Christianæ, *blue morocco* *Amst. Elzev.*	1674	Triphook
	15	-	1830	Idem Liber, *red morocco* - *Amst.*	1684	Heber
	3	-	1831	Grotius de Veritate Religionis Christianæ *Oxon.*	1700	Payne
1	1	-	1832	Gruget l'Heptameron, ou Histoires des Amans Fortunez, 2 vols. *red morocco* - - *Par.*	1697	Drury
	1	-	1833	Gualdi's Life of Donna Olimpia Maldachini	1667	Butler
	8	-	1834	Guarini il Pastor Fido, *cuts, green morocco* *Leide, Elzev.*	1659	Dentley
	9	-	1835	————————, *cuts* - *Parigi,*	1678	Clarke
	16	-	1836	Guicciardini Belgicæ Descriptio Generalis, 2 vols. *plates, blue morocco* - - - *Amst.*	1652	Drury
	11	-	1837	Guichardi Noctes Granzovianæ de antiquis Triumphorum Spectaculis, *green morocco* - *Amst.*	1661	Triphook

£	s.	d.	Lot	Description	Buyer
	5	-	1838	Guide des Chemins de France, de Jerusalem, Rome, &c. *russia* - - - - *Par.* 1586	Heber
	10	6	1839	Guide from the Cradle to the Grave, *cuts, black morocco* 1732	Dibdin
	5	-	1840	Guide to Health, Beauty, Riches, and Honour 1796	Allen
	2	-	1841	Guidi e Zappi, Canzonieri di - *Venezia,* 1789	Warner
	2	-	1842	Guidott's Discourse of Bathe and the Hot Waters there 1676	Drury
	12	-	1843	Guise, les Amours du Grand Alcandre, par Mlle. de, 2 vols. *Par.* 1786	Dulau
	12	-	1844	Gusman de Alfarache, Histoire de l'Admirable, 3 vols. *Brusselles,* 1705	Triphook
	1	-	1845	Guyon de Sardiere, Catalogue des Livres *Par.* 1759	Do.
	6	-	1846	Guyse Legende de Domp Claude de, Abbe de Clury 1581	Payne
	1	-	1847	Gyllius de Constantinopoleos Topographia *Lugd. Bat. Elzev.* 1632	Petrie
1	1	-	1848	Habert, le Combat de Cupido et de la Mort, &c. *wood cuts* - *Paris, par Alain Lotrain, sans date*	Heber
	12	-	1849	Habington's Castara, *second edition* - - 1635	Triphook
	17	-	1850	Hæfteni Regia Via Crucis, *plates, uncut, blue morocco, with joints* - - - - *Antv.* 1728	Chalmers
	9	-	1851	Hæfteni Scola Cordis, *plates* *Antv. Meursais,* 1635	Triphook
	8	-	1852	Hallifax and its Gibbet Law in a true Light 1708	Drury
	11	-	1853	Hall, Mundus alter et idem, sive Terra Australis ante hac semper incognita, *russia* - *Francoforti,* ——	Triphook
	9	-	1854	Hall's History of the Barbarous Cruelties committed by the Dutch in the East Indies - - 1712	Do
	1	-	1855	Halleri Opuscula sua Botanica *Gottingæ,* 1749	Do
1	-	-	1856	Hamilton, Œuvres de, 6 vols. - *Par.* 1749	Drury
	1	-	1857	Hamilton Memoires du Comte de Grammont, 2 vols. in 1 1779	Triphook
1	-	-	1858	Harangues de l'Admirable Crocheteur de Paris, assis sur la Cloche de la Samaritaine.—Response du Crocheteur. Le Voyage de M. Guillaume en l'autre Monde 1612.—Le Surveillant de Charanton 1611—in one vol. *green morocco*	Lepard
	11	-	1859	Hardy, le Reveille-Matin des Courtisans, *red morocco, ruled* - - *Paris, R. Estienne,* 1623	Triphook
	4	-	1860	Harlot's Progress, being the Life of the noted Moll Hackabout - - - - - 1742	Clarke
	6	-	1861	Harmonie des Accords du Soldat François et de ses contredisans - - - *Par.* 1608	Warner
			1862	Harvey's Varieties of Philosophy and Physick 1702	Do.
	14	-	1863	Hattige, ou les Amours du Roy de Tamaran, *blue morocco* *Cologne,* 1676	Strettell
	6	-	1864	Hattige, or the Amours of the King of Tamaran *Amst.* 1680	Triphook

1865 Heath's Brief Chronicle of the late Intestine War, in the three Kingdoms of England, Scotland, and Ireland, with the *frontispiece and portraits, morocco, with joints* 1663

1866 Hecatomphile, ce sont deux Grecques composees, signifiant, Centiesme Amour, *wood cuts, red morocco,* SCARCE *Par. par A. Bonnemere,* 1539

1867 Heineken Idée Generale d'une Collection complette d'Estampes, *russia* - - *Leipsic,* 1771

1868 Heinsii Poemata Auctioria, *red morocco Lugd. Bat.* 1640

1868* Alia editio, *yellow morocco* - *Elzevir,* 1642

1869 Heinsii de Tragœdiæ Constitutione Liber, *red morocco Elzevir,* 1643

1870 ——— Laus Asini, *red morocco* - *Ib.* 1629

1871 Heliodore, les Aventures Amoureuses de Theagenes et Cariclée sommairement descrite et representee par figures par Pierre Valet, *very fine impressions, blue morocco, with joints,* RARE - - *Par.* 1613

1872 ——— Histoire Ethiopique, Amours de Theagenes et Cariclea - - - - - *Par.* 1626

1873 Heliodorus' History of Theagenes and Chariclea 1753

1874 Helisenne de Crenne, les Œuvres de, *wood cuts, yellow morocco* - - *Par. Grouleau,* 1560

1875 Hell upon Earth, or the Town in an Uproar 1729

1876 Help to Discourse, or More Merriment mixt with serious Matter - - - - - 1663

1877 Helth. This is the Myrrour or Glasse of Helth necessary and nedeful for every Person to loke in, that wyll kepe their body from the sycknesse of the Pestilence, &c. *black letter, blue morocco Lond. by Richard Kele, no date*

1878 Another edition, *black letter, title wanting, russia Wyllyam Myddelton, no date*

1879 Hennepin Description de la Louisiane, *blue morocco Par.* 1688

1880 Hennepin's New Discovery of a vast Country in America, *plates* - - - - 1699

1881 Henry III. Protestation et Defense pour le Roy de Navarre, traduicte du Latin intitulé Brutum Fulmen Sixti V. *red morocco* - - - - 1587

1882 Henricus. De Justa et Canonica Absolutione Henrici III. Franciæ et Navarræ Regis - *Lutet.* 1594

1883 Henry IV. Histoire des Amours de - *Leyde,* 1763

1884 Henry VIII. The Practyse of Prelates, whether the Kinges grace may be separated from hys Quene, because she was his brothers wyfe, *Marborch,* 1530. A Treatise of the Cohabitacyon of the faithfull with the unfaithfull, 1555. A Declaration of the then Comma dementes, wants title. *Three Tracts by Tyndale, black letter,* VERY RARE.

£	s	d	Lot	Description	Buyer
2	12	6	1885	Henry VIII. The Determinations of the Universities of Italy and Fraunce that it is so unlefull for a man to marie his brother's wyfe, that the Pope hath no power to dispence therewith, *black letter, russia,* RARE *Berthelet,* 1531	Triphook
1	2	-	1886	Henry VIIIth's Primer, Latin and English, *black letter, imperfect, blue morocco* *Richard Grafton,* 1545	Chalmers
1	12	-	1887	Henry VIII. Doctrine and Erudition for any Christen Man, (commonly called the King's Book) *black letter, wants title, blue morocco* *Berthelet,* 1543	Dr Coombe
4	14	6	1888	Henry VIII. Letters in answere to a certayne Letter of Martyn Luther sent unto hym by the same, and also the copy of the foresayd Luther's Letter, in suche order as hereafter foloweth, *black letter, fine copy, blue morocco,* EXTREMELY RARE. See Dibdin's Ames, Vol. II. p. 488 LONDON, R. PYNSON, *no date*	Triphook
2	8	-	1889	Henry VIII. A Supplycation to our moste Soveraigne Lorde Kynge Henry the Eyght, Supreme Heade, under God, here in Erthe, next and immedyatly of his Churches of Englande and Irelande, *black letter, very fine copy, blue morocco,* RARE - 1544	Heber
	12	-	1890	Henry Frederick, Prince of Scotland, and since of Wales, a True Account of his Baptism, *red morocco* *Edinburgh,* 1703	Triphook
1	15	-	1891	Hentzneri Itinerarium Germaniæ, Angliæ, Italiæ, *red morocco, scarce* - - *Lipsiæ,* 1661	Do
1	1	-	1892	Hentzner's Travels in England, *red morocco* 1797	Do
	2	-	1893	Herbert de Cherbury de Religione Gentilium *Amst.* 1700	Drury
	11	-	1894	Hereford, History and Antiquities of the Cathedral Church of - - - - - 1711	Clarke
	12	-	1895	Hermannidæ Britannia Magna, *maps* - *Amst.* 1661	Triphook
	2	-	1896	Herodiani Historiæ Libri VIII. Gr. Lat. *Lug.* 1624	Clarke
3	13	-	1897	Herodotus Gr. et Lat. ex Edit. Wesselingii et Reitzii, 7 vols. *large paper, yellow morocco* *Edinburgi,* 1806	Triphook
	12	-	1898	Herodoti Historia, Latinè, *blue morocco* *Gryphius,* 1551	Do
	6	-	1899	Heroick Education, or Choice Maximes and Instructions for training up of Youth, *with portrait of William Prince of Orange* - - - 1657	Rodd

Quarto.

£	s	d	Lot	Description	Buyer
3	19	-	1900	Goeteeris, Journael der Legatie en Sweden ende Moscovien, *plates, russia* - *In s'Graven-Hage,* 1619	Clarke
1	15	-	1901	Goldsmith and Parnell's Poems, *with wood cuts by Bewick, green morocco* - - - *Bulmer,* 1795	Drury
3	-	-	1902	Goodwinne's Babel's Balme, or the Honey-Combe of Rome's Religion, translated into tenne English Satyres, by John Vicars, *morocco,* RARE *George Purslowe,* 1624	Thorpe

1903 Gowrie's (The Earle of) Conspiracie against the King's Majestie - - *Valentine Sunnies,* 1603

1904 Greatrak's. A Brief Account ot Mr. Valentine Greatrak's and divers of the strange Cures performed by him, 1666. The Miraculous Conformist, by Henry Stubbe, 1666. Wonders no Miracles, or Mr. V. Greatrate's Gift of Healing examined, 1666, in one volume.

1905 Greene's Tu Quoque, or the Cittie Gallant, by Jo. Cooke, *blue morocco* - *John Trundle,* 1614

1906 ——— (Robert) Ciceronis Amor, Tullies Love, *black letter* - - - *Stansby,* 1611

1907 ——— Groat's Worth of Witte bought with a Million of Repentance, *blue morocco* *by N. O. for Henry Bell,* 1621

1908 ——— History of Dorastus and Fawnia 1703

1909 Greepe's (Thomas) the True and Perfect Newes of the Exploytes performed and doone by that valiant Knight, Syr Francis Drake, not onely at Sancto Domingo and Carthagena, but also nowe at Cales, and upon the Coast of Spayne, 1587, *in verse, black letter, russia,* RARE *J. Charlewood,* 1589

1910 Grevinus de Venenis, *cuts, blue morocco* *Antv. Plantin,* 1571

1911 Gringore, les Fantasies de Mere Sote, avec Privilege daté de Paris, 1516, *black letter, wood cuts, fine copy, blue morocco,* FIRST EDITION, RARE.

1912 Gualterotti, Il Polemidoro, Poema Eroica, *the engraved frontispiece in an unfinished state, green morocco, scarce* *Firenze,* 1600

1913 Guarinus Veronensis de Differentia veri Amici et Adulatoris. Poggius et Aretinus in Hypocritas et Delatores, *editio antiqua, fine copy* *sine ulla nota.*

1914 Guerard Diverses Figures des Cris de Paris. Poilly Jeux d'Enfans - - - - *Par.* 1690

1915 Guevara's Golden Epistles, translated by Edward Fenton, *black letter* - - *R. Newberie,* 1582

1916 ——— Familiar Epistles, translated by Fellowes, *black letter* - - *R. Newberie,* 1584

1917 Guilandini (Melchioris) Papyrus, hoc est Comment. in tria Plinii majoris de papyro capita, *russia* *Venet.* 1572

1918 Guillaume de Palerme, l'Histoire du Noble preux et vaillant Chevalier Guillaume de Palerme et de la belle Melior, *wood cuts, black letter, yellow morocco* *Par. Nicolas Bonfons, sans date*

1919 Gull's (The) Hornbook, by J. Decker, with Notes of Illustration, by Dr. Nott - *Bristol,* 1812

1920 Gysius Korte Schets van het Leeven en Sterven der Martelaaren, *plates* - - *Amst.* 1719

1921 Hackney Coaches, List of the 400 licensed in July and August, 1662 - - - - 1664

£	s.	d.	No.	Lot	Buyer
	4	-	1922	Hackwell's Comparison betweene the dayes of Purim and that of the Powder Treason - *Oxford,* 1626	Drury
1	1	-	1923	Hædus de Amoris Generibus *Tarvisii per Gerardum de Flandria,* 1492	Clarke
	5	-	1924	Hall's Crazy Tales - - - 1762	Rodd
1	16	-	1925	Hamconii Frisia seu de Viris rebusque Frisiæ illustribus libri duo, *plates, red morocco* - *Franekaræ,* 1620	Clarke
4	12	-	1926	Hamilton, Memoires du Comte de Grammont, orné de 72 *portraits, green morocco, gilt leaves* - 1793	Alexander
1	11	6	1927	Harry's (George Owen) Genealogy of James I. 1604	Miller
2	12	6	1928	Harvey's (Richard) Philadelphus, or a Defence of Brutes and the Brutan's History, *black letter, morocco* *John Wolfe,* 1593	Triphook
6	-	-	1929	Hawkins's General History of Music, 5 vols. *russia* 1776	Drury
	14	-	1930	Hayter's Report upon the Herculaneum Manuscripts 1811	Hibbert
3	7	-	1931	Haywood's Philocothonista, or the Drunkard opened, dissected, and anatomized, *with frontispiece, blue morocco* 1635	Clarke
	9	-	1932	Heawood's Manner of the King's Coronation at Manchester, April 23, 1661, *red morocco*	Heber
1	10	-	1933	Hederici Lexicon Græcum, *russia* - *Lond.* 1803	Thorpe
2	16	-	1934	Heinsii Poemata, Gr. et Belg. *plates, fine impressions, blue morocco, with joints* - - *Amst.* 1616	Clarke
1	14	-	1935	Heleine. Le Romant de la Belle Heleine de Constantinople - - *Par. Bonfons,* 1586	Triphook
	18	-	1936	Henrico. La Magnifica et Triumphale Entrata del Re di Francia Henrico Secondo nella Citta di Lyone, alli 21 di Septemb. 1548, *wood cuts, blue morocco* *Lyone Rovillio,* 1549	Drury
	17	-	1937	Henrie. The Order and Solemnitie of the Creation of Prince Henrie, Prince of Wales, &c. on Monday, the 4th of June, 1609, *red morocco* *Britaines Bursse for John Budge,* 1611	Clarke
3	12	-	1938	Hentzner's Journey into England, *morocco, with joints* *Reading,* 1807	Triphook
3	-	-	1939	Herbarius, cum Herbarum Figuris, *fine copy, russia,* RARE, *but wants the first leaf* *Moguntiæ (per P. Schoyffer)* 1484	Cattley
3	4	-	1940	Herbarum, Tractatus de Virtutibus, *cuts,* *Venet.* 1508	Clarke
2	11	-	1941	Heyns Emblemata, Emblemes Chrestienes et Morales, *blue morocco* - - - *Rott.* 1625	Do
10	5	-	1942	Heywood's (John) Parable of the Spider and the Flie, *portrait, wood cuts, black letter, fine copy, red morocco* *Lond. T. Powell,* 1556	Triphook
8	8	-	1943	Heywoode's Workes, a Dialogue conteyning the number of the Effectual Proverbes, concerning two maner of Mariages. With six hundred Epigrammes, *portraits, black letter, fine copy, blue morocco,* RARE *T. Marsh,* 1576	Sketchell

Note	£	s.	d.	Lot	Description	Buyer
	2	14	-	1944	Heywood's Four Prentises of London, with the Conquest of Jerusalem - - - 1632	Booth
	1	-	-	1945	Hexham's Journall of the taking of Venlo, Roermont, Strale, &c. *at Delph, by John Pietersz Walpote,* 1633	Clarke
resold for	1	2	-	1946	Hierusalem, le Grant Voyage de Hierusalem, divisé en deux parties, *black letter, fine copy, with map* *Par. F. Regnault, sans date* — sold the first time for 3.15.– Imperfect.	Laing
		7	-	1947	Hitchins's True Discovery of the Conduct of the Receivers and Thief-Takers in and about the City of London 1718	Drury
	10	15	-	1948	Hoare, The Itinerary of Abp. Baldwin through Wales, by Giraldus de Barri, translated by Sir R. C. Hoare, 2 vols. *large paper, plates, red morocco, with joints* 1806	Milner
	1	1	-	1949	Hocus Pocus Junior, the Anatomie of Legerdemain, *frontispiece* - - - 1634	Clarke
	1	11	6	1950	Hogarth's Analysis of Beauty, *with the large plate, blue morocco* - - - 1772	Hare
	8	10	6	1951	Holinshed's Chronicles of England, Scotland, and Ireland, 6 vols. *russia* - - 1807, &c.	Clarke
	4	6	6	1952	Hollar's Habits of English and Foreign Ladies, 1640, with 28 Plates added, chiefly Views, *mounted on drawing paper*	Arch
	3	18	-	1953	Holy Bull (The) and Crusado of Rome, first published by Gregory XIII. and afterwards renewed and ratified by Sixtus V. *black letter, green morocco* *John Wolfe,* 1588	Longman
	3	6	-	1954	Homelye (An) to be read in the tyme of Pestilence, and a most presente remedye for the same, by Bishop Hooper, *black letter, blue morocco,* RARE *Worceter, by J. Oswen,* 1553	Heber
	13	13	-	1956	Homeri Ilias et Odyssea, Gr. et Lat. cum Scholiis Didymi cura Schrevelii, LARGE PAPER, *red morocco,* VERY RARE, *with Schiavonetti's two plates inserted* *Lugd. Bat.* 1656	Drury

Folio.

Note	£	s.	d.	Lot	Description	Buyer
resold for	131	5		1957	GOWER CONFESSIO AMANTIS Emprynted by me, WILLIAM CAXTON, 1483. A remarkably fine and perfect copy of one of the most interesting and desirable books printed by Caxton, bound in russia. — Sold the first time for 205.16 — Imperfect	Triphook
	4	14	6	1958	Gower's Confessio Amantis, *russia* - *Berthelet,* 1554	Do.
	1	7	-	1959	Granada, Ordenances de la Real Audiencia y Chancilleria da, *russia* - - *Granada,* 1601	Do.
	6	16	6	1960	Gregorii (Sancti Papæ) Expositio in Librum Extremum Ezechielis Prophetæ. *A very ancient Manuscript, upon Vellum, which appears, by the formation of the Capital Letters, to have been written in the 13th Century, red velvet.*	Drury
	4	14	6	1961	Gregorii (Sancti Papæ) Dialogorum Libri Quatuor. *Manuscript of the 14th Century, upon Vellum, in russia.*	Do.

£	s.	d.	Lot	Description	Buyer
	10	-	1962	Gudiel Compendio de Algunas Historias de Espana y de la antigua Familia de los Gironos, *wants title.*	Triphook
1	7	-	1963	Guercino Raccolti di Alcuni Disegni incise in Rame da Bartolozzi et Piranesi.	Parker
13	13	-	1964	Guerino prenominato Meschino, *second edition, the Table is wanting, and the first leaf is very accurately supplied by MS. red morocco, from the Roxburghe Library* *Venezia Gerard. de Flandria,* 1477	Triphook
10	-	-	1965	Guerino chiamato Meschino, *fine copy, red morocco* *Venetia per Jo. Aluiscio Milanesi de Varesi,* 1498	Do
2	14	-	1966	Guevara's Dial of Princes, translated by North, *black letter, red morocco, with joints* - - 1568	Anderdon
	12	-	1967	Guicciardini Descrittione di Tutti i Paesi Bassi, *plates* *Anv.* 1567	Triphook
27	6	-	1968	Guy de Warwick Chevalier d'Angleterre qui en son temps fit plusieurs conquestes en Angleterre, en Allemaigne, &c. *wood cuts, red morocco,* VERY RARE, *from the Roxburghe Library* - *Par. Franç. Regnault,* 1525	Do
34	2	6	1969	Gyron le Courtoys avec la Devise des Armes de tous les Chevaliers de la Table Ronde, WOOD CUTS, EXTREMELY RARE, *a very fine copy, in red morocco, from the Roxburghe Library* - - *Par. Verard, sans date*	Laing
11	11	-	1970	Hamilton's (Sir W.) Campi Phlegræi, COLOURED from Drawings after Nature, *original edition* *Naples,* 1776	Longman
8	10	6	1971	HARRIS'S THIRTY BEAUTIFULLY COLOURED DRAWINGS UPON VELLUM, of English Insects, with the Plants upon which they feed. The original Drawings for his Natural History of English Insects	Triphook
3	-	-	1972	Hay Recueil de Cent Estampes representant differentes Nations du Levant, *red morocco* - *Par.* 1714	Clarke
	13	-	1973	Heisteri Descriptio Novi Generis Plantæ ex Bulbosarum classe, *coloured plates* - - *Brunsvig.* 1753	Cattley
2	2	-	1974	Henrique. Historia de la Vida y Hechos del Rey don Henrique Tercero de Castilla, *russia* *Madrid,* 1638	Heber
5	12	6	1975	Herball, (The Grete) which geveth parfyt knowlege and understandyng of all maner of Herbes, *wood cuts, black letter, russia,* RARE - *Peter Treveris,* 1525	Triphook
2	17	-	1976	Herball, (The Greate) which geveth parfyte knowledge of Herbes, *black letter, russia* - *J. Kynne,* 1561	Do
3	11	-	1977	Herbal, (A.) Manuscript upon VELLUM, with Illuminated Capitals, *russia*	Cattley
3	4	-	1978	Herbert's Travels in Africa and Asia, *frontispiece, plates, russia* - - - 1634	Ponton
1	-	-	1979	Herbier ou Collection des Plantes Medicinales de la Chine, dirigé par Buchoz, *coloured plates* - *Par.* 1781	Cattley
See page 33		-	765	BOCCACIO IL DECAMERONE - VALDARFER, 1471	Longman

End of the Tenth Day's Sale.

ELEVENTH DAY'S SALE.

Octavo et Infra.

£	s.	d.	Lot	Description	Buyer
	2	-	1980	L'Heroine Mousquetaire, ou Histoire veritable de Mademoiselle Christine, Contesse de Meyrac, *plates* *Amst.* 1702	Triphook
	7	-	1981	Herp Directoire des Contemplatifz. Le Mirouer de la Vie de l'Homme et de la Femme. La Seconde Partie du livre appellé le Directoyr doré des contemplatifz, 2 vols. *black letter, red morocco* - *Par.* 1549-52	Do.
	7	-	1982	Herrick's Select Poems - *Bristol,* ——	Do.
	10	-	1983	Hesii Emblemata Sacra de Fide, Spe, Charitate, *blue morocco* - - *Antv. Plantin,* 1636	Clarke
	3	-	1984	Hesiodus Gr. Lat. Schrevelii - *Elzevir,* 1657	Hayes
	2	-	1985	Hexameron Rustique, *red morocco* - *Cologne,* 1671	Triphook
1	1	-	1986	Heywood's Pleasant Dialogues and Dramas, selected out of Lucian, Erasmus, &c. *scarce* - 1637	Clarke
	5	-	1987	Hic, et Ubique Venus, sive Opportunitas Fax Amoris *Lond.* 1667	Perry
	4	-	1988	Hieron's Help to Devotion, *black letter, old stamped binding* - - - - 1619	Christie
	10	-	1989	Hildebrandi Antiquitates Romanæ, *blue morocco* *Trajecti,* 1731	Clarke
	2	-	1991	Hill's Hortus Kewensis - - 1768	Christie
1	1	-	1992	Hillesemii Sacrarum Antiquitatum Monumenta, *plates, blue morocco* - - *Antv. Plantin,* 1577	Hollingworth
	7	-	1993	Hippocratis Prænotiones, cum Versione Foesii, *red morocco* *Amst. Elzevir,* 1660	Black
	3	-	1994	Hippolytus Redivivus, id est Remedium contemnendi Sexum Muliebrem, *red morocco* - - 1644	Clarke
2	18	-	1995	Histoires Prodigieuses, extraictes de plusieurs fameux Autheurs, Grecs and Latins, *wood cuts, blue morocco* *Par.* 1598	Triphook
4	5	-	1996	Histoires Tragiques, 7 vols - *Lyon.* 1616	Lepard
	8	-	1997	——————— extraictes des Œuvres Italiennes de Bandel, par Pierre Boaistuau, *yellow morocco* *Par.* 1559	Triphook
1	10	-	1998	Histoires Galantes, Recueil des, *red morocco* *Cologne, chez Jean le Blanc,* ——	Clarke
	10	6	1999	——————, Facetieuses et Moralles, *green morocco* *Leiden,* 1663	Do.
	2	-	2000	—————— Secrete de Bourgogne, 2 vols. in 1. 2 parts only. *a la Haye,* 1694	Triphook

£	s.	d.	Lot	Description	Buyer
	2	-	2001	Histoire des Favorites sous plusieurs Regnes ——	Warner
3	-	-	2002	———— Ordres Militaires ou des Chevaliers, 4 vols. *Amst.* 1721. Histoire du Clergé Seculier et Regulier, 4 vols. *Amst.* 1716. Histoire des SS. Peres des Deserts, 4 vols. *Anvers.* 1714. 12 vols. *uniform, numerous plates.*	Payne
	11	-	2003	Histoire du Chevalier de Grieux et de Manon Lescaut, 2 vols. - - - *Amst.* 1753	Heber
	14	-	2004	Historia del Emperador Carlo Magno, y de los Doze Pares de Francia, *yellow morocco* - *Barcelona,* ——	Clarke
	5	-	2005	Hobbes le Corps Politique, *red morocco* *Leide, Elsev.* 1653	Black
	1	-	2006	Hoffman's Flora of Germany, for the Year 1800, *boards* —	H.
	2	-	2007	Hogan-Moganides, or the Dutch Hudibras - 1674	
3	4	-	2008	Hogarth illustrated by Ireland, 2 vols. *first edition.* 1791	Payne
	4	-	2009	Holland, Voyage to, in 1690 - - 1691	Clarke
1	17	-	2010	Homeri Ilias et Odyssea, 2 vols. *Aldus. Venet.* 1524. Scholia in Homerum, *Venet. Aldi,* 1521. 3 vols. *red morocco*	Triphook
	2	-	2011	Homeri Ilias, Grecè, 2 vols. - *Glasguæ,* 1747	Hayes
	19	-	2012	——— Batrachomyomachia, Græcè, ex recens. Maittaire, *red morocco* - - *Londini,* 1721	Payne
1	5	-	2013	Homer's Iliad and Odyssey, translated by Pope, 9 vols. 1761	Hayes
1	1	-	2014	——— l'Iliade di Omero tradotta da Melchior Cesarotti, 4 vols. *russia* - - *Venet.* 1795	Milner
	2	-	2015	Homere les Unzieme et Douzieme Liones, traduictz par Salel, *blue morocco* - - *Par.* 1554	Triphook
	6	-	2016	Homme dans la Lune, par Dominique Gonzales *Ib.* 1648	Clarke
2	18	-	2017	Honest Ghost, or a Voice from the Vault, *frontispiece, by Vaughan,* RARE - - - 1658	Rodd
1	4	-	2018	Hoper's Declaration of Christe and of his Offyce, *very fine copy, blue morocco* *Prynted in Zurich by Augustine Fries,* 1547	Heber
	11	-	2019	Hope's Compleat Fencing-Master, *plates* - 1691	Anderdon
	10	-	2020	Hopkins's Flying Pen-Man, or the Art of Short-Writing.	Lewis
2	5	-	2021	Horatii Carmina, *first Aldine edition, in red morocco* *Venet. Aldi,* 1501	Payne
9	5	-	2022	——— *Venetian morocco, by Roger Payne, capitals illuminated* - - *Venet. Aldi,* 1509	Heber
1	16	-	2022*	Horatii Carmina, *printed by Stephens in the Roman letter, red morocco, ruled. Thuanus's Autograph* *Lutet. Steph.* 1613	Payne
2	6	-	2023	Horatii Carmina, *Lutet. Stephani,* 1613. Juvenalis et Persius, *Lutet. Stephani,* 1613. In 1 vol. *large paper, beautifully bound in blue morocco, by Roger Payne*	Triphook
	5	-	2024	Horatii Carmina, *green morocco, with morocco lining* *Amst.* 1625	Heber
	12	-	2025	——— cum Notis Heinsii, 3 vols. *red morocco* *Elzev.* 1625	Hayes

£	s.	d.	Lot	Description	Buyer
1	5	-	2026	Horatii Carmina, Notis Bond, *red morocco, fine copy* *Elzev.* 1678	Lepard
1	2	-	2027	———— *red morocco* *Paris, e Typographia Regia,* 1733	Clarke
	12	-	2028	———— cum Notis Bentleii, Cuninghamii, et Sanadonis, *green morocco* - *Hamb.* 1733	Hollingworth
	12	-	2029	Horatii Opera, a Sandby, 2 vols. in 1, *plates, red morocco* *Londini,* 1749	Hayes
1	13	-	2030	Aliud exemplar, 2 vols *large paper, plates, blue morocco* *Londini,* 1749	Burrell
	3	-	2031	Horatii Poemata - - *Baskerville,* 1777	Evans
	17	-	2032	——— Carmina, *blue morocco* *Paris, Didot.* 1800	Clarke
	9	-	2033	———— in Usum Delphini - 1804	Christie
	4	-	2034	——— Eclogæ ex recens, Zeunii, *interleaved* 1809	Triphook
	2	-	2035	——— Ars Poetica, cum Paraphrasi Sambuci *Antv. Plantin,* 1564	Hollingworth
	5	-	2036	Horace's Poems, translated by Brome, &c. - 1671	Warner
	9	-	2037	——— Odes, Satyrs, and Epistles, translated by Creech, *portrait, red morocco* - *Tonson,* 1711	Do
	6	-	2038	Horace's Works, in Prose, by Smart, 2 vols. - 1756	Heber
	15	-	2039	Horace translated into Verse, with Notes, by Francis, 4 vols. - - - - 1778	Newton
	5	-	2040	Horace, selected Parts of, in English Verse - 1652	Triphook
	4	-	2041	Horn Exalted, or Roome for Cuckolds - 1661	Clarke
	9	-	2042	Horologium Devotionis circa Vitam Christi, *wood cuts, fine copy* - *Paris, per Joh. Gourmont, sine anno*	Do
	7	-	2043	Horozco y Covaruvias Emblemas Morales. *Segovia,* 1591	Triphook
	1	-	2044	Host Synopsis Plantarum in Austria - *Vindob.* 1797	Do
4	5	-	2045	Hours of Recreation, or the Garden of Pleasure, with divers Verses in Italian and English, collected by Sandford, *fine copy, red morocco* - *Bynneman,* 1576	Rodd
	3	-	2046	Howard's Poems and Translations - 1660	Payne
	1	-	2047	Howell's Instructions for Forreine Travell - 1642	Christie
1	11	6	2048	Hoyeri Flammulæ Amoris Versibus et Iconibus Exornatæ, *fine impressions, blue morocco* - *Antverp,* 1629	Triphook
	7	-	2049	Hoym Catalogus Librorum Comitis, à Martin, *with the prices* - - *Par.* 1738	Clarke
	1	-	2050	Huarte Examen de Ingenios para las Sciencias *Leide,* 1652	Triphook
	1		2051	Huet Traité de l'Origine des Romans *Par.* 1711	Christie
			2052	Hughes's Flower Garden - 1672	
	2	-	2053	Hughes's History of Abelard and Eloisa - 1788	Triphook
1	18	-	2054	Hugonis Pia Desideria Emblematis Illustrata, *first edition, plates by Bolswert, fine impressions, blue morocco* *Antv.* 1624	Do
	10	-	2055	————, *blue morocco,* *Ant.* 1628	Clarke
	10	-	2056	Hugonis Pia Desideria, *plates, red morocco* *Ib.* 1632	Do

£	s.	d.	Lot	Description	Buyer
	5	-	2057	Hugonis Pia Desideria, cum figuris æneis, *blue morocco* *Colon. Agripp.* 1635	Clarke
	7	-	2058	Hugonis Pia Desideria, *plates, in blue morocco* *Antv.* 1676	Warner
	6	-	2059	Hugo's Pia Desideria; or, Divine Addresses by Arwaker, *first edition, plates by Sturt, russia* - 1686	Cochran
	3	-	2060	The same, *second edition, plates* - - 1690	Hollingworth
	15	-	2061	Huldericus. An Epistel of moche Learning sent by Huldericus, Bisshoppe of Augusta, unto Nicolas, Bysshoppe of Rome, agaynst the unmarried Chastetie of Pryestes, *black letter*, RARE, *blue morocco.*	Rodd
27	6	-	2062	Hume's History of England and Smollet's Continuation, 16 vols. *Wallis's edition*, LARGE PAPER, *plates*, GREEN MOROCCO - - - - 1803	Thornhill
	3	-	2063	Humours and Conversations of the Town 1693	Hollingworth
1	1	-	2064	Hunter's (John) Poems, *large paper, green morocco* 1805	Newton
1	9	-	2065	Huon de Bourdeaux Histoire de, *blue morocco* *Lyon*, 1606	Heber
	1	-	2066	Husband forc'd to be Jealous - - 1668	Christie
	1	-	2067	Husbandry, Epitome of the Art of - 1685	Triphook
	3	-	2068	Hutchinson's Sermons; or, Faithful Declaration of Christe's Holy Supper, *black letter* - - *J. Day*, 1560	Miller
	19	-	2068*	Hyde de Ludis Orientalibus, 2 vols. *blue morocco* *Oxon.* 1694	Triphook
	1	-	2069	Hygini Fabulæ - - *Lugd. Bat.* 1670	Rodd
1	17	-	2070	Hyll's Epitome of the whole Art of Phisiognomie, *wood cuts, J. Waylande.* Indagine's briefe Introductions unto the Art of Chiromancy and Phisiognomy, translated by Withers, *J. Day*, 1558, in one vol. *red morocco*	Clarke
	8	-	2071	Hyspanius's Treasury of Health, translated by Humfrie Lloyd, *black letter* *Thomas East*, 1585	Triphook
	9	-	2072	Icones Mortis, Inscriptionibus, præter Epigrammata e Gallicis ab Æmylio in Latinum versa, cumulatæ, *blue morocco* - - - *Basiliæ*, 1554	Do
	8	-	2073	Alia editio - - *Coloniæ*, 1555	Black
	8	-	2074	Idol of the Clownes, or Insurrection of Wat the Tyler 1654	Eardley
3	18	-	2075	Ignatius of Loyola's Life, *portrait and plates, blue morocco* 1616	Heber
	6	-	2076	Illustrium Imagines, *blue morocco* *Lugduni*, 1524	Money
2	15	-	2077	Imagination Poetique, traduicte en Vers François des Latins et Grecz, *wood cuts, green morocco* *Lyon*, 1552	Rice
	2	-	2078	Imbert les Egaremens de l'Amour, 3 vols. *Lond.* 1793	Christie
3	-	-	2079	Institution of a Christen Man, conteynynge the Exposition of the Crede, &c. *black letter, fine copy, blue morocco*, RARE *Lond. Berthelet*, 1537	Dr Coombe
	9	-	2080	Instruction (l') de Chevalerie et Exercise de Guerre, *black letter, red morocco* *Estienne, Jehannot, sans date*	Anderdon
	3	-	2081	Intriguing Milliners and Attornies Clerks, with the Lace Women, a Satire - - - 1738	Warner
	10	-	2082	Invasion, Addresses, &c. to the People England and Ireland, at the time of the threatened Invasion 1803	Heber

£	s.	d.	Lot	Description	Buyer
	8	-	2083	Ireland's Case briefly stated, *red morocco, ruled* 1695	Heber
1	11	6	2084	Ireland, the Monastical History of, *plates, green morocco* 1722	Newton
1	11	6	2085	Ireland's Picturesque Views on the River Thames, 2 vols. 1792	Money
	10	-	2086	Ireland's (W. H.) Confessions, &c. 1805	Allen
	11	-	2087	Irish Hudibras, or Fingallian Prince, *russia, with joints* 1689	Hollingworth
	3	-	2088	Irvini de Jure Regni Diascepsis, *blue morocco Elzev.* 1627	Rodd
	5	-	2089	Isidorie. Here be the gathered Counsailes of Saynct Isodorie to informe Man howe he shuld flee Vices and foloweVertues, *black letter*, not mentioned by Mr. Dibdin *T. Berthelet,* 1534	Miller
-	-	-	2090	Italia, Itinerario d', 2 vols. - *Vicenza,* 1538	Withdrawn
	12	-	2091	Italie, Manuel du Voyageur en, *red morocco Par.* 1785	Anderson
	10	-	2092	Italian Dictionary, *blue morocco* - - 1806	Foss
	11	-	2093	Italian Convert, or the Life of Caracciolus, *plates* 1668	Triphook
	17	-	2094	Iver. Le Printemps d'Iver, *yellow morocco Par.* 1575	Lepard
	10	-	2095	Izacke's remarkable Antiquities of Exeter, *red morocco* 1724	Triphook
	18	-	2096	Jablonski Pantheon Ægyptiorum, 3 vols. *gilt leaves Francof.* 1750	Do.
	3	-	2097	Jacob's Plantæ Favershamienses, *russia* - 1777	Do.
	5	-	2098	Jacques. Histoire, Vie et Mort de Jacques V. Roy d'Ecosse - - - *Par.* 1621	A. Boswell
	1	-	2099	Jalousie, Traieté de la, *red morocco* - *Ib.* 1674	Rodd
	8	-	2100	James II. Memoirs of the last 12 Years of his Life 1702	Boswell
1	18	-	2101	Japan, Lettres du, et de la Chine, des Années 1589 et 1590, *ornamented, green morocco* - *Lyon,* 1593	Triphook
	9	-	2102	Jardinier François, *green morocco* - *Par.* 1654	Newton
	1	-	2103	Jardiniere de Vincennes, 2 vols. - *Ib.* 1753	Johnston

Quarto.

£	s.	d.	Lot	Description	Buyer
3	10	-	2104	Homeri Ilias et Odyssea, Gr. 4 vols. in 2, *russia, with joints, the three private plates inserted* - *Oxon.* 1800	Payne
1	6	-	2105	Homeri Ilias, Gr. Lat. cura Clarke, 2 vols. in 1, *best edition Londini,* 1729	Evans
	17	-	2106	Homeri Ilias, Gr. Wolfii, 2 vols. *plates, russia Lipsiæ,* 1804	Heber
6		-	2107	Homeri Batrachomyomachia, cum glossis interlinearibus Charactere rubro distinctis, Græcè, *first edition, red morocco* - *Venetiis, Leonicus Cretensis,* 1486	Payne
1	12	-	2108	Homeri, Speculum Heroicum principis omnium temporum Poetarum. Les 24 Livres d'Homere reduict en Tables demonstratives Figurées, par Crispin de Passe. *Trajecti,* 1613	Triphook

2109 Homer's Iliades (Ten Books of), translated out of French by Arthur Hall, *black letter, with MS. notes by G. Steevens, russia,* RARE - - *R. Newberie,* 1581

2110 Hooghe (Romeyn de) Hieroglyphica of Merkbeelden der oude Volkeren, *fine impressions* - *Amst.* 1735

2111 Hooker's Paradisus Londinensis, or coloured Figures of Plants cultivated in the Vicinity of the Metropolis 1805

2112 Hooper's Godly Confession and Protestacion of the Christion Fayth, *black letter* - *Lond. John Daye,* ——

2113 Hope's Costume of the Ancients, 2 vols. in 1, *large paper, red morocco* - - - - 1809

2114 Horatius, *red morocco* *Birmingham, Baskerville,* 1770

2115 Horace's Satyres Englysshed accordyng to the Prescription of Saint Hierome, by T. Brant, *first edition, blue morocco,* VERY RARE - *Thomas Marshe,* 1566

2116 Horace's Art of Poetry, made English by the Earl of Roscommon - - - 1680

2117 Horsley's Translation of Hosea, with Notes, *blue morocco* 1801

2118 Hortus Floridus in quo rariorum Florum Icones accuratissime deliniatæ exhibentur à C. Passæo *Utrecht,* 1614

2119 Howel's Dodona's Grove, or the Vocall Forrest 1644

2120 Hulsii Tractatus Instrumentorum Mechanicorum, *plates, Thuanus's copy* - *Francof. ad Mænum.* 1605

2121 Hulsii Emblemata, à Crispin de Passæo, *red morocco, with joints* - - - *Amst.* 1624

2122 Hunarry, Five Looks over the Professors of the English Bible - - - - 1642

2123 Hunter's Historical Journal of the Transactions at Port Jackson and Norfolk Island, *plates* - 1793

2124 Huon. Les Prouesses et Faictz du tres preulx noble et vaillant Huon de Bourdeaulx, Per de France, Duc de Guyenne, *black letter* - *Lyon, sans date*

2125 Hyll's Profitable Arte of Gardening, *black letter, green morocco* - *Lond. by E. Allde,* 1593

2126 Hylton's Scala Perfectionis, *blue morocco,* VERY FINE COPY WYNKEN DE WORDE, 1533

2127 Hylton. Hereafter foloweth a devoute Boke, compyled by Mayster Walter Hylton, to a devoute Man in temperall estate, how he shulde rule him, &c. *black letter, blue morocco,* VERY RARE R. PYNSON, 1506

2128 Hymnorum Expositio totius anni in usum Sarum diligentissime recognitorum multis elucidationibus aucta. Expositio Sequentiarum totius anni secundum usum Sarum, *russia,* RARE WYNANDUM DE WORDE, 1517

2129 Icones Historiarum Veteris Testamenti, Latinè et Gallicè, *Lugd. ap. Frellonium,* 1547. Æmilii Descriptio Imaginum in Apocalypsi Johannis, *with plates, Francof.* 1540, in 1 vol.

£	s.	d.	Lot	Description	Buyer
4	5	-	2130	Ides's (Ysbrants) Three Years Travels from Moscow over-land to China, *plates, fine copy, in russia* - 1706	Payne
1	18	-	2131	Iginii Poeticon Astronomicon, *plates, fine copy, in red morocco* - *Venetiis, Erhardus Ratdolt,* 1482	Boswell
1	10	-	2132	Indorum, de Ritu et Moribus, et de Principe eorum Presbytero Joanne. Historia Ladislai, Regis Hungariæ *sine ulla nota (circa* 1490)	Rodd
4	10	-	2133	Insects. Twelve very beautifully coloured Drawings of Insects; ten on vellum; two on paper, mounted on fine drawing paper, *and bound in blue morocco*	Arch
13	-	-	2134	Irelande. the Image of, with a Discoverie of the Irish Woodharne, and their notable aptnesse, celeritie, &c. to Rebellion, made by Jhon Derricke, in Verse, *russia, rare* *Lond. J. Daie,* 1581	Rodd
	1	-	2135	Ireland, Relation of the late Plots in 1641. Letter from Ireland, 1641	Do.
	1	-	2136	Ireland, Declaration of the Parliament concerning the Rebellion - - - 1643	Do.
1	10	-	2137	Jacquin Miscellanea Austriaca ad Botanicam, Chemiam, et Historiam Naturalem spectantia, 2 vols. *coloured plates* *Vindob.* 1781	Cattley
5	2	6	2138	Jacquin Oxalis Monographia Iconibus Illustrata, *coloured plates, russia, with joints* - - *Viennæ,* 1794	Do.
	10	-	2139	Jacquin Collectaneorum Supplementum, *with coloured plates* - - - *Vindob.* 1796	Do.
3	15	-	2140	Jack Puffe. The Birth, Life, Death, Wil, and Epitaph of Jack Puffe, Gentleman, *in russia,* RARE - 1642	Heber
	5	-	2141	James I. His Majesties Speech on the Opening of Parliament, 1603, *blue morocco* - - 1604	Christie
	11	6	2142	Jardin de Plaisance et Fleur de Rethorique, contenant plusieurs beaux Livres, *wood cuts* *Par. Jehan Trepperel, s. date*	Heber
4	4	-	2143	Jehan de Saintre, l'Hystoire et Cronicque du petit, *blue morocco* - - *Par. J. Trepperel, s. date*	Arch
2	3	-	2144	Autre exemplaire, *red morocco* *Par. Jeh. Bonfons,* 1553	Triphook
28	-	-	2145	JERONOMI. Incipit Exposicio Sancti Jeronimi in Simbolum Apostolorum ad Papam Laurentum, *of very great rarity, in a blue morocco case* *Explicit Expositio S. Jeronimi impressa Oxonie et finita,* 1468 THE FIRST BOOK PRINTED AT THE UNIVERSITY OF OXFORD. See the discussions respecting the genuineness of the date in the Bibliotheca Spenceriana, and in Mr. Singer's pamphlet.	Payne
4	16	-	2146	Jerom, the Lyf of Saint, printed by WYNKYN DE WORDE, with Caxton's Device, *russia* *no date*	Rodd
1	-	-	2147	Joachimi Vaticinia, sive Prophetiæ cum Imaginibus Ære incisis, *fine impressions, blue morocco* *Venet.* 1589	Clarke

£	s.	d.	Lot	Description	Buyer
	7	-	2148	Joannis de Tambaco Speculum Patientium, cum Theologicis Consolationibus, *blue morocco* *Nuremb. Pindar,* 1509	Heber
3	15	-	2149	Johannis de Hese, Presbyteri a Hierusalem, Itinerarius Anno 1489, describens Dispositiones Terrarum Insularum, &c. et varii Tractatus de Indorum Moribus, et de Presbyteri Rege, *blue morocco* *Impressi Daventriæ per me* RICHARDUM PAFRAER, 1499	Dibdin
5	15	6	2150	Johannis de Garlandia Synonima, cum Expositione Magistri Galfridi Anglici, *Lond. per Ricardum Pynson,* 1509.—Joannis de Garlandia Multorum Vocabulorum Equivicorum Interpretatio, *Ric. Pynson,* 1514, *in one volume, scarce*	Do.
2	19	-	2151	Johnson's English Dictionary, 2 vols. *russia* 1785	Cochran
1	5	-	2152	Jones's Bathes of Bathes, Ayde and Benefit of the auncient Bathes of Buckstones, *black letter,* 1572.—Jorden's Discourse of Naturall Bathes, 1631.—and other Tracts on Bathing, in one vol. *blue morocco*	Rodd
2	12	6	2153	Jones's Treatise of Patience in Tribulation, 1625.—Teares of the Isle of Wight shed on the Tomb of Henrie Earl of Southampton, &c. in one vol. *red morocco, scarce.*	Longman
	3	-	2154	Jones's Bardic Museum, or Poetical Relicks of Welsh Bards, &c. - - - - 1802	Cattley
3	10	-	2155	Jonson's (Ben.) Hymenæi, or the Solemnities of Masque and Barriers, *green morocco* - - 1606	Jervis
1	1	-	2156	Jonson's (Ben.) Execration against Vulcan, with Epigrams never before published - - 1640	Do.
	14	-	2157	Jonson's (Ben) Catiline, his Conspiracy 1611	Do.
3	4	-	2158	Juan de Persia Relaciones donde se tratan las cosas Notabiles de Persia, *Thuanus's arms, scarce.* *Valladolid,* 1604	Heber

Folio.

£	s.	d.	Lot	Description	Buyer
3	8	-	2159	Heritier Stirpes novæ aut minus cognitæ, *plates, complete, russia, with joints* - - *Par.* 1784	Howarth
17	17	-	2160	Another copy, LARGE PAPER, with a double set of plates, one set first impressions and the other BEAUTIFULLY COLOURED, with gold borders to each plate, 2 vols. *elegantly bound in russia, with joints* - *Par.* 1784	Triphook
3	15	-	2161	Heritier Sertum Anglicum, seu Plantæ rariores quæ in hortis juxta Londinum, imprimis in horto Kewensi excoluntur, 78 *plates, russia, with joints* *Par.* 1788	Cattley
3	18	-	2162	Heritier Cornus, Specimen Botanicum sistens Descriptiones et Icones specierum Corni minus cognitarum, PRINTED UPON VELLUM, with a duplicate set of plates, BEAUTIFULLY COLOURED - - *Par.* 1788	Longman
6	6	-	2163	Herrera Historia general de los echos de los Castellanos en las Islas y Tierra Firme de Mar Oceano, 8 vols. in 4, *blue morocco* - - *Madrid,* 1601-15	Triphook

£	s.	d.	Lot	Description	Buyer
	12	-	2164	Heywood's Hierarchie of the Blessed Angels, *plates* 1635	Longman
	5	-	2165	Hill's Exotic Botany, *plates* - - 1772	Hayworth
22	1	-	2166	Histoire Universelle qui traite de tous les Royaumes et des Roys qui ont regné depuis la Creation du Monde jusques a la Destruction de Jherusalem A magnificent Manuscript of the fifteenth Century, upon vellum. It contains 360 leaves, 98 miniatures, and about 500 illuminated capitals. The six large illuminations, one of which represents the Landing of the Romans in Britain, are painted with great boldness and splendour of colouring, *red morocco*	Longman
15	15	-	2167	Histoire Merveilleuse du Grand Empereur de Tartarie, nommé le Grand Chan, *black letter, wood cuts, fine copy, in green morocco,* EXTREMELY RARE - *Par.* 1524	Triphook
14	3	6	2168	Hogarth's Original Works, *russia* - *Boydell,* 1790	Knell
5	-	-	2169	Holbein, Œuvres de, ou Recueil de Gravures d'après ses plus beaux Ouvrages, avec sa Vie, par C. de Mechél, 4 parts, *fine impressions, russia* - *Basle,* 1780	Anderdon
10	5	-	2170	Holland, Heroologia Anglica, 2 vols in 1, *fine impressions of the plates, russia* - - 1620	Cochran
9	9	-	2171	Hollinshed's Chronicles of England, Scotland, and Ireland, with the Castrations, 3 vols. *russia* - 1586	Alexander
10	10	-	2172	HORATII ODÆ, SATYRÆ, ET EPISTOLÆ, cum scholiis. A Manuscript of the Twelfth Century, upon Vellum, the first twelve Odes supplied in MS. of the fifteenth Century, *russia.*	Payne
3	3	-	2173	Horatii Carmina, cum Commentariis, *wood cuts, red morocco, fine copy* - *Argent. Gruninger,* 1498	Bentham
1	3	-	2174	Horatii Carmina, *fine copy, russia* *Mediolani apud Alex. Minutianum,* 1502	Heber
2	3	-	2175	Howel's Londinopolis, Perlustration of the City of London, *portrait and plan of London, blue morocco, with joints* 1657	Burrell
	19	-	2176	Howel's Morphandra, Queen of the Inchanted Island, *frontispiece by Gaywood, and portrait* - 1560	Anderdon

End of the Eleventh Day's Sale.

TWELFTH DAY'S SALE.

Octavo et Infra.

Price	Lot	Description	Buyer
16 -	2177	Jean danse mieux que Pierre, Pierre danse mieux que Jean, Ils dansent bien tous deux, 5 vols. *Tetonville,* 1719	Triphook
5 -	2178	Jeffries' Treatise on Diamonds and Pearls - 1751	Hollingworth
4 -	2179	Jehosaphat, Life of, *blue morocco* - ——	Payne
12 -	2180	Jenkins, the Learned Judge's Works, *portrait, russia* 1681	Hollingworth
19 -	2181	Jenyns' (Soame) Works, 4 vols. - 1793	Rumboldt
3 -	2182	Jerningham's Poems and Plays, 4 vols. in 2 - 1806	Triphook
5 -	2183	Jesu Christi Vita juxta quatuor Evangelistarum Narrationes, artificio graphices eleganter picta, &c. *wood cuts, blue morocco* - *Antv. apud Cromme,* 1537	Clarke
4 -	2184	Jesu Christi Passio Effigiata, vario Carmine B. Chelidonii, et Ischyrii illustrata.	Triphook
13 -	2185	Jesus Christ, Figures de la Passion de, avec des Explications par Pacot, *with some of Callot's prints inserted.*	Payne
4 -	2186	Jesus Christ our Saviour hath not overcharged his chirche with many Ceremonies, *black letter,* RARE, *blue morocco* *Zurich,* 1543	Hollingworth
1 -	2187	Jesu, Arcana Societatis, Publico bono vulgata - 1635	Triphook
2 -	2188	Jesus, Tres-humble Remonstrance des religieux de la Compagnie de, *red morocco, ruled* - *Bourdeaux,* 1602	D°
1 -	2189	Jesuitarum Mysteria, *russia* - *Lampropoli,* 1633	D°
4 -	2190	Jesuitisme, the Mystery of - - 1658	Rodd
2 -	2191	Jesuite (le) Secularisé, *blue morocco* - *Cologne,* 1683	Triphook
5 -	2192	Jesuites Lettre Mystique touchant la Conspiration derniere avec l'ouverture de la Caballe Mysterielle des Jesuites *Leiden,* 1603	Clarke
	2193	Jesuitiques, Apologie des Anecdotes Ecclesiastiques, du Diocese de Rouen, *green morocco* - 1761	
1 -	2194	Jesuitique, le Cabinet, *russia* - *Cologne,* 1683	Triphook
5 -	2195	Jesuits, the Secret Instruction of the, - 1746	Hollingworth
3 -	2196	Jeu (le) du Prince des Sotz et Mere Sotte, jeu aux Halles de Paris le Mardi Gras, 1511, (reprint)	Triphook
3 -	2197	Jeux (les) de l'Incognu, *plates* - *Par.* 1630	D°
2 -	2198	Joannis de Indagine Introductiones Apotelesmaticæ, *cuts,* *August. Trebocorum,* 1663	D°
2 -	2199	Johnes's Memoirs of the Life of Froissart - 1810	Hollingworth
12 -	2200	Johnson's Dainty Conceits, with a number of rare and witty Inventions, *black letter* *Lond.* 1630	Warder

£	s.	d.	Lot	Description	Buyer
13	13	-	2201	Johnson's Collection of the Works of the English Poets, with Prefaces, Biographical and Critical, 68 vols. 1779	Sir J. Ramsay
	19	-	2202	Johnson's Lives of the Poets, 4 vols. - 1783	Triphook
	9	-	2203	Joli Memoires de Guy, 2 vols - *Geneve*, 1777	D^o.
	4	-	2204	Jones, the Legend of Captain, - 1671	Blundell
	11	-	2205	Jones's Collection of Epitaphs - 1727	Triphook
	13	-	2206	Jonson's (Ben.) Translation of Ovid's Art of Poetry, with other Works, never before printed, *frontispiece* 1640	Rodd
	2	-	2207	Jonstoni Idea Universæ Medecinæ, *green morocco* *Amst.* 1648	Payne
1	5	-	2208	Josephi Opera omnia, Lat. *in curious old morocco binding* *Stoer,* 1595	Heber
	5	-	2209	Josse Grammaire Espagnole - - 1804	Ramsay
	3	-	2210	Josselyn's New-England's Rarities, *cuts* - 1672	Triphook
	18	-	2211	Joujou des Demoiselles, Chansons Joyeuses par un Ane-Onyme, *Par.* 1745. Contes Nouveaux et Nouvelles nouvelles, *Anv.* 1753, 3 vols. in 1	Calkin
1	1	-	2212	Joye's (George) Contrarye to a certayne manis) Consultation: That Adulterers ought to be punyshed wyth Deathe, *black letter,* RARE - *Lond. by G. Joye, no date* See Dibdin's Ames, Vol. III. p. 533, note	Rodd
1	4	-	2213	Joyeuses (les) Aventures et Nouvelles Recreations, *russia,* *Lyon, Rigaud,* 1582	Triphook
	19	-	2214	Joyeuses (les) Narrations advenues de Notre Temps *Lyon,* 1572	D^o.
	3	-	2215	Julii Osequentis Prodigiorum Liber, *wood cuts, green morocco* - - - *Basiliæ,* ——	Heber
	5	-	2216	Jules Obsequent des Prodiges, plus trois livres de Polydore Vergile sur la mesme matiere, *wood cuts* *Lyon, J. de Tournees,* 1555	Triphook
	1	-	2217	Julien les Cesars invitez a la table des dieux par Moret *Par.* 1682	Heber
	12	-	2218	Junii (Hadriani) Emblemata, ejusdem Ænigmatum Libellus - - *Antv. Plantin,* 1565	Clarke
	12	-	2219	Alia editio, *green morocco, with joints* - 1566	Triphook
	9	-	2220	——— *blue morocco* - - 1585	D^o.
	10	-	2221	Junius, 2 vols. - - *Bensley,* 1794	D^o.
1	7	-	2222	Junius' Letters, Woodfall's Edition, 3 vols. *large paper, boards* - - - 1812	Miller
	2	-	2223	Justiniani Institutiones, *blue morocco* - *Elzev.* 1654	Triphook
5	10	-	2224	Justiniani Institutionum Libri quatuor, LARGE PAPER, *very fine copy, green morocco, with joints,* from Col. Stanley's Collection - - *Lugd. Bat.* 1671	Payne
	2	-	2225	Justiniani Institutiones, cura Vinnii - *Elzev.* 1669	Hawtrey
1	1	-	2226	Justinus, *Parisiis,* 1585. Marcus Antoninus de Seipso, *Lugdini,* 1559, 2 vols. in 1, *in old ornamented morocco*	Triphook
	7	-	2227	Justinus et Trogus Pompeius, cum notis Vossii, *red morocco* - - - *Elzev.* 1640	Hawtrey
	3	-	2228	Justus de Alea, *green morocco* - *Ib.* 1642	Rodd

£	s.	d.	Lot	Description	Buyer
	6	-	2229	Justus de Alea, *red morocco* - *Elzev.* 1642	Clarke
	6	-	2230	Juvenalis et Persius, *Aldus*, 1501. Lucanus, *Aldus*, 1502, *the title of the latter MS. red morocco.*	Hawtray
	2	-	2231	Juvenalis et Persii Satyræ, *red morocco, ruled, Lutetiæ R. Steph.* 1544	Triphook
	2	-	2232	Juvenalis et Persii Satyræ, cura Pulmanni, *blue morocco Antv. Plantin,* 1585	Do.
	6	-	2233	Juvenalis et Persius, *green morocco, morocco inside Amst.* 1626	Heber
	1	-	2234	Juvenalis et Persius - - *Elzev.* 1671	Christie
	1	-	2535	——————— *blue morocco* - *Brindley,* 1744	Evans
	14	-	2236	——————— Tabulis Æneis Illustrati, a Sandby, *red morocco* - - *Cantab.* 1763	Hayes
	18	-	2237	Aliud exemplar, *large paper, blue morocco* - 1763	Burrell
	6	-	2238	Juvenalis Satyræ, a Philippe, *blue morocco Lut. Par.* 1741	Triphook
1	5	-	2239	———————, cura Ruperti, 2 vols. - *Lipsiæ,* 1807	Hayes
	3	-	2240	Kanor, a Tale, translated from the Savage - 1750	Christie
	7	-	2241	Kas Emblemata Philosophico-Moralia *Delingæ,* 1692	Triphook
2	12	-	2242	Katherine. A Mervaylous Discourse upon the Lyfe, Deedes, and Behaviours of Katherine de Medicis, Queene Mother, VERY RARE, *blue morocco Heydelberge,* 1575	Rodd
13	10	-	2243	Kelton's Chronycle, with a Genealogie declaryng that the Brittons and Welshemen are lineally descended from Brute, in Verse, *black letter,* VERY RARE, *red morocco, fine copy* - - - *R. Grafton,* 1547	Heber
	15	-	2244	Kempis de Imitatione Christi, *blue morocco, ruled Lugduni, apud Elsevirios,* ——	Clarke
1	1	-	2245	——————————— *red morocco* *Elzev.* 1658	Lepard
	5	-	2246	Idem Liber, *red morocco, ruled* - *Colon.* 1684	Hawtray
	12	6	2247	Kempis de l'Imitation de Jesus Christ, traduit par Ros-Wede, *plates by Callot, splendidly bound in blue morocco Par.* 1664	Christie
	12	-	2248	Kempis's Imitation, or Following of Christ, *black letter* 1567	Triphook
1	-	-	2249	Kidgell's Original Fables, French and English, 2 vols. *red morocco* - - - 1763	Do.
	4	-	2250	Killigrew's Three Plays - - 1665	Do.
	5	-	2251	King's Poems, Elegies, &c. - - 1657	Rodd
	2	-	2252	Another copy - - - 1657	Triphook
	8	-	2253	Kirchmanni de Funeribus Romanorum Libri Quatuor, *plates, blue morocco* - *Lugd. Bat.* 1672	Hollingworth
	6	-	2254	Kitchin Physick, by way of Dialogue - 1676	Triphook
	5	-	2255	Klinkhamer Bybelsche Geschiedenissen des Ouden en Nieuwen Testaments, *plates* - *Amst.* 1748	Do.
	9	-	2256	Knight's Inquiry into the Principles of Taste 1805	Hollingworth
2	4	-	2257	Knox. A Faithful Admonition, by John Knox, unto the Professours of God's Truthe in England, *black letter, blue morocco* - *Imprinted at Kalykone,* 1554	Heber
3	16	-	2258	Knox's Copie of a Lettre delivered to the Ladie Marie, Regent of Scotland, *blue morocco* - *Geneva,* 1558	Rodd

£	s.	d.	No.	Description	Buyer
2	7	-	2259	Knox. Sermon preached by John Knox, in Edenbrough in 1565, *blue morocco* - - 1566	Heber
2	8	-	2260	Knox's Answer to a Letter of a Jesuit named Tyrie, *blue morocco Imprentit at Sanctandrois, by Lekprevik,* 1572	Rodd
	13	-	2261	Knox's Fort for the Afflicted against the Stormes of Tribulation, *blue morocco* - - 1580	Heber
1	9	-	2262	Knox's Notable and Comfortable Exposition upon the Fourth of Mathew, *blue morocco* *Waldegrave,* 1583	Triphook
	10	-	2263	Kolbe. Description du Cap de Bonne Esperance, 3 vols. *plates* - - - *Amst.* 1741	Osborne
	2	-	2264	Kormanni de Virginitatis Jure, Tractatus, *Virginopoli,* 1631	Triphook
	1	-	2265	Kormannus de Virginum Statu ac Jure *Norimb.* 1679	Do
	12	-	2266	Krocker Flora Silesiaca continens Plantas Silesiæ Indigenas, 3 vols. - - - *Uratisl.* 1787	Osborne
3	3	-	2267	Lachrymæ Musarum. The Tears of the Muses exprest in Elegies upon the Death of Henry Lord Hastings, *with frontispiece* - - - 1649	Warder
	6	-	2268	La Combe Dictionnaire des Beaux Arts, *gilt leaves* *Par.* 1659	Anderdon
1	6	-	2269	——————— du Vieux Langage François, 2 vols. - - - *Par.* 1766	Triphook
	8	-	2270	Lactance des Divines Institutions, traduict par René Fame, *wood cuts, green morocco* - *Par.* 1555	Do
	8	-	2271	Ladulfi (Noel du Fail) Discours d'aucuns propos rustiques facecieux, *red morocco* - - 1732	Rodd
5	-	-	2272	Ladulfi Propos Rustiques, *Lyon,* 1547. L'Histoire Plaisante et Facetieuse du Lazare de Tormes, *Paris, Jean Longis.* 2 vols. in 1. *Thuanus's copy, morocco.*	Heber
	7	-	2273	La Fayette, la Princesse de Cleves, *blue morocco* *Par.* 1780	Quatremere
	11	-	2274	Lagrime in Morte di un Gatto, *russia* *Milano,* 1741	Anderdon
	6	-	2275	De Lamarck Flore Françoise ou Description succincte de toutes les Plantes qui croissent naturellement en France, 3 vols. - - *Par.* 1778	Osborne
	5	-	2276	Lambert's Advice of a Mother to her Daughter, *green morocco* - - - 1803	Anderdon
3	9	-	2277	Landi Vita di Cleopatra Regina d'Egitto, PRINTED UPON VELLUM, *with a coloured drawing, yellow morocco* *Parigi,* 1788	Do
16	5	-	2278	Landon, Annales du Musée et de l'Ecole moderne des Beaux-Arts, Recueil de Gravures au trait d'apres les principaux Ouvrages de Peinture, Sculpture, &c. du Musée, 16 vols. *yellow morocco, with joints* - *Par.* 1801	Triphook
	18	-	2279	Landon, Annales du Musée, Salon de 1808, tom. 1, *boards* *Par.* 1808	Do
6	10	-	2280	——— Galerie Historique des Hommes célèbres de tous les Siècles et de toutes les Nations, contenant leurs Portraits, 11 vols. - - *Par.* 1805, &c.	Osborne
	3	-	2281	Langhorne's Poetical Works, 2 vols. - 1766	Money
	14	-	2282	Langueti Epistolæ ad Ph. Sydnæum, *portrait inserted* *Elzevir.* 1646	Anderdon

£	s.	d.	Lot	Description	Buyer
	4	-	2283	Lansdowne Manuscripts, Catalogue of, - 1807	Calkin
	19	-	2284	Laon Relation du Voyage des François fait au Cap du Nord en Amerique, *green morocco* - *Par.* 1664	Hibbert
	12	-	2285	Lara (Cohen de) Comedia Famosa de Aman y Mordechay, &c. *red morocco, rare* - - *Leyde,* 1699	Hawtray
	4	-	2286	L'Arivey Comedies Facecieuses - *Rouen,* 1611	Triphook
	7	-	2287	Larkin's Looking-Glass of the Fathers, with the Characters of Philosophers, Historians, &c. - 1659	Hibbert
	2	-	2288	La Seine Homeri Nepenthes, seu de Abolendo Luctu Liber - - - *Lugduni,* 1624	Payne
1	4	-	2289	Latham's Faulconry, or the Faulcon's Lure and Cure, *cuts, blue morocco* - - - 1658	Rodd
1	4	-	2290	Latham's New and Second Book of Faulconry, *cuts* 1661	Hibbert
	3	-	2291	Laure ou Lettres de quelques Personnes de Suisse, 5 vols. *Lond.* 1787	Triphook
	1	-	2292	Lawrence's Art of Gardening - - 1744	D°
1	18	-	2293	Lawrentius de Sturmarum Sanatione, &c. with a large plate representing Henry IV. of France touching persons afflicted with the Evil, by Firens, *rare* *Par.* 1609	Hibbert
	9	-	2294	Lazarillo de Tormes la Vida de, y de sus fortunas y adversidades - - - *Plantin.* 1602	Hawtray
	14		2295	Lazarillo de Tormes Castigado, *blue morocco,, with joints* *Valencia,* 1602	Rodd
	4	-	2296	——————— - - *Lerida,* 1612	D°
	5	-	2297	——————— por H. De Luna, interprete de la Lengua Espanolo - - *Zaragoca,* 1652	Triphook
	10	-	2298	Lazarille de Tormes Histoire Facetieuse de, *cuts* *Lyon,* 1697	Clarke
1	6	-	2299	——————— la Vie et Aventures de, *cuts* *Brusselles,* 1698	Hibbert
2	2	-	2300	Lazarillo de Tormes, the pleasant History of, drawne out of Spanish by David Rowland of Anglesey, *frontispiece* 1639	Triphook

Quarto.

£	s.	d.	Lot	Description	Buyer
	17	-	2301	Juvenal's Satires, translated, with Notes by Gifford, *blue morocco* - - - - - 1803	Bentham
	7	-	2302	——————— by Hodgson - - 1807	Foss
1	11	6	2303	Juvigny les Bibliotheques François de la Croix du Main et de Du Verdier, 6 vols. - *Par.* 1772	Hayes
1	14	-	2304	Kaempferi Amœnitates Exoticæ et Descriptiones Rerum Persicarum et Ulterioris Asiæ, *fine paper, russia, with joints* - - - *Lemgov.* 1712	Triphook
2	2	-	2305	Kemp's Nine Days Wonder, performed in a Morrice from London to Norwich	D°
1	5	-	2306	Kilburne's Topographie, or Survey of Kent, *portrai* 1659	Foss
	6	-	2307	Klein Descriptiones Tubulorum Marinorum, cum Figuris, &c. *russia, with joints* - - *Gedani,* 1730-1	Christie

£	s	d	Lot	Description	Buyer
3	5	-	2308	Klepisii Poetæ Cæsarii Emblemata Æri incisa, *fine impressions, morocco, with joints* - 1623	Triphook
	5	-	2309	Knight's Description of Latium, *boards* - 1805	Do
2	10	-	2310	Labillardière Novæ Hollandiæ Plantarum Specimen, 2 vols. *plates, elegantly bound in russia, with joints* *Par.* 1804	Loddiges
1	10	-	2311	Lafitau Mœurs des Sauvages Americains, 2 vols. *Par.* 1724	Grant
1	11	6	2312	Lambarde's Perambulation of Kent, *black letter, russia* 1596	Foss
	19	-	2313	Lambert's Description of the Genus Cinchona, *plates, russia, with joints* - - - - 1797	Do
38	17	-	2314	Landon Vies et Œuvres des Peintres les plus celebres, scavoir Domeniquin Raphael, et Poussin, 9 vols. plates in outline, elegantly bound in *fawn coloured morocco*, with joints - - - - - *Par.* 1805-9	Ld Yarmouth
3	16	-	2315	Lascaris Grammatica Græca, cum interpretatione Latina, *russia, first book printed by Aldus* *Venet. Aldus*, 1495	Heber
	3	-	2316	Laud, A briefe Relation of the Death and Sufferings of the late Archbishop of Canterbury - *Oxford*, 1744	Hollingworth
	18	-	2317	Laurembergii Apparatus Plantarius *Francof.* 1654	Triphook
	15	-	2318	Lawyerus Bootatus et Spurratus, or the Long Vacation, a Poem - - - - - 1691	Hibbert
1	7	-	2319	Lebei-Batillii Emblemata, a J. Boissardo delineata et a Theodore De Bry sculpta, *blue morocco* *Francof.* 1596	Triphook
	12	-	2320	Le Clerc le Spectacle de la Vie Humaine, ou Leçons de Sagesse, *plates, blue morocco* - *a la Haye*, 1755	Do
2	8	-	2321	Lederer's Discoveries in three several Marches from Virginia to the West of Carolina, *green morocco* 1672	Warder
	8	-	2322	Legh's Accedens of Armoury, *arms coloured, blue morocco* *Tottel.* 1568	Evans
3	3	-	2323	Le Grand's Fabliaux, or Tales, translated by Way, 2 vols. *red morocco* - - - 1796	Foss
1	3	-	2324	Leicester. A Briefe Report of the Militarie Services done in the Low Countries, by the Erle of Leicester *Arnold Hatfield*, 1587	Hibbert
	2	-	2325	Leighton's Appeal to the Parliament, or Sion's Plea against the Prelacie, *plates* ——	Rodd
	11	-	2326	Lescallier Description Botanique du Chiranthodendron, arbre du Mexique, *coloured plates* - *Par.* 1805	Haworth
1	10	-	2327	Leslæus de Origine Moribus et Rebus Gestis Scotorum, *first edition, blue morocco* - *Romæ*, 1578	Triphook
	13	-	2338	Lesnauderie (Pierre de) la Louange de Mariage et recueil des Hystoires des bonnes Vertueuses, et Illustres Femmes, *black letter* - - - *Par.* 1523	Rodd
	1	-	2329	L'Estranges' further Discovery of the Plot dedicated to Dr. Titus Oates - - - - 1680	Hollingworth
5	7	6	2330	Letters of such True Saintes and Holy Martyrs of God, as in the late bloodye persecution, gave their lyves for the defence of Christe's Holy Gospel, *black morocco* *John Day*, 1564	Clarke

£	s.	d.	Lot	Description	Buyer
	14		2331	Letter. The Copie of a Letter sent out of England to Don B. Mendoza, Ambassadour in France from Spain, declaring the State of England, contrary to the Opinion of Don Barnardin, and of all his Partizans, Spaniards and others, *black letter*, RARE *London, J. Vautrollier*, 1588	Anderdon
	9	-	2332	Letter to the Earle of Leicester, Lieutenant-Generall of all her Majesties forces in the United Provinces, written before, but delivered at his return from thence *Christopher Barker*, 1586	Do
	1	-	2333	Letter. A short Reply to L'Estrange's short Answer to a Litter of Libels - - - 1680	Hollingworth
	1	-	2334	Letter from Amsterdam to a Friend in England 1678	Triphook
			2335	Letters (Two) from Mr. Montagu to the Lord Treasurer 1679	Do
	1	-	2336	Letter Writer (The), A President for Young Penmen 1638	Rodd
	2	-	2337	Leupoldi Ducatus Austriæ filii Compilatio de Astrorum Scientia, decem continens tractatus, *cuts* *August. Vindel. Ratdolt*. 1489	Hibbert
1	1	-	2338	Lewis's History and Antiquities of the Abbey and Church of Faversham, in Kent, *plates* - 1727	Warden
2	15	-	2339	——— of the Isle of Tenet, in Kent, portrait inserted, *red morocco* - 1736	Higgs
1	11	6	2340	Lewkenor's Resolved Gentleman.—This is a Translation of the Romance entitled the "Chevalier Deliberé," and contains two copies of Verses, by R. Dillington and M. Kyffin, of whom see Ritson's Bibliographia Poetica, pp. 188 and 263, *scarce* - - *R. Watkins*, 1594	Hibbert
	18	-	2341	Leycester's Commonwealth, by Robert Parsons the Jesuite - - - - - 1641	Anderdon
1	15	-	2342	Liber Theodoli cum commento incipit feliciter, *fine copy, green morocco*, RARE - *Richard Pynson, sine anno*.	Hibbert
6	8	6	2343	Libro di Battaglia delli Baroni di Francia sotto el nome dello ardito et galiardo Giovini Altobello nelqual molte battaglie et degne cose se puo vedere, *wood-cuts, red morocco*, RARE - - *Venetia, Bindoni*, 1547	Triphook
	4		2344	Limming, A Treatise of the Art of, which teacheth the order in drawing and tracing of Letters, Vinets, &c. 1605	Do
2	2	-	2345	Linché's Fountaine of Ancient Fiction, from the Italian, *blue morocco, with joints* - *Adam, Islip*, 1599	Do
	7	-	2346	Linnæi Musa Cliffortiana Florens Hartecampi, *Lugd. Bat*. 1736. Fungorum Agri Ariminensis Historia a Battarra, *Faventiæ*, 1759, 2 vols. in 1, *plates*.	Osborne
2	13	-	2347	Linnean Society Transactions, 8 vols. *boards* 1791, &c.	Triphook
2	18	-	2348	Lithgow's Adventures in his Travailes from Scotland to the most famous Kingdomes in Europe, Asia, and Affrica, *frontispiece, blue morocco* - - 1640	Clarke
	2	-	2349	Liturgia Inglesa, *blue morocco* *Augustæ, Trinobantum*, 1613	Triphook
6	6	-	2350	Livre (Le) des trois filz de Roy, c'est assavoir de France, d'Angleterre et d'Escosse, lesquelz au service du Roy de Secille eurent de glorieuses victoires contre les Turcz, &c. *wood cuts, black letter* - - *Lyon*, 1508	Hibbert

P

2351 Locke's Works, 4 vols. 1777

2352 Lodge's Catharos, Diogenes in his Singularitie, a Nettle for nice Noses, *black letter, very scarce* *W. Hoskins and J. Danter,* 1591

2353 —— Illustrations of British History, Biography, and Manners, 3 vols. - - - 1791

2354 Loiola. Vita Beati P. Ignatii Loiolæ Societatis Jesu Fundatoris in 79 Imaginibus expressa, Latinis Versibus explicata, with several additional portraits and plates, the whole mounted on drawing paper, *blue morocco, with joints* - - - *Romæ,* 1609

2355 Londini quod Reliquium, or London's Remains, in Latin and English, by Lloyd - - 1667

2356 London. Informations exhibited to the Committee appointed by Parliament to inquire into the late dreadful Burning of London - - 1667

2357 —— (Modern). History and Present State of the British Metropolis - - - 1804

Folio.

2358 Humboldt et Bonpland, Plantes Equinoxiales, 69 plates, LARGE PAPER, *splendidly bound in russia, with joints* *Par.* 1808

2359 Hymni cum Musica. A Manuscript of the Twelfth Century, UPON VELLUM, *russia*

2360 INVASION. A Collection of Caricatures, Addresses to the People, Songs, &c. on the Invasion, inlaid in one large volume.

2361 IRELAND. A Full and Explanatory Account of the Shaksperian Forgery, by myself the Writer, William Henry Ireland.

Ireland's own Manuscript containing his Original Documents, Contracts, and Indentures of Shakspeare, and his Love Verses to Anne Hatherway, with a lock of his hair; illustrated with Drawings by Westall, the Irelands, &c. Portraits and Engravings of many of the principal Persons and Places mentioned by Shakspeare. The whole bound in one volume, and containing a very interesting account of a literary imposition, which deceived several eminent persons.

2362 Jacob's Compleat English Peerage, 3 vols. *plates* 1766

2363 Jacobi Cartusiensis Sermones de præcipuis Festivitatibus Anni, *russia, an early edition* - *sine ulla nota.*

2364 Jacquin Plantarum Rariorum Horti Cæsarei Schænbrunnensis Descriptiones et Icones, 3 vols, COLOURED PLATES, *splendidly bound in russia, with joints* - 1797

2365 Jamblichus de Mysteriis Ægyptiorum, Latinè, *fine copy* *Aldus,* 1497

2366 James I.'s Works, with frontispiece, and portraits, by Passe, *red morocco, with joints* - 1616

2367 Jason et Medée (Le Roman de) par Raoul le Fevre, an ancient edition in a large type, in double columns, *red morocco, the first six leaves manuscript,* VERY RARE *no place or date*

2368 JASON. A BOKE OF THE HOOLE LYF OF JASON, *green morocco,* EXCESSIVELY RARE, PRINTED BY WILLIAM CAXTON *about* (1475)

"This volume is among the scarcest and most interesting of those which owe their first existence, in an English form, to the pen and press of Caxton."—*Bibl. Spenceriana, V.* 4.

2369 Jehan de Saintré, Hystoyre et plaisante Cronique du Petit Jehan de Saintre, *black letter, wood cuts, russia,* VERY RARE - - *Par. Michel le Noir,* 1517

2370 Jeronimi Aureola ex suavissimis salutiferis que Floribus *sine ulla nota*

2371 Jesu Christi Passio Figuris illustrata, *coloured plates, blue morocco* - - - 1509

2372 Jesu. Imago primi Sæculi Societatis Jesu, *plates* *Antv.* 1640

2373 Jones's Antiquities of Stone Heng, *portrait by Hollar* 1655

2374 Jourdain, Les faitz et prouesses du noble et vaillant Chevalier Jourdain de Blaves, *black letter, fine copy, russia,* RARE - - *Par. Michel le Noir,* 1520

2375 JUSTINIANI INSTITUTIONES, cum Scholiis. A beautiful manuscript of the fourteenth century, UPON VELLUM, with miniatures and illuminated capital letters, in very fine preservation, in crimson velvet.

2376 Juvenalis et Persii Satyræ, *fine copy, in russia* *Mediolani apud A. Minutianum sine anno*

End of the First Part.

*** *The Sale of the Second Part will commence on Monday, June* 21.

Printed by W. Bulmer, and Co.
Cleveland Row, St. James's.

WHITE KNIGHTS LIBRARY.

CATALOGUE

OF

THAT DISTINGUISHED AND CELEBRATED

LIBRARY,

CONTAINING

Numerous very fine and rare Specimens from the Presses of

CAXTON, PYNSON, AND WYNKYN DE WORDE, &c.

AN UNRIVALLED COLLECTION OF ITALIAN, SPANISH AND FRENCH ROMANCES OF CHIVALRY, POETRY, AND FACETIÆ.

AN UNIQUE ASSEMBLAGE OF BOOKS OF EMBLEMS, AND BOOKS ORNAMENTED WITH WOOD CUTS.

VERY FINE BOTANICAL WORKS WITH ORIGINAL DRAWINGS.

AND A SELECTION OF RARE, CURIOUS, AND SPLENDID ARTICLES IN EVERY DEPARTMENT OF LITERATURE.

PART II.

WHICH WILL BE

SOLD BY AUCTION,

BY MR. EVANS,

AT HIS HOUSE, No. 26, PALL-MALL,

On Tuesday, June 22, and Ten following Days, Sunday excepted.

Catalogues, Price Two Shillings, and on Large Paper Four Shillings, may be had at the Place of Sale, and of Payne and Foss, 88, Pall Mall. The Books may be viewed Four Days prior to the Auction.

1819.

PART II.

INDEX TO THE DAYS OF SALE.

			£	s.	d.
13th. Day,	Tuesday,	June 22.	544	9	6
14th. Day,	Wednesday,	June 23.	567	6	"
15th. Day,	Thursday,	June 24.	871	6	"
16th. Day,	Friday,	June 25.	472	2	"
17th. Day,	Saturday,	June 26.	385	5	6
18th. Day,	Monday,	June 28.	762	7	6
19th. Day,	Tuesday,	June 29.	1153	14	6
20th. Day,	Wednesday,	June 30.	616	13	6
21st. Day,	Thursday,	July 1.	413	2	"
22nd. Day,	Friday,	July 2.	520	19	"
23rd. Day,	Saturday,	July 3.	668	16	6
			6976	2	"
amt. of Part 1 –			7407	1	6
			£14383	3	6

A

CATALOGUE

OF THE

WHITE KNIGHTS LIBRARY.

PART SECOND.

THIRTEENTH DAY'S SALE.

Each Day's Sale will commence PRECISELY AT HALF PAST TWELVE.

Octavo et Infra.

2377 Le Clerc, Tableaux du Testament, 40 plates, *blue morocco.*

2378 Le Clerc, Figures de la Passion de N. S. Jesus Christ, *blue morocco, with joints.* - - *Paris.*

2379 Le Comte's Journey through the Empire of China, *plates,* 1697

2380 Lee's Introduction to Botany, - 1776

2381 Le Févre, Les Poetes Grecs, *Saumur,* 1664. Le Mariage de Belfegor, 1664, 2 vol. in 1, *gilt leaves.*

2382 Le Fevre, Methode pour commencer les Humanités, 1725. Le Febure, Traité de la Goutte, *Rochelle,* 1720, *in one volume.*

2383 Legende dorée ou sommaire de l'Histoire des freres Mendians de S. Domenique, - *Amst.* 1734

2384 Legouvé, Le Merite des Femmes, Poeme, *blue morocco, Didot,* 1801

2385 Llewellin's Men-miracles, with other Poemes, 1656

2386 Lemnius's Discourse touching Generation, 1664

2387 Le Moyne, la Gallerie des Femmes Fortes, *plates, fine copy, blue morocco,* - *Leiden, Elsevier,* 1660

Q

£	s.	d.	No.	Description	Buyer
	9	-	2388	Lempriere's Classical Dictionary, - 1792	Rodd
	2	-	2389	Lenclos, Memoires sur la Vie de Mlle. Lenclos, *Amst.* 1758	Triphook
	7	-	2390	Lentuli Augustus sive de convertanda in Monarchiam Republica, *green morocco,* - *Elzevir.* 1645	Payne
	8	-	2391	Leonis Africani Africæ Descriptio, *green morocco, ib.* 1632	Parker
	3	-	2392	Leonardus's Mirror of Stones, - 1750	Smith
	8	-	2393	Le Roux, Dictionnaire Comique, Satyrique, Critique, &c. *Amst.* 1750	Dickinson
	2	-	2394	Lery, Histoire Memorable de la Ville de Sancerre, 1574	Heber
	9	-	2395	L'Escale (Le Chevalier de) Le Champion des Femmes, *red morocco,* - - *Paris,* 1618	Triphook
	10	-	2396	Leti, Critique sur les Lotteries, 2 vols. *Amst.* 1697	Clarke
10	-	-	2397	Letter sent by J. B. unto his very frende Maister R. C. wherin is conteined a large discourse of the peopling and inhabiting the cuntrie called the Ardes, and other adjacent in the North of Ireland and taken in hand by Sir Thomas Smith, *black letter,* inlaid in 4to. *russia,* RARE, *H. Binnemann.*	Rodd
	2	-	2398	Lettres Turques, Lettres de Nedim Coggia, 2 vols. in 1. *Amst.* 1750	Clarke
	17	-	2399	Lever's Sermon Preached at Pauls Crosse 14th December 1552, *black letter, fine copy, blue morocco, John Day.*	Triphook
1	-	-	2400	Lewis's History of the Translations of the Holy Bible, 1739	Hancock
3	8	-	2401	Lewis's Life of Maystre Wyllyam Caxton, *portrait, blue morocco,* - - - 1737	Triphook
1	17	-	2402	Lewis's, (M. G.) Monk, 3 vol. 2nd Edition. - 1796	Do.
1	1	-	2403	Lewis's Tales of Wonder, 2 vol. in 1, *large paper,* 1801	Rumboldt
	11	-	2404	Lexiphanes, a Dialogue imitated from Lucian, 1783	Thompson
	2	-	2405	Leycester's Commonwealth, whereunto is added Leicester's Ghost, - - - - 1641	K
2	11	-	2406	Liaisons (Les) Dangereuses, 2 vol. *fine paper, plates, green morocco,* - - *Londres,* 1796	Triphook
	1	-	2407	Libertin (Le) Devenu Vertueux, 2 vol. *Paris,* 1777	Warner
	6	-	2408	Libraries. An Account of all the celebrated Libraries, 1739	Triphook
	3	-	2409	Lightfoot's Flora Scotica, 2 vol. *plates,* - 1792	John
	14	-	2410	Lignaridi Oblectamenta Academica, *cuts, green morocco, Oppenhein.* 1618	Heber
	1	-	2411	Lilly's Anglicus, or an Ephemeris for 1646, 1646	Do.
	11	-	2412	Lindsay's (Sir David) Poetical Works, *black letter, blue morocco,* RARE, - - *Glasgow,* 1696	Hollingworth
	4	-	2413	Lingua, or the Combat of the Tongue and the five Senses for Superiority, - - - - 1657	Osborne
3	1	-	2414	Linnæi Species Plantarum secundum Systema Sexuale curante Willdenow, 5 vol. *fine paper, half bound, uncut, Berol.* 1727	Payne
	2	6	2415	Linnæi Bibliotheca Botanica, - *Amst.* 1751	Smith

£	s.	d.	Lot	Description	Buyer
	4	-	2416	Linnæi Flora Lapponica a Smith, *Londini*, 1792	Osborne
	11	-	2417	Linnæi Genera Plantarum, *russia*, *Holmiæ*, 1764	D°
	5	-	2418	Linnæi Fundamenta Botanica, - *Amst.* 1741	Haworth
	6	-	2419	Linnæi Mantissa Plantarum, - *Holmiæ*, 1767	D°
	1	-	2420	Linnæi Philosophia Botanica, - *Viennæ*, 1755	Osborne
	2	-	2421	Linnæi Philosophia Bòtanica, *russia*, - *ib.* 1763	Triphook
	1	-	2422	Linnæi Philosophia Botanica, - *Vindob.* 1770	Dickenson
	16	-	2423	Linnæi Systema Vegetabilium curante Murray, *russia, with joints*, - - - 1784	Haworth
	6	-	2424	Linneus's System of Vegetables, 2 vol. *Lichfield*, 1783	Osborne
	9	-	2425	Linneus's Families of Plants, 2 vol. *russia*, *ib.* 1787	D°
1	3	-	2426	Linocier, Histoire des Plantes, *wood cuts, red morocco*, *Paris*, 1584	Triphook
	15	-	2427	Lipsius de Magistratibus veteris populi Romani, *Ambergæ* 1608. Lipsii Defensio Postuma, *Plantin*, 1608, 2 vol. in 1. *Thuanus' copy, morocco.*	Clarke
	11	-	2428	Lister's Journey to Paris, - - 1699	King
2	-	-	2429	Liturgia Græca, a Field, *large paper, blue morocco*, *Cantab.* 1665	Hollingworth
	15	-	2430	Liturgia Latina, *plates, blue morocco, ruled*, *Londini*, 1760	Dickenson
	8	-	2431	Liturgia secondo l' uso della Chiesa Anglicana da Montucci, *blue morocco*, - - - 1796	Hollingworth
	5	-	2432	Liturgie de l'Eglise Anglicane, *blue morocco*, 1683	D°
	11	-	2433	Liturgia Ynglesa Hispanizado por Felix de Alvarado, *blue morocco*, Countess of Pomfret's Copy. *Londres*, 1715	Dickenson
	14	-	2434	Lives of Leland, Hearne and Wood, 2 vol. *large paper*, *Oxford*, 1772	Triphook
1	1	-	2435	Livii Historia ex recensione Heinsiana, 3 vol. *Elzevir*, 1634	Hayes
1	19	-	2436	Alia Editio, cum notis Gronovii, 4 vol. *blue morocco*, *Elzevir.* 1645	D°
2	-	-	2437	Livii Historia ex recensione Gronovii, *fine copy, russia*, *ib.* 1678	Payne
1	11	6	2438	Livii Historia cura Ernesti, 5 vol. *Lipsiæ*, 1785	D°
	9	-	2439	Freishemii Supplementum Livianum, *yellow morocco*, *Holmiæ*, 1649	Ramsay
	5	-	2440	Gronovii ad Livii Libros superstites Notæ, *Elzevir*, 1645	Hallam
1	1	-	2441	Livre (Le) de la toute belle sans pair qui est la vierge Marie, *black letter, fine copy, morocco*, *Paris par Jehan Petit, sans date.*	Clarke
	3	-	2442	Livres de Plusieurs Pieces recueilly de divers Autheurs, *russia*, - - *Lyon*, 1548	Triphook
	5	-	2443	Livre sans Nom divisé en cinq Dialogues, *blue morocco*, *Paris*, 1695	D°
	9	-	2444	Livre (le) à la Mode, *red morocco*, *en Europe*, 1759	Allen
	6	-	2445	Livre à la Mode, *green morocco*, - *à Vertefeuille.*	Triphook

1	13	-	2446	Loarte's Instructions how to meditate the Misteries of the Rosarie of the Virgin Mary, *wood cuts, fine copy, blue morocco, with joints, rare,* - *No place or date.*	Clarke
	2	-	2447	Loiola, Stoicus Vapulans, Cancer, et Paria, quatuor Comœdiæ, - - *Londini,* 1648	Heber
	5	-	2448	Lomenii Itinerarium, *red morocco,* *Paris,* 1662	Clarke
	7	-	2449	London, New Remarks on, - - 1732	Allen
	14	-	2450	London, Institution Library Catalogue of, 1813	Triphook
	19	-	2451	Longi Pastoralia de Daphnide et Chloe, cura Boden, *red morocco, fine paper,* - - *Lipsiæ,* 1777	Payne
2	8	-	2452	Longus, Les Amours Pastorales de Daphnis et Chloe, *plates, ruled, elegantly bound in morocco, in compartments, by Monnier,* - - *Paris,* 1732	Triphook
2	4	-	2453	——— ——— ——— traduites par Amyot, decorées de 28 gravures par Audran, après les dessins de Ph. d'Orleans, fine impressions, *blue morocco,* 1718	Do.
	1	-	2454	Longus, Les Amours de Daphnis et Chloé - 1777	Do.
	4	-	2455	Longo, gli Amori Pastorali di Dafni e Cloe, tradotti dal A. Caro, *frontispiece,* - - *Parigi,* 1800	Do.
	1	-	2456	Loredano, La Dianea, *red morocco,* - *Venetia,* 1644	Do.
	5	-	2457	——— Novelle Amorose, *green morocco,* *ib. s. a.*	Do.
	9	-	2458	——— Bizzarrie Academiche, *red morocco,* *ib.* 1642	Calkin
1	2	-	2459	Louenge (La) des Roys de France, *black letter, fine copy,* *Paris, Eustace de Brie,* 1507	Triphook
	11	-	2460	——— des Femmes, extraite du Commentaire de Pantagruel sur l'Androgyne de Platon, *green morocco,* 1551	Heber
4	-	-	2461	Louis XIII. Codicilles de Louys XIII. Roy de France et de Navarre, 2 vol. *red morocco, fine copy,* RARE, 1643	Payne
	1	-	2462	Louis (Le) d'Or Politique et Galant, *Cologne,* 1695	Triphook
1	10	-	2463	Love, the Art of making Love, or Rules for the Conduct of Ladies and Gallants in their Amours, *frontispiece, blue morocco,* - - - 1676	Perry
	12	-	2464	Lovers, the Enchanted, a Pastoral, *frontispiece, blue morocco,* - - - - 1659	Rodd
	3	-	2465	Love, the Garden of. - - *no date.*	Triphook
	5	-	2466	Love and Madness, - - *Ipswich,* 1809	Allen
	6	-	2467	Lover's (The) Miscellany, or Poems on several Occasions, Amorous and Gallant - - 1719	Perry
	2	-	2468	Lovell's Enchiridion Botanicum or Compleat Herball, *Oxford,* 1668	Heber
	6	-	2469	Lowth's Introduction to English Grammar 1762	Triphook
	7	-	2470	Lubini Clavis et Fundamenta Linguæ Græcæ, *red morocco,* *Elzevir,* 1651	Rodd
	13	-	2471	Lucæ (Francisci) Sacrorum Bibliorum Vulgatæ Editionis Concordantiæ, - - *Colon.* 1684	Triphook

£	s.	d.	No.	Lot	Buyer
	14	-	2472	Lucanus, *red morocco,* - - *Aldus,* 1502	Heber
4	4	-	2473	Lucani Pharsalia cum familiari atque perlucida Annotatione Petri Deponte cœci Brugensis, *with ornamented capitals, red morocco,* - *Parrhisiis, Lerouge,* 1512	Lloyd
	4	-	2474	Lucani Pharsalia, 2 vol. *red morocco,* *Brindley,* 1750	Hayes
	1	-	2475	Lucani Pharsalia, - *Glasguæ,* 1785	Do
2	19	-	2476	Lucain, Le Pharsale, par Breboeuf, *thick paper, red morocco,* - - - *Elsevier,* 1658	Clarke
	11	-	2477	Lucas, Voyage dans la Grece, l'Asie Mineure, &c. 3 vol. *Paris,* 1712	Triphook
3	15	-	2478	Lucien de Ceulx qui servent a gaiges es Maisons des gros Seigneurs et Bourgeois, *wood cuts,* *Lyon,* 1536	Heber
	4	-	2479	Lucretius, *blue morocco, with joints,* *Aldus,* 1515	Warner
	4	-	2480	——— de rerum Natura, - *Gryphius,* 1548	Heber
	13	-	2481	——— *red morocco,* *Lut. Par. Coustelier,* 1744	Warner
	9	-	2482	Lucrezio della Natura delle Cose da Marchetti, 2 vol. *plates,* - - - *Amsterdamo,* 1754	Calkin
	1	-	2483	Lucrece traduit par Le Baron de Coutures, 2 vol. *Paris,* 1692	Hayes
	2	-	2484	Ludus Pythagoreus qui Rythmomachia nominatur per C. Buxerium Delphinatem illustratus, *Lutetiæ,* 1556	Payne
	10	-	2485	Luykens's Hundred Plates of Trades, &c. with descriptions in Dutch.	Heber
	11	-	2486	Luikens's Life of Man from beginning to end, *plates, green morocco,* - - - *Amst.* 1719	Clarke
	11	-	2487	Luyken de Beginselen van Gods Koninkryk in den Mensch. *plates,* - - - *Amst.* 1740	Do
	18	-	2488	Lupsete's Exhortation to Yonge Men, perswadyng them to walke in the pathe way that leadeth to honestie and goodnes, black letter, *blue morocco,* RARE, 1534	Triphook
	16	-	2489	Luscinii Joci ac Sales mire Festivi, *green morocco, scarce,* *sine ulla notâ.*	Hibbert
4	5	-	2490	Lyndewode (Wilhelmi) Constitutiones Provinciales Ecclesiæ Anglicanæ, *very fine copy, blue morocco,* *Wynandum de Worde,* 1496	Triphook
1	5	-	2491	Lyre of Love, 2 vol. in 1, *green morocco,* . 1806	Heber
	15	-	2492	Lyttelton, Tenures in Englysshe, *black letter, fine copy,* *T. Petyt.*	Rodd
1	8	-	2493	M's (T.) Lives of Henry Duke of Gloucester, and Mary Princess of Orange, deceased, *frontispiece, blue morocco.*	Clarke
	3	-	2494	Mably, Observations sur les Grecs, *Geneve,* 1749	Triphook
	5	-	2495	——— Entretiens de Phocion, 2 vol. *red morocco,* *Paris,* 1783	Do
1	4	-	2496	Macarronea Latino-Portugueza, *yellow morocco, with joints,* *Lisboa,* 1765-67	Clarke
	3	-	2497	Macer de Viribus Herbarum, *wood cuts, russia,* *sine ulla notâ.*	Triphook

2498 Macer de Viribus Herbarum, *wood cuts, russia, sine ulla notâ.*

2499 ——— *wood cuts,* - - *sine ulla notâ.*

2500 Mackaile's Fons Moffetensis seu Descriptio Fontium Moffetensium in Annandia Scotiæ, *Edinburgi,* 1659

2501 Macrobius et Censorinus, - *Aldus,* 1528

2502 Maddock's Florist's Directory, - 1810

2503 Magaillan's History of China, - - 1688

Quarto.

2504 Long's Voyages and Travels of an Indian Interpreter, 1791

2505 Lonicerus's Roman Catholic Orders, wood cuts of the different habits, with descriptive verses in German, *blue morocco,* - - *Francfort,* 1585

2506 Lopez de Castaneda, History of the Discoverie and Conquest of the East Indies enterprised by the Portingales, translated by Lichefield, *black letter, fine copy, blue morocco,* - - *T. East,* 1582

2507 Louys XI. Chronique Scandaleuse ou Histoire des Estranges faicts arrivez soubs le Regne de Louys XI. *frontispiece, russia,* - - - 1620

2508 Louis XII. La Victoire du Roy contre les Veneciens, par Claude de Seissel, *fine copy, red morocco,* *Paris, A. Verard,* 1510

2509 Lucani Pharsalia cum notis Variorum curante Oudendorpio, *russia,* - - *Lugd. Bat.* 1728

2510 ——— Grotii et Bentleii, *red morocco, with joints,* - *Strawberry Hill,* 1760

2511 Luciani Opera, Gr. et Lat. cum notis Hemsterhuisii et Reitzii, 4 vol. - - *Amstel.* 1743

2512 Lucretius de Rerum Natura, *red morocco, Baskerville,* 1772

2513 ——— cura G. Wakefield, 3 vol. LARGE PAPER, ELEGANTLY BOUND IN GREEN MOROCCO, - - *Londini,* 1796

2514 Ludolphi de Suchen liber de Terra Sancta et Itinerario Iherosolimitano et de aliis mirabilibus quæ inmari conspiciuntur videlicet mediterraneo, *black letter, very fine copy, blue morocco,* RARE - *sine ulla notâ.*

2516 Lux in Tenebris hoc est Prophetiæ Donum quô Deus Ecclesiam Evangelicam (in Regno Bohemiæ) ornare, ac paternè solari, dignatus est. Cotteri Revelationes, *plates, blue morocco,* - - 1657

2517 LYDGATE. The Tale of the Chorle and the Byrd. Emprentyd by me, RICHARDE PINSON, no date, EXTREMELY RARE. Not mentioned by Ames, Herbert, or Dibdin, *red morocco.*

£	s.	d.	Lot	Description	Buyer
17	5	-	2518	**Lydgate.** Lyfe of our Lady, *very fine copy, blue morocco,* RARE, - *R. Redman,* 1531	Triphook
3	3	-	2519	Lylie's Ephues the Anatomy of Wit.—Euphues and his England, 2 vol. in 1, black letter. *G. Cawood,* 1587-88	Do
5	-	-	2520	Lyon. La Merveilleuse Hystoire de l'Esperit qui depuis nagueres c'est apparu au monastere des Religieuses de S. Pierre de Lyon, *wood cuts, black letter, red morocco,* RARE, *Paris,* 1528	Do
	11	-	2521	Mabilionis Iter Italicum Litterarium, *russia,* 1687	Payne
3	10	-	2522	Mabrian, Les proesses et vaillances du Redouté Mabrian le quel fut roy de Jerusalem, *black letter, wood cuts, Paris, J. Bonfons, sans date.*	Heber
	15	-	2522*	Maccii, (P.) Emblemata cum Privilegiis, *Bononiæ,* 1628	Triphook
	7	-	2523	M'Creery's Press, a Poem, *wood cuts, Liverpool,* 1803	Heber
3		-	2524	M'Donald's Dictionary of Practical Gardening, 2 vol. *coloured plates,* - - - 1807	King
1	9	-	2525	Machiavelli, Tutte le Opere di, 2 vol. *red morocco, Roma,* 1550	Triphook
1	11	-	2526	Machiavell's Arte of Warre translated by P. Whitehorne, with an addicion of other like Marcialle feates and experiments, *wood cuts, black letter, red morocco, J. Kingston,* 1562	Heber
	11	-	2527	Machuca, (Capitan don Bernardo de Vargas) Milicia y Descripcion de las Indias, *scarce, Madrid,* 1799	Rodd
3		-	2528	Magnificentissimi Spectaculi, a Regina Regum matre in hortis suburbanis editi, In Henrici Regis Poloniæ invictissimi nuper renunciati gratulationem Descriptio. Io. Aurato Poeta Regio Autore, *wood cuts, red morocco, Paris, Morel.* 1573	Heber
5	10	-	2529	Maguelonne, Hystoire de Pierre filz du Conte de Provence et de la Belle Maguelonne fille du Roy de Naples, *black letter, yellow morocco, scarce, Rouen. pour Michel Angier, sans date.*	Arch
1	19	-	2530	Majeri Emblemata nova de Secretis Naturæ Chymica, *plates, blue morocco,* - *Oppenheimii,* 1618	Triphook
	8	-	2531	Majeri Scrutinium Chymicum per Emblemata illustratum, *green morocco,* - - *Francof.* 1687	Do
	5	-	2532	Majeri Jocus Severus, hoc est Tribunal Æquum, &c. *Francof.* 1617	Do
	15	-	2533	Majeri Septimana Philosophica qua Ænigmata Aureola de omni Naturæ Genere in modum Colloquii proponuntur et enodantur, *yellow morocco,* - *Francof.* 1620	Do
	5	-	2534	Majeri Arcana Arcanissima hoc est Hieroglypica Ægyptio-Græca, - - - *sine anno.*	Clarke
	10	-	2535	Maittaire Annales Typographici ab Artis Inventæ origine ad annum, MD. *russia,* - *Hag. Com.* 1719	Christie

2536 Maldonado, (Lopez) Cancionero, *blue morocco*, *Madrid*, 1586

2537 Malespini, Ducento Novelle, *red morocco*, *Venetia*, 1609

2538 Mallinkrot de Ortu et Progressu Artis Typographicæ, *Col. Agrip.* 1639

2539 Mandevilla (Johanne de) Tractato de le piu Maravegliose cose e piu notabile che si trovino in le parte del Mondo vedute del Cavalier, J. de Madevilla, *fine copy, russia, rarê,* *per Manfredo de Monferato da Strevo de Bonello*, 1496

2540 Mandevilla Itinerario, - *Milano*, 1497

2541 Mandevilla Altra Edizione, *green morocco*, *Bologna*, 1497

2542 Altro Exemplare, - - *Milano*, 1517

2543 Mandeville, Itinerarius domini Johannis de Mandeville militis, *fine copy, blue morocco, with joints*, *sine ulla notâ.*

2544 Mand ville Le Livre du Jehan lequel parle de la terre doultre mer et du Saint Voyage de Hierusalem, *black letter, russia*, - *Paris P. le Noir, sans date.*

2545 Mandevile's Voyages and Travels, *wood cuts,blue morocco*, 1696

2546 Mann's Picture of New South Wales, 1811

2547 Mantelii Speculum Peccatorum aspirantium ad solidam Vitæ emendationem, *plates, green morocco*, *Antverpiæ*. 1637

2548 Manuale ad usum percelebris Ecclesiæ Sarisburiensis, *black letter, russia.* See MS. notes at the end, *Londini*, 1554

Folio.

2549 Kæmpfer Icones Selectæ Plantarum in Japonia, *plates*, *Londini*, 1791

2550 Kircheri Obeliscus Pamphilius hoc est interpretatio Obelisci Hieroglyphici, *plates*, - *Romæ*, 1650

2551 Kircheri Obelisci Ægyptiaci Interpretatio Hieroglyphica, *plate*, - - *ib.* 1666

2552 Kircheri China Illustrata, *plates, vellum*, *Amst.* 1667

2553 Kircheri Latii Descriptio, *Amst.* 1671. Kircheri Museum Celeberrimum Romani Collegii, *Amst.* 1678, 2 vol. in 1, *plates, vellum.*

2553* Kircheri Arca Noe in tres libros digesta, *plates, red momorocco, Colbert's copy*, *Amst.* 1675

2554 Kleedingen van Masquerados. A Collection of Prints of Masquerade Dresses, *fine impressions, vellum.*

£	s.	d.	No.	Description	Buyer
85	1		2555	KNYGHT OF THE TOURE, translated oute of the Frenssh into our Maternall Englysshe tongue, by me WILLIAM CAXTON, - - - 1483 A very fine copy of a book which rarely occurs perfect, *splendidly bound in green morocco, with morocco lining, &c.*	Triphook
1	11	-	2556	Krafftt's Plans of the most beautiful Gardens in France, England, and Germany, in French, English, and German, *Paris*, 1809	Scott
	5	-	2557	Kreuterbuch, a German Herbal, *plates coloured*, *Francof*. 1603	Perry
4	16	-	2558	Laborde, Description d'un pavé en Mosaique, decouvert dans l'ancienne ville d'Italica, *beautifully coloured plates, only* 160 *copies printed*, - *Paris*. 1802	Arch
4	9	-	2559	Lambert's Description of the Genus Pinus, illustrated with figures, directions relative to the cultivation, and remarks on the uses of the several species, - 1805	Johnston
30	19	6	2560	Another Copy, with the plates BEAUTIFULLY COLOURED, of which the number was very small, - 1805	Scott
11	5	-	2561	Lancelot du Lac, Le Roman de, 3 vol. *wood cuts, black letter, fine copy, green morocco*, *Paris, Jehan Petit*, 1520	Longman
12	15	-	2562	Lawrence's (Miss) Collection of Roses, BEAUTIFULLY COLOURED from nature, *russia*, - - 1799	Do
31	10	-	2563	Le Brun Galérie des Peintres Flamands, Hollandois et Allemands, ouvrage enrichi de 201 planches d'aprés les meilleurs tableaux de ces Maitres, 3 vol. *very fine impressions of the plates*, - - *Paris*, 1792	Ld Yarmouth
17	6	6	2564	Le Brun Voyages par la Moscovie en Perse, et aux Indes orientales, 2 vol. *Amst*. 1718. Voyage au Levant, *Paris*, 1714, together 3 vol. *large paper, blue morocco.*	Payne
1	19	-	2565	Le Feron, Catalogue des Noms, Surnoms et Vies des Connestables, Chancelliers, Grands Maitres, &c. de France, avec la Figure et Blasons de leurs armoiries, *blue morocco, with joints*, - - *Paris*, 1599	Hollingworth
15	4	6	2566	Legenda Aurea, The Golden Legende, Finysshed the 27 day of August the yere of our Lord 1527. Imprynted at London in Flete Strete at the sygne of the Sonne by WYNKEN DE WORDE, *elegantly bound in blue morocco.*	Thomson
2	12	6	2567	Leigh's Natural History of Lancashire and Cheshire, and the Peak in Derbyshire, *plates, russia*, - 1700	Scott
2	2	-	2568	Leonardo de Argensola Conquista de las Islas Malucas, *morocco*, - - *Madrid*, 1609	Longman
2	-	-	2569	Leonardus Aretinus de Bello Italico adversus Gothos, *first edition*, Emilianus de Orfinis Fulginas et J. Numeister, 1470	Triphook

2570 Le Plat, Recueil des Marbres Antiques qui se trouvent dans Gallerie du Roy de Pologne à Dresde, *fine impressions, privately printed only for presents, russia,* Dresde, 1733

2571 Lepolemo, El Libro del invencible Cavàllero Lepolemo Cavallero de la Cruz, *rare,* - *Sevilla,* 1548

2572 L'Espinette du jeune prince conquerant le Royaulme de Bonne Renomme (par Simon Bougoine), *wood cuts, fine copy, blue morocco, by Derome,* RARE, *Paris, A. Verard,* 1508

2573 LETELTUN Tenuris new correcte, *fine copy, russia,* VERY RARE. See Dibdin's Ames, Vol. II. p. 459, PYNSON, 1516

2574 Licetus de Lucernis Antiquorum reconditis, *plates, red morocco,* - - *Utini,* 1652

2575 Linschoten's Voyages into the East and West Indies, *with the plates belonging to the original Dutch edition, fine copy, russia,* - - *Printed by Wolfe,* 1598

2576 LISUARTE. El Octavo Libro de Amadis: que trata de las estrañas avēturas y grandes proezas desunieto Lisuarte, y de la muerte del inclito rey Amadis, en Castellano por Juan Diaz, *Sevilla,* 1526.—El noveno Libro de Amadis de Gaula: qui es la cronica del Cavallero de la ardiente espada Amadis de Grecia; hijo de Lisuarte, *Sevilla,* 1542, 2 vol. in 1, *wood cuts, fine copies, yellow morocco,* VERY RARE.

FOURTEENTH DAY'S SALE.

Octavo et Infra.

2577 Magia (De) in Lingua Malabarica, written on the bark of a tree and enclosed in a morocco case.

2578 Magius de Tintinnabulis et de Equuleo, *plates, blue morocco,* - - *Amst.* 1664

2579 Maire (Le) Voyages aux Iles Canaries, Cap Verd, &c. *Paris,* 1695

2580 Maire de Belges, Le Promptuaire des Conciles de L'Eglise Catholique, avec les Scismes et la difference diceulx, *wood cuts, blue morocco,* - - *Lyon,* 1532

2581 Maison des Jeux Academiques, - *Paris,* 1665

2582 Man's Benefit of Procreation. - 1739

2583 Manchini, The Apology, or the Genuine Memoires of Madam Maria Manchini, - - 1769

2584 Manetti Viridarium Florentinum, sive conspectus Plantarum in Horto Cæsareo Florentino, *Florentiæ.* 1751

2585 Manfredi, Carcer d'Amore, *wood cuts, Venet. Bindoni.* 1533

2586 Manteaux (Les), *red morocco, à la Haye,* 1746

2587 Marconville de la Bonté et Mauvaistie des Femmes, *green morocco,* - - - *Lyon,* 1573

2588 Marconville de l'Heur et Malheur de Mariage, *green morocco,* - - - *ib.* 1573

2589 Marguerite de Valois, Reine de Navarre, Contes et Nouvelles, 2 vol. *plates, red morocco* - *Amst.* 1708

2590 Marguerite Reine de Navarre, Nouvelles de, 3 vol. *large paper, fine impressions of the plates,* - *Berne,* 1780

2591 Margaret de Valoys, Queen of Navarre's Heptameron, or the History of the Fortunate Lovers, *scarce,* 1654

2592 Marguerites de la Marguerite des Princesses tres illustre Royne de Navarre, 2 vol. in 1, *fine copy of the best Edition, rare,* - - - *Lyon,* 1547

2593 Marguerite, Le Tombeau de Marguerite de Valois Royne de Navarre, *fine copy, green morocco, Paris,* 1551

2594 Marguerite, Memoires de la Reyne Marguerite, *ib.* 1661

2595 Mariage, Les quinze Joyes de Mariage, *red morocco, à la Haye,* 1726

2596 ———-- Plaisant Contract de Mariage passé nouvellement à Aubertvilliers entre Nicolas grand Jean et Guillmette Ventruë, *green morocco, with joints, Paris,*

2597 Mariage, Le, 2 vol. - - *Paris,* 1769

2598 Marigny, Le Pain Benit de Mons. l'Abbé, - 1673

2599 Marino, La Galeria del Cavalier Marino, 2 vol. *gilt leaves, Venetia,* 1635

2600 ——— La Lira Rime del Cavalier Marino, 2 vol. *russia, Milano,* 1617

2601 ———La Murtoleide Fischiate, *blue morocco, Spira,* 1629

2602 ———L'Adone, Poema Heroico del C. Marino, 4 vol. *Parigi.* 1678

2603 ———La Strage de gl'Innocenti, - *Venetia.*

2604 Marivaux, Œuvres Complettes, 12 vol. *blue morocco, Paris,* 1781

2605 Markham's Hunger's Prevention, or the whole Art of Fowling, *cuts,* - - - 1655

2606 Marlborough, Lediard's Life of John Duke of Marlborough, 2 vol. *plates, red morocco,* - 1743

2607 ————— Milner's Journal of the Duke of Marlborough's Wars, - - - 1733

£	s.	d.	Lot	Description	Buyer
	5	-	2608	Marlborough, La Conduite le Duc du Marlborough dans la presente Guerre, - - *Amst.* 1712	Triphook
	1	-	2609	——— ———The Information against the Duke of Marlborough, and his Answer.	Do.
	11	-	2610	——— ———Memoirs of the Life and Conduct of Sarah, late Duchess of Marlborough, - 1744	Clarke
	2	-	2611	——— ——— Account of the Conduct of the Dowager Duchess of Marlborough, 1742	Triphook
	3	-	2612	——— ——— Remarks upon the Account, &c. 1742	Do
1	10	-	2613	——— ———The Opinions of Sarah, Duchess-Dowager of Marlborough, - - - 1788	Molteno
	3	-	2614	——— ——— No Queen or no General, proving the necessity of Displacing the D— of M——borough, 1712	Triphook
	7	-	2615	——— ——— Her Grace of Marlborough's Party Gibberish explained, - - - 1742	Do.
	3	-	2616	——— ——— Vindication of the Duchess Dowager of Marlborough, - - 1742	Do
	1	-	2617	——— ——— A Continuation of the Review of a late Treatise, entituled an Account of the Conduct of the Dow—r D—— of M——— &c. - 1742	Do.
1	-	-	2618	——— ——— The Sarah-ad; or, a Flight for Fame, a Burlesque Poem, - - 1742	Clarke
	8	-	2619	——— ——— The Will of Sarah, late Duchess Dowager of Marlborough, - - - 1744	Molteno
1	-	-	2620	——— ——— The Secret History of Queen Zarah, *blue morocco, with joints,* - - 1705	Thornhill
	10	-	2621	——— ——— The Secret History of Queen Zarah, 1749	Molteno
	7	-	2622	Marmion Travestied, - - 1809	Hollingworth
1	14	-	2623	Marmite (La) Retablie par les Miracles du Pere Marc d'Aviano. *Cologne,* 1684. Onquant pour la Brulure ou le Secret pour empecscher les Jesuites de bruler les Livres, 1669, Veron ou le Hibou des Jesuites. Le Mercure Postillon. *Liege,* in one vol. *red morocco.*	Triphook
	4	-	2624	Marolles, Catalogue des Livres d'Estampes et de Figures en Taille-douce, *red morocco,* - *Paris,* 1666	Heber
	8	-	2625	Marolles, Catalogue de Livres d'Estampes, *red morocco,* *ib.* 1672	Payne
	9		2626	Marot, Les Œuvres de Clement Marot faictes en son adolescence, *wood cuts, morocco, with morocco lining,* *Paris, D. Janot,* 1538	Triphook
	14	-	2627	——— Les Œuvres de Clement Marot, *red morocco, ruled,* - - - *Paris, Bignon,* 1542	Heber
	12	-	2628	——— ——— 2 vol. *green morocco,* - - - *à la Haye,* 1700	Warner
2	15	-	2629	Marot (Jean) Sur les deux heureux Voyages de Genes et Venise, *Paris, par Tory,* 1532. Le Recueil des Œuvres	Clarke

de Jehan Marot de Caen, *Paris, Tory,* in one vol. *yellow morocco, scarce,*

2630 Marottes a Vendre ou Triboulet Tabletier, *one of six copies, printed upon pink paper,* *Londres R. Triphook.*

2631 Marseilles, Account of the Plague at 1721

2632 Marsh's Survey of the Turkish Empire and Government, *yellow morocco, with joints,* - - 1663

2633 Marston's (John) Tragedies and Comedies, *red morocco, rare,* - - - 1633

2634 ——— ——— Tragedies and Comedies, 1633

2635 Martelli Opere, Corrette, *red morocco,* *Firenze, Giunta,* 1548

2636 ——— Stanze e Canzoni, *Venetia, Pincio,* 1533

2637 Marthe, Les Chastes Amours d'Helene de Marthe, recherchée de plusieurs Amans, - *Paris,* 1597

2638 Martialis Epigrammata, - - *Aldus.* 1501

2639 Martialis Epigrammata, ex museo Scriverii, *yellow morocco,* - - *Elzevir.* 1664

2640 Martialis Epigrammata, 2 vol. *blue morocco, Paris,* 1754

2641 Martialis Epigrammata cura Smids, 2 vol. *ruled, half bound, uncut,* - - *Amstel.* 1701

2642 Martin, Le Papillon de Cupido, - *Lyon,* 1543

2643 Martinet, Emblemes Royales à Louis le Grand, *plates, Paris,* 1673

2644 Martiniere, Voyage des pays Septentrionaux, *ib.* 1682

2645 Martyn's Observations on the Æneid of Virgil, *red morocco,* - - - 1770

2646 ——— Flora Rustica, 4 vol. *coloured plates,* 1792

2647 ——— Language of Botany, - 1793

2648 ——— Thirty-eight Plates, intended to illustrate Linnæus's System of Vegetables, - - 1788

2649 Mary Queen of Scots. Buchanan's Detectioun of the Duinges of Marie Quene of Scottes, touchand the murder of hir husband, and hir conspiracie, adulterie and pretensed mariage with the Erle of Bothwell, *black letter,* - - - *no date,*

2650 ——— ——— Martyre de la Royne d'Escosse, Douairiere de France, avec son Oraison Funebre, *blue morocco,* RARE, - - *Edimbourg.* 1588

2651 Mascardi's Relation of Fieschi's Conspiracy against Genoa, translated by Hare, - - - 1693

2652 Masaniello. The remarkable History of the Rise and Fall of Masaniello, the Fisherman of Naples, by Giraffi, translated by Howell, - - 1664

2653 Another Copy, - - - 1756

2654 Mason's Poems, - - - 1779

£	s.	d.	Lot	Description	Buyer
2	1	-	2655	Masques, Mommerie, Bernez et Revernez es Jours gras de Caresme prenant, L'Origine des, *red morocco, scarce,* 1609	Heber
3	18	-	2656	Massinger's Plays, with Notes, critical and explanatory, by Gifford, 4 vol. - - - 1805	Gen. Mead
	7	-	2657	Mastigophore (Le) ou Precurseur du Zodiaque, traduit par Victor Grévé, *red morocco. This Book was suppressed.* De Bure, No. 3945, - - - 1609	Dulau
1	8	-	2658	Mathias, Componimenti Lirici de' più Illustri Poeti d'Italia, 3 vol. - - - 1802	Dibdin
1	19	-	2659	——— Aggiunta ai Componimenti Lirici, 3 vol. *green morocco,* - - - 1808	Do.
	5	-	2660	——— Canzoni e Prose Toscane, - 1808	Triphook
	17	-	2661	Matrimony. A Ryght Godly Treatise of Matrimony, compiled by Wolfgangus Musculus, translated by Richard Ryce, *black letter, russia,* RARE, *no place or date.*	Thornhill
	6	-	2662	——— The present State of, - - 1739	Major Hay
	7	-	2663	——— The Fifteen Comforts of, - 1721	Arch
	1	-	2664	Mattuschka Enumeratio Stirpium in Silesia sponte crescentium, - - *Uratislaviæ.* 1779	Triphook
2	16	-	2665	Maundevile's (Sir John) Voiage and Travaile to Hierusalem, &c. *blue morocco,* - - 1727	Clarke
	7	-	2666	Maundrell's Journey from Aleppo to Jerusalem, *Oxford,* 1703	Hodgson
	1	-	2667	Maurice duc de Bouillon, Memoires de, *Amst.* 1691	Triphook
	3	-	2668	Maurice's Poems, - - 1800	Heber
	4	-	2669	Maximi Tyrii Dessertationes, Gr. Lat. *ruled, Oxon.* 1677	Christie
	4	-	2670	Mayerus Ludus Serius or Serious Passe Time, 1654	Do.
1	11	-	2671	Mazot le Tableau de la Croix representé dans les Cérémonies de la St. Messe, *plates, red morocco, with clasps, Paris.* 1651	Clarke
	2	-	2672	Medulla Oratoria ab Petr.—Adolpho, *green morocco, Elzevir,* 1656	Christie
5	10	-	2673	Medici (Lorenzo di) Stanze Belissime et ornatissime intitulate Le Selve d'Amore, *fine copy, yellow morocco, with joints, very rare,* - - *Venet. Rusconi,* 1522	Heber
	7	-	2674	Medley (The Historical and Poetical) or Muse's Library, 1738	Triphook
	2	-	2675	Megiseri Icones et Vitæ Paparum, *wood cuts, Franc.* 1602	Do.
	8	-	2676	Meibomius de Flagrorum usu in re Veneria, *blue morocco, Lond* 1665	Do.
	9	-	2677	Meibomius et Bartholinus de Flagrorum usu in re Medica et Veneria, *green morocco,* - *Francof.* 1670	Christie
2	19	-	2678	Meichsneri Thesaurus Sapientiæ Civilis sive Vitæ Humanæ ac Virtutum et Vitiorum Theatrum, *plates, fine copy, green morocco* - - - *ib.* 1626	Clarke

2679 Melampus's Contemplation of Mankinde, englished by Thomas Hyll, *black letter, cuts, blue morocco,* *Lond. by W. Seres,* 1571

2680 Melancton. The Epistle of Philip Melancton, made unto oure late Sovereygne Lord Kynge, Henry the eight, for revokinge and abolishing of the Six Articles, &c. *black letter,* RARE - - *Printed at Weesell,* 1547

2681 Melandri Jocorum et Seriorum Centuriæ aliquot, 2 vols. *red morocco, ruled,* - *Francof.* 1626

2682 Mellini Descrizione dell' Entrata della Reina Giovanna d'Austria et dell' Apparato fatto in Firenze nella venuta, et per le Nozze di S. Altezza et Francesco de Medici. Giunta 1566. Descrizione degl' intermedii rappresentati colla Commedia nelle nozze del Principe di Firenze 1566 in one vol.

2683 Memoires du Marquis de Bénavidés, 2 vol. *Paris,* 1754

2684 ——— du Comte de Claize, par De Catalde, *Amst.* 1738

2685 ——— de la Marquise de Orémy, 2 vol. *Lyon,* 1766

2686 ——— du Chev. du Gonthieu, par De la Croix, *Amst.* 1766

2687 ——— de Mademoiselle de Montpensier, 7 vol. *Londres,* 1746

2688 ——— de M. de Montresor, 2 vol. *green morocco,* *Leyde,* 1665

2689 ——— de la Regence du Duc d'Orleans, 3 vol. *red morocco,* - - - *Amst.* 1729

2690 ——— d'un Favory du Duc d'Orleans, *yellow morocco,* *Leyde,* 1668

2691 ——— du Chevalier de St. George *Cologne,* 1712

2692 ——— de l'Academie des Colporteurs, *plates,* 1748

2693 ——— Historiques et Secrets concernant les Amours des Rois de France, *green morocco,* - *Paris,* 1739

2694 Menagii Poemata, *red morocco, with joints,* UNCUT, *Elzevir,* 1663

2695 Menckenii de Charlataneria Eruditorum Declamationes Duæ, *frontispiece* - - - *Lipsiæ,* 1715

2696 Mendoça (Gonçalez de) Historia de las Cosas mas notables Ritos y Costumbres del Reyno de la China, con un Itinerario del nuevo Mundo, *russia,* *Anvers,* 1596

2697 Mendoça (Lopez de) Proverbios. Coplas de Mingo Revulgo, *green morocco, with joints, scarce,* *ib.* 1594

2698 Menestrerii Philosophia Imaginum, *plates,* *Amst.* 1695

2699 Menzini l'Arte Poetica Italiana in Cinque Canti 1804

2699* Mercurius Rusticus, The Country's Complaint, recounting the Sad Events of this unparralel'd Warr, frontispiece by Marshall, - - - 1646

£	s.	d.	Lot	Description	Buyer
	18	-	2700	Merigot Promenades ou Itineraire des Jardins de Chantilly, *plates*, - - - *Paris*, 1791	Triphook
4	14	6	2701	Merlino, Historia di, *wood cuts, red morocco*, RARE, *Venetia, per Roffinelli*, 1539	Heber
	11	-	2702	Merlin revived in a Discourse of Prophecies and Predictions, with Lilly's Hieroglyphicks, exactly cut, *russia*, 1683	Christie
	1	-	2703	Meroveus a Prince of the Blood Royal of France, a Novel, 1682	Triphook
1	11	-	2704	Merouée fils de France, *red morocco*, - *Lyon*, 1678	Chamier
			2705	Merryland, a New Description of, 1741. The Potent Ally, or Succours from Merryland. Merryland Displayed. Description of the Roads which lead to Merryland, 1743, *in one volume*.	
	5	-	2706	Messie. Les Diverses Leçons de Pierre Messie Gentilhomme de Sevile, *red morocco*, - *Lyon*. 1570	Triphook

Quarto.

£	s.	d.	Lot	Description	Buyer
	4	-	2707	Marchand, Histoire de l'Origine et des premiers progrès de l'Imprimerie, - - *à la Haye*, 1740	Triphook
1	15	-	2708	Marcus. Evangelium secundum Marcum cum glossis. A Manuscript of the 13th Century, upon vellum, *blue morocco, with joints*	Do.
10	10	-	2709	Marcus Paulus de Venetiis de Consuetudinibus et condicionibus orientalium regionum, *very fine copy, blue morocco*, EXTREMELY RARE, *sine ulla nota*	Payne
	2	-	2710	Margarita Philosophica nova cui insunt sequentia. Epigrammata in commendationis Operis, Institutio Grammaticæ Latinæ, Precepta Logices, &c. *Argent. Gruninger*, 1512	Heber
2	15	-	2711	Marguerite de Valois Royne de Navarre, l'Heptameron des Nouvelles, *scarce*, - *Paris*, 1560	Triphook
	13	-	2712	Markham's Cavelarice, or the English Horseman, *no date*	Anderdon
	7	-	2713	Marlborough Garland, a Real Anecdote from common Life - - - - - 1795	Triphook
1	6	-	2714	Marozzo Bolognese, Mastro generale de l'Arte de l'Armi Opera Nova, *plates*. *Mutiæ in ædibus Anton. Bergolæ Sacerdotis*, 1536	Do.
	1	-	2715	Marston's Malcontent, *rare*, - - 1604	Rodd
	4	-	2716	Marten's Familiar Letters to his Lady of Delight 1663	Triphook
4	4	-	2717	Martialis Epigrammata cum Vita Calderini, *fine copy*, sine ulla nota. The character resembles that used by Vindelin de Spira in his Dante of 1477	Do.

2718 Martial's Epigrams, with a Comment by Elphinstone, 1782

2719 Martin de Cordova. Jardin de las nobles Donzellas, *fine copy*, RARE, - - - 1542

2720 Martius de Homine - *Venet. per I. Rubeum*, 1476

2721 Martyn's Universal Conchologist, exhibiting the figure of every known Shell, accurately drawn and painted after nature, 2 vol. 160 *plates, red morocco*, - 1789

2722 Martyn's English Entomologist, exhibiting all the Cleopterous Insects found in England, COLOURED PLATES, *green morocco*, - - - 1792

2723 Martyn's Forty-four beautifully COLOURED DRAWINGS of Plants, *with a gold border to each, red morocco*, 1725

2724 MARY OF NEMMEGEN. Here begynneth a lyttell story that was of a trwethe done in the lande of Gelders of a Mayde that was named Mary of Nemmegen that was the dyvels paramoure by the space of VII yere longe, *wood cuts*, EXTREMELY RARE. *Imprynted at Antvarpe by me* IOHN DUISBROWGHE.

2725 Mary Queene of Scots. A Defence of the Honorable Sentence and Execution of the Queene of Scots, together with the Answere to certaine objections made by some of her Favourites, *fine copy, morocco, ruled*, RARE, *London, Iohn Windet*, 1587

2726 Mascall's Country-Mans new art of Planting and Graffing 1651

2727 Mason's Costume of China, illustrated by sixty coloured engravings, with explanations in English and French, *red morocco*, - - - - 1800

2728 Matheolus. Le Livre de Matheolus qui nous monstre sans varier les biens et les vertus qui vieignent pour soy marier, *wood cuts, red morocco*, - *sans date*

2729 Mathias, Canzoni Toscane - *Londra*, 1805

2730 Mathieu's Heroyk Life and Deplorable Death of Henry IV. translated by Grimeston - *G. Eld.* 1612

2731 Mathieu's Unhappy Prosperitie expressed in the Histories of Ælius Sejanus and Philippa, translated by Sir T. Hawkins - - - - 1632

2732 Maurice's Grove Hill, a Descriptive Poem, *wood cuts, green morocco*, - - - 1799

2733 Maurice's Poems and Miscellaneous Pieces - 1779

2734 Meermanni Origines Typographicæ, 2 vol. in 1, *Hag. Com.* 1765

2735 Meisneri Thesaurus Philo-Politicus, 2 vol. *plates*, *Francofurti*, 1624

2736 Meliadus. Histoire des hauts et chevalereux faicts d'armes du Prince Meliadus dit le Chevalier de la Croix, fils unique de Maximian Empereur des Allemaignes, *morocco*, - - - *Paris, Bonfons*, 1584

£	s.	d.	Lot	Description	Buyer
	2	-	2737	Mentelus de vera Typographiæ Origine, *Paris*, 1650	Triphook
1	11	-	2738	Mercerii Emblemata Latinis versibus explicata, *blue morocco*, - - - - - 1592	Clarke
	10	-	2739	Mercurius Trismegistus Latinè, *Venet.* 1481. Beroaldus de Felicitate, *Bononiæ*, 1495. Bossi in Jesu Christi Passione sermo, *Bonon.* 1495. Philippi Adhortatio ad quendam Theodosium Judæum, *Venet.* 1499, *morocco.*	Heber
	6	-	2740	Mercurialis (Hieronymus) de Arte Gymnastica, *cuts, morocco*, - - - - *Juntas*, 1573	Do
	10	-	2741	Alia editio, *plates, blue morocco, with joints*, *Amst.* 1672	Triphook
1	5	-	2742	Mercurie's Message, or the copy of a Letter sent to Archbishop Laud, 1641. An Answer to Mercurie's Message, 1641. Mercurie's Message defended, 1641, 3 vol.	Taylor
	5	-	2743	Mercurie's Message, 1641	Triphook
	10	-	2744	Mercurius Aquaticus, or the Water Poet's Answer to all that hath or shall be Writ by Mercurius Britannicus, 1643	Perry
	11	-	2745	Merian's Dance of Death, plates, with explanatory verses in German, - - - *Franfort*, 1696	Laing
1	-	-	2746	Merian, Icones Biblicæ, *fine impressions, blue morocco, with joints*, - - - *Strasbourg*, 1627	Triphook
3	10	-	2747	Merlino, La Vita de, et de le sue Prophetie historiade, *wood cuts, black morocco*, - *Venetia*, 1507	Do
2	19	-	2748	Merlin. Sensuit les Prophecies de Merlin, *black letter, blue morocco*, - - *Paris*, 1528	Do
	10	-	2749	Merlin's Life, his Prophecies and Predictions Interpreted, and their truth made good by our English Annals, *frontispiece*, - - - - - 1641	Perry
	2	-	2750	Merrett's View of the Frauds and Abuses committed by Apothecaries - - - 1670	Heber
	19	-	2751	Merry-Man (Doctor) or nothing but Mirth, being a Poesie of Pleas and Poems, and Witty Jests	Perry
3	3	-	2752	Michaux Flora Boreali-Americana, 2 vol. *fine paper, plates, russia, with joints*, - - *Paris*, 1803	Scott
1	1	-	2753	Mignerak La Pratique de l'Aiguille Industrieuse, *with patterns*, - - - - - - *Paris*, 1605	Triphook
3	4	-	2754	Milton's Paradise Lost and Regained, 2 vol. *blue morocco*, *Baskerville*, 1759	Do
1	1	-	2755	Milton's Paradise Regained, and Samson Agonistes, *first edition*, - - - - 1671	Knell
	5	-	2756	Mirabilis Annus, or the year of Prodigies and Wonders, *frontispiece*, - - - - - 1661	Christie

Folio.

£	s.	d.	Lot	Description	Buyer
18	-	-	2757	Livre (Le) des fais d'armes et de Chevalerie, *wood cuts, fine copy, green morocco*, VERY RARE, *Paris, par Anthoine, Verard*, 1488	Triphook

2758 Lobel (Mathias de) Kruydtboeck, a Herbal in Dutch, *wood cuts, coloured, elegantly bound in russia, Antwerpen Plantyn,* 1581

2759 Loggan Oxonia Illustrata, *fine copy, splendidly bound in russia with joints,* - - - *Oxon.* 1675

2760 London, Pine and Tinney's 24 Sheet plan of London, *coloured,* - - - 1746

2761 Loubere's Historical Relation of the Kingdom of Siam, *plates,* - - - 1693

2762 Lower's Relation of the Voyage and Residence of Charles II. in Holland, *Portrait and Plates, blue morocco, with joints,* - - *Hague,* 1660

2763 LUIS DE ESCOBAR. Las quatro cientas Respuestas con las cient Glosas o Declaraciones assi en Prosa como en Metra *Valladolid en Casa de Fernandez de Cordova,* 1550, La Segunda Parte de las quatro cientas Respuestas *Valladolid,* 2 vol. VERY RARE, *russia,* 1552

2764 Luyken, Icones Biblicæ Veteris et N. Testamenti, *Amst.*

2765 Luzon de Millares Idea Politica Veri Christiani sive Ars Oblivionis, isagogica ad artem Memoriæ, *plates, russia, with joints,* - - - *Bruxellis,* 1665

2766 LYF OF OUR LADY, made by dan John Lydgate, Enprynted by WYLLYAM CAXTON, - *no date.*
This Copy wants the Table and six leaves at the end.

2767 Mabillon de Re Diplomatica cum Supplemento, *large paper,* - - - *Paris,* 1581

2768 Mabrian. Histoire singuliere et fort recreative contenant la reste des faitz et gestes des quatre filz Aymon, &c. semblablement La Cronique et hystoire du chevaleureux prince Mabrian, Roy de Hierusalem, *first edition, wood cuts, fine copy, blue morocco,* RARE,
Paris, par J. Nyverd, pour Galliot du Pre.

2769 Autre Edition, *wood cuts, red morocco, Paris, J. Nyverd,* 1530

2770 Madien. La conqueste de Grece faicte par le trespreux et redouté en chevalerie Philippe de Madien, *fine copy, blue morocco,* RARE, - - *ib.* 1527

2771 MANDEVILLE. Cy Commence le Livre des parties d'outre mer le quel fut fait et ordonné par Messire Jehan de Mandeville. Chevalier qui fut nes en Angleterre dans la ville que on dist Sainct Albain. A splendid Manuscript of the 15th Century, upon vellum; the first page contains a large Miniature, beautifully painted with borders of flowers, &c. and the Arms of the person for whom it was written. The capital letters illuminated. *Elegantly bound in red morocco, by Hering.*

£	s.	d.	Lot	Description	Buyer
3	-	-	2772	Manerbi Legendi di tutti li Santi della Romana Sedia, *blue morocco, - Venet. N. Jenson, senz' anno.*	Longman
4	16	-	2773	Mariana, Historia General de España, 2 vol. *red morocco, Toledo,* 1601	Triphook
4	5	-	2774	Marlborough, Life and Military History of the Duke of, *plates, and portrait inserted, red morocco, with joints,* 1754	Natton
2	5	-	2775	——— The Anthem performed at the Funeral of the Duke of, set to music by Bonancini, *splendidly bound in red morocco.*	Payne
16	16	-	2776	Marmol, Descripcion General de Affrica, 3 vol. *red morocco.* The third volume is very scarce, *Grenada,* 1573, *et Malaga,* 1599	Do
3	3	-	2777	Martial d' Auvergne, Les Vigilles de la Mort de Charles VII. *wood cuts, fine copy, Par. Pierre le Caron, sans date.*	Triphook
2	-	-	2778	Martyn, Historia Plantarum Rariorum, COLOURED PLATES, *russia, with joints, - - Lond.* 1728	Longman
4	10	-	2779	Masson Stapeliæ Novæ or a Collection of several new Species of that Genus discovered in the interior of Africa, *coloured plates, russia, with joints,* - 1796	Scott
9	-	-	2780	Masuccio, Il Novellino, nel quale si contengono cinquanta novelle, *wood cuts, fine copy, green morocco,* VERY RARE, *Venet. Greg. de. Gregorii* 1492	Triphook
1	7	-	2781	Martinæ Elogia et Icones Principum omnium Reipublicæ Venetæ, *plates, fine impressions, russia, with joints, Patavii,* 1659	Clarke
8	15	-	2782	Mayer's Views in Egypt, COLOURED after *the original Drawings, green morocco,* - 1801	Nattons
8	10	-	2783	Meliadus, Les Nobles faits d'Armes du Vaillant Roi Meliadus de Leonnoys, *black letter, fine copy, blue morocco, Paris, D. Janot.* 1532	Triphook
24	3	-	2784	Melusine, L'Histoire de, nouvellement corrigée, *wood cuts, fine copy, russia,* VERY RARE, *Paris, Pierre le Caron, sans date.*	Hibbert
	11	-	2785	Menetreii Symbolica Dianæ Ephesiæ Statua, *plates, red morocco, - - - Romæ,* 1688	Triphook

FIFTEENTH DAY'S SALE.

Octavo et Infra.

£	s.	d.	Lot	Description	Buyer
3	5	-	2786	Mestastasio, Opere, 12 vol. *red morocco*, *Londra*, 1784	Triphook
1	13	-	2787	———— Opere Postume, 3 vol. *Vienna*, 1795	D°
	2	-	2788	Methodists (The), a Satirical Poem, *Reading.*	Allen
	9	-	2789	Meurier Recueil de Sentences Notables, Dicts et Dictons communs, &c. - - *Anvers.* 1556	Rodd
	10	-	2790	Meursii ad Phædri Fabulas Animadversiones; Fabellæ et Ænigmata Veterum Poetarum. Ori Apollinis de Sacris Ægyptiorum notis libri duo, Iconibus illustrati, *Paris*, 1754. Orus Apollo, *Lugduni*, 1542, in one vol. *morocco.*	Clarke
	7	-	2791	Meursii Græcia Ludibunda, sive de Ludis Græcorum. Souterii Palamedes, *blue morocco*, *Elzevir*, 1625	Payne
	19	-	2792	——— Elegantiæ Latini Sermonis, *Lug. Bat.* 1774	Triphook
	15	-	2793	———— *blue morocco.* ————	D°
	12	-	2794	Alia Editio *red morocco*, - - 1781	D°
1	2	-	2795	Meursius François ou Entretiens Galans d'Aloysia, *Cythere*, 1795	D°
2	2	-	2796	Meygra Entrepriza catoliqui Imperatoris, quando de Anno domini mille ccccxxxvi. veniebat per provensam bene corrossatus impostam prendere fransam, &c. per A. Arenam, *original edition, red morocco,* RARE, *Avenione*, 1537	D°
2	2	-	2797	Meynier, la Naissance et les Triomphes esmerveillables du Dieu Bacchus, *plates, blue morocco.*	D°
	15	-	2798	Michælis Apelles Symbolicus, 2 vol. *many plates*, *Amstel.* 1699	Rogers
	5	-	2799	Microcosmographie, or a Piece of the World discovered, by E. Blount, *blue morocco*, - - 1629	Triphook
	7	-	2800	Midwife. The Complete Midwife's Practice enlarged, *plates*, - - - 1680	D°
2	1	-	2801	———— (The) or the Old Woman's Magazine, 3 vol.—	Knell
1	1	-	2802	Military Discipline, wherein is most Martially shone the Order of Drilling for the Musket and Pike, *seventy-seven plates, red morocco, with joints.*	Triphook
1	-	-	2803	Milne's Botanical Dictionary, - 1805	Warder
1	16	-	2804	Milton's Paradise Lost and Regained, by Newton, 4 vol. in 3, - - - - - 1778	Ward
5	10	-	2805	Milton's Poetical Works, with Notes and Illustrations, by Todd, 6 vol. *large paper, blue morocco, with joints*, 1801	Johnston

£	s	d	Lot	Description	Buyer
3	-	-	2806	Milton's Paradise Lost, *cuts, Addison's copy, Tonson,* 1711	Wellesley
	13	-	2807	——————— *green morocco, Dublin,* 1724	Triphook
	10	-	2808	——————— - *Glasgow,* 1750	Do
	1	-	2809	Ministry, The New, a Collection of all the Satyrical Poems, Songs, &c. since the beginning of 1742, 1742	Allen
	4	-	2810	Mirabeau, Errotika Biblion, - - 1792	Triphook
	1	-	2811	Miracle. Histoire du Très-Saint Sacrement de Miracle, *plates,* - - - *Bruxelles.*	Warner

Manuscripts of the Bible, &c. Missals, and Offices of the Church.

£	s	d	Lot	Description	Buyer
	13	-	2812	Biblia Latina, *on vellum, with illuminated capitals.* ——	Triphook
1	7	-	2813	The Book of Psalms, on vellum, *red morocco.* —— July 26, 1728. Examined this MS. by Wickliff's Bible in Queen's Colledge, Oxon. and find it the same. Jo. Ames. See Note.	Heber
3	13	6	2814	Les Sept Pseaumes de la Penitence. A modern MS. on vellum, delicately written, with the capitals illuminated in gold, and each page surrounded by a gold border, *red morocco, with blue morocco lining.*	Jarman
9	14	-	2815	Explication de l'Oraison Dominicale Presentée à Monseigneur, le Prince de Galles. Beautifully written on vellum, by Berthelet, in 1692, for Prince James, son of James the Second, with eight highly coloured and splendid miniatures. Each page is encircled with a border of gold, *bound in red morocco, with the Royal Arms.*	Triphook
18	-	-	2816	Epistolæ Sancti Pauli ad Romanos, &c. a beautiful specimen of Calligraphy, on vellum, with illuminated capitals and gold borders to all the pages, bound in red morocco. At the beginning of the volume is the following note: "The two Paintings in this Book of St. Paul and St. Jerome, with the Flowers and Insects on the borders, were painted by the celebrated French Artist, Marolles, and the MS. was written by the famous Writing Master, Monchaussée."	Do
1	1	-	2817	Missale Romanum of the Fifteenth Century, on vellum, *with four paintings, yellow morocco, ruled.*	King
6	12	-	2818	Missale Ecclesiæ Romanæ cum Psalmis, MS. of the Fifteenth Century, upon vellum, with 45 miniatures, and painted borders, and Arms of the Family for whom it appears to have been executed, *red morocco, with clasps.*	Arch
8	8	-	2819	Officium B. M. Virginis cum Calendario, with 16 paintings and borders of flowers, &c. *bound in satin.*	Jarman
16	5	6	2820	——————— secundum Consuetudinem Romanæ Curiæ, a beautiful MS. of the Fifteenth Century, on vel-	Triphook

lum, with illuminated capitals, and borders of flowers. It contains ten miniatures, very splendidly executed, which are said to have been painted by Girolamo, the son of Francesco dai Libri, bound in crimson satin, with silver gilt ornaments, &c. with a Virgin and Child engraved on silver on one side.

2821 ———————— an Italian manuscript of the Fifteenth Century, upon vellum, with the capital letters painted with great taste and delicacy. See MS. Note, *blue morocco.*

2822 Missale sive Officium Beatæ M. Virginis cum Calendario. A very beautiful Book of Offices, executed at Bruges in 1531. It contains 32 miniatures of the Birth and Passion of Christ, of the Twelve Apostles, &c. painted with a taste and delicacy of execution far superior to the generality of Flemish Missals. The Calendar is also ornamented with appropriate emblematic devices to each month. It is said to have been executed for the celebrated Diana of Poitiers. It concludes thus: " Author ac scriptor hujus operis presentis nomen est ei, Antonius Van Damme moram trahens Brugis anno 1531, *bound in red velvet, enclosed in a silver gilt fillagree case, and a blue morocco case.*

2823 Horæ B. M. Virginis, MS. of the Fifteenth Century, upon vellum, with illuminations and borders of flowers, *calf.*

2825 Missale Romanum cum Calendario, on vellum, with 14 miniatures, and illuminated capitals and borders, *blue morocco.*

2826 Officium Beatæ Mariæ Virginis cum Calendario. A beautiful specimen of Italian Calligraphy of the beginning of the Sixteenth Century. It has 16 large miniatures very splendidly painted and illuminated with arabesque borders to the opposite pages, in gold and colours. *In very rich old morocco binding, in compartments with clasps, in the finest preservation.*

2827 Heures à l'Usaige de Romme, printed upon vellum, with engraved borders, and illuminations, *coloured, red morocco, in compartments,* *Paris, Hardouyn, sans date.*

2828 Missale Romanum, printed upon vellum, with illuminations and engraved borders, *a very fine copy in old binding in compartments; ruled,* *Paris, Simon Vostre, sans date.*

2829 ———————— printed upon vellum, with cuts, *en couleur de gris, black morocco, Paris, Hardouin sans date.*

2830 ———————— on paper, with plates and engraved borders, *ruled,* - *Simon Vostre, sans date.*

2831 Horæ Beatissimæ Virginis Mariæ, printed upon vellum,

with coloured plates, and illuminated capitals, bound in old morocco, with morocco lining, in compartments, *Antverp, Plantin,* 1570

2832 Mizard, Secrets de la Lune, opuscule non moins plaisant que utile, - - *Paris,* 1571

2833 Mocquet's Travels and Voyages in Africa, Asia, and America, translated by Pullen, *plates,* - 1696

2834 Moench, Methodus Plantas Horti Botanici Marburgensis describendi, *russia,* - *Marburgi,* 1794

2835 Moise, Rose d'Amore raccolte nel Giardino delle Muse, *Vicenza,* 1615

2836 Moliere, Œuvres de, par Bret, 6 vol. *best edition, red morocco, fine copy,* - - *Paris,* 1773

2837 Moliere's Works, in English and French, 10 vol. *plates,* 1755

2838 Molimbrochius's Curiosities of Scurvy Grass, englished by Sherley, - - 1676

2839 Molinet, les Faitz et Dictz de, one leaf MS. *Paris,* 1537

2840 Moncada, Expedicion des los Catalanes y Aragoneses contra Turcos y Griegos, - - *Madrid,* 1777

2841 Moncrif, les Chats, *cuts,* - *Rotterd.* 1728

2842 Moncrife, Essais sur la Necessité et sur les Moyens de plaire, *red morocco,* - - *Amst.* 1738

2843 Monde (Le) des Cornuz où sont specifiées diverses Manières de Cornes, - - - *sans note.*

2844 Money Masters all Things, or Satyrical Poems, 1698

2845 Monpensier, La Princesse de, *red morocco,* *Paris,* 1674

2846 Montague's (Lady Mary W.) Works, 5 vol. 1803

2847 Montaigne, Essais de, 10 vol. *thick paper, portrait inserted, Londres,* 1754

2848 Montaigne, Le Proumenoir de Monsieur de, *blue morocco, Rouen,* 1607

2849 Montalte, Les Lettres Provinciales, *yellow morocco, Cologne,* 1657

2850 Montani Humanæ Salutis Monumenta, *many plates, blue morocco, with joints,* *Antverp. Plantin,* 1751

2851 Montemayor, La Diane de, 3 vol. *red morocco, Paris, Bonfons,* 1587

2852 ———————— Espagnol et François, par Pavillon, *red morocco,* - *Paris.* 1603

2853 Montesquieu, Le Temple de Gnide, *plates, green morocco, Paris,* 1796

2854 Monti, La Rivoluzione Francese, - 1804

2855 Mont-Sacre. Les Amours de Cleandre et Domiphile, *Paris,* 1598

2856 Montenay, Cent Comparaisons de Vertus et Emblemes Chrestiens avec des Vers Latins, Espagnols, Italiens, Allemans, Anglois et Flamands, *portrait and many plates, green morocco*, - - *Franckf.* 1819

2857 Montigny, L'Ombre de Necrophone Vivant Chartier, *green morocco*, - - - *Rouen*, 1622

2858 Moralistes Anciens, Collection des, 15 vol. *green morocco*, *Paris*, 1782, &c.

2859 Mori Epigrammata, *frontispiece with portrait, by Marshall*, *Londini*, 1638

2860 Mori Utopia, *blue morocco*, - *Amst. Janson*, 1631

2861 Morisoti Henricus Magnus, *old ornamented binding, red morocco, ruled*, - - *Geneve*, 1627

2862 Morlini Novellæ cura Caron, *calf extra, by Roger Payne*, *Paris*, 1799

2863 Mors. The Complaynt of Roderyck Mors, somtyme a gray fryre, unto the parliament howse of Ingland, his natural cuntry, EXCESSIVELY RARE, *inlaid, russia, Imprinted at Savoy, per Franciscum de Turona, no date.*

2864 Mortimer's Lectures on Commerce, Politics and Finances, 1801

2865 Motte, Fables Nouvelles dediées au Roy, *plates, red morocco*, *Amst.* 1727

2866 Mouhy, les Delices du Sentiment, *sans date.*

2867 Moulin, Le Rabelais Reformé, *Brusselle*, 1620

2868 Moult, Les Propheties Perpetuelles de, *Paris*, 1741

2869 Moyen de Parvenir (par Beroalde), 2 vol. in 1, *sans date.*

2870 Moyne, Saint Louys ou la Sainte Couronne Reconquise, Poeme Heroique, *plates, red morocco*, *Paris*, 1666

2871 Mugetto, Le Barbet Mignon, 2 vol. in 1, *Francof.* 1749

2872 Mulieres Homines non esse Disputatio Perjucunda, *red morocco*, - - *Hagæ Com.* 1641

2873 Muret, Ceremonies Funebres de toutes les Nations, *black morocco*, - - *Paris*, 1679

2874 Mureti et Turneri Epistolæ et Hymni, *Ingolst.* 1584

2875 Murray, Prodromus Designationis Stirpium Gottingensium, *Gottingæ*, 1770

2876 Murtola Canzonette ed altre Rime, *Venezia*, s. a.

2877 Musæi Opusculum de Herone et Leandro, Græce, *green morocco*, - - *Venet. Aldi.* 1517

2878 Musæ Etonenses, 2 vol. - *Londini*, 1755

2879 ———— 2 vol. - - *ib.* 1795

2880 Muse Folastre, 2 vol. in 1, *blue morocco*, *Rouen*, 1608

2881 Muses Gaillardes des plus beaux Esprits de ce temps, *green morocco* - - - - *Paris*, 1609

2882 Muses en Belle Humeur ou Chansons et autres Poesies Joyeuses, - - *Ville Franche*, 1742

2883 Autre Exemplaire, - - *ib.* 1742

T

£	s.	d.	No.	Description	Buyer
	11	-	2884	Muse in Good Humour, or Collection of Comic Tales, 2 vol. - - - 1751	Allen
1	8	-	2885	Musarum Deliciæ, the Muses Recreation, - 1655	Rodd
	10	-	2886	Musgrave, Belgium Britannicum, *many plates,* 1719	Anderson
3	-	-	2887	Musick, The Praise of, (by Joseph Barnes), *green morocco, black letter,* - - *Oxenford,* 1586	Triphook
1	9	-	2888	Naogeorgii Judas Iscariotes Tragœdia, et duæ Sophoclis Tragœdiæ, Ajax Flagellifer et Philoctetes, ab eodem autore carmine versæ, *russia,* - *Stutgardiæ.*	Rodd
	2	-	2889	Naufrage des Isles Flottantes ou Basiliade du celebre Pilpai, 2 vol. - - - *Messine,* 1753	Triphook
	17	-	2890	Naunton's Fragmenta Regalia, or Observations on the late Queen Elizabeth, her Times and Favourites, *morocco,* 1650	Payne
	13	-	2891	Navarre, Les Poesies du Roy de Navarre, 2 vol. *Paris,* 1742	Hare
	13	-	2892	Navarre, l'Histoire du Royaume de Navarre, *russia, Paris,* 1606	Rodd
	3	-	2893	Neandri Græcæ Linguæ Erotemata cum præfatione Melanchthonis, *russia,* - - *Basil.* 1561	Do
	3	-	2894	Needham de Inscriptione quadam Ægyptiaca Taurini inventa, - - - *Romæ,* 1761	Hare
	1	-	2895	Neri de Arte Vitraria, Libri VII. - *Amst.* 1686	Heber
	14	-	2896	Neve's Cursory Remarks on some of the Ancient English Poets, particularly Milton, - - 1789	Jewis
1	5	-	2897	Neugebaveri Electorum Symbolorum Heroicorum Centuria Gemina, *plates, red morocco, with joints, Francof.* 1619	Clarke
	5	-	2898	Nevizani Sylvæ Nuptialis Libri sex, *Lugduni,* 1545	Hallam
	17	-	2899	Newton's Compleat Herbal, *plates, russia,* 1752	Heber
	6	-	2900	Nichols's Select Collection of Poems with Notes Biographical and Historical, 4 vol. - - 1780	Christie
	5	-	2901	Nigroni Dissertatio Subsesiva, *blue morooco, with joints, Delingæ,* 1621	Triphook
	6	-	2902	Nile. A short relation of the River Nile, of its Source and Current, - - - 1669	Hare
	8	-	2903	Nine par M. D. B. 2 vol. - - *Amst.* 1756	Hancock
			2904	Nobbes's Compleat Troller, - - 1682	
	18	-	2905	Nobilitie. A Treatise of the Nobilitie of the Realme — Of the Baronage of England when they sit in Parliament, 1642, in 1 vol. *russia.*	Hay
	4	-	2906	Noble, Histoire Secrete des conspirations des Pazzi contre les Medicis, - - *Paris,* 1698	Johnston
1	7	-	2907	Nonnus, Les Dionysiaques ou les Voyages, les Amours et les Conquestes de Bacchus aux Indes, *plates, by Crispin de Passe, purple morocco,* - *Paris,* 1625	Triphook
	13	-	2908	Nostradamus, Les Vrais Centuries et Propheties, *yellow morocco,* - - - *Amst.* 1668	Christie

£	s.	d.	Lot	Description	Buyer
	13	-	2909	Nourjahad, the History of, *green morocco*, 1792	Allen
1	18	-	2910	Novelle Scelte Rarissime stampate a spese di XL. Amatori, 1814	Triphook
4	-	-	2911	Novelle tre dell' Ingratitudine, dell' Avarizia de' Principi Moderni, e dell' Eloquenza. "A very rare edition, printed in the 16th Century, without date, place, or name of the Printer. The Novels are ascribed to Marco de Mantoa," *bound in russia*, Stanley Catalogue.	Hare
	7	-	2912	Novels. A Banquet for Gentlemen and Ladies, consisting of nine Tragi Comical Novels, - 1718	Christie
	3	-	2913	——— Twelve delightful Novels displaying the Stratagems of Love and Gallantry, - - 1719	Triphook
	7	-	2914	Nugæ Venales sive Thesaurus Ridendi et Jocandi, 1689	Rodd
	1	-	2915	Nuit (La) et le Moment, - - 1786	Triphook
	17	-	2916	Nyenborg Variarum Lectionum Selecta figuris æneis applicata, *green morocco*, - *Groningæ*, 1660	Do
2	1	-	2917	Obedience of a Christen Man, and how Christen rulers ought to governe, where in also (yf thou marke diligently thou shalt fynde eyes to perceave the crafty conveyaunce of all jugglers, *black letter*, RARE, *At Marlborow in the lande of Hesse*, 1528	Clarke
	6	-	2918	Obliging Husband and Imperious Wife, - 1722	Perry
	18	-	2919	Obsopæus de Arte Bibendi, *blue morocco, with joints*, *Francof.* 1578	Triphook
3	15	-	2920	Officers of the Kingdom as they are placed by Act of Parliament, A. 31 Hen. 8. A manuscript on vellum, with the arms of all the great officers emblazoned, *blue morocco*.	Percival

Quarto.

£	s.	d.	Lot	Description	Buyer
3	3	-	2921	Miroir de la Cruelle et Horrible Tyrannie Espagnole perpetree au Pays Bas, par le Tyran Duc d'Albe et autres.—La deuxiesme partie de les Tyrannies commises aux Indes Occidentales par les Espagnols, *plates, blue morocco*, *Amst.* 1620	Hibbert
1	14	-	2922	Mirrour of Princely deedes and Knighthood: wherein is showed the worthinesse of the Knight of the Sunne, and of his brother Rosicleer, &c. translated by Tyler, *Thomas East.*	Triphook
3	3	-	2923	Mischle, Liber typis hebraicis impressus, *wood cuts, russia.*	Do
18	-	-	2924	Mirrour, (The) of Majestie or Badges of Honour conceitedly emblazoned with emblems annexed, poetically unfolded, *red morocco*, RARE, - *W. Jones*, 1619	Perry

Missals and Offices of the Church, &c.

5	15	6	2925	A Manuscript of the 15th century upon vellum, in glass case, one side of which contains the Horæ Beatæ Mariæ Virginis, the other, Precationes Christo et Matri.	Booth
	10	6	2926	Missale Romanum, a manuscript upon vellum of the 15th century, with illuminations, several in an unfinished state, *red morocco.*	Rodd
2	2	-	2927	Missale Ecclesiæ Romanæ on vellum, with two large illuminations, and borders of flowers, &c.	Jarman
10	-	-	2928	Missale in Lingua Germanica, a MS. of the 15th century, upon vellum, with nine large Paintings, and Capitals tastefully illuminated, *bound in velvet.*	Do.
3	15	-	2929	Pontificale Romanum, a Manuscript of the 15th century upon vellum, with the Capital Letters richly illuminated in gold and flowers, splendidly bound in purple velvet.	Triphook
13	2	6	2930	Precationes Piæ, a MS. on vellum, with nine large splendidly painted Miniatures and borders of flowers to each page, *red morocco.*	Do.
7	17	6	2931	Missale Romanum cum Festis Sanctorum et Calendario, a Manuscript of the 14th century upon vellum. It contains a great many Miniatures painted in a very curious and fanciful Stile of Illumination. Each Month of the Calendar is ornamented with appropriate Emblematical Devices. See MS. note at the beginning, *red morocco.*	Arch
57	15	-	2932	Missale Ecclesiæ Romanæ, a very beautiful Flemish Manuscript of the 15th century upon vellum. It has 21 large Miniatures, which are painted (especially the Figures of the Apostles) with a correctness and delicacy of finish very rarely seen in Missals of this description, *bound in red velvet, with gold ornaments, and a blue morocco case.*	Triphook
53	11	-	2933	Officium Beatæ Mariæ Virginis secundum Consuetudinem Romanæ Curiæ, cum Calendario. A most splendid Manuscript of the beginning of the 16th century, upon vellum. It contains six large Miniatures with Groups of figures, &c. on the borders of a very brilliant and elaborate execution. The Capital Letters are also richly illuminated with figures, &c. and the Signs of the Zodiack are painted to each month of the Calendar, *bound in blue velvet, with gold ornaments, in a red morocco case.*	Do.
18	-	-	2934	Psalterium Latine, a Manuscript of the 15th century, upon	Do.

£	s	d	Lot	Description	Buyer
				vellum, with very delicate Paintings of Groups of Figures and Landscapes, in the Capital Letters, and Borders richly illuminated with Figures, Candelabras, &c.	Triphook
1	14	-	2935	Moerman Apologi Creaturarum, *plates, red morocco, with joints,* - - *Plantin, sine anno.*	Do.
	4	-	2936	Moine (Pierre le) Devises Heroiques et Morales, expliquées par vers, *red morocco,* - *sans date.*	Do.
3	15	-	2937	Molitormii's (Ulricus) De Lamiis et Phitonicis mulieribus, *wood cuts, blue morocco, fine copy,* RARE, *impressum Coloniæ apud conventum predicatorum in destolckgasse per me Cornelium de Zyrichzee,* - - 1489	Clarke
	2	-	2938	Monardus's Booke which treateth of two Medicines most excellent against all Venome, the Bezaar Stone and the hearbe Escuerconera, *black letter,* - 1580	John
	19	-	2939	Monde, L'Ymage de, *black letter, Paris, Trepperel, sans date*	Booth
	8	-	2940	Monk's (General) Letters and Declarations, 1660	
4	11	-	2941	Montaigne, Essais de, cinquiesme édition augmentée d'un troisieme Livre, *portrait, red morocco, Paris, sans date.*	Heber
1	5	-	2942	Montaneæ Emblematum Christianorum Centuria, *blue morocco, with joints,* - *Heidelbergæ,* 1602	Triphook
	10	-	2943	Montelion, the Knight of the Oracle, The Famous History of, - - - *no date.*	Hay
	15	-	2944	Montesquieu, Le Temple de Gnide avec figures gravées, par Le Mire, *large paper, red morocco, Paris,* 1772	Black
4	14	6	2945	Moor's Hindu Pantheon, *plates, russia,* - 1810	Cochran
2	-	-	2946	Morelli Thesaurus, *portrait, russia,* - *Etonæ,* 1764	Barclay
3	13	6	2947	Morgant, Histoire de Morgant le Geant et de plusieurs autres Chevaliers et Pers de France, *wood cuts, blue morocco,* - - - *Troyes,* 1608	Arch
2	5	-	2948	Mori. Prima Parte delle Novelle di Ascanio de' Mori da Ceno, *red morocco, scarce,* - *Mantova,* 1585 *There never was a second part published.*	Black
1	6	-	2949	Morin. Declaration de Morin sur la Revocation de ses pensees, 1649. Declaration de Morin, de sa Femme et de Mlle. Malherbe touchant ce qu'on les accuse de faire une Secte Nouvelle. Arrest de la Cour de Parlement, qui condamme Morin, 1663. Procez verbal et execution de mort du meme Morin, 1663, *green morocco.*	Triphook
4	10	-	2950	Morley's Madrigals to Foure Voices with some Songs added by the author, *T. Este,* 1600, *the two last pages manuscript.*—Morley's Madrigals, first Booke, *T. Est,* 1594. Two Copies, the last of which is supplied in MS. *red morocco.*	Perry
	5	-	2951	Moro, Rappresentatione del Figliuolo Prodigo, *Venetia,* 1585	Triphook

£	s.	d.	No.	Lot	Buyer
	6	-	2952	Morritt's Vindication of Homer, and Bryant's Observations, *Eton*, 1799	Payne
1	2	-	2953	Morton's New English Canaan, containing an Abstract of New England, - - *Amst.* 1637	Cochrane
19	19	-	2954	Morlini Novellæ, *first edition, very fine copy, morocco, from the Roxburghe Collection,* EXTREMELY RARE, *Neapoli in ædibus Joan. Pasquet de Sallo,* 1520	Triphook
	4	-	2955	Morwing's Booke of Destillatyon, *black letter, John Day,* 1565	Edwards
	12	-	2956	Motte (De La) Fables Nouvelles, *large paper, plates, Paris,* 1719	Triphook
	14	-	2957	Moyne (Le) de l'Art des Devises avec divers recueils de Devises du mesme Auteur, *blue morocco, Paris,* 1666	Edwards
6	12	6	2958	Muld Sacke, or the Apologie of Hic Mulier to the late Declamation against her, *portrait on the Title, russia,* RARE, - - - 1620	Clarke
	6	-	2959	Mundus Muliebris, or the Ladie's Dressing Room unlocked and her Toilette spread, - - 1690	Triphook
	2	-	2960	Mundinus de Omnibus humani Corporis interioribus Membris, - *Argent. Martinus Flack.* 1513	Heber
1	10	-	2961	Mundus Parvus, *plates, fine impressions, blue morocco, with joints,* - - *Francof.* 1618	Edwards
1	1	-	2962	Murner Logica Memorativa, cum jucundo pictas matis exercitatio, *wood cuts, Argent. Gruninger,* 1509	Arch
	6	-	2963	Musæum Hermeticum Reformatum et Amplificatum, *Francof.* 1677	Triphook
1	8	-	2964	Musæi Moschi et Bionis quæ extant omnia, Gr. Lat. cura Whitfordi, *plates, blue morocco, Londini.* 1659	Edwards
1	7	-	2965	Musicæ Antiquæ Auctores Septem, Gr. et Lat. Meibomii, 2 vol. *russia,* - - *Elzevir.* 1652	Calkin
6	16	6	2966	Music, a Compleat Collection of Haydn, Mozart and Beethoven's Symphonies, 6 vol. *half bound in russia.*	Jarvis

Folio.

£	s.	d.	No.	Lot	Buyer
2	15	-	2967	Mer des Histoires depuis la Creation du Monde, 2 vol. *russia, with joints, ruled, Paris, N. Couteau,* 1543	Rodd
9	9	-	2963	Merlin, Les Prophecies de, *fine copy, from the Roxburghe Collection,* RARE, - *Paris, Verard,* 1498	Triphook
9	9	-	2969	Michault (P.) Doctrinal du Temps present, *wood cuts, remarkably fine copy, red morocco,* EXTREMELY RARE, *sans aucune note.*	Do.
	6	-	2970	Michele, Diario del' ultimo Viaggio Bottanico fatto da Pier Antonio Michele nel 1736, per lo Stato Veneto.	Smith

£	s.	d.	Lot	Description	Buyer
				Martini Catalogo al Fasciculo di Monte Baldo delle Piante Naturali, 2 vol. *manuscript on paper.*	
15	15	-	2971	Miller's Gardener's Dictionary, by Martyn, 4 vol. *russia, with joints,* - - - 1807	Barclay
16	16	-	2972	Milles et Amys, le quel racompte les gestes et haulx fais du chevalier Miles tres renomme et de Amys, &c. *wood cuts, fine copy, very rare,* *Paris, Verard, sans date.*	Hibbert
5	7	6	2973	Missale Ecclesiæ Noviomensis, a Manuscript upon vellum of GREAT ANTIQUITY. It is of an oblong form, and appears by the Capital Letters and singular Illuminations to have been written in the 11th Century, *bound in red velvet.*	Payne
35	14	-	2974	Missale ad Usum Ecclesiæ Portugallensis. A most splendid Manuscript upon vellum, executed in 1557, for John the Fourth, King of Portugal, and Catherine his Queen. It contains above a THOUSAND ILLUMINATIONS painted with a great variety, richness and brilliancy of colouring, and each page is surrounded with a border and other ornaments of gold, *bound in red morocco.*	Triphook
4	4	-	2975	Monde. L'Œuvre qui a pour Titre Le Monde plein de Fols, curious grotesque plates, with borders after designs by Van Sasse, with descriptions in French, German and Dutch verse, - - *no date.*	Sir J. G. Egerton
22	1	-	2976	Murphy, a Collection of Quotations from a variety of Authors on Wit, Humour, Ridicule, Burlesque, Raillery, Causes of Laughter; on Comedy and Farce; on the Characters of Falstaff, Abel Drugger, and Don Quixote; on Shakspeare and Ben Jonson. A Manuscript of 500 pages in the hand writing of Arthur Murphy, and appears to have been made with a view to some publication on the above subjects.	Payne
15	-	-	2977	MYRROUR OF THE WORLD, or thymage of the same, FIRST EDITION, two leaves wanting, and two supplied by Manuscript, *red morocco,* WILLIAM CAXTON, 1481	Triphook
55	13	-	2978	MYRROUR OF THE WORLD, *wood cuts, second edition, very fine copy, in blue morocco,* WILLIAM CAXTON, 1481	Do.
7	10	-	2979	Mystere des Actes des Apostres, 2 vol. in 1. *black letter, wood cuts, red morocco,* *Paris, par N. Cousteau,* 1537	Do.
15	-	-	2980	Mystere de la Conception et Nativite de la Vierge Marie avec la Nativité, &c. de Jesus Christ, 3 Mysteries in 1 vol. *wood cuts, fine copy, blue morocco,* *Par. M. le Noir,* 1507	Do.
10	-	-	2981	Napoleon, Tableaux Historiques de ses Campagnes en Italie, *plates, russia,* - - *Paris,* 1806	Sir J. G. Egerton
2	2	-	2982	Nicolo, di Nicolai, Le Navigationi et Viaggi nella Turchia *plates,* - - *Venetia,* 1580	Heber

£	s.	d.	No.	Description	Buyer
1	3	-	2983	Nephi (Augustini) Icones Regum Hispanorum et Portugallensium, *fine impressions*, MS. Title, *Romæ*, 1684	Hay
1	1	-	2984	North's (Lord) Forest of Varieties, 3 Parts, 1645	Edwards
1	-	-	2985	North Britain, The, 4 vol. - - 1769	Black
	19	-	2986	Octavii Boldonii Theatrum Temporaneum Æternitati Cæsaris Montii Sacrum, *many plates, blue morocco*, *Mediol*. 1636	Triphook
19	19	-	2987	Oeder Icones Plantarum sponte nascentium in Regnis Daniæ et Norvegiæ, 19 Fasciculi, 6 vol. *fine copy with coloured plates, splendidly bound in russia, with joints*, *Hauniæ*, 1762, 1794	Cochran
3	5	-	2988	Olaus Magnus de Gentibus Septentrionalibus, *plates, red morocco, ruled*, - - *Romæ*, 1555	Payne
1	2	-	2989	Olao Magno Historia delle Genti Settentrionali, *plates*, *Vinegia*, 1565	Hibbert
4	4	-	2990	Ordonnances de l'Ordre de la Toison d'Or, *beautifully printed* UPON VELLUM, *red morocco, in a red morocco case*, - - *Le Noir*, 1523	Triphook for Watson Taylor Esq

SIXTEENTH DAY'S SALE.

Octavo et Infra.

£	s.	d.	No.	Description	Buyer
	3	-	2991	Officium Hebdomade Sanctæ Secundum consuetudinem Sanctæ Romanæ Ecclesiæ, . - *Venetiis*. 1561	Triphook
	7	-	2992	Officium Beatæ Mariæ Virginis, *russia*, *Paris. Kerver*, 1577	Do
	2	-	2993	Offitio della Chiesa per tutto l'anno, *red morocco*, *Parigi*. —	Do
	8	-	2994	Ogden's Sermons, 2 vol. - *Cambridge*, 1786	Hitchcock
	10	-	2795	Olaus Magnus de Gentibus Septentrionalibus, *Antv*. 1562	Heber
15	4	6	2996	Olivier de la Marche, Le Chevalier Delibere, A MANUSCRIPT UPON VELLUM, with fifteen large Illuminations, *red morocco*. Scriptum Bruxellæ Anno Millesimo quingentesimo quadragesimo VII.	Triphook for W. Taylor Esq
	4	-	2997	Olivier, La Pandore de Janus Olivier, pere spirituel et evesque d'Agan, *red morocco*, - - *Paris*. 1542	Do
1	2	-	2998	Olympes (Le Grand) des Histoires Poetiques du Prince de Poesie Ovide Naso en sa Metamorphose, *wood cuts, red morocco*, - - - *Paris*. 1543	Do

£	s.	d.	No.	Description	Buyer
	4	-	2999	Olympo. Opera Nuova chiamata Pegasea, per Baldassare Olympo delli Alessandri da Sasso Ferrato, *red morocco*, *Vineg. Bindoni*. 1524	Triphook
	2	-	3000	Omphalii Prolegomena in Ciceronis pro Cecinna Orationem, *Colinæus*, 1535. Sambuci Tirnaviens de Imitatione a Cicerone petenda Dialogi tres, *Antv*. 1563.	Heber
	14	-	3001	Ophiomaches, or Deism Revealed, 2 vol. *blue morocco*, 1749	Evans
2	-	-	3002	Opuscles d'Amour, par Heroet, La Borderie et autres Divins Poetes, *morocco, ruled*. - - *Lyon*. 1547	Rice
	1		3003	Oracle (l') consulté par les Puissances de la Terre, *green morocco*, - - - *Rome*. 1688	Triphook
	1	-	3004	Ordene (l') de Chevalerie, - - *Paris*. 1759	Rodd
1	1	-	3005	Ordynaunces that the Emperour hath caused to be red and declared in his presence to the States of his countrees of those partyes at theyr assemblynge to his Magestye in 1531, &c. *black letter, blue morocco*, *Robert Wyer*	Do
	3	-	3006	Ori Apollinis Hierogliphica Gr. *Basiliæ*. Idem Latinè. *Paris*. 1521. Hippocratis Aphorismi, *Haganoæ, russia*.	Heber
	2	-	3007	Ori Apollinis Hieroglyphica, Gr. et Lat. *cuts, blue morocco*, - - - *Romæ*, 1597	Triphook
	8	-	3008	Ori Apollinis Selecta Hieroglyphica, Gr. et Lat. *cuts, red morocco*, - . - *Romæ*. 1606	Clarke
	4	-	3009	Ori Apollinis de Sacris notis et Sculpturis libri duo, Gr. et Lat. *cuts*, - - *Paris. Kerver*, 1551	Triphook
	8	-	3010	Orus Apollo de Hieroglyphicis notis a Bernardino Trebatio latinitate donatus, - *Paris. R. Steph*. 1531	Clarke
			3011	Ori Apollinis de Sacris Ægyptiorum notis Libri, Lat. et Fr. *cuts, red morocco*, - *Paris*. 1574	
	16	-	3012	Orus Apollo les Sculptures ou Graveures Sacrées, *cuts, morocco*, - - - *Paris. Kerver*. 1553	Triphook
6	-	-	3013	Orphica cum notis H. Stephani, Eschenbachii, Gesneri, Tyrwhitti, recensuit Hermannus, LARGE VELLUM PAPER, on which only TWELVE COPIES were printed, *blue morocco, with joints*, - - *Lipsiæ*. 1805	Perry
	11	-	3014	Orthodox Communicant (The), with plates, engraven by Sturt, - - - 1721	Do
	1	-	3015	Osmont Dictionnaire Typographique, 2 vol. *Paris*. 1768	Triphook
	3	-	3016	Ossian's Poems, 3 vol. - - 1796	Dickenson
	18	-	3017	Ossian, Poesie di, di Cesarotti, 4 vol. - *Padova*. 1773	Calkin
	19	-	3018	Othonis. Incipiunt Opera super constitutiones provinciales et Othonis, *black letter, red morocco*, *per me Wynandum de Worde*, 1517	Rodd
	4	-	3019	Oufle, a History of the Ridiculous Extravagancies of Monsieur Oufle, - - - 1711	Triphook
1	10	-	3020	Overbury (Sir Thomas), his Wife, with Additions of new Newes and divers more Characters, *red morocco, with joints*, - - - - 1618	Clarke

U

£	s.	d.	Lot	Description	Buyer
	3	-	3021	Overbury (Sir Thomas), his Wife, with Additions of new Newes and divers more Characters, Calf - - - 1618	Perry
3	10	-	3022	Ovidii Opera, 3 vol. *green morocco*, *Aldus*. 1515-1516	Payne
3	3	-	3023	Ovidii Opera, 3 vol. *old morocco binding*, - *Antv*. 1561	Heber
1	11	6	3024	Ovidii Opera, ex recens Heinsii, 3 vol. *blue morocco, morocco inside*, - - *Elz*. 1629	Triphook
1	-	-	3025	Ovidii Opera, 3 vol. *blue morocco*, - *Amst*. 1713	Evans
	8	-	3026	Ovidii Opera, 4 vol. *blue morocco*, *Brindley*, 1745	Triphook
	11	-	3027	Ovidii Metamorphoses, *red morocco*, - *Aldus*, 1502	Heber
	6	-	3028	Ovidii Metamorphoses, *wood cuts, red morocco*, *Paris*. 1570	Triphook
	7	-	3029	Ovide, Metamorphoses d', en vers François, par Marot et Aneau, *wood cuts and borders, green morocco, Lyon*. 1556	Do
1	-	-	3030	Ovide, Les Metamorphoses en vers François, par Habert, 3 vol. *cuts, green morocco*, - - *Par*. 1587	Do
	6	-	3031	Ovide, Metamorphoses en Rondeaux, 2 vol. *plates*, *Amst*. 1697	H.
	10	6	3032	Ovidii Nasonis Metamorphoses Argumentis Brevioribus ex Luctatio Grammatico collectis expositæ, *plates, morocco*, *Antv. Plantin*. 1591	Triphook
	4	-	3033	Ovid's Epistles, translated by several Hands, *cuts*, *Tonson*. 1720	Heber
4		-	3034	Ovid's Elegies, by C. Marloe. Epigrams, by I. Davis, *scarce*, - - *at Middleburgh*,	Perry
	5	-	3035	Ovide Travesty ou les Metamorphoses Burlesques, *frontispiece*, - - - *Paris*. 1659	Clarke
	11	-	3036	Ovidio Istorico, Politico, Morale brevamente spiegato, e delineato con Artificiose figure, *cuts*, - *Venet*. 1688	Molteno
	5	-	3037	Ovington's Essay upon the Nature and Qualities of Tea, *blue morocco*, - - - 1709	Christie
	11	-	3038	Oweni Epigrammata, *red morocco*, - *Elzevir*. 1628	Lepard
	9	-	3039	———————, *blue morocco*, *Elzevir*. 1647	Triphook
	10	-	3040	———————, *red morocco*, - *Lugduni*. 1668	Heber
	3	-	3041	Oxford Sausage, boards - - *Oxford*, ——	
	5	-	3042	Another copy. Calf - - - *ib* ——	Dickenson
	3	-	3043	Pædiani Expositio in quatuor Orationes M. T. Ciceronis, *Venet. Aldi*. 1522	Heber
	2	-	3044	Palæphati de Incredibilibus Liber, Græce et Latine, Tollii, *blue morocco*, - - *Elzev*. 1649	Payne
	4	-	3045	Pagan's Description of the Country of the Amazons, translated by Hamilton, - - - 1661	Christie
	12	-	3046	Palais Royal, Histoire du, *blue morocco*, *sans date*.	Booth
	1	-	3047	Palais du Silence, Conte Philosophique, 2 vol. *Amst*. 1754	Rodd
	5	-	3048	Palatines, State of the, for Fifty Years past. ——	Dickenson
			3049	Pallavicino, Opere Scelte di, 2 vol. - *Villefranca*. 1673	
1	14	-	3050	Palmerin d'Angleterre, Histoire du Preux Vaillant et tres Victorieux Chevalier, 2 vol. *red morocco*, *Paris*. 1574	Rodd

£	s.	d.	Lot	Description	Buyer
	2	-	3051	Palmestry and Physiognomy, the Book of, englished by Withers. - - - - 1651	K.
	6	-	3052	Panthot, Traité des Dragons et des Escarboucles, *green morocco*, - - - *Lyon.* 1691	Triphook
	2	-	3053	Panurge, Le Nouveau, avec sa Navigation en l'Isle Imaginaire, - - - *Lyon.* 1616	Heber
	6	-	3054	Parabosco, gli Diporti di, *russia*, - *Venetia*, 1586	Triphook
2	3	-	3055	Paradin, Devises Heroiques, *many plates, blue morocco*, *Lyon. I. de Tournes.* 1551	Molteno
	5	-	3056	Paradin, Devises Heroiques et Emblemes augmentées, *blue morocco*, - - - *Paris.* 1614	Triphook
	5	-	3057	Paradini et Symeonis Symbola Heroica ex Gallico Idiomate in Latinum traducta, *plates, blue morocco*, *Antverp. Plantin.* 1562	Do
	5	-	3057	Paradini et Symeonis Symbola Heroica, *red morocco*, *Ib.* 1563	Heber
	2	-	3058	Idem Liber, *calf* - - *Antverp. Plantin.* 1600	Christie
	11	-	3059	Paradoxes contre la Commune Opinion en forme de Declamations Forenses, *green morocco, ruled*, *Paris. Estienne.* 1554	Triphook
5	12	6	3060	Parangon de Nouvelles, Honnestes et Delectables, *wood cuts, Lyon.* 1532. Les Parolles Joyeuses des Nobles Anciens par Petrarcque, in 1 vol. *red morocco*, *Lyon.* 1532	Heber
	10	-	3061	Paris. La Fleur des Antiquitez, Singularitez et Excellences de la Noble Ville de Paris, *blue morocco, ruled*, *Paris.* 1543	Clarke
	1	-	3062	Paris, Voyage Pittoresque de *plates*, *Paris. sans date.*	Johnston
	1	-	3063	Parismus, Prince of Bohemia, - - 1724	Christie
	6	-	3064	Park's Travels into Africa, - - 1800	King
	4	-	3065	Parny, Poesies Erotiques, *thick paper, vellum, Paris.* 1778	Triphook
7	7	-	3066	Parrot's Laquei Ridiculosi, or Springes for Woodcocks *very scarce, G. Steevens's copy, blue morocco*, *London.* 1613	Rodd
	14	-	3067	Parson's Leicester's Common-Wealth, and Leicester's Ghost, *portrait of the Earl of Leicester, by Marshall*, 1641	Blundell
2	14	-	3068	Parthenia Sacra, or the Mysterious Garden of the Sacred Parthenes, *many plates, red morocco, scarce*, *John Cousturier*, 1633	Clarke
	17	-	3069	Paschalius de Coronis, *blue morocco, by Derome*, *Lugd. Bat.* 1681	Triphook
	1	-	3070	Parthenius Nicaensis de Amatoriis Affectionibus Latine, *Froben.* 1531	Heber
	8	-	3071	Pasori Manuale Græcarum Vocum N. Testamenti, *blue morocco*, - - - *Elzev.* 1640	Clarke
1	5	-	3072	Pasquillorum Tomi Duo, *Eleutheropoli (Basil)* 1544	Payne
1	15	-	3073	Pasquille, Les Visions de, avec le Dialogue de Probus, *red morocco*, - - - - 1547	Heber

3074 Pasquin, Les Risees de, dans l'Ambassade de M. de Crequi à Rome, *red morocco*, - *Cologne*, 1647

3075 Passe Partout Galant, - *a Constantinople*, ——

3076 Passions Personify'd in Fables. *no date.*

3077 Pastissier François tres utile a toute sorte de Personnes, *blue morocco*, - - *Amst. Elzevier.* 1655

3078 Paterculi Historia notis Vossii, *red morocco*, *Lugd. Bat. Elzevir.* 1639

3079 Idem Liber, *red morocco*, - *Ib. Elzev.* 1664

3080 Alia Editio, *yellow morocco*, - *Ib. Elzev.* 1678

3081 Paterculi Historia Romana notis Ruhnkenii, 2 vol. *russia*, *Lugd. Bat.* 1779

3082 Pathelin, La Farce de Maistre Pierre, *red morocco*, *Paris.* 1723

3083 Pathwaye to perfect Knowledge, *black letter, wants title, blue morocco.*

3084 Patin, Relation des Voyages en Allemagne, Angleterre, Hollande, &c. *plates*, - - *Amst.* 1695

3085 Patrick, History of the Life and Death of St. of Ireland, *green morocco.* - - - *Lond.* 1685

3086 Patte, La, du Chatte, Conte Zinzimois, 1741. Gaudriole, Conte, *Haye*, 1746, in 1 vol.

3087 Patten's Expedition into Scotland, of Prince Edward, Duke of Somerset, Uncle unto Edward VI. EXTREMELY RARE, *fine copy, red morocco, with Portrait of Edward VI.* - - *London, R. Grafton*, 1548

3088 Paul, La Vie de Pere, traduit de l'Italien, *Elzev.* 1661

3089 Pauli Thomæ Engolismensis Poemata - 1593

3090 Paulo, Historia de las Grandezas de las Provincias Orientales sacada de Marco Paulo, por Don Martin de Bolea, *green morocco*, - - *Caragoça*, 1601

3091 Pays, Amitiez, Amours, et Amorettes, par Mr. Le, *Amst.* 1693

3092 Peacham's Period of Mourning in Memorie of the late Prince, - - - 1789

3093 Pecke's Parnassi Puerperium, or some Well-Wishers to Ingenuity, in Epigrams from Martial, More, &c. *blue morocco*, - - - 1659

3094 Peerage of England, Scotland, and Ireland, 3 vol. 1778

3095 Pegme, Le, de Pierre Coustau mis en Francoys par Lanteaume de Romieu, Gentilhomme d'Arles, *wood cut borders to all the pages, many plates, green morocco*, *Lyon. Bonhomme*, 1555

3096 Pentateuch, The, translated by Tindal, *black letter, wood cuts, some leaves supplied from another edition, blue morocco. Printed at Marlborow, in the Land of Hesse*, 1530

3097 Percel, Gordon de, de l'Usage des Romans, 2 vol. *Amst.* 1734

3098 Percey's Compleat Swimmer, or the Art of Swimming, *blue morocco*, - - - 1658

3099 Percy's Reliques of Ancient English Poetry, 3 vol. 1775

3100 Perefixe Histoire du Roy Henry le Grand, *red morocco*, *Elzevier*. 1661

3101 Perefixe Histoire de Henri le Grand, UNCUT, *portrait inserted, blue morocco, with joints*, - *ib*. 1679

3102 Peretti, Vocabulario Poetico, - - 1800

3103 Perez Cartas de Antonio, Secretario de Estado del Don Phelippe II. *Paris*. Perezii ad Comitem Essexium et ad alios Epistolæ, *Paris*, in 1 vol. *morocco, ruled*.

3104 Periandri Noctuæ Speculum *wood cuts*, *Francof*. 1567

3105 Perieres, Bonaventure des, Les Contes et Nouvelles Recreations de, 3 vol. *green morocco*, - *Amst*. 1735

3106 Perriere, La Morosophie en Cent Emblemes par Guillaume de la, *blue morocco, with wood cut borders*, *Lyon*. 1553

3107 Perriere Guill. de la, Les Considerations des quatre Mondes, *with borders round the pages, blue morocco*, *ib*. 1552

3108 Peru La Chronica del, por Pedro de Cieça de Leon, *Anvers*. 1554

3109 Peruse, Les Œuvres de Jan de la, *red morocco*, *Lyon*. 1577

3110 Pescatore, la Morte di Ruggiero continuata a la Materia de l'Ariosto, *wood cuts, fine copy, morocco, with joints*, *Vinegia*. 1549

3111 Petit, L'Heure du Berger, *blue morocco*, *Paris*, 1664

3112 PETRARCHA, Triomphi e Sonetti, a very beautiful Italian Manuscript of the beginning of the 16th Century, upon vellum. *It is written in a very delicate and legible hand, and the titles to the different chapters are illuminated in letters of gold, splendidly bound in morocco.*

3113 Il Petrarcha con Nuove Dichiarationi, *Lyone, Rovillio*, 1551

3114 ——————— con Annotationi di Bembo, *Venetia, Bevilacqua*, 1562

3115 Il Petrarcha con Dichiarationi non più stampate, *red morocco*, *Venetia Nicolini*, 1573

3116 Petrarcha, Rime Scelte di, - *Londra*. 1801

3117 Petrarque, Les Triumphes traduictes en Vers, par le Baron d'Opede, *wood cuts, yellow morocco*. *Paris. Janot. s. date*.

3118 Petrarque, Les Triumphes en Prose, *wood cuts, green morocco*, - - - *Paris, Janot*. 1539

3119 Petrarque, Les Triumphes en Prose, 2 vol. *wood cuts*, *Paris, Groubleau*, 1554

3120 Petrarque, Toutes les Evvres Vulgaires de, en Vers Francoys par Vasquin Philieul, *morocco*, *Avignon*, 1555

3121 Petronii Arbitri Satyricon et Priapeia notis Variorum, *russia*, - - - *Amst. Bleau*. 1669

3122 Petronii Satyricon, *red morocco*, UNCUT, *Amst*. 1677

£	s.	d.	Lot	Description	Buyer
	16	-	3123	Petrone, La Satyre de, traduite en François avec le Texte Latin, 2 vol. *plates, blue morocco* *Cologne*, 1694	Triphook
	10	-	3124	Peyreri Præadamitæ Exercitatio in Versus Epistolæ Pauli et Systema Theologicum, 1655. Hilperti Disquisitio de Præadamitis in 1 vol. *red morocco*, *Amst.* 1656	Do

Quarto.

£	s.	d.	Lot	Description	Buyer
	12	-	3126	Nazari della Tramutatione Metallica sogni tre, *Bres.* 1572	Heber
3	15	-	3127	Needle, a Schole House for the, *plates, russia*, 1624	Triphook
1	15	-	3128	Nef (Le Grant) des folz du monde, *wood cuts, black letter, yellow morocco*, title manuscript, - *Lyon*. 1529	Do
1	13	-	3129	Nef (La) des Princes et des batailles de Noblesse, *wood cuts, black letter, scarce*, - - *Lyon*. 1502	Arch
1	5	-	3130	Neperi Logarithmorum Canonis Descriptio, *russia*, *Edin*. 1614	Do
1	1	-	3131	Nevell (Mr.) The Generous Usurer in Thames Street, who alloweth his Maid usually a Black Pudding to Dinner, 1641	Clarke
	4	-	3132	Newes from France, a Relation of the Fire at Paris the 7th March, 1618, - - 1618	Anderdon
	13	-	3133	News from Hell, Rome and the Innes of Court, by J. M. (supposed to be John Milton), *scarce*, - 1642	Perry
15	15	-	3134	New Custome, a new Enterlude, no less wittie than pleasant, *black letter*, VERY RARE, - - 1573	Heber
17	17	-	3135	Nichols's Progresses and Public Processions of Queen Elizabeth, 2 vol. *plates, russia*, - 1788	Booth
	2	-	3136	Nicols's Faithful Lapidary, - - 1659	John
1	1	-	3137	Nicolai, Le Navigationi et Viaggi nella Turchia, di Nicolo di Nicolai, *plates after Titian, russia*, *Anversa*. 1576	Triphook
	7	-	3138	Nicolay, Les Navigations Peregrinations et Voyages faicts en la Turquie, - - *ib*. 1576	Arch
	7	-	3139	Nicolai Commentatio de Ritu Antiquo et Hodierno Bacchanaliorum, - - *Helmestadii*, 1679	Payne
4	8	-	3140	Niebuhr Voyage en Arabie avec le Recueil de Questions par Michaelis, 4 vol. *plates*, - *Amst*. 1766, &c.	Do
12	5	-	3141	Niger's (Franciscus) Tragedie, entituled Freewyl, translated by Henry Cheeke, *black letter*, RARE, *about* 1589	Heber
2	6	-	3142	Norden's Speculum Britanniæ, *maps, blue morocco*. ———	Booth
	5	-	3143	Norden's Christian Comfort unto all English Subjects not to dismaie at the Spanish Threats, 1596	Rodd
3	10	-	3144	Nosce Teipsum, by John Davys, 1602. Davies's Mirum in Modum, a Glimpse of God's Glorie and the Soule's Shape, 1602, *two scarce Poems*.	Perry
1	13	-	3145	Novelle (Cento) Amorose de i Signori Accademici Incogniti, *red morocco*, - - *Venet*. 1651	Burrell

3146 Novelle Otto, LARGE PAPER, *red morocco, with joints,* RARE, - - - *Londra,* 1790

3147 Nychodemus Gospell, *wood cuts, red morocco, fine copy,* VERY RARE, - WYNKYN DE WORDE, 1511

3148 Ochine's Tragoedie, or Dialoge of the unjuste usurped primacie of the Bishop of Rome, translated by Ponet, *black letter,* - - *Gwalter Lynne,* 1549

3149 Office (The) of the Holy Week according to the Missal and Roman Breviary, enricht with many Figures, *blue morocco,* - - - *Paris,* 1670

3150 Oger le Dannois Duc de Dannemarche qui fut l'un des douze Pers de France, *wood cuts, blue morocco,* *Troyes.* 1610

3151 Oh Read over D. John Bridges, for it is a worthy Worke, an Epitome of his fyrste Booke against the Puritanes, *black letter, red morocco.*

3152 Old Newes newly revived, or the Discovery of all Occurrences happened since the Beginning of the Parliament, 1641

3153 Oppianus de Piscatu et de Venatione, Gr. et Lat. *Paris, Turnebus,* 1555

3154 Oppianus de Venatione Bodino interprete, cum comment. ejusdem, *red morocco, ruled,* *Lutet. Vascosan,* 1555

3155 Oratio Dominica C. L. Linguis Versa, edente J. J. Marcel, *blue morocco, with joints,* - - *Paris,* 1805

3156 Orapollinis Hieroglyphica, Gr. et Lat. curante de Pauw, *Traj.* 1727

3157 Orders appointed by his Majestie to be observed, for preventing the Dearth of Graine and Victuall, 1630

3158 Oræi Eicones Mysticæ, *plates, blue morocco, with joints,* *Francof.* 1620

3159 Orio, Le Iscrittioni poste sotte le vere Imagini de gli Huomini Famosi, *red morocco, Fiorenza, Torrentino,* 1552

3160 Orme's History of the Military Transactions of the British Nations in Indostan, 3 vol. - - 1780

3161 Ornatus and Artesia, The most pleasant History of, *see MS. note,* - - - - 1683

3162 O'Rourke's Treatise on the Art of War, - 1778

3163 Otia Sacra, (Poems) *plates by Marshall,* - 1648

3164 Ovalle Historica Relacion del Reyno de Chile, *morocco,* *Roma.* 1646

3165 Ovidii Metamorphoses, Figuræ elegantissime a Cr. Passæo laminis æneis incisæ, *russia, with joints,* *Colon.* 1607

3166 Ovidii Metamorphoses Figuris expressa, *Augsb.* 1681

3167 Oxford. Answer of the Chancellor, &c. of the University of Oxford to the Petition, Articles of Grievance, and Reasons of the City of Oxon, - 1678

3168 Paley's Moral and Political Philosophy, - 1786

£	s.	d.	Lot	Description	Buyer
7	-	-	3169	Panzer Annales Typographici ab Artis Inventæ Origine ad Annum 1536, 11 vol. - *Norimb.* 1793-97	Arch
	5	-	3170	Parable of the Wycked Mammon, *black letter. Prynted at Malborowe, in the Land of Hesse, by Hans Luft,* 1528	Rodd
1	1	-	3171	Paracelsi Prognosticatio Figuris illustrata, *wood cuts, inlaid, bound in red morocco,* - *sine nota.*	Payne
1	-	-	3172	Aliud Exemplar Figuris æneis illustrata, *red morocco,* *sine anni nota.*	D°
32	-	6	3173	Paradyse of Daintie Devises, 1600. The Workes of a young Wyt, trust up with a Fardell of prettie Fanices, by N. Breton, title MS. 1577. Southern's Poems, addressed to the Earl of Oxenford, wanting the title. Watson's Centurie of Love, made perfect in Mr. Steevens's hand-writing, 4 vol. in 1, interleaved with curious notes and illustrations, by G. Steevens, Mr. Ritson, Mr. Parke, Sir W. Musgrave, and Lord Orford.	Triphook
3	10	-	3174	Paradyse of Daintie Devises, the title and several leaves supplied by MS. with numerous manuscript additions and explanations, *russia.*	Perry
8	12	6	3175	Paris, Tableau Historique et Pittoresque de, 2 vols. VELLUM PAPER, *numerous plates, green morocco, with joints,* - - - *Paris,* 1806	Triphook
4	16	-	3176	Paris e Viena, Innamoramento de, novamente Historiado, *wood cuts,* RARE, - - *Vinetia,* 1511	D°
1	1	-	3177	Parismus of Bohemia, the Famous, Delectable, and Pleasant History of, *russia,* - - 1681	Warrender
1	8	-	3178	Parke's Travels into Africa, *plates,* - 1799	D°

Folio.

£	s.	d.	Lot	Description	Buyer
16	5	-	3179	Orme's Collection of British Field Sports, illustrated with beautifully coloured Engravings, 1807. Orme's Oriental Field Sports, with Forty beautifully coloured Engravings, in 1 vol. *splendidly bound in russia, with joints,* 1807	Triphook
7	17	6	3180	Orose, les Histoires du Paul, traduites en François, 2 vol. *wood cuts, fine copy, ruled,* *Paris, Verard, sans date.*	Arch
	10	6	3181	Ortus Sanitatis de Herbis et Plantis, &c. *wood cuts, red morocco, with joinis,* Imperfect. - resold - 1517 (sold first time for 1.11 -)	Haworth
39	18	-	3182	OVERLAET, One Hundred and Twenty five admirable Drawings in Pen and Ink, by Overlaet, of Antwerp. They consist either of Copies or Imitations from various Masters, and are drawn with very great spirit and accuracy, *bound in russia,* - 1755, 1761	Payne

3183 Ovidii Metamorphoseon Libri Quindecim, *very fine copy in red morocco,* 'of this extremely rare and beautiful impression of the Metamorphoses of Ovid.' See Biblioth. Spencer, vol. 2, page 204, *sine ulla nota, sed circa* 1472

3184 Ovidio Methamorphoses Vulgare, *wood cuts, splendidly bound in green morocco, Venetia per Zoane Rosso,* 1497

3158 Ovide. La Bible des Poetes Metamorphozé, *wood cuts, Paris, Philippe le Noir,* 1523

3186 Pallas, Flora Rossica jussu Catherinæ Secundæ, 2 vols. in 1, *coloured plates, russia, with joints, Petropoli,* 1784

3187 Palisot-Beauvois, Flore d'Oware et de Benin en Afrique, vol. 1, *coloured plates, russia, with joints, &c. Par.* 1805

3188 Paris, Versailles, St. Cloud, &c. Vues de, · 1658

3189 Paris. Etudes prises dans le bas Peuple ou les Cris de Paris en cinq Suites, *plates, russia, with joints, ib.* 1737

3190 Parkinson's Theatrum Botanicum, or Herball, *plates,* 1640

3191 Parkinson's Garden of Pleasant Flowers, *russia, with joints,* - - - 1629

3192 Parr. The Life of the Old, Old, very Old Parr. A Manuscript, by Ireland, illustrated with Portraits of Parr, and of the Kings and Queens in whose Reign he lived. There are Portraits of Richard the Third by Cross, of Queen Elizabeth by Marshall, and of Howard Earl of Surry, by Hollar, &c. *bound in russia.*

3193 Parthenia, or the Maydenhead of the first Musicke that ever was printed for the Virginals, composed by Bird, Bull, and Gibbons, ingraven by William Hole, VERY RARE, - - - 1611

3194 Passaiges d'Oultre Mer faictz par les François contre les Turcqz et Mores oultre Marins, *black letter, Michel le Noir,* 1518

3195 Patina, Pitture Scelte e Dichiarate, *very fine impressions, with the Family of More, hog-skin, with joints, Colonia,* 1691

SEVENTEENTH DAY'S SALE.

Octavo et Infra.

3196 Phædri Fabulæ, *Paris,* 1629, Petronii Satyricon, *Plantin,* 1614, in one vol.

3197 Phædri Fabulæ ex recens. Laurentii, *vellum, Amst.* 1667

3198 ——— cura Maittaire, *blue morocco, Lond.* 1713

3299 Phædri Fabulæ et Syri Sententiæ, *red morocco,* *e Typogr. Regia.* 1729

3200 Phedre, Les Fables de, avec le Latin, *red morocco, with red morocco lining,* - *Paris,* 1647

3201 ——————— avec Figures en Taille-douce, *blue morocco,,* - - - *ib.* 1669

3202 Philippi (Beroaldi) Epistolæ, *red morocco,* *Parisiis, Johannes Lambert, s. anno.*

3203 Philippes's Treatise on the Defence of the Honour of the Right High &c. Marie Queene of Scotland, with a Declaration of her right to the Crowne of England, VERY RARE, *venetian morocco,* - *Leodii.* 1571

3204 Phillips's Complete Collection of the Poets, 1675

3205 Philocophus or the Deafe and Dumbe Man's Friend, *blue morocco,* - - - 1648

3206 Philomathi Musæ Juveniles, *green morocco, with joints,* *Colon.* 1645

3237 Philothei Symbola Christiana, *many plates,* *Lugd. Bat.* 1682

3238 Physiophili Opuscula a Martio, *Augustæ Vindel.* 1784

3209 Phytologia Britannica Latine et Anglice, *interleaved,* 1650

3210 Piccolomini, La Sphere du Monde par, traduitte par J. Goupyl, *ruled,* - - *Paris,* 1550

3211 Pibrac, Les Quatrains du Sieur, enrichis de Figures, *blue morocco,* - - - *ib.* 1640

3212 Pieces Nouvelles et Galantes en Prose et Vers, 2 parts in one, *blue morocco,* - *Cologne,* 1667

3213 Pierii Dissertatio pro Sacerdotum Barbis, *Leodii.* 1643

3214 Pierre, J. de la, Le Grand Empire de l'un et l'autre Monde divisé en trois Royaumes, *frontispiece and portraits by Passe, red morocco,* - - *Paris,* 1636

3215 Pignorii Symbolicæ Epistolæ, *red morocco,* *Patavii* 1629

3216 Pilpay, Les Fables de, ou la Conduite des Roys, *Paris,* 1698

3217 Autre Exemplaire, *yellow morocco,* - *ib.* 1698

3218 Pindari et Octo Lyricorum Carmina, 2 vol. *red morocco,* *Steph.* 1600

3219 Pindari Carmina Græce, *blue morocco,* *Oxon.* 1808

3220 Pinelliana Bibliotheca a Jac. Morellio descripta, 6 vol. *Venet.* 1787

3221 ——————— *with the prices* - 1789

3222 PITOCCO. Orlandino, composto per Limerno Pitocco da Mantoa, Teofilo Folengi. ORIGINAL EDITION, VERY RARE, *from Col. Stanley's Collection, blue morocco,* *Vinegia Gregorio de Gregori,* 1526

£	s.	d.	Lot	Description	Buyer
	5	-	3223	Plague, Collection of Pieces relating to the, of 1665, and the Plague of Marseilles, - 1721	Triphook
	5	-	3224	Planquais' Spanish and English Grammar, 1807	Dickenson
	11	-	3225	Another Copy, *blue morocco,* - - 1807	Triphook
	3	-	3226	Plantarum Historia cum Figuris, *russia,* *Lugduni,* 1557	Christie
	1	-	3227	——— Catalogus Oxoniensium, - 1648	Triphook
	1	-	3228	——— circa Harefield Fasciculus, - 1737	
	7	-	3229	Plat's Garden of Eden, or Description of Flowers and Fruits, *green morocco,* - - 1659	D°
1	8	-	3230	Platonis Opera Latine a Ficino, 5 vol, *red morocco, ruled, Lugduni.* 1550	D°
	7	-	3231	Plauti Comœdiæ, *red morocco,* - *Venetiis, Aldi.* 1522	D°
	1	-	3232	Plauti Comœdiæ a Camerario, vol 1, *red morocco, Antwerp. Plantin,* 1566	Warner
	12	-	3233	Plauti Comœdiæ, *red morocco,* *Amst. Elzev.* 1652	Payne
	8	-	3234	Plauti Comœdiæ ex recens. Gronovii, 2 vol. *blue morocco, Amst. Wetstein.* 1721	Triphook
2	15	-	3235	Plinii Historia Naturalis, 3 vol. *Elzevir,* 1535,—Plinii Epistolæ, *Elzev.* 1640, 4 vol. *splendidly bound in green morocco.*	D°
	3	-	3236	Plot, The, in a Dream, or the Discoverer in Masquerade, 1682	Warner
	2	-	3237	Pluton Maltotier, Nouvelle Galante, - *Cologne.* 1708	D°
	2	-	3238	Poems upon several occasions, - 1673	Triphook
	5	-	3239	Poems, a volume of, containing Beaumont's Bosworth Field, 1710,—Congreve's Temple of Fame, 1709,—Howard's Duel of the Stags, 1709,—Addison's Letter from Italy,—Earl of Mulgrave's Essay on Poetry,—Phillips's Poems,—Dryden's Absolam and Architophal,—Overbury's Wife, &c. - - 1709	Christie
	3	-	3240	Poesies, Recueil de Diverses, *yellow morocco,* *Leide.* 1652	Payne
	7	-	3241	Poesies Diverses (de Frederic le Grand) 2 vol. *green morocco,* - - - *Berlin,* 1762	Triphook
	10	-	3242	Poesies, Nouvelles, Galantes, Critiques, Latines et Françoises, *yellow morocco,* - *Londres, s. date.*	Warner
	1	-	2343	Poesies du XII. XIII. et XIV. Siecle Extraits de, *Lausanne,* 1759	Triphook
	9	-	3244	Poesie, Introduction à la, *blue morocco,* *Paris,* 1620	Payne
	19	-	3245	Poesis Tacens, Pictura Loquens, Formis Æneis delineata, *blue morocco,* - - *Dilingæ,* 1630	Clarke
	18	-	3246	Poetes Provensaux, Les Vies des plus Celebres et Anciens, *green morocco,* - - *Lyon,* 1575	Triphook
1	14	-	3247	Poetes François, Recueil des plus belles Pieces des, depuis Villon jusqu'à Benserade, par Babin, 5 vol. *russia, Paris,* 1692	Warner
	2	-	3248	Poet's Ramble after Riches, - - 1710	Clarke
	2	-	3249	Poetical Recreations, in two Parts, - 1688	Perry

3250 Poetry, Beauties of, Displayed, 2 vol. - 1757

3251 Pogonologie ou Discours Facetieux des Barbes, *yellow morocco*, - - - *Rennes*, 1589

3252 Poggio, Facetie di, Historiate, *red morocco*, *Vinegia, Bindoni*, 1547

3253 Pointer's Account of the Roman Pavement at Stunsfield, 1713

3254 Poissenot, L'Esté de, en trois Journees, *red morocco*, *Paris*, 1583

3255 Polidori Novelle Morali, 2 vol. *blue morocco*, *Lond.* 1804

3256 Politiano, Stanze di Messer Angelo, *red morocco*, *Vineg. Nic. Zoppino*, 1524

3257 Politiano Stanze di, *red morocco*, *Vinegia, Aldo*, 1541

3258 Political Merriment, or Truths told to some Tune, 1714

3259 Pollnitz, Memoires du Baron de, 5 vol. *Londres*, 1747

3260 Pompadour, Lettres de Madame la Marquise de, 3 vol. in 2, *red morocco*, - - *ib.* 1771

3261 Pompe, Contes et Historiettes Divertissantes, *red morocco*, *Paris*, 1688

3262 Pomponatii Tractatus de Immortalitate Animæ, *green morocco*, - - 1534

3262* Pomponius Mela de Situ Orbis, *Lugd. Bat.* 1743

3263 Ponet's (Busshop of Winchester) Apologie aunsweringe by Scriptures and aunceant Doctors a blasphemose Book by Gardiner and other Papists, *black letter*, VERY RARE, *blue morocco*, - *no date or place.*

3264 Pontani Opera Omnia, 3 vol. *red morocco*, *Venet. Aldi*, 1519

3265 Pontani Amores, *red morocco*, - *ib.* 1518

3266 Poole's English Parnassus, or a Helpe to English Poesie, 1657

3267 Pope's Works, with Notes, by Warton, 9 vol. *London*, 1797,—Pope's Homer's Iliad and Odyssey, with Notes by Wakefield, 11 vol. 1796, together 20 vol. *uniform, in russia.*

3268 Pope, Additions to the Works of, 2 vol. - 1776

3269 Porcelli, Basinii et Trebani Opuscula, *Colin.* 1539,—Mureti Juvenilia, *Paris*, 1553,—Sepini Amatoria, *Paris*, 1553, in one vol. *russia.*

3270 Porta, La Fisonomia dell'Huomo et della Celeste Fisonomia, *many plates, red morocco*, - *Venetia*, 1652

3271 Porta, La Magie Naturelle traduite de Latin, *red morocco*, *Lyon*, 1608

3272 Porter's Life of St. Edward the Confessor, - 1710

3273 Post of the World, containing the Antiquities of the most famous Cities in Europe, - *London, East*, 1576

3274 Postelli Concordia Alcorani et Evangelistarum, *Par.* 1543

£	s.	d.	Lot	Description	Buyer
	15		3275	Postelli Syriæ Descriptio, *apud Hier. Gormontium,* 1540	Clarke
	18	-	3276	Postellus de Fœnicum Literis seu de prisco Latinæ et Græcæ Linguæ Charactere, *red morocco,* *Paris, Gaultherot,* 1552	Triphook
	5	-	3277	Postel, Les tres-Merveilleuses Victoires des Femmes du Nouveau Monde, *red morocco,* - *Paris,* 1553	Do
	8	-	3278	Pot Pourri, Ouvrage Nouveau de ces Dames et de ces Messieurs, *green morocco,* - *Amst.* 1748	Do
1	3	-	3279	Pot Pourri a qui on voudra, *plates by Eisen, red morocco,* *Paris,* 1764	Arch
1	5	-	3280	Pourtraits Divers, *plates by le petit Bernard, red morocco,* *Lion. J. de Tournes.* 1557	Triphook
	2	-	3281	Pourtraits de la Cour pour le present, *blue morocco,* *Cologne.* 1667	Clarke
	1	-	3282	Pratensis de Arcenda Sterilitate, *Amst. Bleau.* 1657	Warner
sold for 2	5	-	3283	Prayer. The Booke of Common Praier and Administracion of the Sacramentes, *black letter,* RARE, *in blue morocco,* *in Ædibus R. Graftoni,* 1553 (Imperf.t — sold first time for 5.15.6 — The first small prayer)	Payne
5	5	-	3284	——— The Primer and Catechisme set forth at large with many Godley Prayers, *black letter, without date.* The Epistles and Gospels of every Sonday in the yeare, *John Awdely,* 1563, in 1 vol. *blue morocco, with joints,* RARE.	Do
	8	-	3285	——— The Primer imprinted by R. Grafton, 1546, *reprinted.*	Cochran
	10	-	3286	——— The Book of Common Prayer, *Barker,* 1638	Rodd
1	11	6	3287	——— The Book of Common Prayer, *plates by Sturt, red morocco, ruled,* - - *Oxford,* 1712	Cochrane
1	11	-	3288	——— Another Edition, *with plates by Sturt, red morocco,* 1717	Payne
	18	-	3289	——— The Book of Common Prayer, French and English, *red morocco,* - - *Oxford,* 1717	Arch
3	18	-	3290	——— The Book of Common Prayer, large 8vo. *in blue velvet, with a blue morocco cover,* *Cambridge, Baskerville,* 1761	Major Hay
1	19	-	3291	——— Another edition, *blue morocco, Baskerville,* 1762	Cochran
	18	-	3292	——— The Book of Common Prayer, *red morocco,* Jarvis. London, 1791	Warner
1	9	-	3293	——— The Book of Common Prayer, *green morocco,* 1792	Triphook
	10	-	3294	——— Another Copy, *blue morocco,* - 1798	Cochran
	14	-	3295	——— Another, *blue morocco,* - Lucellon 1799	Triphook
1	16	-	3296	——— The Book of Common Prayer, by Reeves, *with a set of wood cuts inserted, splendidly bound in yellow morocco,* - - - 1802	Johnston
	13	-	3297	——— Another Edition, *blue morocco,* - 1803	Cochran
	14	-	3298	Prayers used by William III. *blue morocco,* 1704	Johnston

£	s.	d.	Lot	Description	Buyer
	12	-	3299	Priapeia sive Diversorum Veterum Poetarum in Priapum Lusus, *red morocco, ruled, scarce,* *Venet. Aldi.* 1534	Triphook
	7	-	3300	——— ——— ——— cum Commentariis Scaligeri, *blue morocco,* - - *Patavii,* 1664	D^o.
	1	-	3301	Priapeia cum Notis, - - *sine anno.*	D^o.
	4	-	3302	Priapeia di Guterry Clugnicese. La Camilletta di Guttery Clugnicese, in 1 vol. - - *Parigi.* 1586	Rodd
	11	-	3303	Prideaux, La Vie de Mahomet, *plates, blue morocco,* *Amst.* 1699	Cochran
1	4	-	3304	Primaleon de Grece, L'Histoire de, 3 vol. in 4, *green morocco,* - - - *Lyon,* 1572	Triphook
	4	-	3305	Prince Apprius, Histoire de, tire d'un MS. Persan, 1728	Christie
	1	-	3306	Prince, The Perplex'd, - - *no date.*	Christie
	5	-	3307	Princesse, The Idea of a Perfect, in the Life of St. Margaret, - - - - - 1661	Rodd
	14	-	3308	Princesses Malabares, Les, ou le Celibat Philosophique, *green morocco,* - - - 1734	Arch
	11	-	3309	Prior's Poems, *blue morocco,* - *Tonson,* 1717	Major Hay
	2	-	3310	Pritii Introductio in Lectionem N. Testamenti, *Lipsiæ,* 1722	Cochran
	8	-	3311	Processus Juris Joco-Serius, - *Hanoviæ,* 1611	Triphook
	2	-	3812	Procez Criminel fait a Pierre Barriere dit la Barre, *Paris,* 1593, Arrest de la Cour contre Jean Chastel, 1594.—Amour d'un, Pere envers son Prince, 1595, in 1 vol. *red morocco.*	D^o.
2	-	-	3315	Procez et Amples Examinations sur la Vie de Caresme, Prenant, et plusieurs autres brochures libres, *red morocco.*	Lepard
	13	-	3316	Prognostication, a General, for ever, *Edinburgh,* 1619	Rodd
1	-	-	3317	Prologues non tant Superlifiques que Drolatiques, *russia,* *Rouan,* 1610	D^o.
	3	-	3318	Prologues tant Serieux que Facecieux, *Rouen.*	Triphook
	6	-	3319	Autre Examplaire, *russia,* - *Rouen,* 1610	D^o.

Quarto.

£	s.	d.	Lot	Description	Buyer
2	14	-	3320	Parke's Historie of the Great and Mightie Kingdome of China, translated from the Spanish, *black letter, green morocco* - - - 1588	Warden
	12	-	3321	Parkyns's Inn-Play, or Cornish-Hugg Wrestler, *plates, blue morocco,* - - - 1727	Triphook
	2	-	3322	Parliaments, The manner of holding, and other Parliamentary Tracts, - - - 1641	Major Hay
	7	-	3323	Parliamentary Tracts, Collection of, relative to Charles I. 2 vol. - - - 1641-2	Triphook

£	s.	d.	Lot	Description	Buyer
	4	-	3324	Parliaments Unspotted. Bitch in Answer to Prince Robert's Dog called Boy, - - 1643	Triphook
	1	-	3325	Parliament, The Judgements of the Lords assembled in, 1747	
	4	-	3326	Parliament of Ladies, - - 1647	Rodd
	3	-	3327	———— and Character of a Town Gallant, 1647	Do.
	6	-	3328	Parran, Traité de la Musique Theorique et Pratique, *Paris*, 1639	Triphook
5	18	-	3329	Pasquil's Passe, and passeth not, set downe in three Pees, Passe, Precession and Prognostication, by Nicholas Breton), *green morocco*, - *London*, 1600	Perry
	11	-	3330	Paulo Jovio, Dialogue des Devises d'Armes et de' Amours trad. par Phileul, avec les Devises de Symeon, *plates*, *Lyon. Guill. Rouille*, 1561	Triphook
	3	-	3331	Paulus Pater de Typis Literarum Germaniæ, *Lipsiæ*, 1710	Do.
5	5	-	3332	Peacham's Minerva Britanna, or a Garden of Heroicall Devices furnished with Emblemes impressed of sundry Natures, *fine impressions, green morocco*, *London*, 1612	Lepard
5	15	6	3333	Peele's Love of King David and Fair Bethsabe, with the Tragedie of Bethsabe, - - 1599	Jervis
	9	-	3334	Pegasus, or the Flying Horse from Oxford, *no date.*	Booth
	15	-	3335	Peil Tabula exhibens Processum seu Ordinem Ultimi Divini et Criminalis Judicii, *plates, blue morocco*, *Cliviæ*, 1625	Triphook
8	-	-	3336	Pembroke (Countess of), Discourse of Life and Death by Mornay, and Antonius, a Tragedy by Garnier, both done in English, - *W. Ponsonby*, 1592	Rodd
	3	-	3337	Penna, (Lorenzo), Li Primi Albori Musicali, *cuts of Musick*, *Bologna*, 1696	Christie
	12	-	3338	Peristromata Turcica Præsentem Europæ Statum Ingeniosis Coloribus repræsentans et Germania Deplorata, *vellum*,	Rodd
4	-	-	3339	Perotti Grammatica, Ars Metrica, &c. cum Textu Jodoci Badii Ascensii, *black letter, very scarce*, *Londini per Wynundum de Worde*, 1512	Do.
	1	-	3340	Pescetti, Il Cesare, Tragedia, - *Verona*, 1594	Triphook
1	15	-	3341	Pesto, Raccolta degli Antichi Monumenti della Città di, e di Pozzuolo, Cuma, et fra Girgenti Segeste e Selinunte, *many plates, blue morocco*, - *Roma, s. a.*	Collins
	1	-	3342	Peters (Hugh), Conference between the Old Lord Protector and the New General, - 1660	Rodd
	2	-	3343	Petition of the Gentle Women, &c. 1641.—Discoverie of six Women Preachers, 1641.	Christie
1	1	-	3344	Petrarcha, Sonetti e Trionifi, con l'Espositione di Gesualdo, *russia*, - - *Vinegia, Giolito*, 1553	Triphook

1	-	-	3345	Petrasancta de Symbolis Heroicis, *fine impressions of the plates, red morocco, with joints.* *Antverp.* 1634	Triphook
	19	-	3346	Ejusdem Alia Editio, *blue morocco, with joints, Amst.* 1682	Barker
	1	-	3347	Petrifications, Memoires pour servir à l'Hist. Naturelle de, *plates,* - - *Haye,* 1742	Triphook
	8	-	3348	Petter, Klare Ondevrichtinge de Worstel-Konst, *plates by Romeyn de Hooge, and portrait inserted, Amst.* 1674	Giles
	4	-	3349	Phædri Fabulæ, *russia,* - *Rob. Stephani,* 1617	Barclay
1	-	-	3350	Phædri Fabulæ notis Hoogstratani, *large paper, plates, Amst.* 1701	Do.
	6	-	3351	Phalaridis Epistolæ Latine ex Versione Aretini, *Florent. per Ant. Venetum, sine anno.*	Johnston
	12	-	3352	Philelfi Fabulæ, *first edition, wanting the last leaf, which contains the Colophon, russia,* - *Venet.* 1480	Triphook
	16	-	3353	Phillips's History and Antiquities of Shrewsbury, *plates, Shrewsbury,* 1779	Booth
	7	-	3354	Picquet. Shufling, Cutting and Dealing in a Game at Picquet, acted from 1653, 1658. - 1659	Perry
7	-	-	3355	Pierce Plowman, The Vision and Crede of, newlye imprynted after the Authour's Olde Copy, *fine copy, green morocco,* EXTREMELY RARE, *London, Owen Rogers,* 1561	Jarvis
	10	-	3356	Pierre de Provence et la Belle Maguelonne, *Paris, Bonfons, sans date.*	Triphook
1	15	-	3357	Pigafetta's Report of the Kingdom of Congo, translated by A. Hartwell, *plates,* - - 1597	Arch
	3	-	3358	Pignoria, Le Origini Padova, *plates, blue morocco, Padova,* 1625	Triphook
	18	-	3359	Pignori Mensa Isiaca qua Sacrorum apud Ægyptios Ratio et Simulacra explicantur, *numerous plates, russia, Venet.* 1605	Cochran
	14	-	3360	Aliud Exemplar, *plates,* - - *Amst.* 1669	Do.
5	10	-	3361	Pilgrymage of Perfeccyon very profytable for all Christen People to rede, with the Exposicyon of the Ave and the Creed, &c. *black letter, curious wood cuts,* VERY RARE, *Wynkyn de Worde,* 1531	Longman
4	5	-	3362	Pilkington's Turnament of Tottenham, published by W. Bedwell, *green morocco, with joints,* - 1631	Booth
	11	-	3363	Plantæ Clematidis Altera Species, Flore Purpureo, *plates, blue morocco,.*	Triphook
1	12	-	3364	Pistles and Gospels of every Sonday and Holy Day in the Yeare, *black letter, blue morocco, with joints. Abraham Veale, no date.*	Cochran
	19	-	3365	Plates, an oblong Volume of, Christ's Passion, &c. *By Callot and others, no date.*	Johnston
7	-	-	3366	Plates. A Volume of Emblematical Plates, from Old Masters, with Descriptions in Latin, *inlaid and bound in russia.*	Booth

£	s.	d.	No.	Lot	Buyer
7	-	-	3367	Plays.—Cupid's Whirligig, 1616.—Heywood's Woman kilde with Kindnesse, 1617, in one vol.	Booth
12	12	-	3368	——— The Shoo-Maker's Holyday, or the Gentle Craft, a Comedy, 1618.—Field's Amends for Ladies, a Comedie, 1618.—Chapman's May Day, a Witty Comedie, 1611.—Cupid's Whirligig, 1616, 4 plays in one vol. *russia.*	Kuell
1	16	-	3369	Plowden's Historical Review of the State of Ireland, 2 vol. in 3, - - - - 1803	Christie
1	11	6	3370	Poems, Collection of Manuscript, with a Table of the Contents, *blue morocco.*	Triphook
1	-	-	3371	——— a Collection of Poems and Poetical Epistles, &c. published from 1772 to 1780, 3 vol.	Perry
	3	-	3372	Poetry of Nature, selected from the Caledonian Bards. —	Booth
4	14	6	3373	Pogii Facetiarum Libri, A VERY RARE EDITION, *in russia,* - *Mediolani Scinczenceller,* 1481	Triphook
1	17	-	3374	Pogii Historiæ Convivales, Orationes, Epistolæ, &c. *venetian morocco,* *Parisiis a Johanne Parvo, sine anno.*	Do
1	10	-	3375	Pois, Le, Discours sur les Medailles et Gravures Antiques, *fine copy in red morocco, with portrait,* *Paris,* 1579	Clarke
1	1	-	3376	Politiano, Stanze di, cominciate per la giostra del magnificho Giuliano di Piero de Medici, et la Favola d'Orfeo, *Fiorenza, senza anno.*	Triphook
1	2	-	3377	Pomponius Mela et Alii de Situ Orbis, *very fine copy in red morocco,* - *Venetiis. Ratdolt,* 1482	Arch
	4	-	3378	Pontani Libri de Liberalitate, de Beneficentia, &c. *Neapoli per J. Tresser et Mart. de Amsterdam,* 1498	Triphook
6	6	-	3379	Ponthus. Histoire de Ponthus, Fils du Roy de Galice et de la Belle Sidoyne, Fille de Roy de Bretagne, *wood cuts, fine copy.* - *Paris, Michel le Noir, sans date.*	Do
1	14	-	3380	Pontificiorum Omnium Habitus cum Versibus Modii et Figuris Ammoni, *blue morocco, with joints,* *Francof.* 1588	Arch

Folio.

£	s.	d.	No.	Lot	Buyer
	14	-	3381	Penæ et Mathiæ de Lobel Stirpium Adversaria Nova, *plates, russia,* - - *Londini,* 1571	Arch
16	5	6	3382	Perceforest. La tres-elegante, delicieuse et tres-plaisante Histoire du tres noble Perceforest, Roi de la Grande Bretagne, 6 vol. in 3, *black letter, fine copy, red morocco,* *Paris, Gourmont,* 1531	Booth
18	18	-	3383	Perceval le Galloys, Tres plaisante et recreative Histoire de, *black letter, fine copy, blue morocco,* *Paris,* 1530	Triphook
6	-	-	3384	Petrarcha, le Sue Rime, 2 vol. *splendidly bound in green morocco, &c.* - *Parma, Bodoni,* 1799	Col. Hay
	2	-	3385	Peutinger, Inscriptiones Vetustæ Romanæ in Augusta Vin-	Johnston

deliçorum, *Schœffer*, 1520. Antiquitates in Urbe Moguntina, *Mogunt.* 1525, in one vol.

3386 Phebus des Deduitz de la Chasse des Bestes Sauvaiges et des Oyseaulx de Proye, *wood cuts, Paris, J. Trepperel, sans date.*—Le Livre du Roy Modus, et de la Royne Racio lequel fait mention commant on doit deviser de toutes manieres de Chasses, *curious wood cuts*, RARE, *Chambery, Ant. Neyret*, 1486

3387 Philelfi Satyræ, *first edition, red morocco, ruled, Mediolani, Christof. Valdarpher*, 1476

3388 Pigage, La Galerie de Dusseldorf, *plates, fine impressions, russia*, - - - *Basle*, 1778

3389 PILPAI FABULÆ. Hic est, Liber PARABOLARUM ANTIQUORUM SAPIENTIUM, et vocatur Liber Belile et Dimne, et prius quidem in Lingua fuerat Indorum translatus, &c. *wood cuts, fine copy, splendidly bound in red morocco, sine ulla notâ, sed circa* 1480

A book of very great rarity and curiosity. Panzer and Santander only mention one Latin edition of these celebrated Fables in the Fifteenth Century. See Panzer, Vol. IV. p. 106, and Santander, Vol. II. p. 376.

3390 Pilpai Fabulæ, another edition of the 15th century, *with wood cuts, russia*, - - *sine ulla notâ.*

3391 Pilpay, Favolas o Exemplario contra los Engannos y Peligros del Mundo, transferido en nuestra Lengua Castellana, *wood cuts, fine copy*, VERY RARE, *Emprentado enla Ciudad de Saragoça de Aragon*, 1531

3392 Piranesi, Vedute di Roma, 2 vol. *original edition, very fine impressions, uncut.* - - *senz' anno.*

3393 Pisani (Bartholomei), Summa de Casibus Conscientiæ, *Paris, Martinus et Ulricus Crantz, sine anno.*

3394 Pittoni, Imprese di Diversi Principi, Duchi, &c. con Stanze di Dolce, *russia*, - *Venezia senza anno.*

3395 Plans of Fortifications, &c. A large Collection of Drawings of Plans of Cities, Fortified Places, Battles, &c. with Plates of Towns, Fortifications, and Extracts of celebrated Battles, Sieges, &c. in four large volumes.

3396 Plantarum Historia Generalis plusquam mille Imaginibus Illustrata, 2 vol. *splendidly bound in russia, with joints, Lugduni, Rovillii*, 1587

EIGHTEENTH DAY'S SALE.

Octavo et Infra.

£	s.	d.	Lot	Description	Buyer
8	10	6	3397	Propertii Carmina, recensuit, illustravit, Kuinoel, 2 vol. *large paper, blue morocco, with joints,* EXTREMELY RARE, - *Lipsiæ.* 1805	Knell
3	10	-	3398	Protestant's Vade Mecum, or Popery displayed in its proper Colours, in thirty Emblems, *fine impressions, red morocco,* - - - 1680	Triphook
	8	-	3399	Proverbes, Dictionnaire des, François, *yellow morocco, Brusselles,* 1710	Dulau
	13	-	3400	Prudentii et aliorum Carmina, *a counterfeit of the Aldine Edition, printed at Lyons, red morocco.* *sine anno.*	Triphook
4	-	-	3401	Prudentii Carmina Heinsii, UNCUT, *green morocco. Amst. Elzev.* 1667	Arch
	4	-	3402	Psalmanaazar's Description of Formosa, - 1705	Giles
	11	-	3043	Psalmanaazar, Description de l'Isle Formosa, *plates, red morocco,* - - - *Amst.* 1708	Boswell
	7	-	3404	Psalmorum Davidis Liber, Græce et Latine, *blue morocco, Antverp. Plantin.* 1584	Heber
1	-	-	3405	Psalmi Davidis, Latine, *in rich binding in morocco, with morocco lining, ruled,* - *Rob. Steph.* 1556	Do
	8	-	3406	Psalterium Davidis, *blue morocco, Lugd. apud Elsev.* 1653	Triphook
	1	-	3407	Psalmen Davidis, *black morocco,* - *Leyden,* 1643	Christie
2	12	6	3408	Psalmes of David, after the Translation of the Great Bible, *black letter, in blue morocco,* - - 1553	Cochran
1	11	-	3409	Psalmes of David, in four Languages, *blue morocco,* 1643	Do
	13	-	3410	Pseaumes de David en Vers François, *bound in tortoise-shell, with silver clasps,* - - *Amst.* 1730	Triphook
1	11	6	3411	Pseaume 118, Heures Canoniales contenues dans le. The binding is worked on blue and yellow beads, with the words Ouvrage de Marguerite Genevieve de la Briffe, Comtesse de Choiseul fait par Elle le 1. Mars, 1758.	Do
1	1	-	3412	Ptholomeus, The Compost of, Prince of Astronomye, *black letter, wood cuts, russia, ruled, London, R. Wyer, no date.*	Arch
	7	-	3413	Puces, L'Origine des, - - *Londres,* 1749	Perry
	5	-	3414	Pulci, Sonetti di Franco e di Luigi, - 1759	Heber
	2	-	3415	Pulteney's View of the Writings of Linnæus, 1781	K
	5	-	3416	Pursuits of Literature, - - 1798	Christie
	16	-	3417	Another Copy, *red morocco,* - - 1801	Ponton
	3	-	3418	Irish Pursuits of Literature, - - 1799	Bentham
2	19	-	3419	Puteani Bruma sive de Laudibus Hiemis, *plates by Sadeler, white morocco,* - - *Monaci,* 1619	Clarke

3420 Puteani Ænigma Regium, *plates by Sadeler*, *Mon.* 1623

3421 Puttane. La Rettorica delle Puttane, *red morocco*, *Villa Franca*, 1673

3422 Puttanismo Moderne con il Novissimo Parlatorio. ———

3423 Quadriga Æternitatis sive Universi Generis Humani Meta, *plates by Sadeler, fine impressions, red morocco*, *Monaci.* 1619

3424 Quarles's Emblemes, *first edition, portrait and plates by Marshall and Simpson, russia*, - 1635

3425 Quarles's Emblemes, - - *no date*

3426 Quarles's Argalus and Parthenia, - 1677

3427 Queen's Closet Opened, Secrets in Physick, &c. 1671

3428 Querelle de Gaultier-Garguille et de Perrine sa Femme, *Vaugirard*,

3429 Queries humbly proposed to Count Zinzendorf, 1755

3430 Question Curieuse si M. Arnauld est Heretique, 1690. Avis sur la Maniere de Precher, 1733, in 1 vol.

3431 Quevedo l'Aventurier Buscon, Histoire Facecieuse, *Paris*, 1639

3432 Quinti Curtii Historia Alexandri, *red morocco*, *Elz.* 1633

3433 Rabelais, Les Œuvres de, 2 vol. *Amst. Elzevir.* 1663

3434 Autre Edition, 2 vol. *red morocco, ruled*, *ib.* 1666

3435 Autre Exemplaire, 2 vol. *red morocco*, - *ib.* 1675

3436 Le Rabelais Moderne ou les Œuvres de Rabelais mises à la portée de la plupart des Lecteurs avec des Notes, &c. 8 vol. *green morocco*, - - *Amst.* 1752

3437 Rabelais' Works, translated with Notes by Ozell, 5 vols. *plates*, - - - - - 1737

3438 Rabelais, Pantagruel, Roy des Dipsodes, restitue à son naturel, *yellow morocco*, - - *Lyon.* 1542

3439 Rabelais, La Plaisante et Joyeuse Histoyre du grand Geant Gargantua, *Valence*, 1547. Second et Tiers Livre de Pantagruel, 1547, in 1 vol. *wood cuts, red morocco.*

3440 Rabelais, Les Croniques du Roy Gargantua, *red morocco*, *Troyes, s. d.*

3441 ——— Entretien de Rabelais et de Nostradamus, de Scarron et de Moliere, *Cologne*, 1690. L'Ombre de Charles Quint, - - - 1688

3442 Rabelais, Les Songes Drolatiques de Pantagruel, in 120 plates, *very rare, green morocco*, - *Paris*, 1565

3443 Rabelais, Les Horribles Faictz et Prouesses de Pantagruel par Alcofrybas Nasier, *red morocco*, *Paris. s. date.*

3444 Rabelais, La Schiomachie et Festins faits a Rome au Palais du Cardinal du Bellay, - - *Lyon* 1549

3445 Rabelais Resuscite ou les Faicts du Grangosier Roy de Place vuide, *red morocco*, - *Paris*, 1614

3446 Rabutin, Hist. Amoureuse des Gaules, avec la Clef, *Elzev. s. date.*

3447 Rabutin Histoire Amoureuse des Gaules, 2 vol. *Col.* 1722

3448 Raclot, Vie de l'Empereu Charles V. 2 vol. *plates, Brusselles,* 1700

3449 Radcliffe's Italian, 3 vol. - - 1797

3450 Radcliffe's Mysteries of Udolpho, 4 vol. - 1795

3451 Ræmondi Fabulæ Joannæ Papæ quæ Pontificis Sedem occupasse credita est, *red morocco, scarce, Burdig.* 1606

3452 Raeuschel, Nomenclator Botanicus, - *Lipsiæ.* 1797

3453 Ragot, Les Ruses et Finesses de, - *Paris,* 1573

3454 Raii Angliæ Plantarum Catalogus, *Londini.* 1670

3455 Raii Synopsis Methodica Stirpium Britannicarum, *ib.* 1724

3456 Raimond Comte de Barcelonne, Nouvelle Galante, *Amst.* 1698

3457 Rainold's Refutation of Mr. Whitaker's Labours to Deface the late English Translation of the New Testament, *Paris,* 1583

3458 Raleigh's (Sir Walter) Instructions to his Sonne, 1633. The Advice of a loving Son to his aged Father, 1632, in 1 vol. *red morocco.*

3459 Ramsay's Collection of Songs, vol. 1, - 1750

3460 Randolph's Poems, *frontispiece, russia,* - 1652

3461 Rapini Hortorum Libri, *green morocco, Lugd. Bat.* 1668

3462 Rastel's Treatise, intitled Beware of Mr. Jewel. *Antverp, Fouleri,* 1566

3463 Ratts Rhimed to Death, or the Rump Parliament hang'd up in the Shambles, *blue morocco,* - 1660

3464 Ravanne, Memoires du Chevalier de, 2 vol. *Leige,* 1740

3465 Ravisii Epistolæ, - - - *Paris,* 1559

3466 Ray's Collection of English Proverbs, *Cambr.* 1670

3466* Another Copy, *russia,* - - *ib.* 1678

3467 Ray's Collection of English Words not generally used, 1674

3468 Raymond's Itinerary through Italy, - 1648

3469 Raynal, Histoire Philosophique et Politiqne des Etablissemens et du Commerce des Européens dans les deux Indes, 10 vol. and atlas in 4to. - *Geneve,* 1780

3470 Rawlinson's Catalogue of Books, *priced,* 1721

3471 Reading School Poems, Odes, &c. *red morocco,* 1804

3472 Rebellions, History of the, from the Norman Conquest to the present Times, - - 1717

3473 Recit Veritable de la Venue d'une Canne Sauvage en la Ville de Montfort, *russia,* - - *Rennes,* 1652

3474 Recreations Geographiques et Historiques, *many plates.* –

3475 Recreations Françoises ou Recueil des Contes à Rire, *Paris,* 1658

3476 Recreation, Devise et Mignardise Amoureuse, *red morocco, ib. s. d.*

3477 Autre Exemplaire, *wood cuts, Paris,* 1596. Le Blason des Fleurs, *wood cuts, Paris, s. d.* in one vol. *blue morocco.*

£	s	d	Lot	Description	Buyer
	9	-	3478	Recueil des Airs et Chansons du Theatre Italien gravez par M. H. 3 vols. - - - *Amst.* 1701	Christie
2	3	-	3479	Recueil de toutes Chroniques et Hystoires depuis le Commencement du Monde jusqu'au Temps Present, *black letter, blue morocco, Anvers. par Martin l'Empereur,* 1534	Arch
	13	-	3480	Recueil de ces Dames, *red morocco,* *Brusselles.* 1745	Ld Yarmouth
1	12	-	3481	Recueil des Faceties, contenant Le Blason des Barbes de maintenant. La Cholere de Mathurine. La Moustache des Filous arraché. Les Espices. Les Prognostications de Roupieux—Pasquin de Cour—La Promenade du Pre aux Clercs—La Camarade de l'Ante-Christ, in 1 vol.	Arch
3	10	-	3482	Recueil de la Diversité des Habits qui sont de present en Usage es Pays d'Europe, Asie, Afrique, &c. 61 plates, *printed in the cursive letter,* *Paris, Breton,* 1562	Heber
2	15	-	3483	Autre Exemplaire, 61 plates, *green morocco,* *ib.* 1564	Johnston
	14	-	3484	Recueil de Diverses Pieces Comiques, Gaillardes et Amoureuses, *russia,* - - *Leide,* 1699	Chamier
	1	-	3485	Recueil de Plusieurs Pieces servans à l'Histoire Moderne, *Cologne,* 1663	Triphook
1	7	-	3486	Recueil de tout Soulas et Plaisir et Paragon de Poesie, *red morocco,* - - - *Paris,* 1563	Heber
	5	-	3487	Redi, Soldani, Rosa, Menzini, &c. - *Venezia,* 1789	Christie
	3	-	3488	Redi, Bacco in Toscana, - *Londra.* 1804	Heber
5	19	-	3489	Regnier, Les Fortunes et Adversitez de feu noble homme Jehan, *black letter, curious wood cuts, red morocco, fine copy, very scarce,* - - 1526	Clarke
1	4	-	3490	Regnier, Les Satyres et Autres Œuvres de, *yellow morocco,* *Elsev.* 1652	Triphook
	10	-	3491	Regrets Fecetieux et Plaisantes Harengues Funebres, *red morocco,* - - - *Paris,* 1576	Do.
	10	-	3492	Reichard, Guide des Voyageurs en Europe, 2 vol. *Weimar.* 1802	Money
	4	-	3493	Rei Venaticæ Autores Antiqui, - *Elsev.* 1653	Booth
1	10	-	3494	Reifenbergii Emblemata Politica, *many plates, yellow morocco,* - - *Amst.* 1632	Clarke
2	3	-	3495	Reiss gesert durch Ober-und Neider Tutchland, *numerous plates, blue morocco,* - *Nuremb.* 1686	Arch
1	1	-	3496	Relandus de Religione Mohammedica, *portrait and plates, yellow morocco,* - *Trajecti.* 1717	Christie
1	5	-	3497	Relation Historique de l'Amour de l'Empereur de Maroc pour la Princesse de Conty, *Cologne,* 1707. Le Siecle d'Or de Cupidon, 1712 *blue morocco.*	Ld Yarmouth
1	2	-	3498	Relation and Journall of the Entertainment of Prince Charles at Madrid, *inlaid, red morocco,* *J. Haviland,* 1623	Barker
	2	-	3499	Religieuse Interesseé et Amoureuse, *Cologne.* —	Triphook
	5	-	3500	Religion, Le Triumphe de la, sous Louis le Grand, *Paris,* 1687	Barker

3501 Religious Customs, and Manners of Sundry Nations, *blue morocco*, - - - 1683

3502 Remains of Perron, Thuanus, &c. - 1707

3503 Renouard Annales de l'Imprimerie des Alde, 2 vol. in 1, *fine paper, blue morocco*, - *Paris*, 1803

3504 Renoult, Les Aventures de la Madona et de François d'Assise, *plates, red morocco*, - *Amst.* 1701

3505 Responce Bonne a tous Propos, - *Lyon*, 1567

3506 Retz, Memoires du Cardinal de, et de Joli, 7 vol. *green morocco, by Derome, fine copy*, - *Amst.* 1731

3507 Reusneri Aureola Emblemata Stimmeri Iconibus exornata, *wood cuts, with borders round the pages*, *Argent*, 1591

3508 Reveil Matin pour reveiller les pretendus scavans Matematiciens de l'Academie Royale, par M. Bertrand, *Hamb.* 1674.—Suite du Reveil Matin, *ib.* 1675, in one vol. *blue morocco.*

3509 Reynold's Garden of Love, a pleasant History, *no date.*

3510 Reyrac, Hymne au Soleil: Premiere Epreuve d'une Nouvelle Presse de l'Imprimerie Royale, *red morocco*, *Paris*, 1783

3511 Rhead's Description of the Body of Man, *plates*, 1616

3512 Ricaut, Histoire de l'Etat present de l'Empire Ottoman, *plates, blue morocco*, - *Amst.* 1670

3513 Riccoboni, Œuvres Complettes de, 8 vol. *blue morocco, plates*, - - - - 1790

3514 ——— Lettres de Sophie de Vallière a Louise de Canteleu, 2 vol. - - - 1772

3515 Rich's Book of Psalms in Short Hand Writing, *portrait, red morocco.*

3516 Richelieu, Mazarin et Colbert, Tableau de la Vie et Gouvernement, *red morocco*, - *Cologne*, 1693

3517 Autre Exemplaire, *red morocco*, - *ib.* 1694

3518 Richelieu, Journal du Cardinal de, 2 parts in one, *red morocco, portrait*, - - *Amst.* 1764

3519 Ridley's Declaration of the Lordes Supper, *blue morocco, scarce*, - - *Abr. Veale*, 1586

3520 Rime Scelti di diversi Autori di nuovo corretti e ristampate, 2 vol. *beautiful copy in very rich old binding in morocco, fleur-de-lisé, ruled; from Col. Stanley's Collection*, *Venetia, Giolito*, 1588

3521 Altro Esemplare, 2 vol. *vellum*, - *ib.* 1588

3522 Rinnucci, Le Capucin Escossois, - *Paris*, 1664

3523 Rire, Traité des Causes Physiques et Morales du, *Amst.* 1768

3524 Ritson's Pieces of Ancient Popular Poetry, *London*, 1791

3525 Another copy, *in very rich and splendid binding in compartments*, - - - *ib.* 1791

£	s.	d.	Lot	Description	Buyer
5	5	-	3526	Ritson's English Anthology, 3 vol.—Robin Hood, 2 vol. —Minot's Poems, 6 vol. *uniform, extra bound,* 1793-95	Arch
2	5	-	3527	——— Ancient English Metrical Romances, 3 vol. *red morocco,* - - - - - 1802	Do
	15	-	3528	——— Bibliographia Poetica, or Catalogue of Engleish Poets, - - - - - 1802	Do
	6	-	3529	Rival Princes, by Mrs. Clarke, - - 1810	Bentham
	11	-	3530	Roberts's Adventures of an English Merchant taken Prisoner by the Turks of Argiers, - 1670	Rodd
	12	-	3531	Robbing of the Nunnery, a Ballad, - 1786	Heber
	6	-	3532	Robin Hood's Garland.	Perry
26	15	6	3533	ROBINSON. Handfull of Pleasant Delites, containing New Sonnets and delectable Histories in divers kindes of Meeters, by Clement Robinson, and divers others - 1584 This is presumed to be the ONLY PERFECT COPY of a very interesting Collection of Old Poetry, which acquires additional interest from the allusion made to the First Poem in the Collection, by the frantic Ophelia when strewing the flowers in her phrenzy: "There's Rosemary, that's for remembrance." &c. See Hamlet, Act IV. Scene V.	Do.

Quarto.

£	s.	d.	Lot	Description	Buyer
1	2	-	3534	Porcacchi Funerali Antichi di Diversi Popoli et Nationi, con Figure di Porro, *fine copy, blue morocco, with joints,* *Venet.* 1574	Evans
1	11	6	3535	Porri, Vaso di Verita intorno all' Origine, Nascita, &c. dell' Antichristo, *plates, by Porro, blue morocco,* *Venet.* 1597	Payne
	7	-	3536	Porta della Celeste Fisonomia con Figure, *red morocco,* *Padova,* 1616	Dulau
9	9	-	3537	Porter's Pleasant Historie of the Two Angrie Women of Abington, *scarce,* - - - - 1599	Jervis
5	15	6	3538	Prayer Book, Queen Elizabeth's Book of Christian Prayers, *wood cut, borders, blue morocco, with joints,* 1590	Barker
1	14	-	3539	Prayer Book, The Book of Common Prayer, *London, Cawood,* 1571.—The Psalms of David, *imperfect,* 1571, *blue morocco.*	Cochran
	9	-	3540	Prayer, The Book of Common, *black morocco,* 1639	Do.
1	16	-	3541	——— The Book of Common, *red morocco,* 1696	Do.
12	-	-	3542	——— The Book of Common, by Sturt, *large paper, plates, red morocco, ruled,* - - 1717	Do.
	14	-	3543	——— Book, *black morocco,* - 1730	Heber
3	15	-	3544	Prayers, The Posie of Flowred, disposed in fourme of	Triphook

the Alphabet of the Queene her most excellent Majesties name, inlaid in 4to. *blue morocco,* *London, Wykes.*

3545 Prieres du Matin et du Soir, *plates, by Coypel, red morocco, ruled,* - - - *sans date.*

3546 Primer (Queen Mary's) in Englishe and Latin, set out along after the Use of Sarum, *wood cuts, blue morocco,* VERY RARE, - *Kyngston and Sutton,* 1577

3547 Printing, Decree of Starre-Chamber concerning, 1637

3548 Projector's Downfall, or Time's Changeling, 1642

3549 Prophecie of all Transactions past and to come, in Verse, written in the Time of Elizabeth, - 1659

3550 Pruthenii Trilogium Animæ, *russia, Noremb. Coburger,* 1498

3551 Prynne's Opening of the Great Seale of England, 1643

3552 Psalterium, Græce, *fine copy, red morocco,* *Venet. in Ædibus Aldi, sine anno.*

3553 Psalme LI. St. Hierom of Ferrarye's Exposicyon of, and Meditacyō on the Psalme in te Domine Speravi, *black letter, very rare, russia,* *Imprynted in Parys,* 1538

3554 Purgatorye. Here begynneth a lytell boke, that speketh of Purgatorye, and what Purgatorye is, and in what place and of the paynes that be therin, &c. in verse, VERY RARE, *fine copy, blue morocco,* *Imprynted by Robert Wyer, no date.*

3555 Puttenham's Arte of English Poesie in three Bookes: the first of Poets and Poesie, the second of Proportion, the third of Ornament, *first edition, rare, in russia,* *London, Field,* 1589

3556 Pym's Speeches delivered in Parliament, 2 vol. 1641

3557 Quench-Coale, or Inquiry where the Lord's Table ought to be situated, - - - - 1637

3558 Quintiliani Opera cum Notis Burmanni, 3 vol. large paper, *russia, with joints,* - - *Lugd. Bat.* 1720

3559 Rabutin, Commentaires sur les Guerres de Henry Second, *Paris, Vascosan,* 1555

3560 Rademaker, Kabinet van Nederlandsche Outheden en Gezichten, 300 plates, - *Amst.* 1731

3561 Rappresentazione Sacre.—A Collection of Ninety-eight early Italian Mysteries, many of them with wood-cuts, 2 vol. *vellum,* EXTREMELY RARE,

3562 Rare en Tout, Comedie, - - 1677

3563 Rastell's Pastime of the People, *russia,* - *Lond.* 1811

3564 Raynalde's Birth of Mankynde, otherwyse named the Woman's Booke, *black letter, blue morocco,* 1565

3565 Record's Whetstone of Witte, the Second Parte of Arithmetike, *black letter,* - *Kyngston,* 1557

3566 Recueil de Figures Historiques, Symboliques et Tragiques pour servir à l'Histoire du XVIII siecle, *Amst.* 1762

3567 Reformatio Camaldulensis Ordinis a Leone X. et Romualdi Vita, - - *Florent.* 1513

3568 Reges, Reginæ et Alii in Westmonasterio Sepulti, cum Epitaphiis, *large paper,* - *Londini,* 1603

3569 Regicides, Trial, &c. of the Twenty-nine, - 1660

3570 Regnault, Discours du Voyage d'Outre Mer au Sainct Sepulchre de Jerusalem, *wood cuts, fine copy, ruled,* *Lyon,* 1573

3571 Renealmi, Blaesensis, Specimen Historiæ Plantarum, *cuts,* *Paris,* 1611

3572 Renversement de la Morale Chrétienne par les Desordres du Monachisme, *plates by Hemskirk, blue morocco,* *sans date.*

3573 Reusneri Emblemata Varia, - *Francof.* 1581

3574 Reynard the Fox, in Two Parts, with the Shifts of Reynardine, *one leaf MS.* - - 1681

3575 ——————— The Delectable History of, *russia,* 1694

3576 Reynolds's Death's Vision, in a Sacred Poem, 1709

3577 Ricchi, Comedia intittolata I Tre Tiranni, *plates,* *Vinegia, Bern. de Vitali,* 1532

3578 Riche's Allarme to England, with a Short Discourse on Warlike Discipline, - 1578

3579 Richeome's Pilgrime of Loreto performing his Vow, *Paris,* 1630

3580 Rime de gli Academici Occulti con le loro Imprese et Discorsi, *large paper, blue morocco, with joints, Brescia,* 1568

3581 Rinaldo di Monte Albano Paladino, Inamoramento di, *wood cuts,* - - *Venetia,* 1533

3582 Ringhieri, Cento Giuochi Liberali' *ornamented binding in compartments,* - - *Bologna,* 1551

3583 Ripa, Nova Iconologia, *many plates, red morocco,* *Padova,* 1618

3584 Ripa's Iconologia, or Moral Emblems, illustrated by Three Hundred and Twenty-six Plates, *blue morocco, with joints,* 1709

Folio.

3585 PLANTS.—A Collection of FORTY FIVE PLANTS, painted with exquisite delicacy on vellum, by A. LEE, 1772. The name is affixed to each figure, mounted on Drawing Paper, with a border to every page, from the Earl of Bute's Collection.

3586 ——— A Collection of FORTY SIX very large drawings of PLANTS, by J. MILLAR. The subjects were collected by Captain William Miller, of the Alert, who by Order of Sir Robert Harland, surveyed the Coasts of the Island of Ceylon. These Plants are very beautifully painted on vellum, mounted on fine drawing paper, with borders to the pages, from the Earl of Bute's Library.

3587 PLANTS.—A Collection of FORTY-EIGHT DRAWINGS of Plants, on vellum, by TAYLOR, with the name to each, drawn and painted with admirable delicacy of finish and beauty of colouring, mounted on drawing paper, and splendidly bound in red morocco, from the Earl of Bute's Library.

3588 ——— A volume containing SIXTY-TWO DRAWINGS of Plants of the Genus Pinus, by FRANCIS BAUER, the greater part very highly and beautifully coloured.

3589 ——— A Portfolio containing FORTY-TWO most exquisite and delicately coloured drawings, copied by Artists engaged expressly for the purpose from the rarest and most beautiful Plants in the Botanic Garden at White Knights.

3590 ——— Another Collection consisting of FIFTY-EIGHT Drawings of a smaller size.

3591 ——— Another Portfolio containing a Profusion of Drawings, either in outline or in an unfinished state.

3592 ——— A Volume containing EIGHTY-NINE Drawings of Plants, by the DUCHESS OF MARLBOROUGH, painted in a most delicate and beautiful manner.

3593 ——— A Volume containing Eight most exquisite and highly finished Drawings of Plants, upon vellum, with a border of gold round each page, *bound in russia, with joints.*

3594 A HORTUS SICCUS, in Seven Volumes, containing above Nine Hundred Specimens of Grasses, &c. with their Latin and English names, and an Index to each volume.

3595 A Volume containing FIFTY-NINE coloured Drawings of Flowers and Fruits, with two portraits of Mandarins, in old morocco binding in compartments.

3596 A Collection of THREE HUNDRED AND THIRTY-TWO most delicate and beautiful Chinese Paintings, mounted on fine Drawing Paper, and elegantly bound in four volumes, in russia, with joints. The first volume has Eight Drawings of the various stages of the Silk Worm, Fruits of China, and Figures of their Birds, splendidly coloured, and concludes with Six Paintings of Chinese Vessels. The second volume contains the insects of China, with the different leaves and flowers on which they feed, and the third and fourth, Chinese Flowers.

3597 A Collection of EIGHTEEN very beautifully coloured Draw-

£	s.	d.	Lot	Description	Buyer
				ings of Plants, upon vellum, by John Bolton, of Halfax, in a portfolio. - - 1794	Triphook
3	3	-	3598	Pluvinel, Instruction du Roy en l'Exercice de Monter à Cheval, François et Allemand, *plates after Pass, by Merian, very fine impressions,* - *Francf.* 1628	Do
	3	-	3599	Poems, a volume of, containing Oliver Cromwell's Ghost.—Two Dialogues.—Fire Side.—Odes on Poetry and Pleasure, - - - 1754	Rodd
	1	-	3600	——— Secretary Janus.—The Nowiad.—The Apostates.	Do
	1	-	3601	——— containing, the Merry Campaign, the Malecontent, &c.	Do
2	15	-	3602	Poems and Ballads, a volume of, with Caricature Prints, 1681	Perry
37	10	-	3603	Polindo. Historia del Invencible Cavallero Don Polindo y de las Maravillosas Fazannas y Estrannas Aventuras que andando por el Mundo acabo, *fine copy, blue morocco,* VERY RARE, - - *Toledo,* 1526	Heber
4	10	-	3604	Poliphili Hypnerotomachia, *plates, green morocco, Venet. Aldi,* 1499	Payne
3	17	-	3605	Poliphile, Discours du Songe de, *plates, green morocco, Paris, Kerver,* 1554	Rogers
6	6	-	3606	POLYCHRONICON AB R. HIGDEN. A Latin Manuscript of the Fourteenth Century, upon vellum. "It finishes at the year 1352, but the copy from which Caxton printed was continued to the year 1357, from this addition to the History, we may presume that this Manuscript was the first copy which R. Higden exhibited of his work." See MS. Note by Bryant.	Triphook
94	10	-	3607	——— in whiche book ben comprised briefly many wonderful historyees, 2 vol. *fine copy, splendidly bound in green morocco, with morocco lining, Fynsshed, per Caxton,* 1482	Payne

NINETEENTH DAY'S SALE.

Octavo et Infra.

£	s.	d.	Lot	Description	Buyer
	3	-	3608	Robinson's Treatise on the Virtues of a Crust of Bread, 1756	Triphook
	1	-	3609	Robison's Proofs of a Conspiracy against all Europe, 1797	Clarke
1	3	-	3610	Roche's Discarded Son, or the Haunt of the Banditti, 5 vol. - - - - 1807	Triphook

£	s.	d.	Lot	Description	Buyer
	7	-	3611	Roche's Maid of the Hamlet, 2 vol. - 1800	Natton
	7	-	3612	——— Vicar of Lansdowne, 2 vol. - 1800	Do.
	7	-	3613	Rochefoucault, Memoires de, *blue morocco,* *Haye,* 1689	Collins
	7	-	3614	Rocoles, La Fortune Marastre de plusieurs Princes et Seigneurs, *red morocco* - *Leide,* 1684	Freeling
	4	-	3615	Rocsort, Nouveaux Recits Moralisez, *red morocco,* *Paris,* 1574	Triphook
	13	-	3616	Rodomontades Espagnolles, Espagnol et François, *wood cuts, red morocco,* - - *Rouen,* 1650	Laing
	12	-	3617	Roger Bon Temps en Belle Humeur, *blue morocco,* *Cologne,* 1670	Triphook
	17	-	3618	Rohan, Voyage de Duc de, en Italie, Allemagne, Angleterre, &c. *green morocco, ruled,* - *Elzev.* 1646	Rodd
	3	-	3619	Rolli, Le Canzonette e Cantate di, *red morocco,* *Londra,* 1727	Christie
1	2	-	3620	Rojas, El Viage entretinedo de, con una exposicion de los Nombros Historicos y Poeticos que no van declarados, *red morocco,* - - *Lerida,* 1615	Rodd
	3	-	3621	Roman Bourgeois, Le, Ouvrage Comique. *Paris,* 1666	Triphook
1	1	-	3622	Rommant de la Rose, *wood cuts, red morocco,* *Paris, Galliot du Pre,* 1529	Evans
2	-	-	3623	Roman de la Rose avec des Notes, 4 vol. *blue morocco, with joints,* - - - *Paris,* 1735	Johnstone
	4	-	3624	Romances and Novels, a new Collection of, 1780	Christie
1	2	-	3625	Romans.—Hist. de Pierre de Provence et de la Belle Maguelonne—Hist. de Jean de Paris—La Vie de Tiel Ulespiegle—Richard sans Peur—Vie du Gargantuas—Robert le Diable—La Belle Heleine—Hist. de Fortunatus. 8 Romances, in 1 vol. - *Troyes, s. d.*	Arch
	9	-	3626	Romans et Contes de M. de ——— 2 vol. *red morocco,* *Londres,* 1767	Triphook
1	13	-	3627	Romani Institutiones Christianæ Æneis Formis Canisii expressæ, *numerous plates,* - *Antverp.* 1589	Payne
	5	-	3628	Roma Illustrata sive Breviarium Romanarum Antquitatum Fabricii, *yellow morocco,* *Amst. Elzev.* 1657	Christie
	3	-	3629	Romanorum Imperatorum Libellus cum Imaginibus, *Argent,* 1526	Triphook
	12	-	3630	Rome, Reliques of, gathered out of Chronicles and Histories, by T. Becon, *black letter, blue morocco,* *J. Day,* 1563	Cochran
4	-	-	3631	Rome—The Hystorie of the Seaven Wise Maisters of Rome, *black letter, wood cuts, blue morocco,* *T. Purfoot,* 1633	Triphook
	8	-	3632	Another Copy, *black letter, wood cuts,* - 1661	Do.
	6	-	3633	Another Edition, - - - 1684	Rodd
	3	-	3634	Another Copy, - - - *no date.*	Warren
	4	-	3635	Rome—History of the Seven Wise Mistresses of Rome, *cuts,* - - - - - 1712	Triphook

£	s.	d.	Lot	Description	Buyer
	3	-	3636	Romney Marsh, Charter of, *Wolfe,* 1597	Rodd
2	6	-	3637	Romyshe Fox. The Huntyng and Fynding out of the Romyshe Fox, which more then seven yeares hath bene hyd among the Bishoppes of England, &c. *black letter,* VERY RARE, *blue morocco. Imprynted at Basyll,* 1543	Heber
1	6	-	3638	——— The Rescuynge of the Romishe Fox, by Steven Gardiner.—The Second Course of the Hunter of the Romishe Fox, *black letter,* VERY RARE, *blue morocco, Winchester, by me, Hanse Hit Prif.* 1545	Cochran
2	-	-	3640	Another Edition, *blue morocco,* *ib.* 1545	Do
	17	-	3641	Ronsard, les Odes de Pierre de, *venetian morocco, ruled, Paris,* 1550	Triphook
1	10	-	3642	Ronsovinus's English Man's Doctor, or the Schoole of Salerne, translated by Sir J. Harington, *blue morocco,* 1624	Rodd
	4	-	3643	Rosamond and Jane Shore, the History of, 1723	Anderdon
1	2	-	3644	Rosarii Antithesis de præclaris Christi et indignis Papæ Facinoribus, *plates, blue morocco, Per Zach. Durantium,* 1558	Heber
1	8	-	3645	Rose's English Vine Yard vindicated, *green morocco, Lond.* 1666	Anderdon
	3	-	3646	Rose's Elements of Botany, - - 1775	K.
1	1	-	3647	Ross's View of all Religions in the World, *blue morocco,* 1653	Warner
	18	-	3648	Rose's Mel Heliconium, or Poeticall Honey, *red morocco,* 1646	Triphook
	12	-	3649	Rosset, L'Admirable Histoire du Chevalier de Soleil, 8 vol. in 29,—vol. 3 *imperfect,* - *Paris,* 1643	Do
	17	-	3650	Rostgaard, Deliciæ quorundam Poetarum Danorum 2 vols. *green morocco,* - - - *Lugd. Bat.* 1693	Heber
	11	.	3651	Roulliard, La Magnifique Doxologie du Festu, *red morocco,* - - - - - *Paris,* 1610	Do
	17	-	3652	Roulliard, Le Lumbifrage de Nicodeme Aubier, *yellow morocco,* - - - - *s. date.*	Do
1	5	-	3653	Rousseau, Julie ou la Nouvelle Heloise, 6 vol. *plates, red morocco,* - - - *Amst.* 1761	Triphook
	2	-	3654	Rousseau, Dictionnaire de Musique, - *Paris,* 1768	Warner
-	13	-	3655	Rousseau, Elements of Botany, translated by Martin, 1791	K.
	2	.	3656	Rowzee's Treatise on the Vertues of Tunbridge Water, 1632	Anderdon
14	-	-	3657	Roy.—Rede me, and be nott wrothe, For I saye no thynge but trothe, *First edition, blue morocco,* VERY RARE, *no date.*	Rodd
18	-	-	3658	Roy.—The Boke. Reade me, frynde, and be not wrothe, For I saye nothynge but the trothe. *Second edition, red morocco,* VERY RARE. *Printed at Wesell in the yeare of our Lorde* 1546	Triphook for W. T. Esq

* 3655. With Martyn's 38 plates coloured - vide Lot 3647-8

3659 Roy (Alard le) La Vertu Enseignée par les Oiseaux, *blue morocco*, - - - *Liege*, 1653

3660 Royal Sufferer, a Manual of Meditations and Devotions, *blue morocco*, - - - 1699

3661 Rudimenta Antiquæ Linguæ Britannicæ (a Davis), 1621

3662 Rump Parliament, a Collection of Songs and Ballads upon the, - - - - 1660

3663 Russel's History of Modern Europe, 4 vol. 1779

3664 Russia, a Voyage to, - - 1739

3665 Saavedra. El Peregrino Indiano, par Antonio de Saavedra Guzman, *yellow morocco, with joints*, *Madrid*, 1599

3666 Saavedra Faxardo, Idea Principis Christiano-Politici, *red morocco, with joints*, - - *Amst.* 1660

3667 Sacheverell's Sermon before the House of Commons, May 29, 1713, - - - 1713

3668 Sackville Lord Buckhurst's Tragedie of Ferrex and Porrex, *black letter*, RARE, *red morocco*, *John Daye*, 1571

3669 Sacræ Scripturæ Locorum quorundam Versio Metrica, *Oxon.* 1736

3670 Sacrobosco. La Sphere de Jean de Sacrobosco, augmentée de nouveaux Commentaires, *yellow morocco, with joints*, *Paris*, 1576

3671 Sadeleri Zodiacus Christianus, seu signa 12. divinæ Prædestinationis, &c. *blue morocco, with joints*, *Monaci.* 1618

3672 Sagard, le Grand Voyage du Pays des Hurons, avec un Dictionnaire de la Langue Huronne, *morocco*, VERY RARE. From the Stanley Collection, No. 1112. *Paris*, 1632

3673 Sage (Le) Histoire de Gil Blas de Santillane, LARGE PAPER, *proof plates before the letter*, - *Paris*, 1795

3674 Saint Amant, Moyse Sauvé, Idyle Heroique, *yellow morocco, with joints*, - - - *Leyde.* 1654

3675 St. Disdier La Ville et la Republique de Venise, *red morocco, with joints*, - *Amst. Elzevir.* 1680

3676 St. Olon, The Present State of the Empire of Morocco, *cuts*, - - - - - 1695

3677 Saint Pierre's Studies of Nature, by Hunter, 6 vol. 1796

3678 Saint-Real, Œuvres de, 6 vol. *plates*, - *Amst.* 1740

3679 St. Real's History of the Conspiracy of the Spaniards against Venice, - - *Glasgow*, 1752

3680 Saintré. Histoire et plaisante Cronique du Petit Jehan de Saintré, 3 vol. - - *Paris*, 1724

3681 Salgado Symbiosis Papæ et Diaboli ut et Cardinalis et Morionis, *plates*, - - *Londini.* 1681

3682 Sallengre, Histoire de Pierre de Montmaur, 2 vol. in 1, *à la Haye*, 1715

3683 Sallustius cum veterum Historicorum Fragmentis, *red moroco* - - - *Elzevir.* 1634

3684 Sallustius, *red morocco, with joints,* *Edinburgi.* 1744

3685 Salmasii de Annis Climactericis et antiqua Astrologia Diatribe, *blue morocco, with joints, Lugd. Bat. Elz.* 1648

3686 Salmigondis (Le), Œuvres Morales, Physiques, Critiques et Burlesques, - - *Francfort.* 1740

3687 Salter's Caliope's Cabinet Opened and Reviewed, 1674

3688 Sambuci Emblemata et aliquot Nummi Antiqui, *plates, green morocco, with joints,* - *Antv. Plantin.* 1566

3689 Sambuci Emblemata, &c. *plates, blue morocco, with joints, ib.* 1584

3690 Sammarthani Poemata, - *Lutetiæ.* 1597

3691 Sandys's Christ's Passion, a Tragedy, *frontispiece,* 1698

3692 Sanfrein, ou mon dernier sejour à la Campagne, *Amst.* 1765

3693 Sannazaro, Arcadia del, *fine copy, in old stamped binding, Aldus.* 1534

3694 Sanson, Voyage ou Relation de l'Etat Present de Perse, *plates,* - - - *Paris,* 1695

3695 Sapet, Les Enthousiasmes ou Eprises Amoureuses de P. de Sapet, *green morocco,* RARE, - *Paris,* 1556

3696 Sarendip. Le Voyage et les Aventures des trois Princes de Sarendip, *plates,* - - *Amst.* 1721

3697 Sattire. Sette Libri di Sattire raccolti per Sansovino, *Venetia.* 1563

3698 Satiræ duæ Hercules tuam fidem sive Munsterus Hypobolimæus, et Vergula Divina, - *Elzevir.* 1617

3699 Satyres (Les) Bastardes, et autres Œuvres folastres du Cadet Angoulevent, *blue morocco, by Padeloup, Par.* 1615

3700 Satyre Menippée de la Vertu du Catholicon d'Espagne, *blue morocco,* - - *Ratisbonne,* 1664

3701 Satyriques (Les) Grotesques du Temps présent, passé, et à venir. *Paris,* 1631. A Manuscript with 139 coloured Drawings of most grotesque Figures, in the manner of the Songe Drolatiques de Pantagruel, with some Verses of Introduction. See MS. Note at the beginning, *red morocco.*

3702 Saunger, Les Decades de l'Esperant, *cuts, red morocco, Rouen, sans date.*

3703 Sauvigny, Theatre de, 6 vol. *plates, blue morocco, Paris,*

3704 Savaron Traitté contre les Masques, *Paris,* 1608. Traicté contre les Duels, 1614. Discours et Ordonnance du Roy contre les Duels, 1614. Remonstrance au Roy contre les Duels par Roland, 1625. Phase utriusque Foederis auctore Hemeræo, 1628. Savaron Traitté des Confrairies, 1604. Les Chassier Observations de la Digamie, 1601. 7 Tracts in 1 vol. *green morocco.*

3705 Savigny, Histoire Naturelle et Mythologique de l'Ibis, *plates,* - - - *Paris,* 1805

3706 Savoy. Memoirs of the Transactions in Savoy during the War, *russia,* - - - 1697

3707 Savoye, Relation de la Cour de, ou les Amours de Madame Royale, - - *Par.* 1667

3708 —— Le Cavalier de, ou Response au Soldat François, *Bruxelles,* 1706

3709 Scachi. Libro da Imparare Giochare a Scachi, in lingua Spagnola, et Italiana novamente Stampato, *red morocco, with joints,* RARE, - *senza nota.*

3710 Scaligeri (J. C.) Lacrymæ, Prosopopœia Francorum Regis Fr. Valesii incomparabili virtute Viri atque illustrissimi, Deflet Carolum Ducem a Longavilla, qui ad Ticenum interfectus fuit, *blue morocco,* VERY RARE, *Paris, Vascosan,* 1534

3711 Scarron, Œuvres de, 10 vol. - *Amst.* 1737

3712 Scarron, Roman Comique, 2 vol. in 1, *Rouen,* 1781

3713 Scarron's Novels, - - - 1665

3714 Scarron's Unexpected Choice, translated by J. Davies, 1670

3715 Scelte di Facetie, Buffonerie, Motti e Burle, *green morocco, Verona,* 1586

3716 Schopperi Opus Poeticum de Admirabili Fallacia et Astutia Vulpeculæ Reinikes, *cuts, russia,* *Francof.* 1567

3717 Schopperus's Fable of Reinard the Fox, done into English Verse, - - - - - 1706

3718 Schopperus de Omnibus Illiberalibus sive Mechanicis Artibus, *plates, red morocco,* - - *Francof.* 1574

3719 Schotti Itinerarium Italiæ, - - *Amst.* 1655

3720 Schurman (Annæ Mariæ) Opuscula *Traj. ad Rhen.* 1652

3721 Scopoli Flora Carniolica exhibens Plantas Carnioliæ Indigenas, 2 vol. *plates,* - *Vindobonæ,* 1772

3722 Scot's Philomythie, or Philomythologie, wherein outlandish Birds, Beasts, and Fishes are taught to speake true English plainely, *frontispiece, fine copy, russia,* 1616

3723 Scotch Politics, or the Satirical History of the Year 1762, in Twenty-five Plates by Darley.

3724 Scotland Delineated, - - *Edinburgh,* 1791

3725 Scotland. Memorialls of the Government of the Royall Burghs of Scotland, - - *Aberdeen,* 1685

3726 Scoto Nuovo Itinerario d'Italia, 2 vol. *plates, Padova,* 1646

3727 Scott's Essay of Drapery, or the Compleate Citizen, *blue morocco, frontispiece,* - - *London,* 1635

Quarto.

3728 Ripa, Cæsar. Historiæ et Allegoriæ projectæ et designatæ ab Eichler, inventæ ab Hertel, *in Ten Parts, very fine impressions of the plates, splendidly bound, red morocco, with joints,* - - *August. Vindel. s. a.*

£	s.	d.	Lot	Description	Buyer
6	10	-	3729	Robert Le Diable, La Vie de, *black letter red morocco*, *Jeban Herouf. sans date.*	Triphook
14	-	-	3730	Robin the Divell. The Famous, True, and Historicall Life of Robert, Second Duke of Normandy, surnamed Robin the Divell, interspersed with Poetry, EXTREMELY RARE, - - - *Busbie*, 1591	Heber
	11	-	3731	Robinson's Anatomy of the English Nunnery at Lisbon, 1623	Hibbert
4	8	-	3732	Robinson's Handefull of Pleasant Delites, &c. a MS. copy from the very rare Edition of 1584, *blue morocco.*	Jervis
1	7	-	3733	Roger, Le Theatre de l'Idolatrie, ou Les Vies et les Mœurs des Bramins, *plates, blue morocco*, *Amst.* 1670	Cochran
4	6	-	3734	Rollenhagii Nucleus Emblematum Selectissimorum, 2 vol. *fine impressions, blue morocco*, *e Museo Crispiani Passæi, Ultraj.* 1613	Triphook
10	15	-	3735	Romæ, Historiæ Septem Sapientium, a very ancient Edition without date, place, or printer, *fine copy, red morocco.*	Do
10	15	-	3736	——— Alia Editio, *with curions wood cuts, blue morocco*, *sine ulla nota.* Neither of these Editions appears to be mentioned by Bibliographers.	Hibbert
1	2	-	3737	Rome. The Sum of the Actes and Decrees made by dyvers Byshopes of Rome, *black letter, inlaid*, *T. Gybson*, 1538	Cochran
	11	-	3738	Round Head, an Exact Description of, *russia*, 1642	Perry
2	12	-	3739	Rossi, Scherzi Poetici e Pittorici sopra Amore, *plates, russia*, - - *Parma, Bodoni*, 1795	Calkin
2	-	-	3740	Altro Esemplare, plates coloured in the Etruscan manner, *russia*, - - - 1795	Longman
	6	-	3741	Rosset, Le Romant des Chevaliers de la Gloire, *Paris*, 1612	Triphook
7	17	6	3742	Rowland's Famous History of Guy Earle of Warwick, in Verse, *russia, with joints*, - - 1667	Freeling
1	15	-	3743	Rowley's Poems, with a Commentary by Milles, *yellow morocco*, - - - 1782	Hodd
2	2	-	3744	Romant des Trois Pelerinaiges de l'Homme durant quest en Vie—de l'ame separée du Corps et de notre Seigneur Jesus Christ, *blue morocco*, *Paris, Petit, sans date*	Triphook
8	-	-	3745	Romans, Collection des—Histoire du Roy Artus, *Paris*, 1584. Tristan de Leonnois, 1586. Hist. de Prince Meliadus, 1584. La Fleur des Batailles. Doolin de Mayence, *sans date.* Olivier de Castille, 1587. Robert le Diable, *sans date.* Richard sans Peur, *sans date.*—7 Romances in 1 vol. *morocco.*	Longman
2	15	-	3746	Romans, Collection de—Maugis d'Augremont. Gallien Restaure Valentine et Orson. Morgant le Geant.—4 Romances in 1 vol. *wood cuts, yellow morocco, with joints*, - - *Troyes*, 1668, &c.	Laing

3747 Romances, a Collection of 13, in 1 vol.—Reynard the Fox. Don Bellianis of Greece. The Unhappy Hunting of Chevy Chase. Elizabeth and the Earl of Essex. Drake's Voyages round the World. Arthur and the Knights of the Round Table. Nine Worthies of the World. Hero and Leander. Seven Wise Masters of Rome. Seven Champions of Christendom. Fair Rosamond. Sir Rich. Whittington. Life and Death of Captain Hind.

3748 Romances, a volume of 5,—containing Floridon and Lucina, 1663. Tom a Lincoln. The Golden Eagle, 1672. History of Cleotreton and Cloryana. Parismus, Prince of Bohemia.

3749 Rump Parliament, Collection of Pamphlets relating to the, in 10 volumes,—containing The Acts and Monuments of the Rump. The Debates and Conferences of the Rump. The Character of the Rump. The Rump's Proverbs. Qualifications for the Rump. Rump's Funeral Sermon, by Feacke. The Rump, or the Mirror of the Times, a Comedy. The Tragedie of the Rump. The Rump's Last Will. Ghost of the Rump and Tom Tel-Troth, - - - 1660

3750 Rupert's (Prince) Malignant She Monkey, an Exact Description of, - - - - 1643

3751 Rusher's Collects of the Church, in Verse, - 1790

3752 RUSSELL. Propositio Clarissimi Oratoris Magistri Johannis Russell, decretorum doctoris ac adtunc Ambassiatoris Christianissimi Regis Edwardi dei gracia Regis Anglie et Francie, ad illustrissimum principem Karolum ducem Burgundie super susceptione Ordinis garterii etc.

Without Printer's name, date, or place, but printed by Caxton in 1469 or 1470.

The only Copy known of a Tract of the very first curiosity and importance to Collectors of early English printing. The Duke of Burgundy, to whom this Epistle is addressed, was created a Knight of the Garter in 1469, consequently this Oration was printed either in that year or in 1470. It is therefore not only Unique, but is the FIRST SPECIMEN OF THE PRESS OF CAXTON. Bound up in morocco, with a MS. partly on vellum and partly on paper; for the Contents of which, see the New Edition of Ames, vol. 1. p. 14.

3753 S. (W.) Examination of certayne ordinary complaints of divers of our countrymen in these our Dayes, *black letter, yellow morocco,* - - *T. Marshe,* 1581

3754 Saavedra Idea de un Principe Politico Christiano, representada en Cien Empresas, *blue morocco,* *Monaco,* 1640

3755 Sack. A Preparative to Study, or the Vertue of Sack, 1641

£	s.	d.	No.	Description	Buyer
9	-	-	3756	Sadeler, Theatrum Morum, *first impressions, red morocco, ruled,* - - - *Pragæ*, 1608	Sir J. G. Egerton
1	8	-	3757	Sainct Gelais, La Chasse et le depart d'Amours, *wood cuts, Paris, Trepperel, sans date.*	Rodd
	13	-	3758	St. Michel, L'Institution et Or onnances des Chevaliers de l'ordre des tres chrestiens Roys de France. Manuscript upon vellum with illuminated Capitals, *in old ornamented binding.*	Freeling
1	1	-	3759	Saix (Antoine du) Petitz Fatras d'ung Apprentis, surnommé Lesperonnier de discipline, *red morocco, Paris*, 1537	Rodd
1	-	-	3760	Salazar, Cythara de Apollo, varias Poesias y Comedias, 2 vol. - - - *Madrid*, 1604	Dunbar
	8	-	3761	Salmacida Spolia, a Masque, - - 1639	Rodd
2	12	6	3762	Salsmannus. Liber Genesis æreis formis a Cr. Passæo expressus versibusque tam Latinis quam Germanicis ornatus per G. Salsmanum, *russia, Arnheimii*, 1616	Hibbert
33	12	-	3763	SALTWOOD, a Comparyson bytwene IV byrdes; the Larke, the Nyghtyngale, the Thrusshe and the Cucko, for theyr syngynge who should be chauntoure of the quere, *black letter, russia,* EXTREMELY RARE, *John Mychel, no date.*	Evans
	2	-	3764	A Satyr against Satyrs, or St. Peter's Vision transubstantiated, - - - 1680	Hibbert
5	15	6	3765	Saviolo (Vincentio) his Practise of the use of the Rapier and Dagger, of Honor and honorable quarrels, *wood cuts,* RARE, - - *John Wolfe*, 1595	Smith
	2	-	3766	Scala et Hun (Pauli Principis de) Explanatio Imaginum Joachimi Abb. Florensis, Calabriæ et Anselmi Episcopi Marsichani, *plates*, - - *sine anno.*	Triphook
1	1	-	3767	Scaligeri La Nobilta del Asino, *plates, blue morocco, Venetia*, 1599	Hibbert
4	4	-	3768	Schmidel, Vera Historia Admirandæ cujusdam Navigationis in Americam, *plates, red morocco, Noribergæ*, 1599	Triphook
1	3	-	3769	Schoonhovii Emblemata, cum eorundem ejusdem Auctoris Interpretatione, *fine impressions, blue morocco, Goudæ*, 1618	Bentham
1	1	-	3770	Alia Editio, *blue morocco*, - *Amst.* 1648	Longman
	5	-	3771	Scotch and English, an unhappy Game at, *Edinburgh*, 1646	Hibbert
3	9	-	3772	Scotland, The Complaynt of, written in 1548, with a Preliminary Dissertation and Glossary, *russia, with joints, Edinburgh* 1801	Cochran
	6	-	3773	Scott's Marmion, *boards*, - - 1808	Henry
	10	-	3774	Sebastiano a Matre Dei, Firmamentum Symbolicum, *plates, Lublini*, 1652	Payne
1	2	-	3775	Sebastian. A Discourse concerning the Successe of the King of Portugal Don Sebastian from his Voyage into Affricka when he was lost in the battle against the Infidels in the year 1578, unto the 6th of January 1601, 1601	Cribb

Folio.

3776 Porta de Furtivis Literarum Notis *Neapoli*, 1602

3777 Prayer, The Booke of the Common Prayer and Administracion of the Sacramentes, *black letter*, RARE, *Whitchurche*, 1549

3778 Prayer, The Book of Common Prayer and Administration of the Sacraments, *frontispiece*, by Loggan, *large paper*, *very fine copy, in blue morocco, with joints*, 1662

3779 Prempart's Relation of the Siege of the Citie called Busse, *maps and plans*, - - *Amst.* 1630

3780 Preux, Le Triumphe des Neuf Preux, avec l'Hystoire de Bertram de Guesclin, *wood cuts, fine copy, red morocco*, *Michel le Noir*, 1507

3781 Primaleon, Los Tres Libros del muy efforçado Cavallero Primaleon (de Grecia) et Polendos su hermano, hijos del Emperador Palmerin de Oliva, *wood cuts, fine copy, blue morocco*, VERY RARE, *from Col. Stanley's Collection*, *Venez. Nicolini de Sabio*, 1534

3782 PRINTS. A Collection of Forty Eight Portraits of Eminent Men and Remarkable Characters.

3783 PRINTS. A Volume of French Prints engraved by Mariette, &c. containing Masquerade Characters, Portraits of French Actresses, Emblematical Figures and Miscellaneous Prints, *fine impressions bound in russia*.

3784 PRINTS A Collection of Three Hundred and Forty Two Portraits, some of Eminent Characters, but principally of Highwaymen, Impostors, Gypsies, Criminals, Conspirators, Persons tried for Treason, &c. with some original Drawings, *in one very large volume*.

3785 Psalterium Latine, a Manuscript of the 15th century upon vellum with the initial Letters splendidly illuminated, *bound in red morocco*.

3786 Psalterium Quincuplex, *blue morocco, ruled*, *Genuæ, Porrus*, 1516

3787 PYLGREMAGE OF THE SOWLE, which Book is ful of devoute Materes touchyng the Sowle, *with many Songs and Poems attributed to Lydgate, fine copy, but wanting the last leaf*, EXTREMELY RARE, CAXTON, 1483.—Here begynneth a lityll treatise shorte and abredged spekynge of the ARTE AND CRAFTE TO KNOWE WELL TO DYE. W. CAXTON, 1490, *very fine copy of a Tract* OF EXCESSIVE RARITY, *in 1 vol. russia*.

3787 Quatriregio del Decursu della Vita Humana di Fred. Frezzi (Nicolo Malpigli) in rime, *fine copy, black morocco*, RARE, *Milano, Antonio Zarotto*, 1488

£	s.	d.	No.	Description	Buyer
11	0	6	3788	Reali di Franza, comenzado da Constantino Imperatore secondo molto Lezende che io ho attrovute e racolte insieme. *Venetia, per Christophalo da Pensis da Mandello,* 1499	Hibbert
	14	-	3789	Recorde's Castle of Knowledge, *R. Wolfe,* 1556	Rodd
9	15	-	3790	Recueil des Histoires Troiennes par Raoul le Fevre, *wood cuts, blue morocco,* RARE, *Paris, Verard, sans date.*	Triphook
30		-	3791	Recueil of the Histories of Troye, translated by Wyllyam Caxton, *very fine copy in blue morocco,* RARE, *Wyllyam Copland,* 1553	Do
2	2	-	3792	Recueil des Histoires Romaines, *wood cuts, Paris, G. Eustace,* 1513	Hibbert
33	1	6	3793	REGNAULT DE MONTAUBAN, Cy finist l'Istoire du Noble et Vaillant Chevalier Regnault de Montauban, *sans date.* A very ancient edition with wood cuts and singular Capital Letters, *fine copy, red morocco,* EXTREMELY RARE.	Do.
80	-	-	3794	Redouté, Les Liliacées, 5 vol. *coloured plates, splendidly bound in russia,* - - *Paris,* 1802, &c.	Sir S. Clarke
15	15	-	3795	Redouté et Decandolle Plantarum Succulentarum Historia. Histoire des Plantes Grasses, 20 Livraisons on LARGE VELLUM PAPER, *splendidly bound in russia, Parisiis,* 1799	Triphook
	14	-	3796	Reynolds's Triumphs of God's Revenge against Murther, *plates,* - - - 1704	Rodd
	3	-	3797	Ripa, Iconologie, ou Explication des Emblemes, Images, &c. &c. *Paris,* 1636	Triphook
13	-	-	3798	Robert, Recueil des Plantes, dessinées et gravées par l'Ordre du Roi (Louis XIV.) 3 vol. *largest paper.*	Hibbert
100	-	-	3799	ROMANS, RECUEIL DES ROMANS DES CHEVALIERS DE LA TABLE RONDE, à savoir Le San-Graal, Merlin, et Lancelot du Lac. A very valuable Manuscript upon vellum, containing more than Seven Hundred Miniatures, illuminated in gold and colours, from the Roxburghe Library. See the Catalogue No. 6093, 3 vol. *red morocco.*	Triphook
11	11	-	3800	Rousseau, La Botanique, par Redouté, VELLUM PAPER, *plates beautifully coloured, splendidly bound in russia, Paris,* 1805	Do.
	9	-	3801	Ruffi, Histoire de la Ville de Marseille, *Marseille,* 1642	Heber
9	19	6	3802	Ruiz et Pavon, Prodromus et Novarum Generum Plantarum Peruvianarum et Chilensium Descriptiones et Icones, 3 vol. *russia,* - - *Madrid,* 1794-8	Loddiges
2	2	-	3803	Rusconi, Architettura di, *plates, Thuanus's copy, Venet. Giolito,* 1590	Payne
73	10	-	3804	ROYAL BOOK, OR A BOOK FOR A KYNG, reduced out of Frensshe into Englysshe by Caxton and fynysshed. *A perfect copy in russia, with wood cuts,* - 1484	Hibbert
	13	-	3805	Ryff Newe Distillier Buch, *many plates, Francf.* 1597	Longman

TWENTIETH DAY'S SALE.

Octavo et Infra.

£	s.	d.	Lot	Description	Buyer
1	10	-	3806	Scott's Minstrelsy of the Scottish Border, 3 vol. *green morocco*, - - - *Kelso*, 1802	Henry
1	5	-	3807	Scott's, Sir Tristrem, a Metrical Romance, *blue morocco*, *Edinburgh*, 1804	Hodson
21	10	-	3808	SCOTTES. An exhortacion to the Scottes, to conforme them selves to the honorable expedient and Godly Union betwene the twoo realmes of Englande & Scotlande. R. Grafton 1547. An Epistle or exhortation sent from the Lord Protector to the Nobilitie, &c. of Scotlande. R. Grafton 1542. 2 vol. in 1, *black letter, fine copies, morocco, from the Roxburghe Collection,* VERY RARE	Triphook
	3	-	3809	Scriptores varii Argumentorum Ludicrorum et Amœnitatum, - - - - *Lugd. Bat.* 1623	Christie
	15	-	3810	Scripture. Common places of Scripture set forth by Erasmus Sarcerius, translated into English by Richard Taverner, *black letter*, - - *Thomas East*, 1577	Cochran
5	10	-	3811	Sea-Man's Triumph, declaring the actions of such Gentlemen Captaines and Sailers as were at the takinge of the great Carrick, lately brought to Dartmouth, with the manner of their flight, and names of men of accompt, *black letter,* VERY RARE, *red morocco*, *London*, 1592	Payne
	4	-	3812	Secret (Le) des Cours, ou les Memoires de Walsingham, *Cologne*, 1695	Anderdon
2	-	-	3813	Sectes. The Original & Sprynge of all Sectes & Orders, by whome, whan or were they beganne, *black letter,* RARE, *Southwarke, by I. Nicolson, for Jhon Gough*, 1537	Cochran
	11	-	3814	Secundi (Johannis) Opera, *blue morocco, with joints*, *Paris*, 1561	Heber
	4	-	3815	——————— Opera, emendata, et aucta, *green morocco*, - - - - - *ib.* 1582	Triphook
	6	-	3816	——————— Opera, ex museo Scriverii, *Lugd. Bat.* 1631	Christie
			3817	——————— Opera, *red morocco*, *Paris*, 1748	
	15	-	3818	Secundus's Kisses, with an Essay on his Life and Writings, 1778	Triphook
	12	-	3819	Seduction, The Case of, being an Account of the Proceedings against the Reverend Abbé Claudius Nicholas des Rues, for committing Rapes upon 133 Virgins, 1732	Do.
	3		3820	Segrais, Zayde, Histoire Espagnole, 2 vol. *green morocco*, *Paris*, 1671	Do.

£	s.	d.	Lot	Description	Buyer
	5	-	3821	Seiz, Annus Tertius Sæcularis inventæ Typographicæ, *Harlemi*, 1741	Payne
	4	-	3822	Seldenus de Successionibus ad Leges Ebræorum in bona defunctorum, *yellow morocco*, - *Elzevir*, 1638	Do.
	7	-	3823	Selector (The), *red morocco*, - - 1804	H.
	4	-	3824	Semelion, Histoire Veritable, *blue morocco*, *à Constantinople cette Année presente.*	Triphook
	3	-	3825	Senarii in Horti Spectaculum, *blue morocco*, *Lutetii*, 1609	Do.
2	12	6	3826	Senecæ Opera Omnia, 4 vol. *red morocco, ruled*, *Elzevir*, 1640	Do.
1	19	-	2827	Alia Editio, 4 vol, *blue morocco, with joints*, *ib.* 1659	Cochran
	5	-	3828	Senecæ Tragœdiæ, *red morocco*, - *Aldus*, 1517	Triphook
	6	-	3829	Senecæ et aliorum Tragœdiæ, *blue morocco*, *Amst.* 1664	Do.
1	6	-	3830	Senecæ Tragœdia Nona quæ Octavia nominatur, *blue morocco*, RARE, - *Paris, Brunello*, 1533	Heber
	13	-	3831	Seneca, Le Tragedie di, tradotte da Dolce, *blue morocco*, *Venet. Giolito*, 1560	Do.
	4	-	3832	Seneque, les motz dorez des quatre Vertus Cardinales compose par Claude de Seissel, *black letter, red morocco*, *Paris, par Simon du Bois*, 1527	Triphook
	4	-	3833	Sententiæ Singulis versibus contentæ, juxta ordinem literarum, ex diversis Poetis, Gr. Lat. - *Paris* 1540	Heber
	2	-	3834	Senofonte Efesio, Gli Efesiaci di, da Salvini, *Parigi*, 1800	Triphook
	19	-	3835	Septuaginta Græca -*Londini, Daniel*, 1653	Christie
1	2	-	3836	Septuaginta Græca *Cantab. Field*, 1665	Cochran
12	18	-	3837	Sepulveda, Romances Nuevamente sacados de Historias Antiguas de la Cronica de España compuestos por Loreçco de Sepulveda, annadiose el Romance de la Conquista de la ciudad de Africa en Berveria, y otros diversos. *blue morocco, morocco inside*, RARE, *Anvers*, 1580	Hare
	19	-	3838	Seraphina d'Amore dove se contiene Sonetti, Strambotti, &c. - - - *Venet. Roffinello*, 1544	Do.
	2	-	3839	Serasquier Bassa, an Historical Novel of the Times, 1685	H.
	5	-	3840	Sermon des Quakers de Londres, par le frere E. Elwall, *red morocco*, - - - 1737	Do.
	4	-	3841	Serre (de La) Les Delices de la Mort, *plates, black morocco*, - - - - *Bruxelles*, 1631	Heber
	16	-	3842	Seward's Anecdotes of Distinguished Persons, 4 vol. 1796	Triphook
	15	-	3843	Seyssel (Claude de) La Grand Monarchie. La Loi Salique, premiere loy des François, *yellow morocco, scarce*, *Paris, par Denys Janot, sans date*	Clarke
	7	-	3844	Shaftsbury's Rawleigh Redivivus, or the Life and Death of Anthony, late Earl of Shaftsbury, - - 1683	Hare
2	10	-	3845	Shakespear's Works, by Pope, 8 vol. in 16, *Glas.* 1766	Triphook
11	-	-	3846	———— Comedies, Histories and Tragedies, by Capell, 10 vol. *blue morocco, with joints*, - *Tonson*, 1767	Arch

£	s.	d.	Lot	Description	Buyer
2	10	-	3847	Shakespeare. Capell's Prolusions, *blue morocco, with joints,* *Tonson,* 1760	Arch
	12	-	3848	———— Dramatic Works. *red morocco,* *Stockdale,* 1784	Evans
3	-		3849	———— Plays by Johnson and Steevens, 10 vol. 1785	Cuthell
8	10	6	3850	———— Plays, Wallis's Edition, 10 vol. *large paper, green morocco, with joints,* - - *Bensley,* 1803	Triphook
2	8	-	3851	———— Twenty Plays from the Original Editions, by Steevens, 4 vol. - - - 1766	Jervis
	7	-	3852	Shee's Elements of Art, a Poem, - - 1809	Johnstone
	7	-	3853	—— Rhymes on Art - - - 1805	Triphook
	2	-	3854	Ship (The Modern) of Fools, - - 1807	Harry
	3	-	3855	Sibthorp Flora Oxoniensis - - *Oxon.* 1794	Booth
	2	-	3856	Siden's History of the Sevarites or Sevarambi 1665	Triphook
	1	-	3857	Sidney's (Sir P.) Almanzor and Almanzaida, a Novel, 1678	Money
1	-	-	3858	Silius Italicus, *red morocco,* - - *Aldus,* 1523	Triphook
17	5	-	3159	SILVA DE VARIOS ROMANCES en que estan recopilados la mayor parte de los Romances Castellanos que hasta agora se han compuesto. Hay al fin algunas canciones y coplas graciosas y sentidas, *blue morocco,* VERY RARE, *Caragoça,* 1550	Heber
	2	-	3860	Simpson's Treatise of Algebra, - 1667	John
	7	-	3861	Simolachri Historie e Figure de la Morte, *plates, russia,* *Lyone, Frellone,* 1549	Triphook
2	-	-	3862	Skelton's Pithy, Pleasaunt, and Profitable Works, *russia,* *London,* 1736	Do.
1	6	-	3863	Sleidanus de quatuor summis Imperiis, *Elzevir,* 1631	Clarke
			3864	Smid's Pictura Loquens sive Heroicarum Tabularum Schoonebeeck Enarratio et Explicatio, *large paper, green morocco,* - - - - *Amst.* 1695	
	2	-	3865	Smith's (Capt A.) Thieves Grammar ——	Warner
	11	-	3866	Smith's Inquiry into the Nature and Causes of the Wealth of Nations, 3 vol. - - - 1796	Rodd
	16	-	3867	Smith's Exotic Botany, the Figures by Sowerby, vol. 1, 1804	Loddiges
	13	-	3868	Smith, Flora Britannica, 3 vol. - *Londini,* 1800	Do.
	1	-	3869	Smith's Tracts relative to Natural History - 1798	Triphook
	19	-	3870	Smyth's Defence of the Sacrifice of the Masse, *black letter,* *John Herforde,* 1546	Cochran
1	10	-	3871	Smythe's Assertion and Defence of the Sacramente of the Aulter, *black letter, fine copy, blue morocco,* *John Herforde,* 1546	Heber
1	10	-	3872	Smyth's brief Treatyse settynge forth divers Truthes necessary both to be beleved of Chrysten people, and kepte also, *black letter, blue morocco,* *Thomas Petit,* 1547	Do.
12	-	-	3173	Sneyders Amoris Divini et Humani Effectus varii, emble-	Payne

matis sacræ scripturæ sanctorumque P. P. Sententiis ac Gallicis versibus illustrati, Anno, 1626. The plates (56 in number) printed upon vellum, and beautifully coloured by SNEYDERS HIMSELF. The Latin and French verses, &c. in Manuscript upon vellum, bound in *green morocco*, AN UNIQUE COPY.

3874 Sneyders, Amoris Divini et Humani Antipathia, *plates*, *Antverpiæ*, 1629

3875 Solanges, Memoires du Marquis de, 2 vol. *Amst.* 1766

3876 Somervile's Chace. Hobbinol, or the Rural Games, *plates*, 1757

3877 Somervile's Chace, *blue morocco*, - 1805

3878 Somneri Vocabularium Anglo-Saxonicum, *Oxon.* 1701

3879 Somner's Treatise of the Roman Ports and Forts in Kent, *Portrait*, - - - - *Oxford*, 1693

3880 Sonan, Chriserionte de Gaule, *blue morocco*, *Lyon*, 1620

3881 Song of Solomon, in English Meeter, *Edinburgh*, 1701

3882 Sonnini, Voyage en Egypte, 3 vol. and Atlas, in 4to. *Paris*, 1799

3883 Sophoclis Tragœdiæ Septem, Gr. *first Edition*, *russia*, *Aldus*, 1502

3884 Sophocles, ex Editione Brunck, 2 vol. *blue morocco*, *Oxon.* 1809

3885 Sorbiere, Relation d'un Voyage en Angleterre, *Paris*, 1664

3886 Sorbin, dit de Saincte Foy, Histoire de Charles IX. où sont contenués plusieurs choses merveilleuses advenues durant son regne, à bon droit dit le Regne des merveilles, *yellow morocco*, - - - - - *ib.* 1574

3887 Souhait. Les Divers Souhaits d'Amour - *ib.* 1599

3888 Source (La) d'Honneur pour maintenir la corporelle élégance des dames en vigueur, *black letter, title* MS. *Lyon*, 1543

3889 Southey's Thalaba the Destroyer, 2 vol. - 1801

3890 ——— Specimens of the later English Poets, 3 vol. *green morocco*, - - - - - 1807

3891 Southouse's Surveigh of the Monastery of Faversham, 1671

3892 Spanish Novels (Three Ingenious) ———

3893 Spanish (The) Gallant, by Gracian de Antisco, translated by Style, - - - - - 1640

3894 Spectator (The) 8 vol. ———

3895 Spelte, La Sage Folie, Fontaine d'Allegresse, Mere des plaisirs, Reyne des belles humeurs, traduitte par Garron, *red morocco*, - - - - *Rouen*

3896 Spence's Parallel, in the manner of Plutarch, between Magliabechi & Hill, *red morocco, with joints*, *Strawberry Hill*, 1758

	8	-	3897	Spençer's (W. R) Poems, - - - 1811	Heber
1	-	-	3898	Spenser's Works, by Hughes, 6 vol. - 1750	Rodd
9	-	-	3899	——— Works, by Todd, 8 vol. *large paper, yellow morocco,* - - - - 1805	Triphook
	1	-	3900	Spigelii Isagoges in rem herbariam, *blue morocco, Elzevir,* 1633	D°
	2	-	3901	Spon de l'Origine des Etrennes, - *Paris,* 1781	Giles
	5	-	3902	Sportsman's (The Young) Instructor, by G. M. *green morocco,*	Triphook
	4	-	3903	——— Delight and Instructor, by G. M. *red morocco,*	Rodd
	16	-	3904	Stael's (Mad. de) Corinna, or Italy, 3 vol. - 1807	Hay
2	12	-	3905	Stalbridge's Epistel Exhortatorye of an Inglyshe Chrystian unto his derely-beloved countrey of Ingland, against the pompouse popysh Bishops thereof, *black letter, fine copy, blue morocco,* RARE, - - *no date or place*	Cochran
	4	-	3906	Stanyan's Grecian History, 2 vol. - 1781	Evans
1	16	-	3907	Stanze Amorose sopra gli Horti delle donne et in lode della Menta, da Tansillo *red morocco,* - *Venetia,* 1574	Payne
1	17	-	3908	Altro esemplare, *yellow morocco,* - 1574	Triphook
	4	-	3909	Statii Sylvæ, Thebais, Achilleis. - *Aldus,* 1502	Heber
	19	-	3910	Alia Editio, *red morocco,* - - *ib.* 1519	D°
	14	-	3911	Statius, *red morocco,* - *Paris, Colinæus,* 1530	Triphook
	5	-	3912	Statius, *green morocco, morocco lining, Amst.* 1624	Heber
	3	-	3913	Statius cum Notis Stephens, *russia, Cantab.* 1651	Evans
1	19	-	3914	Statius ex recens. Gronovii, *green morocco, morocco lining, Elzevir.* 1653	Triphook
-	-	-	3915	Steeven's (George) Catalogue of the Library of, with the Prices and Purchasers Names. - 1800	Passed
	14	-	3916	Stengelii, Ova Paschalia sacro Emblemate inscripta descriptaque, *plates, yellow morocco, Ingolstadii,* 1672	Triphook
	5	-	3917	——— Corona Lucida in Cœlo jam fulgens, olim in Terris conserta, *plates, blue morocco, Vindel.*	Rodd
1	1	-	3918	——— Josephus hoc est Sanctissimi Educatoris Christi Historia, *plates, red morocco, Monaci,* 1616	Triphook
	10	-	3919	Stephani, Paralipomena Grammaticarum Gr. Linguæ Inst. 1581, De Puerili Græcarum Literarum doctrina Liber. 1555, 2 vol. in 1, *morocco, with joints.*	D°
	2	-	3920	Stephani et Brounei Catalogus Horti Botanici Oxoniensis, *russia,* - - *Oxon.* 1658	Money
	4	-	3921	Stephens's Essayes and Characters Ironical and Instructive, - - - - 1615	Rodd
	7	-	3922	Stewart's Genealogy of the Stewarts refuted, *Edinburgh,* 1799	D°
	18	-	3923	Stolcii Hortulus Hermeticus Flosculis Philosophorum Cupro incisis conformatus, &c. *white morocco, Francofurti,* 1627	Triphook
	5	-	3924	Strange (John) Catalogue of the Library of, 1801	Mitchell

£	s.	d.	Lot	Description	Buyer
	4	-	3925	Straparola. Le Piacevoli Notti di Giovan Fr. Straparola da Caravaggio, 2 vol. - - *Luca*, 1551	Triphook
	15		3926	Straparola. Le Piacevoli Notti di, *blue morocco*, RARE, *Vineg.* 1560	Payne
	15	-	3927	Altro Esemplare, *green morocco*, - *Venet.* 1608	Triphook
1	6	-	3928	Straparole. Les Nuicts Facetieuses du J. F. Straparole, 2 vol. *yellow morocco*, - *Paris*, 1585	Do.
1	1	-	3929	Autre Edition, 2 vol. *blue morocco*, - - 1726	Do.
	2	-	3930	Stubbe, Fraus Honesta, Comœdia Cantabrigiæ olim acta, *Londini*, 1632	Clarke
	10	-	3931	Suave, Devis sur la Vigne, Vin et Vendanges, *Paris*, 1550	Triphook
	8	-	3932	Suede. Histoire de la Vie de la Reine de Suede, *blue morocco*, - - - *Fribourg*, 1667	Payne
	1	-	3933	Suetonii Opera, - - *Paris*, 1644	Rodd
	2	-	3934	Suisse. Formulaire de Consentement des Eglises Reformées de Suisse sur la Doctrine de la Grace Universelle, et autres pieces, - - 1695, &c.	Triphook
	9	-	3935	Sulpitii Severi Opera Omnia, *blue morocco*, *Elzevir.* 1643	Cochran
1	19	-	3936	Summe (The) of the Holy Scripture, and Ordinarye of the Chrystian teachying the true Christian Fayth, by the whiche we be all justified, *black letter, blue morocco, with joints*, - - - 1548	Do.
	9	-	3937	Supper (The) of the Lorde after the true meaning of the Sixte of John, and the XI of the fyrst Epistle to the Corinthians, by John Fryth, *black letter, blue morocco, with joints*, - - - - - 1533	Rodd
1	16	-	3938	Supplication of the poore Commons, wherunto is added the Supplication of Beggars, *black letter, blue morocco, fine copy*, - - - *no date.*	Heber
1	14	-	3939	Supplication that the Nobles and Commons of Osteryke made lately by their Messaungers unto Kynge Ferdinandus in the Cause of the Christen Religion, *black letter, blue morocco*, RARE, - - *no date.*	Cochran
1	1	-	3940	Surrey. Poems of Henry Howard, Earl of Surrey, with the Poems of Sir Thomas Wiat, *russia, with joints*, 1717	Rodd
	18	-	3941	Surveyinge, by Fitzherbarde, *black letter, green morocco, fine copy*, - - - *Berthelet*, 1539	Triphook
	9	-	3942	Susii Opuscula Litteraria, - *Antverpiæ*, 1620	Heber

Quarto.

£	s.	d.	Lot	Description	Buyer
	15	-	3943	Secret (le) des Secretz, Aristote qui ensegne a cognoistre la complecion des hommes et des femmes, *russia*, *Cy fine le petit monde, sans date.*	Rodd
	5	-	3944	Seduli Imagines Sanctorum, cum Elogiis, *Antv.* 1602	Clarke

£	s.	d.	Lot	Description	Buyer
3	11	-	3945	Segura. Processo de Cartas de Amores, *fine copy, scarce,* *Toledo*, 1548	Heber
6	-	-	3946	Sëir Mutagharin, or View of Modern Times, being an History of India for 1781-82, 3 vol. *Calcutta*, 1789	Do
4	-	-	3947	Selman. The Araignment of John Selman who was executed neere Charing Crosse, 7th of January, 1612, for a Fellony committed in the King's Chapell, at White-Hall, *black letter, inlaid, red morocco,* *T. Archer*, 1612	Rodd
2	2	-	3248	Seven Champions of Christendom, the Famous History of the, *black morocco,* - - 1670	Triphook
1	6	-	3949	Another edition, - - - 1705	Do
	16	-	3950	Seven Champions of Christendome, by John Kirke, acted at the Cocke-Pit, - - 1638	Hibbert
6	-	-	3951	Seynt Kateryne, Lyf and Martyrdom of, *manuscript upon vellum,* from the Towneley Library, *blue morocco.*	Do
1	5	-	3952	Shakspeare's Merchant of Venice, - 1637	Jervis
1	1	-	3953	———— Love's Labours Lost, - 1631	Triphook
10	-	-	3954	———— King Richard the Second, - 1598	Jervis
18	7	6	3955	———— Henry the Fourth, Part I. - 1599	Do
	3	-	3956	———— Henry the Fourth, Part I. - 1639	Rodd
10	10	-	3957	———— Romeo and Juliet, *inlaid, rare,* 1599	Jervis
1	-	-	3958	———— Romeo and Juliet, - 1637	Hay
	12	-	3959	———— Othello, - - 1630	Jervis
2	5	-	3960	———— Pericles, *red morocco,* - 1609	Do
	9	-	3960	———— Pericles, - - 1630	Triphook
5	5	-	3961	———— Sir John Oldcastle, *red morocco,* 1600	Jervis
37	-	-	3962	———— Sonnets, never before Imprinted, *inlaid, red morocco,* VERY RARE, - - 1609	Do
16	16	-	3963	Shepeherdes, The Kalender of, *wood cuts, imperfect,* *Wynkyn de Worde*, 1528	Do
1	7	-	3964	Sidney. Exequiæ Illustrissimi Equitis D. Philippi Sidnæi, Peplus Ph. Sidnæi, - - *Oxon.* 1587	Dr Butler
2	15	-	3965	Sight of the Transactions of these latter yeares emblamized with engraven plates, which men may read without spectacles, collected by John Vicars, *blue morocco, ruled,* 1647	Cochran
1	14		3966	Another copy, - - - 1647	Rodd
2	9	-	3967	Sibyllarum (XII.) Icones a Cr. Passæo delineati, ac tabulis æneis in lucem editi. *fine impressions, blue morocco,* 1601	Hibbert
1	1	-	3968	Silvius (Æneas) de duobus Amantibus, Euriolo et Lucretia, *red morocco,* - - *sine ulla notâ.*	Triphook
1	3	-	3969	Sketches of William Pitt and Charles James Fox, of Lord Nelson and of Burke, *with portraits,* - 1807	Do
	9	-	3970	Smith's Common-wealth of England, and maner of Government thereof *black letter,* - *Val. Simmes*, 1594	Heber
11	-	-	3971	Smith's Select Views in Italy, *red morocco, with joints,* 1792	Do
3	-	-	3972	Somervile's Chase, *wood cuts, green morocco, Bulmer,* 1796	Bulmer

3973 Somerville, History of Political Transactions from the Restoration, to the Death of William III. 1792

3974 Sonnerat, Voyage aux Indes Orientales et à la Chine, 2 vol. *plates*, - - - *Paris*, 1782

3975 Sonnerat, Voyage à la Nouvelle Guinée, *plates*, *ib.* 1776

3976 Sorowes Joy, or a Lamentation of our late deceased Sovereigne, Elizabeth, with a Triumph for the prosperous succession of our gracious King James, &c. *very fine copy, with portraits of Elizabeth and King James inserted, blue morocco*, RARE, *Printed by John Legat, Printer to the Universitie of Cambridge*, 1603

3977 Southerne's Treatise concerning the right use and ordering of Bees, *black letter*, - *T. Orwin*, 1593

3978 Spectacle de la Vie Humaine ou Leçons de Sagesse exprimées avec art en 103 Tableaux en Taille douce, avec des explications, par le Clerc, *blue morocco, with joints*, *la Haye*, 1755

3979 Speculum Religiosorum et Speculum Christianorum, a Manuscript of the Fourteenth Century, upon vellum, written by John Watson, contains several English Prayers in verse. See Watson's History of Poety, Vol. II. p. 194, *blue morocco, with joints*.

3980 Spencer's Faerie Queene, Colin Clout's come home again.—Complaints.—Tears of the Muses and other Poems, in 2 vol. FIRST EDITIONS, *fine copies, blue morocco*, RARE, 1590-96

3981 ——— Shepherd's Calendar, *black letter, blue morocco, rare*, - - - - - 1597

3982 Spiegel der Spaensche tierannye geschiet in Westindien, *plates*, - - - - *Amst.* 1620

3983 Spiegel der Deugden en Konsten. Miroir des Vertus et des Arts, *plates, red morocco, with joints*, *Leyden*, 1721

3984 Spiegel Teucht door Z. G. H. P. H. S. *plates*, 1610

3985 Spinniker Leerzaame Zinnebeelden, 2 vol. *plates*, *Haarlem*, 1757

3986 Spinola Funerali nella morta del Cardinale H. Spinola Arcivescovo di Genova, *plates, venetian morocco, senz' anno.*

3987 Statutes and Orders relative to the Plague, 1630

3988 Statuts de l'Ordre de Saint Esprit, - *Paris*, 1788

3989 Staunton's Account of Lord Macartney's Embassy to China, 2 vol. and atlas, fol. - 1797

3990 Stella. Les Jeux et Plaisirs de l'Enfance, *fine impressions, blue morocco*, - - *Paris*, 1657

3991 Stow's Annals of England, *russia*, *R. Newbery*, 1592

3992 Strafforde's (The Earl of) Passage over the Styx described, 1641

Strawberry Hill Publications.

£	s.	d.	Lot	Description	Buyer
9	12		3993	Gray's Odes, 1757. To Mr. Gray on his Odes.—Poems, by Anne Chamber, Countess Temple, 1764.—Verses sent to Lady Charles Spencer, with a painted Taffety.—Poems, by the Rev. Mr. Hoyland, 1769.—The Muse recalled, an Ode, by Sir W. Jones, on the Marriage of the present Earl Spencer, 1781.—Bishop Bonner's Ghost, 1789.—Rules relative to Strawberry Hill.—To Lady Horatia Waldegrave, on the Death of the Duke of Ancaster.—The Press at Strawberry Hill, to the Duke of Clarence.—The Press, to Miss Mary and Miss Agnes Berry.—The Magpie and her Brood.—Epitaph on a Canary Bird.—Epitaph on a Woman who sold Earthen Ware, *many of these being single leaves, are very scarce, red morocco, with joints.*	Triphook
3	8	-	3994	Life of Edward, Lord Herbert of Cherbury, *portrait, red morocco, with joints.* 1764	Do.
2	15	-	3995	Hamilton, Mémoires du Comte de Grammont, *portrait, red morocco, with joints,* - - 1772	Do.
1	5	-	3996	Miscellaneous Antiquities, two Numbers.—Copies of Seven Letters from King Edward VI, to Barnaby Fitz-Patrick, *red morocco,* - - - 1772	Do.
3	3	-	3997	Description of Strawberry Hill, *red morocco,* 1774	Dorrant
2	5	-	3998	Another Edition, with plates, *red morocco, with joints,* 1784	Triphook
1	2	-	3999	Walpole's Essay on Modern Gardening, with a French Translation by the Duc de Nivernois, *red morocco, with joints,* - - - - - 1785	Do.

Folio.

£	s.	d.	Lot	Description	Buyer
	17	-	4000	Saavedræ Symbola Christiano-Politica, *many plates, hog skin,* - - - *Brux.* 1649	Johnstone
1	5	-	4001	Saint-Gelais. Le Vergier d'Honneur, *wood cuts,* *Paris, s. date.*	Heber
sold for 47	7	-	4002	Saint Non, Voyage Pittoresque de Naples et de Sicile, 5 vol. PROOF IMPRESSIONS of the plates, with the double plates of the Sicilian Coins, *very fine copy, in red morocco,* — *Paris,* 1781-86 (Imperfect - Sold first time for £50. 18. 6)	Payne
9	9	-	4003	Salade, laquelle fait mension de tous les Pays du Monde, *wood cuts, Michel le Noir,* 1521.—La Grant Nef des Folz du Monde, *wood cuts, scarce, Geoffry Marnef,* 1494, *in one vol. red morocco,*	Hibbert
5	-	-	4004	Salmon's English Herbal, or History of Plants, *fine copy, splendidly bound in hog skin, with joints,* - 1710	Triphook

£	s.	d.	Lot	Description	Buyer
6	16	6	4005	SALUSTIO. La Conjuracion de Catalina y la Guerra de Jugurta translated by the Infant Don Gabriel of Spain, with an Appendix, by Bayer, on the Phœnician Coins. *One of the copies of the first distribution, in red morocco,* *Madrid,* 1772	Triphook
3	13	6	4006	Sandoval, Chronica del Inclito Emperador don Alonso VII, *russia,* - - - *Madrid,* 1600	Hibbert
3	15	-	4007	Sandrat, Academia Artis Pictoriæ in Lingua Germanica, *first impressions of the plates, russia,* *Nureb.* 1675	Mason
	19	-	4008	Saunders's Physiognomie and Chiromancie, 1671	Foss
3	4	-	4009	Saxonis Grammatici Historia Danica ex Recogn. Stephanii, *red morocco,* - - *Soræ,* 1644	Payne
3	15	-	4010	Schedel, Chronicarum Liber, *plates uncoloured,* *Nuremb. Koburger,* 1493	Carpenter
	18	-	4011	Scheffer's History of Lapland, *plates, red morocco,* *Oxford,* 1674	Evans
64	1	-	4012	SCOTLAND, THE HISTORY AND CHRONICLES OF, compilit be the Noble Clerk Maister, Hector Boece, Channon of Aberdene, translatit laitly in our vulgar and common langage, be Maister John Bellendene, Archdene of Murray. A book of EXTRAORDINARY RARITY, *morocco,* *Imprinted in Edinburgh by me Thomas Davidson,* (*about* 1536)	Appleyard for Earl Spencer
18	7	6	4013	SHAKESPEARE'S Comedies, Histories, and Tragedies, *first edition, morocco,* - - - 1623	Arch
5	2	6	4014	——— Comedies, Histories, &c. *second impression, morocco,* - - - 1632	Do
14	10	-	4015	——— *third impression, morocco,* - - - 1664	Do
4	16	-	4016	——— *fourth impression, morocco,* - - - 1685	Do
	11	-	4017	Shaw's Travels in Barbary and the Levant, *Oxford,* 1738	Foss
1	18	-	4018	Simon, Noticias Historiales de las Conquistas de Tierra-Firme en las Indias Occidentales, *morocco,* *Madrid,* 1627	Triphook
1	11	6	4019	Shepheard's Kalendar, *black letter, wood cuts,* 1618	Rodd
4	5		4020	Silvius (Æneas) de Duobus Amantibus Eurialo et Lucretia et de Amoris Remedio. A very ancient edition in double columns, without signatures, numerals, or catch-words, *red morocco,* - - *sine ulla notâ.*	Heber

TWENTY-FIRST DAY'S SALE.

Octavo et Infra.

4021 Sutton's Disce Mori, Learne to Die, *black letter*, 1600

4022 Swartz Observationes Botanicæ, *plates*, *Erlangæ*, 1791

4023 Swift's Works by Sheridan and Nichols, 19 vol. *large paper*, 1801

4024 Swift's Gulliver's Travels, 2 vol. - 1776

4025 Swift, Le Conte du Tonneau, 2 vol. *à la Haye*, 1732

4026 Swinton's Travels into Norway, Denmark, and Russia, 1792

4027 Sylvester's Parliament of Vertues Royal, 2 vol. RARE, *no date.*

4028 Sylvester's Poems collected in one volume, *blue morocco*, 1615, &c.

4029 Symbola Divina et Humana Pontificum, Imperatorum, Regum, *plates*, *blue morocco*, *with joints*, *Arnheima*, 1666

4030 Symbola Principum Italiæ, *plates*, *yellow morocco*, *Amst.* 1686

4031 Symon's Synopsis Plantarum Insulis Britannicis Indigenarum, - - - 1798

4032 Tabarin. Recueil Général des Œuvres et Fantaisies de Tabarin, *yellow morocco*, - - *Rouen*, 1627

4033 Table (A) collected of the yeres of our Lorde God, and of the yeres of the Kingdom of England from William the Conqueror, &c. *black letter*, - *J. Waley*, 1558

4034 Tableau (Le) des Piperies des Femmes Mondaines, *red morocco*, - - *Cologne*, 1685

4035 Tablettes Géographiques pour l'Intelligence des Historiens et des Poetes Latins, 2 vol. - *Paris*, 1755

4036 Tacitus ex Lipsii accuratissima Editione, 2 vol. *red morocco*, *Elzevir*, 1634

4037 Tacitus ex Lipsii editione cum Not. Grotii, 2 vol. *red morocco*, *by Padeloup*, - - *Elzevir*, 1640

4038 Savilius in Tacitum et Comment. de Militia Romana, *red morocco*, - - *Elzevir*, 1649

4039 Taciti Opera ex Editione Gronovii, 4 vol. *Glasguæ*, 1753

4040 Taciti quæ extant Opera recensuit Lallemand, 3 vol. *red morocco*, - - *Parisiis*, 1760

4041 Tahureau. Odes, Sonnets et autres poesies Gentiles et Facetieuses de Jacques Tahureau, - *Lyon*, 1574

4042 Tales of the Genii, 2 vol. - - 1781

4043 Tales of the Genii, translated from the Persian, by Sir C. Morell, *large paper*, *plates*, *red morocco*, 1805

4044 Talleyrand de Perigord's Memoirs, 2 vol. 1805

£	s.	d.	Lot	Description	Buyer
	5	-	4045	Tansillo, Il Vendemiatore, - - *senza nota.*	Hare
	1	-	4046	Tansillo, Il Vendemiatore.	Dunbar
	3	-	4047	Tant mieux pour elle, Facetie faite en 1762 attribuée à l'Abbé de Voisenon.	Triphook
13	10	-	4048	Tartaria, Doi Itinerarii in Tartaria, per Alcuni Fratri mandati da Papa Innocentio IV. nella detta Provincia de Scithia per Ambasciatori, *blue morocco,* *Venet. per N. da Sabio,* 1537	Hare

19£ in Col. Stanley's Sale.

"This curious little volume is of rare occurrence, Mr. Crofts had written in his Copy, "Liber Rarissimus, quippe cujus apud Bibliographos nullibi fit mentio." But that accurate Italian scholar does not appear to have been acquainted with the contents of the Volume, or he would probably have stated, that it contained the first edition in Italian, of the Travels of Carpini, who went through Poland and Russia to Tartary in the year 1247." Stanley Catalogue.

£	s.	d.	Lot	Description	Buyer
	9	-	4049	Tasso, Rime di Bernardo Tasso, *Vinegia, Giolito,* 1560	Hare
1	1	-	4050	——- Il Goffredo, overo Gierusalemme Liberata del Torquato, *red morocco,* - - 1652	Triphook
	17	-	4051	——- Gierusalemme Liberata, 2 vol. *Elzevir,* 1678	Lepard
	11	-	4052	Tasse, La Hierusalem delivreé, en vers François, 2 vol. *cuts, green morocco,* - - *Paris,* 1671	Heber
	7	-	4053	Tasso, Aminta, Favola Boschereccia, *morocco,* *Venet, Aldo,* 1583	Triphook
	7	-	4054	Tasso, Aminta, *red morocco,* *Leida, Elsevir,* 1656	Money
	4	-	4055	Tasso, Aminta, - - *Elsevir,* 1678	Lepard
	5	-	4066	Tasso, Aminta, *frontispiece,* - *Parigi,* 1800	Warner
	3	-	4057	Tasse Rouzi Friou Titave aux Femmes ou aux Maris pour donner a leurs Femmes, - *Paris,* 1713	Triphook
	12	-	4058	Tavannes, Memoires de, *portrait,* *Cologne,* 1691	Clarke
	11	-	4059	Taverner's Garden of Wysdome conteynyng pleasaunte floures, that is to saye propre and quicke sayinges of Princes, &c, *black letter,* - *J. Kynge.*	Triphook
1	2	-	4060	Tavernier, Voyages en Turquie, en Perse, et aux Indes, 3 vol. *plates,* - - - *Paris,* 1679	Warner
	15	-	4061	Taxe de la Chancellerie Romaine ou Le Banque du Pape, *blue morocco,* - - *Paris,* 1744	Triphook
	15	-	4062	Taxe des Parties casuelles de la Boutique du Pape, Lat. et Fr. *red morocco,* - - *Lyon,* 1564	D°
1	-	-	4063	Taylor's (J. The Water Poet) Memorial of all the English Monarchs (151) from Brute to King Charles in Heroicall Verse, *wood cuts, portrait,* - - *London.* 1630	D°
1	7	-	4064	——— Wit and Mirth, being 113 Pleasant Tales and Witty Jests, *portrait in pen and ink.* - 1635	Heber
	6	-	4065	Taylor's Essay on Stenography, or Short hand writing, 1786	Cochran

£	s.	d.	Lot	Description	Buyer
	5	-	4066	Tayssonniere, Les Amoureuses occupations de Guillaume de la Taysonniere de Chanein, *red morocco, rare*, *Lyon*, 1555	Triphook
	10	-	4067	Teagueland Jests, or Dear Joy's Bogg Witticisms, *blue morocco.*	Booth
	1	-	4068	Teate's Ter Tria, or the Doctrine of the Three Sacred Persons, Father, Son and Spirit. - - 1669	Christie
3	-	-	4069	Teixeira Relaciones de los Reyes de Persia y de Harmuz y de un Viage dende la India Oriental hasta Italia por tierra, *Amberes*, 1610. Politica Specialis gemina, Prior Polonica, opus posthumum Keckermanni, Posterior Germanica, studio Alstedi, *Hanov.* 1611, in one volume, *Thuanus's Copy, scarce.*	Triphook
	12	-	4070	Temple of the Fairies, 2 vol. *wood cuts*, - 1804	Heber
	3	-	4071	Templum Musicum, or the Musical Synopsis of Alstedius, *frontispiece*, - - - 1664	Christie
1	15	-	4071*	Terentii Comœdie, per P. Malleolum recognite, annotatæque, *Paris*, 1499	Heber
	3	-	4072	Terentii Comœdiæ, *red morocco*, bad copy - *Aldus*, 1517	Triphook
	8	-	4073	Terentii Comœdiæ Sex ex recens. Heinsiana, *red morocco*, *Elzevir*, 1635	Young
	8	-	4074	Terentii Comœdiæ Sex, *red morocco*, by Du Seuil, - *Elzevir*, 1661	Payne
	15	-	4075	Terentii Comœdiæ, accesserunt Variæ Lectiones, 2 vol. in 1, *plates*, - - *Londini, Sandby*, 1751	Hayes
1	1	-	4076	Aliud Exemplar, 2 vol. LARGE PAPER, *blue morocco*, 1751	Burrell
	5	-	4077	Terentii Comœdiæ, *red morocco*, *Baskerville*, 1772	Money
	7	-	4078	Terentio, Locutioni di: overo Modi Famigliari di dire: scielti da Aldo Mannucci, *blue morocc*, *Vinetia*, 1585	Triphook
	16	-	4079	Novum Testamentum Græcè, *fine copy, blue morocco*, *Basil. Bebelius*, 1535	Heber
1	11	6	4080	N. Testamentum Græcum, 2 vol. *morocco*, *R. Stephani*, 1546	H. Holland
1	3	-	4381	N. Testamentum Græcè et Latinè, Erasmi, *yellow morocco*, *Lugd. per Tornæsium*, 1559	Heber
	7	-	4082	N. Testamentum, Gr. - *R. Stephani*, 1568	Triphook
	7	-	4083	N. Testamentum, Gr. - - 1569	Christie
	18	-	4084	N. Testamentum, Gr. - *Lugd. Bat. Elzevir*, 1624	Triphook
1	2	-	4085	N. Testamentum, Gr. *red morocco*, - *Sedani*, 1628	Cochran
1	14	-	4086	N. Testamentum, Gr. ex regiis aliisque optimis editionibus, 2 vol. *red morocco*, - - *Elzevir*, 1633	Payne
	7	-	4087	N. Testamentum, Gr. - - *Elzevir*, 1641	Money
	10	-	4088	N. Testamentum, Gr. - *Elzevir*, 1670	Payne
2	2	-	4089	N. Testamentum Græcum cura Maittaire, *large paper, ruled, red morocco*, - - *Tonson*, 1714	Hibbert
	2	-	4090	Novum Testamentum Interprete Beza, *Amst.* 1679	Cochran
	8	-	4091	N. Testamentum Armenice, *plates, fine copy, in morocco.* —	Do.

£	s.	d.	Lot	Description	Buyer
6	6	-	4092	N. Testamentum, Gr. cura Griesbach, 2 vol. *russia, with joints*, - - *Halæ Sax.* 1796, &c. This Copy was presented by the Duke of Grafton to Professor Porson, and has a few Notes in the hand writing of the Professor,	Triphook
5	2	6	4093	The New Testament both in Latin and English after the vulgare texte, which is red in the Churche, translated by Myles Coverdale, *blue morocco, the two first leaves slightly injured, Paris, Regnault for Richard Grafton*, 1538	Heber
3	1	-	4094	——————— in Englishe after the Greeke translation annexed wyth the Translation of Erasmus in Latin, *blue morocco*, - *Londini*, 1550	Do.
4	-	-	4095	The New Testament faithfully translated out of Greke, and perused by the commaundement of the kynges majestie and his honourable counsell and by the authorised, *black letter, fine copy, blue morocco, R. Jugge*, 1553	Cochran
1	4	-	4096	The New Testament, *black letter, red morocco, C. Barker*, 1581	Heber
	17	-	4097	The New Testament, *black letter, blue morocco, Edinburgh*, 1643	Cochran
	5	-	4098	——————— Tindal's Edition, *very imperfect.* ——	Evans
	13	-	4099	Le Nouveau Testament, bound in Tortoise-shell, with silver corners, hinges, and clasps, *Charenton*, 1656	Triphook
	12	-	4100	Le Nouveau Testament, 2 vol. *plates*, *Mons.* 1710	Warner
	18	-	4101	Il Nuovo Testamento tradotto di Græco in Vulgare Italiano per Brucioli, *wood cuts, red morocco, Lyone, Rovillio*, 1549	Triphook
	11	-	4102	Il Nuovo Testamento, Lat. et Volgare, 2 vol. *uncut, Rovillio*, 1558	Do.
	7	-	4103	Altro Esemplare, 2 vol. *blue morocco*, 1558	Christie
	17	-	4104	Het Nieuwe Testament, de CL. Psalmen Davids, *with engraved silver clasps, corners and ornaments*, *Amst.* 1633	Triphook
	4	-	4105	Figures du Nouveau Testament, *Lyon, Tournes*, 1579	Evans
	6	-	4106	Testamentum cujusdam monachi Cartusiensi in extremis laborantis, *Paris, De Marnef*, Speculum Religiosorum, Speculum Ecclesie et Speculum Sacerdotum, *Denis Roce*, in 1 vol. *fine copies, blue morocco*,	Johnston
	10	-	4107	Testament of the Twelve Patriarchs the Sons of Jacob, translated by Rob. Grosthead, *black letter, wood cuts, red morocco*, - - 1660	Triphook
	1	-	4108	Testament Politique de Charles duc de Lorraine et de Bar, *map*, - - - *Lipsic*, 1696	Christie
	5	-	4109	Tetons (Les), Ouvrage Curieux Galant et Badin, *Amst.* 1720	Warner
	7		4110	Texier, Les Colons de toutes Couleurs, 3 vol. *plates*, *Berlin*, 1798	Christie

£	s.	d.	Lot	Description	Buyer
1	13	-	4111	Theatre de la Foire ou l'Opera Comique par Le Sage et D'Orneval, 5 vol. *plates*, - - *Amst.* 1723	Ld Beauchamp
1	2	-	4112	Theocriti Carmina cum Scholiis Græcis, *fine copy, red morocco*, - - *Romæ, Calliergus*, 1516	Payne
1	-	-	4113	Theologia Sacris Bibliorum Figuris illustrata, *fine impressions, blue morocco*, - - 1738	Clarke
	9	-	4114	Theophile, Le Parnasse Satyrique du Sieur Theophile, *red morocco*, - - - 1677	Triphook
	3	-	4115	Theophraste des Odeurs mis de Grec en notre langue Francoyse par J. de l'Estrade, *Paris, G. Guillard*, 1556	Do.
	15	-	4116	Thevenot's Art of Swimming, *plates, blue morocco*, 1699	Do.
1	16	-	4117	Thevenot, Voyages en Europe en Asie et en Afrique, 5 vol. *plates*, - - - *Paris*, 1689	Ld Beauchamp
	13	-	4118	Thevet, Les Singularitez de la France Antarctique, autrement nommée Amerique, &c. *wood cuts, fine copy, blue morocco*, - - - *Anvers*, 1558	Lepard
	5	-	4119	Thomson's Seasons, - - 1799	Money
	9	-	4120	Thresor des Recreations, contenant Histoires facetieuses et honnestes propos, &c. - - *Rouen*, 1611	Triphook
3	14	-	4121	Thucydides, Gr. et Lat. ex Edit. Wassii et Dukeri, 6 vol. *large paper, yellow morocco*, - *Edinburgi*, 1804	Do.
	9	-	4122	Thunberg's Travels in Europe, Africa and Asia, 3 vol. ——	Do.
	4	-	4123	Thunberg, Flora Japonica, *plates*, - *Lipsiæ*, 1784	Loddiges
	1	-	4124	Thunberg, Prodromus Plantarum Capensium, *Upsaliæ*, 1794	
	5	-	4125	Tibulli et Propertii Opera ex Editione Broukhusii, *Glasguæ*, 1753	Triphook
	6	-	4126	Tilliot (Du), Memoires pour servir à l'Histoire de la Fete des Foux, - - *Lausanne*, 1751	Major Hay
	3	-	4127	Tim Bobbin's Miscellaneous Works. ——	Warner
1	-	-	4128	Tiraboschi, Storia della Poesia Italiana ripubblicata da Mathias, 4 vol. *portrait*, - - *Londra*, 1803	Do.
	12	-	4129	Tiran le Blanc, Histoire du Chevalier, 2 vol. in 1, *red morocco*, - *Londres.*	Triphook
	9	-	4130	Tocsain (Le) contre les Massacreurs et auteurs des Confusions en France, *green morocco*, - *Reims*, 1579	Clarke
	6	-	4131	Tombeau (Le) de la Melancolie, ou le vray moyen de vivre joyeux, *red morocco*, - *Paris*, 1635	Triphook
	6	-	4132	Tonnelier (Justin), Discours Fantastiques de, *blue morocco*, *Paris*, 1597	Dunbar
1	15	-	4133	Tooke's Life of Catherine II. Empress of Russia, 3 vol. 1798	Leake
	10	-	4134	Tour (La) Tenebreuse et les Jours Lumineux, Contes Anglois, - - - *Amst.* 1706	Warner
	4	-	4135	Tours (Les) Industrieux, Subtils et Gaillards de la Maltote, Nouvelles Galantes, *green morocco*, *Paris*, 1708	Triphook
	13	-	4136	Tournefort, Elements de Botanique, 3 vol. *plates, russia*, *Paris*, 1694	Loddiges

£	s.	d.	Lot	Description	Buyer
	3	-	4137	Tourterelles (Les) de Zelmis, *Poeme, red morocco.* ——	Warner
	3	-	4138	Tractatus de ymitatione Cristi, cum Tractatulo de Meditatione Cordis, *blue morocco,* - - 1487	Rodd
	13	-	4139	Tractatus Lacrymæ et Risus Democriti, *Paris,* 1623.—Puteanus de Risu, *Lovanii,* 1612.—Cenomanica, 1632, in one vol. *yellow morocco.*	Heber
1	-	-	4140	Tractatus de Arte bene vivendi beneque moriendi, *Paris,* 1494. De Munditia et Castitate Sacerdotum. Liber de Vilitate Conditionis humane a Lothario Dyacono, &c. *Pet. Levet.* 1495. Secundum Legem debet mori Johannes decimonono, in one volume.	Payne
1	9	-	4141	Tractatus varii. Confessio utilis et Necessaria Fr. Anthonii Farenii.—Modus Confitendi, *Par. D. Roce.* Interrogationes et doctrine quibus quilibet sacerdos debet interrogare suum confitentem,—De preceptis decalogi, de Confessione et de Arte Moriendi.—Thesaurus Incomparablis.—Speculum Ecclesiæ et Speculum Sacerdotum, *Denis Roce,* in one vol. *red morocco.*	Do.
	12		4142	—————— Speculum Tragicum auctore J. D. Delph. Bat. 1602.—Bebelii Facetiæ, *Tubingæ,* 1561.—Joannis Dantisci de Nostrorum Temporum Calamitatibus Sylva, *Colon.* 1530.—Æquitatis Discussio super Cons. Cardin. Antv. 1539.—XXI. Articuli Anabaptistarum, per Cochleum confutati, 1534.—Prognosticatio Johannis Leichtenbergers, *cuts,* 1528.—Erasmi Epistolæ duæ, *Colon.* 1530, in one vol. *morocco.*	Triphook
1	19	-	4143	Tractatus Varii de Pulicibus, *red morocco.* ——	Heber
1	7	-	4144	Tracts. The oration at Joyner's Hall, Sept. 24, 1733, on the Plurality of Worlds, &c.—Wit and Mirth to Perfection.—Shon ap Morgan.—Delights for Young Men and Maids.—Art of Gossipping.—Life of Charlotte Crutchey.—Coachman's and Footman's Catechism.—History of Thomas Hickathrift, &c. &c.	Perry
1	10	-	4145	Tracts on the Invasion, 3 vol. - 1803	Booth
	12	-	4146	Tracts.—Robinson's Account of Sweden, 1694.—Benson's Letter to Sir J. Bankes, 1711.—Puffendorf, on the Alliance between Sweden and France, 1719.—Molesworth's Observations on an English Merchant's Remarks, &c. 1717.—Molesworth's Account of Count Patkul.—Letter to Timothy Goodwin, 1717.—Memoirs of Sweden, 1719.	Payne
	7	-	4148	Tracts.—Christmas Entertainments, 1796.—History of the Haveral Wives.—The Laidly Worm.—Dun's Garland, 1742, &c.	Perry
1	8	-	4149	——— A Collection of Penny Histories, &c. Charles XII.—The Poets Jests.—Montelion.—Travels of Sir John Mandeville, &c. &c. in 2 vol.	Do.
12	12	-	4149	Tracts. A complete Collection of all the Tracts, both	Evans

printed and manuscript, concerning MARY TOFT, the celebrated Rabbit Woman, collected by G. STEEVENS, ESQ. with a Drawing of her portrait; to which has been added a curious original letter from Mr. HOWARD, the Accoucheur, to the DUKE OF ROXBURGHE, then Secretary of State, detailing the whole circumstances of the case, *russia*. From the Roxburghe Collection. } Evans

11 | - | 4150 ——— Sir R. Manningham's Diary, concerning Mary Toft, 1726.—Braithwaite's Remarks on a short Narrative of an extraordinary Delivery of Rabbits, performed by J. Howard.—Ahler's Observations concerning Mary Toft, 1726.—Howard's Short Narrative.—Depositions relative to Mary Toft.—The Sooterkin Dissected.—The Anatomist Dissected.—Mr. St. Andre's Case and Depositions. } Do.

2 | - | 4151 ——— Holyday's Persius.—Carrell's Deserving Favorite, 1659.—Morisoti Liber Amatorius, *Lugd.* 1558.—The Fair Circassian, 1743. } Heber

3 | - | 4152 ——— History of Adolphus, Prince of Russia, 1691.—De Foe's True born Englishman, 1708.—Lucretius, a Poem, against the Fear of Death, 1709.—Moderation displayed, 1709.—Blenheim, 1709.—Addison's Campaign, 1710. } Johnstone

4 | - | 4153 ——— Two Epistles to Mr. Pope, 1730.—The Royal Martyr, 1719.—A Key to the Lock, 1715.—The Battle of the Sexes, 1724.—Harlequin Horace, 1731.—Scarborough Miscellany, 1732.—Rape of the Lock, 1714.—The Raven and the Black Bird, 1715.—The Tunning of Elinor Rumming, 1718. } Christie

15 | - | 4154 Tragœdiæ Selectæ Æschyli, Sophoclis, Euripidis, cum duplici interpretatione Latina, una ad verbum, altera carmine, 3 vol. *yellow morocco*, - *H. Steph.* 1567 } Triphook

3 | - | 4155 Tragedie Varie. Thieste di Dolce, Venetia, Giol. 1544.—La Sophonisba del Caleotto Carretto, *Venet. Giolito*, 1546.—Romilda di Cesari, *Venet. Bindoni*, 1551.—Scilla di Cesari, *Ven.* 1552, *in one volume, blue morocco.* } Dunbar

7 | - | 4156 ————— Hecuba, Thyeste, Ifigenia di Dolce.—Orbecche di G. Cinthio.—La Sophonisba del Trissino, *Venet. Giolito*, 1549, &c. } Triphook

19 | - | 4157 Traicte (Petit) contenant en soy la Fleur de toutes joyeusetez en Epitres, Ballates et Rondeaux, &c. *Paris*, 1535 } Rodd

1 | 1 | - | 4158 Traités Diverses. Le Fondement et Origin des Tiltres de Noblesse, &c. Paris, 1535.—Le Blason des Armes, avec les Armes des Princes et Seigneurs de France, *Lyon, par Claude Nourry.*

1 | - | 4159 ————— Hist. Entiere du Procez de Charles Stuart, Roy d'Angleterre, 1650.—Traitte des Anciennes Ceremonies, - - - *Amst.* 1646 } Christie

£	s.	d.	Lot	Description	Buyer
	2		4160	Traités Diverses. Recueil de Diverses Pieces servant à l'Histoire de Henry III, Roy de France, Cologne, 1663.—Discours Merveilleux de la Vie de Catharine de Medicis, 1663.	Johnstone
	1		4161	——— La Modestie Chretienne, 1678.—L'Epée de de l'Eternel et de Gedeon, Amst. 1698.—Le Triomphe de la Paix, 1698.—Refutation du Plaidoyer de M. Talon, 1688.—Traitée des Miracles, Roterdam, 1545.	Triphook
	1	-	4162	——— Histoire du Prince Charles et de l'Imperatrice douairiere, Cologne, 1676.—Le Tombeau des Controverses, Amst. 1673.—Hist. du Siege de Montauban, Leyden, 1623.	D^o
	9	-	4163	Trappe. Les Veritables Motifs de la Conversion de l'Abbé de la Trappe, *blue morocco*, - *Cologne*, 1685	Arch
	5	-	4164	Travels of Tom Thumb over England and Wales, 1746	Foss
	7	-	4165	Treasure of Pore Men, a good Booke of Medycines, *black letter, russia*, - - *W. Powell*, 1551	Barker
1	11	6	4166	Treasure (The) of Gladnesse, *black letter, fine copy, blue morocco, with joints*, - *J. Charlewood*, 1566	Cochran
	19	-	4167	Treatise concernynge the division between the Spiritualtie and Temporaltie, *black letter*, *J. Berthelet.*	Rodd
2	-	-	4168	Treatise (A) shewing that Pictures and other Ymages which were wont to be Worshipped are in no wise to be suffered in the Temples or Churches of Christen Men, *black letter, fine copy, blue morocco*, *Printed for W. Marshall.*	Cochran

Quarto.

£	s.	d.	Lot	Description	Buyer
2	18	-	4169	Strutt's Sports and Pastimes of the People of England, *coloured plates, red morocco*, - - 1801	Collins
11	-	-	4170	Strutt's Complete View of the Dress and Habits of the People of England, 2 vol. *coloured plates, russia*, 1796	Dorrant
5	7	6	4171	Strutt's Biographical Dictionary of Engravers, 2 vol. in 1, *russia*, - - - - - 1785	Cochran
	5	-	4172	Struys, Voyages en Moscovie, en Tartarie, en Perse, aux Indes, et en plusieurs autres pais etrangers, *plates*, *Amst.* 1681	Johnston
5	5	-	4173	Struys's Voyages and Travels, *plates, blue morocco, with joints*, - - - - 1684	Barker
	9	-	4174	Suarez de Mendoza y Figueroa, Eustorgio y Clorilene, Historia Moscovica, - *Caragoça*, 1665	Triphook
1	7	-	4175	Summers's History of the Life and Death of Will Summers, King Henry the Eighth's Jester, *portrait and plates inserted, title reprint*, - - 1676	Booth
	4	-	4176	Surey (The) Demoniack, *frontispiece*, - 1699	Sedgwick
	3	-	4177	——— Vindication of, - 1698	D^o
1	2	-	4178	Sutcliffe's Practice, Proceedings, and Lawes of Armes, *black letter, blue morocco*, *C. Barker*, 1593	Christie

£	s.	d.	Lot	Description	Buyer
	5	-	4179	Sylvester's Lachrimæ Lachrymarum, or the Distillation of Teares shede for the untymely Death of Prince Henry, *scarce*, - - - 1612	Christie
	4	-	4180	Sylvester's Elegie and Epistle on the Death of Sir William Sidney, - - 1613	Do
	19	-	4181	Symbola et Emblemata jussu atque Auspiciis Imperatoris Moschoviæ, *russia*, - - *Amst.* 1705	Johnstone
1	1	-	4182	Symeoni Le Satire alla Berniescha, con una elegia sopra alla morte del Re Francesco Primo, *red morocco*, RARE, *Turino*, 1549	Triphook
	15	-	4183	Symeoni, Dialogo Pio et Speculativo, *plates, fine copy, blue morocco, ruled*, - *Lyone, Roviglio*, 1560	Do
	15	-	4184	Symeon, Les Illustres Observations Antiques en son dernier Voyage en Italie l'an, 1557, *plates, russia*, *Lyon*. 1558	Heber
1	19	-	4185	Symes's Account of an Embassy to the Kingdom of Ava, *plates*, - - - - 1800	Rawlinson
36	15	-	4186	Taciti (C. Cornelii) Opera, recognovit, emendavit, supplimentis explevit, notis, dissertationibus, Tabulis Geographicis illustravit, Brotier, 4 vol. LARGE PAPER, *red morocco, with joints*, - *Parisiis*, 1771	Payne
	9	-	4187	Tactique Prussienne ou Système Militaire de la Prusse, 2 vol. *plates*, - - *Paris*, 1804	Triphook
	9	-	4188	Tagliente, La vera arte delo excellente Scrivere de diverse varie sorti di Literi li quali se fano per Geometrica Ragione, *plates*, - - *Antverpiæ*, 1545	Rodd
	9	-	4189	Tamerlan. The History of the Great Emperour Tamerlane, 1597	Hay
	2	-	4190	Tanner's Mirror for Mathematiques, - 1587	Heber
1	-	-	4191	Tarbat's (Viscount) Vindication of Robert III. King of Scotland, from the Imputation of Bastardy, *Edinburgh*, 1695	Hay
1	8	-	4192	Tasso, La Gierusalemme Liberata, con le Figure di Bernardo Castello, *fine copy, red morocco*. *Geneva*, 1590	Triphook
	2	-	4193	Taxe Cancellarie Apostolice et Taxe sacre penitentiarie itidem aplice, - - - *Paris*, 1520	Do
	16	-	4194	Taylor's (John) Heaven's Blessing and Earth's Joy. A relation of the supposed Sea Fights, Fire Works, with Encomiasticke Verses on the Marriage of the Two Peerlesse Paragons of Christendome, Fredericke and Elizabeth, *red morocco*, RARE, - - 1613	Rhodes
1	1	-	4195	Tempe Restored, a Masque, - - 1631	Do
2	10	-	4196	Novum Testamentum Græcè ex recensione Griesbach, tom. 1 and 2, with two plates after Carlo Dolce and Guido, *elegantly bound in red morocco, with joints*, *Lipsiæ*, 1803-4	Triphook
	9	-	4197	Testament, (The New), translated by Tindal, *black letter, wood cuts, title manuscript*, - - 1536	Evans

£	s.	d.	Lot	Description	Buyer
5	18	-	4198	Testament (The New), both Latine and Englyshe, faythfully translated by Myles Coverdale, *fine copy, blue morocco, with joints,* RARE, *Southw. by J. Nicolson,* 1538	Cochran
6	16	6	4199	——————— translated out of the Greke, with the Notes and Expositions of the Darke Places, *wood cuts,* - - *Richard Jugge.*	G. Hibbert
	11	-	4200	——————— in Irish, - *Lond.* 1681	Triphook
	14	-	4201	Le Nouveau Testament, - *Amst.* 1714	Sedgwick
	3	-	4202	Thalii Sylva Hercynia sive Catalogus Plantarum sponte nascentium in Montibus et Locis vicinis Hercyniæ, *cuts, Francof.* 1588	Clarke
	10	-	4203	Theatre d'Histoire, ou les Aventures du Chevalier Polimantes Prince d'Arfine, *red morocco, Bruxelles,* 1613	Triphook
2	3	-	4204	Theatrum Crudelitatum Hæreticorum nostri Temporis a Verstegan, *fine impressions, red morocco. Antverpiæ.* 1592	Cochran
	6	-	4205	Theocriti Carmina, Gr. - *Paris, Wechel,* 1543	Payne
1	11	6	4206	Thevet's New Found Worlde, or Antarctike, wherin is contained wonderful and strange Things, *black letter, blue morocco, H. Bynneman,* 1568	Triphook
2	5	-	4207	Thomas's Historie of Italie, a Boke excedyng profitable to be redde, *black letter, russia,* - *T. Berthelet,* 1549	Booth
18	18	-	4208	THORDYNARY OF CRYSTEN MEN, *very fine copy, wood cuts, russia,* EXTREMELY RARE, WYNKYN DE WORDE, 1506	Hibbert
1	1	-	4209	Thurci Epistole per Laudinium Hierosolimitanum equitem aggregate, *wood cuts,* - *Lugduni,* 1520	Rodd
	5	-	4210	Thyrsis, De Veldgezangen van, *plates, Leyden,* 1702	Johnston
1	5	-	4211	Thurston's Religious Emblems, with Descriptions, by the Rev. J. Thomas, *blue morocco,* - 1810	Cochran
	6	-	4212	Tilliot (Du) Memoires pour servir à l'Histoire de la Fête des Foux, *plates,* - - *Lausanne,* 1741	Triphook
1	10	-	4213	Timberlake's True and Strange Discourse of the Travailes of two English Pilgrimes to Gaza, Grand Cayro, Alexandria, and other Places, *inlaid,* RARE, - 1620	Do.
7	7	-	4214	Tirante il Bianco valorosissimo Cavaliere, *beautiful copy, in old stamped binding,* - *Vineg. Sessa,* 1538	Clarke
	8	-	4215	Tobacco, the Touchstone or Trial of, whether it be good for all Constitutions, with a Word of Advice against immoderate Drinking and Smoaking. Portrait of James I. inserted, - - - 1676	Gaskoin
	3	-	4216	Tonge's Jesuitical Aphorismes, or a Summary Account of the Doctrine of the Jesuites, - 1679	Triphook
	1	-	4217	Tookes's History of Cales Passion, or, as some will byname it, the Miss-taking of Cales, - 1659	Hay
1	15	-	4218	Topographer (The), containing a Variety of Original Articles, illustrative of the Local History and Antiquities of England, *plates,* - - 1791	King

£	s.	d.	Lot	Description	Buyer
	3	-	4219	Torquemada's Spanish Mandevile of Miracles, 1618	Triphook
2	15	-	4220	Tournefort, Relation d'un Voyage du Levant, 2 vols. *plates, fine paper,* - - *Paris,* 1717	Loddiges
	6		4221	Tournefort Institutiones Rei Herbariæ, 3 vol. *plates, Parisiis,* 1700	Sir J. G. Egerton
1	5	-	4222	Tractatus de Turcis, *russia, by R. Payne. Nuremb.* 1481	Clarke

Folio.

£	s.	d.	Lot	Description	Buyer
2	10	-	4223	Smith's (Captain) Travels and Adventures, *Lond.* 1630 Smith's Historie of Virginia, *frontispiece and portrait of C. Smith,* in 1 vol. *russia, the plates inlaid,* 1624	Triphook
2	4	-	4224	Smith, Plantarum Icones hactenus Ineditæ Fasciculus 1. *russia, with joints,* - - - 1789	Loddiges
1	-	-	4226	Solorzano Emblemata Regio Politica, *plates, Matriti,* 1653	Triphook
5	18	-	4227	Solvyns, Les Hindous, Description de leurs Mœurs, Coutumes, Ceremonies, &c. 4 vol. *coloured plates.* The four last Livraisons of the Second Volume, and the whole of the Third, are wanting, - *Paris,* 1808	D°
3	3	-	4228	Speculum Humanæ Salvationis. A very curious Manuscript upon vellum. The Drawings are of the same Subjects, with Descriptions beneath as in the following article, but are of much ruder and more ancient execution, *blue morocco.*	Evans
	5	-	4229*	Speculum Regiminis Principum sive Cato Moralisatus, *sine ulla nota.*	Rodd
42	-	-	4229	Speculum Humanæ Salvationis, one of the earliest Specimens of Printing from Wood Blocks, *blue morocco, with the cuts uncoloured,* from the Merly Library.	Triphook
5	-	-	4230	Speed's Prospect of the most Famous Parts of the World, 1631. Speed's Theatre of Great Britain, 1627, in 1 vol. *maps, fine copy, in russia, with joints.*	Knell
	19	-	4231	Spenser's Faerie Queen, and other Poems, 1617	D°
1	2	-	4232	Sperling Judicium Paridis XX. Emblematibus Illustratum cum Germanis et Latinis Versibus, *Aug. Vindel. s. a.*	Cicognani
1	12	-	4233	Stackhouse's Nereis Britannica, containing all the Species of Fuci, with Descriptions in Latin and English, *russia, with joints,* - - - - 1801	Triphook
	13	-	4234	Statii Silvæ, printed with Catullus, Tibullus, and Propertius, by John de Colonia, *fine copy, red morocco, Venetiis* 1475,	Heber
4	16	-	4235	Statutes Vieu Abregement des Statutes, *red morocco,* without place or date, but supposed to be printed by Lettou and Machlinia.	Triphook
	5	-	4236	Stoeffler, Calendarium Romanum, *Oppenheym per Iac. Robel,* 1518	Sir J. G. Egerton

4237 STONE-HENG. Inigo Jones's Stone-Heng Restored, *portrait by Hollar*, 1725. Charleton's Antiquity of Stone-Heng, *portrait by Lombart*, 1725. Webb's Vindication of Stone-Heng Restored, 1725, 3 vol. in 1, *in russia.*

4238 Stow's Chronicle of England, by Howes, - 1615

4239 Swayne's Gramina Pascua, or Specimens of Pasture Grasses, 1790

4240 Sweertii Florilegium de variis Floribus et Plantis, cum figuris ad vivum delineatis, *blue morocco, Francof.* 1612

4241 TABLE RONDE. Ce sont les Noms, Armes et Blasons des Chevaliers et Compaignons de la Table Ronde au Temps que ilz jurerent la Queste du Sainct Graal a Camaloth le Jour de la Pentecoste, *red morocco*, from the Roxburghe Library. A Manuscript upon vellum, with the Arms richly emblazoned. The writer concludes thus:—"Ay cerche et concueilli les Noms et Armes des Chevaliers tant ou Livre de Maistre Helye, Maistre Robert de Borron, Maistre Gaultier Moab le Bret que de Maistre Rusticien de Pise qui en parlent en leurs Livres."

4242 Tasso's Godfrey of Boulogne, *portrait of Godfrey by Pass, red morocco,* - - - 1624

4243 Taylor the Water Poet's Workes, *frontispiece, russia,* 1630

4244 Tempest's Cryes of London, *good impressions,* 1711

4245 Temporum Fasciculus, *Lovanii per Joh. Veldener,* 1476

4246 Terentii Comœdiæ cum Scholiis, *wood cuts, red morocco, Argent. Gruninger,* 1499

4247 Terentii Comœdiæ cum Comment. Donati, *in rich old binding,* - - *Paris, Steph.* 1529

4248 Teurdanncth. The Adventures of the Renowned Chevalier, *first edition, plates, red morocco, Nuremb.* 1517

4249 Theatrum Omnium Scientiarum in Instauratione Innici de Guevaræ in Neapol. Academiæ, *many plates, Neapoli.* 1650

4250 Theatro Moral de la Vida Humana en Cien Emblemas, con el Enchiridion de Epicteto y la Tabla de Cebes, *fine impressions, red morocco,* - - *Brusselas,* 1672

TWENTY SECOND DAY'S SALE.

Octavo et Infra.

4251 Tressan (Comte de) Histoire de Robert surnommé le brave, *large paper,* - - *Londres,* 1800

4252 Tressan (Comte De) Histoire du Petit Jehan de Saintré, *blue morocco,* - - *Paris,* 1791

4253 Trismegistus (Hermes) The Works of, in Manuscript, divided into Seven Books. London, written by John Raymond. 1649, *blue morocco.*

4254 Trissino, La Italia Liberata da Gothi, 3 vol. in 1, *yellow morocco, with joints,* - - *Roma,* 1547

4255 Tristan. Le Livre du Nouveau Tristan, par Jean Maugin, *blue morocco,* - - *Lyon,* 1577

4256 Triomphes de l'Abbaye des Conards sous les resueur en decimes fagot Abbé de Conards, &c. *yellow morocco, rare,* *Rouen,* 1587

4257 Triumphes de la Noble et Amoureuse Dame, et l'Art de Honnestement Aymer, par Bouchet, *very fine copy, green morocco, with joints,* - - - *Paris,* 1545

4258 Trotter's Memoirs of C. J. Fox, - 1811

4259 Trovamalæ Liber qui Rosella Casuum appellatur, *mo-morocco, with joints,* - - *Paris,* 1515

4260 Turner's Huntyng of the Romyshe Wolfe, *black letter, fine copy, blue morocco, scarce,* - *no place or date.*

4261 Turner's Botanist's Guide through England & Wales, 2 vol. - - - - 1805

4262 Turpin, La Chronique de, Archevesque et Duc de Reims, *Paris,* 1583

4263 Tusser's Five Hundred Points of Husbandry, 1744

4264 Tutti i trionfi, carri, mascherate, o canti carnascialeschi andati per Firenze dal tempo del Magnifico Lorenzo vecchio de Medici raccolti per N. Lasca. Fiorenza, Torrentino, 1559. Canzoni dell' Ottonaio. Fiorenza, 1560, 2 vol. *The first, in old stamped morocco, the second in green morocco, rare.*

4265 Tutti i triomfi, carri, mascherate, canti carnascialeschi, 2 vol. *red morocco,* - *Cosmopoli, (Lucca).* 1750

4266 Tyndal's Obedyence of a Chrysten man, *W. Copland,* 1561. Tyndal's Parable of the wicked Mammon. *W Coplande,* 2 vol. in 1, *black letter.*

4267 Tyndal's Exposicion upon the 5th, 6th, and 7th Chapters of Mathew, *black letter, wood-cut inserted, blue morocco, rare.*

4268 Ulitii, Venatio Nova Antiqua, *red morocco, Elzevir,* 1645

4269 Uranckryck en zijn Steden, *numerous plates, blue morocco,* - - - *Amst* 1662

4270 Ursini Arboretum Biblicum præcipuis Emblematibus et Arboribus ære incisis exornatum, 2 vol. *Norimb.* 1699

4271 Urynges. Here begynneth the Seynge of Urynes, &c. *black letter, J. Waley.* A Catalogue of Herbes and their

Properties, *black letter, imperfect. W. Copland. No date.*

4272 Vænii (Ottonis) Emblemata Amatoria, *Amst.* 1618

4273 Vænii Emblemata Horatiana Imaginibus in æs incisis Latino Germanico Gallico et Belgico Carmine illustrata, *large paper, red morocco,* - - *Amst.* 1684

4274 Vænii Emblemata Horatiana in quatuor Linguis, *green morocco,* - - - *Amst.* 1684

4275 Vagabond ou l'Histoire de ceux qui courent le monde aux despens d'autruy, *yellow morocco,* - *Paris,* 1644

4276 Valcourt, Memoires de Mademoiselle de, 2 vol. *Amst.* 1767

4277 Valerius Maximus, - - *Venet. Aldi.* 1534

4278 Valerii Maximi Dicta, Factaque Memorabilia, *in very rich old binding in morocco, with fleurs de lis on the sides, ruled,* - - - *Ludg. Gryphii,* 1581

4279 Idem Liber, *red morocco,* - *Amst. Elzev.* 1690

4280 Vallensis (Rob.) de Veritate et Antiquitate Artis Chemicæ, *red morocco,* - - *Paris, Morel.* 1561

4281 Valliere, Catalogue des Livres de Monseigneur le Duc de la, 3 vol. *red morocco, with the prices in MS. Par.* 1783

4282 Valpy's Plays, altered from Shakspeare, *blue morocco,* 1803

4283 Varenii Geographia Generalis, *yellow morocco, Amst. Elzevir,* 1650

4284 Aliud Exemplar, *green morocco,* - - *ib.* 1670

4285 Varthema, Itinerario de, nella Arabia deserta e felice nella Persia, nella India e nella Ethiopia, EXCESSIVELY RARE, *blue morocco,* - *Rome, per Guillireti,* 1517

The first edition of these Travels mentioned by Haym, is printed at Venice, in 1518.

4286 Vaughan's Silex Scintillans, or Sacred Poems, 1650

4287 Vavassore, Opera nova laquale tratta de le figure del Testamento Vecchio e Nuovo, *black letter, with very curious and spirited wood cuts, blue morocco, &c. Vinegia, senza anno.*

4288 Vaugondy Dictionnaire Geographique, &c. de la Suisse, *Géneve,* 1776

4289 Vecchii Clericus Deperrucatus, *plates, Amstel. s. anno.*

4290 Vecellio Habiti Antichi delineate dal Gran Titiano, *Venetia,* 1664

4291 Vegetii et Aliorum de Re Militari Libri cum Comment. *wood cuts, red morocco,* - *Plantin,* 1592

4292 Veillées, Les, de Thessalie, 2 vol. *red morocco, Par.* 1731

4293 Venette's Conjugal Love Revealed, - *no date.*

4294 Venezia. Forestiere Illuminato intorno le Cose più rare, e curiose della Città di Venezia, *plates, uncut, Venezia,* 1740

4295 Venus Physique, *blue morocco,* - - 1745

4296 Verboquet, les Delices ou Discours Joyeux et Recreatifs de, *green morocco,* - - - *Paris,* 1630

4297 Verdizotti, Cento Favole Bellissime, *wood cuts,* *Venetia,* 1661

4298 Vergilius, Polydorus, de Inventoribus Rerum, *red morocco,* *Amst. Elzev.* 1671

4299 Vergil, The Notable Work of Polidore, abridged, by T. Langley, *black letter,* *London, J. Tisdale, no date.*

4300 Verien, Livre Curieux et Utile composé de trois Alphabets de Chiffres, accompagné des Devises, Emblemes, &c. *Paris, s. d.*

4301 Verronis Friburgensis Physicorum Libri X. *Lond. Bynneman,* 1581

4302 Versailles, Labyrinthe de, *plates, red morocco, Paris,* 1679

4303 Verville (Beroalde de) Le Voyage des Princes Fortunez, *red morocco,* - - - *ib.* 1610

4304 Viaggi fatti da Vinetia alla Tana in Persia, in India, &c. *Vinegia, Aldo,* 1543

4305 Vidæ Hieronymi Carmina, *Antwerp. Plantin,* 1567

4306 Vigelli Speculum Stultorum et Ovidii Libri tres de Vetula, *plates,* - - *Wolferbyti,* 1662

4307 Vilrain's Epitome of Essais, Englished out of Latin, 1654

4308 Villinovan L'Ecole de Salerne avec les Moyens de se passer de Medécin, *yellow morocco, with joints, Par.* 1672

4309 Villon, Les Œuvres de François, *blue morocco,* *ib.* 1723

4310 Vincentius Lirinensis of the Natioun of Gallis, for the antiquitie & veritie of the catholik fayth. Translatit into Scottis be Niniane Winzet, a catholik Priest, VERY RARE, *Antwerp, Æg. Diest,* 1563

4311 Virgilii Opera, best Aldine Edition, LARGE PAPER, *red morocco, but wanting the four leaves containing the Errata & Date,* - - *Venetiis. Aldi,* 1514

A book of very great Rarity, on Large Paper.

4312 Virgilii Opera Pulmanni, *green morocco, with morocco lining,* - - - *Amst.* 1625

4313 Virgilii Opera ex recensione Heinsii, *red morocco,* *Amst. Elzev.* 1676

4314 Virgilii Opera ex recens. Phillippe, 3 vol. *plates, red morocco,* - - - *Lutet. Paris,* 1745

4315 Virgilii Opera cum Figuris a Sandby, 2 vol. *red morocco,* *Londini,* 1750

4316 Virgilii Opera cum Figuris a Sandby, 2 vol. royal 8vo. *large paper, blue morocco,* - - *ib.* 1750

4317 Virgilii Opera ex Antiquis Monimentis Illustrata a Justice, 5 vol, *plates, red morocco,* - - *sine anno.*

4318 Virgilii Opera, *blue morocco,* - *Paris, Didot,* 1798

4319 Virgilii Opera ex recensione et cum notis Heyne, 6 vol. *Best Edition, finest paper, plates, elegantly bound in blue morocco, with joints,* - - *Lipsiæ,* 1800

4320 Virgil's Works, translated by Dryden, 3 vol. *large paper, red morocco, wanting the plates,* - - 1709

4321 Virgil's Works, translated by Dryden, 4 vol. *plates,* 1772

4322 Virgile, L'Eneide de, translatee de Latin en François, par Louis des Masures, *wood cuts, blue morocco, ruled,* *Lion, J. de Tournes,* 1560

4323 Virgil's Georgicks & Bucolicks, by Martyn, 2 vol. *plates,* 1749

4324 Virgile, Les Eglogues de, traduites en Vers François, par Richer, *blue morocco,* - - *Rouen,* 1717

4325 Virgile, Les Georgiques de, par De Lille, *Paris,* 1782

4326 Virgil, The Passion of Dido, translated from, by Waller & Godolphin, - - - - - 1658

4327 Virgilius, The Life & Death of, reprinted by Mr. Utterson, *only* 50 *copies printed, blue morocco,* - 1812

4328 Visionnaires ou Lettres sur l'Heresie Imaginaire, *splendidly bound in red morocco,* - *Liege, Elzev.* 1667

4329 Visschers Zinne-Poppen, *many plates, blue morocco,* *Amst.* 1678

4330 Vitruvii de Architectura Libri, *wood cuts,* *Florent. Junta,* 1522

4331 Vivarii de Arte Mendicandi Libri Quatuor, *Pragæ,* 1585

4332 Vives. Introduction to Wysedome, BLACK LETTER, *John Daye.*

4333 Vivre, Lettres Missives Familieres et Deux Livres de l'Utilite du Train de Marchandise, *printed partly in the cursive letter,* - - - *Rotterdam.*

4334 Voisenon, Le Sultan Misapouf, 2 vol. *red morocco,* *Londres,* 1767

4335 Volpii. La Libreria de' Volpi e la Stamperia Cominiana, *Padova,* 1756

4336 Volpi, Rime del - - - *ib.* 1741

4337 Voltaire, La Henriade, 2 vol *red morocco,* *Paris,* 1770

4338 Voltaire, La Pucelle, *plates, red morocco,* *ib.* 1775

4339 Voltaire, Zadig, Histoire Orientale, - 1748

4340 Autre Exemplaire, *red morocco,* - - - 1799

4341 Voltaire, Histoire de Charles XII. 2 vol. in 1, *Amst.* 1739

4342 Vosgien, Dictionnaire Geographique Portatif, *russia,* *Haie,* 1748

4343 Voyage Nouveau, du Nort, - *Amst. s. date.*

4344 Voyage d'Espagne, Relation du, 2 vol. in 1, *Haye,* 1693

4345 Voyage to Buenos Ayres, and by Land to Potosi, *map,* 1716

4346 Voyage de Campagne, 2 vol. in 1, - *ib.* 1700

£	s.	d.	Lot	Description	Buyer
	13	-	4347	Wafer's Voyage and Description of the Isthmus of America, - - - - - - 1704	Blaquiere
	8	-	4348	Walker's Descriptive Catalogue of a choice assemblage of Pictures, *blue morocco,* - - 1807	Do.
1	10	-	4349	Wallace. The Life and Acts of the most famous and valiant Champion Sir William Wallace, *black letter, red morocco,* - - - - - - *Glasgow.*	Triphook
	9	-	4350	Wallace's Description of the Isles of Orkney, *Edin.* 1693	Rodd
1	3	-	4351	Waller's Poems, with his Life, *portraits,* *Tonson,* 1711	Blaquiere
	16	-	4352	Waller's Poems, *yellow morocco, with joints,* *ib.* 1712	Thornton
2	2	-	4353	Walpole's Fugitive Pieces in Verse and Prose, *red morocco, with joints,* - - *Strawberry Hill,* 1758	Dorrant
6	16	6	4354	——— Mysterious Mother, a Tragedy, *red morocco,* *ib.* 1768	Triphook
	2	-	4355	——— Castle of Otranto, - - 1782	Anderdon
1	10	-	4356	——— Castle of Otranto, *green morocco,* *Parma, Bodoni,* 1791	Triphook
	17	-	4357	Castle of Otranto, *with coloured plates, and borders,* 1796	Calkin
	16	-	4358	Walpoliana, 2 vol. ———	Blaquiere
	4	-	4359	Walter's Flora Caroliniana, *plates,* - - 1788	Mokay
	10	-	4360	Walton's Experienced Angler, *plates,* - 1662	Hancock
1	2	-	4361	——— Compleat Angler, *plates,* - - 1668	Triphook
1	6	-	4362	——— Cotton's and Venable's Universal Angler, *plates, fine copy,* - - - - 1776	Blaquiere
1	3	-	4363	Walton & Cotton's Complete Angler, by Hawkins, *plates, russia,* - - - - 1760	King
	18	-	4364	Another Edition, *russia,* - - - 1766	Hay
	9	-	4365	Walton, Cotton, & Browne's Compleat Angler, 1772	Hancock
	5	-	4366	Warde's Translation of Arcandam's Astrologie and Physiognomy, *black letter, cuts, russia,* - 1652	Blaquiere
	1	-	4367	Ward's Vulgus Britannicus, or the British Hudibras, 1711	Christie
	5	-	4368	Ward's Woe to Drunkards, - - 1627	Clarke
	2	-	4369	Warder's True Amazons, or the Monarchy of Bees, *portrait,* - - - 1713	Anderdon
1	2	-	4370	Watkins's Biographical, Historical, and Chronological Dictionary, *russia,* - - - 1806	Blaquiere
	12	-	4371	Watson's History of the Art of Printing, *Edin.* 1713	Cochran
	5	-	8372	Watson's Apology for the Bible - - 1796	Calkin
	14	-	4373	Watson's Chemical Essays, 5 vol. - 1782	Hancock
	2	-	4374	Wedderburni Persius Enucleatus, *uncut,* *Elzevir,* 1664	Payne
	1	-	4375	Wegweiser zür Höffligkeit, - - 1646	Rodd
	4	-	4376	Welsh Legends, a Collection of Popular Oral Tales, 1802	K.
	7	-	4377	Werke (A) for Housholders, or for them that have the guydyng or governaunce of any company, *black letter, blue morocco,* - - *R. Redman,* 1537	Rodd
	2	-	4378	Werther traduit de l'Allemand, *Maestricht,* 1776	Thornton

4379 Wesley's Maggots, or Poems on Several Subjects, *portrait*, 1685

4380 West, Catalogue of the Library of J. West, 1773

4381 Westhovii (Willichii) Cimbri Emblemata, *cuts*, *Hafniæ*, 1640

4382 Westminster, Antiquities of St. Peter's, or the Abbey Church of Westminster, *plates, blue morocco, with joints*, 1711

4383 Westminster Drollery, or a Choice Collection of the newest Songs and Poems both at Court and Theatres, 2 vol - - - 1671

4384 Weston's Universal Botanist & Nurseryman, 4 vol. 1770

4385 Wharton's Calendarium Ecclesiasticum & Gesta Britannorum, *interleaved, blue morocco*, - - 1657

4386 Wheatley's (Phillis) Poems on Various Subjects, 1773

4387 Wheelwright's Poems, Original and Translated, 1810

4388 White's (Peter) Discoverie of the Jesuitical Opinion of Justification, guilefullie uttered by Sherwine at the time of his execution, *black letter, blue morocco*, *John Wolfe*, 1582

4389 Whyte's (Peter) Answere unto certaine crabbed questions pretending a reall presence of Christ in the Sacrament, *blue morocco*, - *John Wolfe*.

4390 White's Hocus Pocus, or a Rich Cabinet of Legerdemain Curiosities ———

4391 ———— Cabinet, with Variety of Inventions, *frontispiece*, 1668

4392 White's Bampton Lecture Sermons, - 1792

4393 ———— Naturalist's Calendar, - 1795

4394 Whitworth's Account of Russia, as it was in 1710, *red morocco, with joints*, - - *Strawberry Hill*, 1758

4395 Wicklieffe's Wicket faythfully overseene and corrected after the originall and firste copie.—The Protestacion of John Lassels lately burned in Smythfelde; and the Testament of W. Tracie expounded, by W. Tyndall and John Frythe.—A Supplication of the Poore Commons, *black letter, fine copies, blue morocco, with joints*, *no place nor date.*

4396 Histoire du Wiclefianisme, - *Lyon*, 1682

4397 Wilkes's Correspondence, 5 vol. - 1805

Quarto.

4398 Tracts. South Musica Incantans sive Poema exprimens Musicæ Vires, Oxon. 1667. The Conflagration of

London, Poetically Described in Lat. and Eng. 1667. London's Remains in Lat. & Eng. 1667. Londini Renascentis Imago Poetica, 1668. The Plague at Athens, by Th. Sprat 1667, in 1 vol. *blue morocco.*

4399 Tracts. The Copie of a Letter sent out of England to to Don Bernardin Mendoza, declaring the State of England, &c. 1588.—Certaine Advertisements out of Ireland, concerning the Losses and Distresses happened to the Spanish Nation upon the west coast of Ireland, 1588. The Earle of Essex's Treasons, Arraignement, and Conviction, 1601, in 1 vol.

4400 Tracts. The English Schoolmaster, by Edward Coote, 1669. Rarities in the Anatomie Hall at Leyden, by Blancken, 1712. Rive's Twelve Rules, introducting to the Art of Latine, 1620.

4401 Tracts. Characters at the Hot-Well, Bristol, 1723. Εικων βασιλικη τριτη, or the Picture of the late King James, drawn to the Life, 1697.

4402 Tragius de Stirpium, quæ in Germania nascuntur, usitatis nomenclaturis, &c. *wood cuts, coloured, russia, sine anno.*

4403 Triall of Treasure, a New and Merry Enterlude, newly set foorth, and never before this Time imprinted, *black letter, red morocco,* VERY RARE, *Thomas Purfoote,* 1567

4404 Triomphi di Carlo di Messer Fr. di Ludovici Vinitiano, Poema ; *red morocco, scarce, Vinegia, Bindoni,* 1535

4405 Triumphs of Paris at the Reception of their Majesties of France, - - - 1660

4406 Triumphe (Le) des Dames, *black letter, Paris, pour P. Sergent, sans date.*

4407 Trombelli, Arte di Conoscere l'Eta de' Codici Latini e Italiani, - - - - - - *Bologna,* 1756

4408 Troye, Les Cent Hystoires de, *black letter, wood cuts, blue morocco,* - *Paris, par P. le Noir,* 1522

4409 Troy, The Destruction of, in Three Books, 1663

4410 Tuccaro, Trois Dialogues de l'Exercice de Sauter, et Voltiger en l'Air, *plates,* - *Paris,* 1599

4411 Tuberville's Noble Art of Venerie or Hunting, *wood cuts,* 1611

4412 Turner's Account of an Embassy to Tibet, *plates,* 1800

4413 Turpin. Cronique et Histoire faite et composée, par Reverend Pere en Dieu Turpin, Archevesque de Reims, l'ung des pairs de France, *black letter, blue morocco, Paris, par P. Vidove,* 1527

4414 Tusser's Five Hundred Points of good Husbandry, *black letter,* - - - 1614

4415 Tusser's Five Hundred Points, edited by Mavor, *large paper, russia,* - - - 1812

£	s.	d.	Lot	Description	Buyer
3	19	-	4416	Typus Occasionis in quæ receptæ commoda, neglectæ vero incommoda, personato schemate proponuntur, *fine impressions of the plates, russia,* *Antverpiæ*, 1603	Clarke
	3	-	4417	Ubaldino's Discourse concerning the Spanish Fleete invadin England in 1588, *imperfect, black letter.*	Triphook
	19	-	4418	Væmii, Q. Horatii Flacci Emblemata, *fine impressions,* *Antv.* 1612	Booth
1	1	-	4419	Alia Editio, *blue morocco,* - *Bruxelles*, 1683	Hayes
2	5	-	4420	———— 2 vol. *morocco,* - *Florentiæ*, 1777	Blaquiere
	11	-	4421	Væmii Emblemata sive Symbola a Principibus, viris Ecclesiasticis, aliisque usurpanda, *blue morocco, with joints,* *Bruxellæ*, 1624	Do.
	18	-	4422	Væmii Amoris Divini Emblemata, *fine impressions, red morocco,* - – *Antverpiæ*, 1615	Triphook
1	9	-	4423	Alia Editio, *blue morocco,* - *ib.* 1660	Blaquiere
	10	-	4424	———— with descriptions in Dutch, *Amsterdam*, 1683	Gaskoin
	14	-	4425	Væmii Amorum Emblemata a Weigel, *sine anno.*	Calkin
2	-	-	4426	Venius. Les Emblemes de l'Amour Humain, · *Brusselles*, 1668	Do.
3	3	-	4427	Valentin et Orson. L'Histoire des Deux Nobles et Vaillants Chevaliers, *black letter,* *Paris, sans date.*	Rodd
	10	-	4428	Valentin et Orson, l'Histoire de, *Rouen, sans date.*	Blaquiere
	10	-	4429	Valeriani Joathas Rotatus, *russia, by R. Payne, ruled,* *Romæ*, 1512	Triphook
3	13	6	4430	Valerius (Johan) born without Arms. Prints exhibiting several of his Performances, *blue morocco, with joints.*	Booth
2	12	6	4431	Valle. Les Apologues et Fables de Laurens Valle Translatees de Latin en François, *black letter, wood cuts,* *sans date.*	Triphook
1	2	-	4432	Van de Vennes Taffereel van de Belacchende Werelt, *plates,* *Graven-Hage*, 1635	Booth
	3	-	4433	Van Sloetten's Description of the Isle of Pines, *frontispiece,* 1668	Rodd
2	12	6	4434	Vander Veens Zinne Beelden oft Adams Appæl, *plates, fine impressions, red morocco,* - *Amst.* 1642	Triphook
	11	-	4435	Varamundus Frisius, de Furoribus Gallicis, *a curious Tract attributed to Fr. Hotman. See De Bure, No.* 5230, *green morocco,* - *Edimburgi*, 1573	Rodd
	10	-	4436	Varchi Sonetti Spirituali, *Giunta*, 1573.—Boezio, tradotto, Varchi Firenza, 1551, 2 vol. in one.	Rice
5	-	-	4437	Varchi's Blazon of Jealousie, *green morocco, with joints,* 1613	Triphook
3	3	-	4438	Vasari. Le Vite de' più eccellenti Pittori, Scultori e Architettori, 3 vol. *best edition, russia, Fiorenza, Giunta*, 1568	Payne

Folio.

£	s	d	Lot	Description	Buyer
2	2	-	4439	Theseus de Cologne. Histoire du Noble Chevalier, *two leaves, MS. red morocco, Paris, Ant. Bonnemere,* 1534	Payne
6	12	-	4440	Thucydidis, Historia, Gr. Latine, ex recens. Dukeri, *russia, Amstel.* 1731	D°.
	13	-	4441	Thucydides, translated by T. Nicolls, *black letter,* 1550	Rodd
	10	-	4442	Thunberg, Icones Plantarum Japonicarum, *Upsaliæ,* 1794	Money
3	17	-	4443	Tim Bobbin's Human Passions Delineated in 120 figures, Droll, Satyrical and Humorous, - 1772	Blaquiere
1	-	-	4444	Tod's Plans, Elevations, &c. of Hot-Houses and Green-Houses, - - - 1807	Mead
2	5	-	4445	Todentanz, Der sogenannte, *many plates, black morocco, with morocco lining,* - - *Wien.* 1767	Blaquiere
3	13	6	4446	Toison d'Or, composé par Guillaume jadis Evesque de Tournay, auquel sont contenus les Magnimimes Faictz des Maisons de France, Bourgogne, &c. 2 vol. *black letter, wood cuts, red morocco, Paris. Le Rouge,* 1530	Booth
2	-	-	4447	Tom Thumb, Compleat History of, - 1729	Heber
1	5	-	1448	Traités, Recueil de, contenant—L'Art de bien Vivre, *wanting the Title.*—L'Art de bien Mourir.—Traité des Paines d'Enfer et de Purgatoire.—L'Advenement de l'Antechrist, in 1 vol. *curious wood cuts, Paris, Verard,* 1492	Triphook
21	10	6	4442	Tristan Fils du Noble Roy Meliadus et Chevalier de la Table Ronde, 2 vol. in 1, *red morocco,* EXTREMELY RARE, *Paris, Ant. Verard, sans date.*	Heber
4	5	-	4453	Tristan, Premier Livre du Nouveau, Prince de Leonnois, *green morocco,* - - *Paris,* 1554	Triphook
	15	-	4451	Triumphant Love invested by Victorious Virtue, a Ballet at the Nuptials of Lord Christian Ludowick, &c. in German, *many plates, russia,* - *Nuremb.*	Blaquiere
8	10	6	4452	Troye, Epistre que Othea la Deesse envoya à Hector avec Cent Histoires, *wood cuts, fine copy, Phil. Pigouchet, sans date.*	Triphook
1	4	-	4453	Turner's most excellent and perfecte Homish Apothecarye, or Homely Physick Booke, translated out of the Almaine Speech.—Turner's Book on the Nature of Bathes in England, *in one vol. russia, Collen, Arnold Birckmann,* 1561-2	Gaskoin
	3	-	4454	Turre, (Georgii a) Universa Natura Plantarum, *russia, Patavii,* 1685	Rodd
	14	-	4455	Typotii Symbola Divina et Humana, Pontificum Imperatorum et Regum, 2 vol. in 1, *many plates, Francof,* 1642	Blaquiere
3	16	-	4456	Ulloa (Don Antonio de) Relacion Historica del Viage à la America Meridionale, 4 vol. in 2, *Madrid,* 1748	Young
	6	-	4457	Ulstadii (Philippi) Cœlum Philosophorum seu de Secretis Naturæ, *wood cuts, russia, Argentorati,* 1528	Heber
	13	-	4458	Utino (Leonardi de) Sermones aurei de Sanctis, 1474	Triphook

£	s.	d.	Lot	Description	Buyer
2	2		4459	Valerian vulgairement nommé Pierius, Les Hieroglyphiques, autrement Commentaires des Lettres et Figures Sacrees des Egyptiens et autres Nations, *wood cuts, russia*, *Lyon*, 1615	Christie
1	5		4460	Valturio, Opera de Facti e Precepti Militari translata per Ramusio, *plates, red morocco*, - *Verona*, 1483	Booth
	16	-	4461	Vega's (Garcilaso de la) Royal Commentaries of Peru, by Ricaut, - - - 1688	Young
23	2	-	4462	Ventenat, Jardin de la Malmaison, WITH ONE HUNDRED AND TWENTY BEAUTIFULLY COLOURED PLATES, *elegantly bound in russia*, - *Paris*, 1805-7	Triphook
7	17	6	4463	Ventenat, Description, des Plantes Nouvelles et peu connues, cultivées dans le Jardin de J. M. Cels, *with one hundred plates, from drawings by Redouté*, *Paris*, 1801	Blaquiere
9	19	6	4464	Vere's (Sir Francis) Commentaries, published by Dillingham, LARGE PAPER, *fine impressions of the plates, russia*, RARE, - - *Cambridge*, 1657	Payne
11	-	-	4465	Vergier, Le Songe du Vergier, a manuscript on vellum of the fifteenth Century, bound in purple velvet, with gilt clasps and corners.	Longman
1	1	-	4466	Vigon's Workes of Chirurgerye, *black letter, russia*, *E. Whytchurch*, 1543	Gaskoin
1	2	-	4467	Viola Sanctorum, *editio Antiqua, russia*, *sine ulla notâ, sed typis Bernardi Richel.*	Booth
4	4	-	4468	Virgille, Les Œuvres de, translatees de Latin en Francoys, *black letter, ruled*, *Paris, Galliot du Pre*, 1529	Triphook
4	-	-	4469	——— Les Eneydes de, translatez de Latin en François, par Octavian de Sainct Gelais revues et cottez par Jehan Divry, *black letter, fine copy, morocco*, RARE, *Paris, pour Antoine Verard*, 1509	Do.
88	4	-	4470	VYRGYLES ENEYDOS. Here fynysheth the boke of Eneydos, compyled by Vyrgyle whiche hathe be translated oute of latyne in to frenshe, and oute of frenshe reduced into Englysshe by me WYLLIM CAXTON the XXII daye of Juyn, the yere of our Lorde 1490, A VERY FINE AND PERFECT COPY, EXTREMELY RARE, *russia*.	Evans
24	3	-	4471	Visconti, Il Museo Pio Clementino, 6 vol. *plates*, *Roma*, 1782-98	Blaquiere
32	11	-	4472	VITAS PATRUM. The Lives of holy Faders lyvynge in deserte, translated out of Frensshe in to Englysshe by Wyllyam Caxton of Westmynstre late deed, and fynysshed it at the laste daye of his lyff, *wood cuts, blue morocco, fine and perfect copy*, VERY RARE, WYNKYN DE WORDE, 1495. "This is one of Wynkyn de Worde's most magnificent Typographical Productions. It is ornamented with a great number of wood cuts." Mr. Dibdin's Ames, vol. 2, p. 49.	Payne

TWENTY-THIRD DAY'S SALE.

Octavo et Infra.

£	s.	d.	No.	Description	Buyer
	4	-	4473	Wilkins's Mathematical Magick, - 1648	Clarke
	6	-	4474	Willemet, Herbarium Mauritanianum, *Lipsiæ*, 1796	Gaskoin
			4475	Willis's Pathologiæ Cerebri et Nervosi generis Specimen, *red morocco*, - - *Elzevir*, 1668	
4	-	-	4476	Willis's History of the Mitred Parliamentary Abbies and Conventual Cathedral Churches, 2 vol. 1712	Dorrant
3	13	6	4077	Willis's Survey of the Cathedral Churches of St. Davids, of Llandaff, St. Asaph, and of Bangor, 4 vol. *russia, with joints*, - - - 1717, &c.	Payne
	5	-	4478	Wilson's Biographical Index to the House of Commons. —	Heber
	2	-	4479	Winchilsea's (the Earl of) Account of the late Earthquake and Eruption of Mount Ætna, *plate*, - 1669	Do.
	4	-	4480	Windsor (The) Medley. - - 1731	Gaskoin
	6	-	4481	Wine and Women, or a Briefe Description of the common courtesie of a Courtezan, - - 1647	Triphook
	4	-	4482	Winstanley's Lives of the most Famous English Poets, 1687	Do.
	9	-	4483	Wits Triumph, or Ingenuity displayed in his Perfection, 1712	Perry
	5	-	4484	Wits Commonwealth, newly corrected and amended. ——	Triphook
1	15	-	4485	Wither's Abuses Stript and Whipt, or Satyrical Essays, *portraits inserted*, 1615. A Satyre dedicated to James Ist. 1616. Shepheard's Hunting, 1615. Browne's Shephearde's Pipe, 1614. Shephearde's Pipe Eglogues by Brooke, Wither and Davies, 1614, in one vol. *blue morocco*, VERY RARE.	
	3	-	4486	——— Satyre dedicated to his most excellent Majestie, 1615	Heber
	3	-	4487	——— Satyre written when he was Prisoner in the Marshalsey, for his first Booke. - 1622	Perry
	2	-	4488	——— Britain's Remembrancer, - 1628	Henry
3	-	-	4489	——— Psalmes of David, *blue morocco*, RARE, *printed in the Netherlands*, - - 1632	Arch
	18	-	4490	——— Juvenile Poems, *portrait*, - - 1633	Warder
	4	-	4491	——— Campo-Musæ, or Field Musings, 1643	Miller
	3	-	4492	——— Campo-Musæ, - - 1644	Heber
	3	-	4493	——— Fides Anglicana, or a Plea for the Publick Faith of these Nations, - - - 1660	Do.
	5	-	4494	——— Speculum Speculativum, or a Considering-Glass, 1660	Do.

4495 Wither's Crums and Scraps lately found in a Prisoner's Basket in Newgate, - - 1661

4496 ——— Divine Poems (by Way of Paraphrase) on the Ten Commandments, - - 1728

4497 Withering's Arrangement of British Plants according to the Linnæan System, 4 vol. *plates*, - 1796

4498 Witt's Recreations refined and augmented with Ingenious conceits, *russia*, - - 1654

4499 Witt's Recreations, - - 1667

4500 Witty Apophthegms by King James, King Charles, &c. *yellow morocco*, - - - 1658

4501 Wood's Bow-mans Glory, or Archery revived, *blue morocco*, 1682

4502 Wood's Stone Henge, *plates*, - - 1747

4503 Wolley's Queen-Like Closet, or Rich Cabinet stored with all manner of rare Receipts, *frontispiece*, 1672

4504 Woolsey, the Life and Death of Cardinal Woolsey, *portrait*, 1667

4505 Woolridge's Art of Gardening, - - 1688

5506 Worcester's (Marquis of) Century of Inventions, *red morocco*, - - - - - 1746

4507 Another Edition, *red morocco*, *Glasgow*, 1767

4508 Another Edition, *red morocco*, - 1763

4509 World (The), by Adam Fitz-Adam, 4 vol. 1789

4510 Wright's Complete Fisher, or the Art of Angling, *red morocco*.

4511 Wynman, Colymbetes, sive de Arte Natandi, *red morocco*, *scarce*, - - *August. Vindel*, 1538

4512 Xenophon's Treatise of Housholde, translated out of the Greke Tongue into Englysshe, by Gentian Hervet, *black letter*, *russia*, - - *Berthelet*, 1537

4513 Yeux, Les, Le Nez et les Tetons, Ouvrage Curieux et Galant, *red morocco*, - - *Amst.* 1735

4514 Young's Night Thoughts, 2 vol. in 1 *plates*, *blue morocco*, 1800

4415 Young's Rural Œconomy, - - 1773

4516 Yriarte La Musica Poema, *plates*, *blue morocco*, *Madrid*, 1779

4517 Zang-en Speel Œffening, - *Haarlem*.

4518 Zappi, Rime di Felice e di Faustina Martati, *Nizza*, 1781

4519 Zeeusche Nachtegael, *plates*, *green morocco*, *Rotterd.* 1632

4520 Zincgrefii Centuria Emblematum Ethico-Politicorum, *plates*, *Heidel.* 1681

4521 Zingis, a Tartarian History, - - 1692

4522 Zuallardo, Il Devotissimo Viaggio di Gierusalemme, *maps and plates*, *Venetian morocco*, - *Roma*, 1595

4523 Zwinglys (Bisshoppe of Zuryk) Rekening and Declaration of his Faith and Belief sent to Charles V. that nowe is Emprowr of Rome, *black letter*, *blue morocco*, *Imprinted at Zuryk*, 1543

4524 HEARNE. T. Livii Foro-Juliensis Vita Henrici Quinti, LARGE PAPER, *russia*, - - *Oxon*. 1716

4525 ——— Textus Roffensis, LARGE PAPER, *russia*, *Oxon*. 1720

4526 ——— Collection of Antiquarian Discourses, LARGE PAPER, *red morocco*, - - *Oxford*, 1720

4527 ——— Antiquities of Glastonbury, LARGE PAPER, *russia*, - - *Oxford*, 1722

4528 ——— Robert of Gloucester's Chronicle, 2 vol. LARGE PAPER, *russia*, - - *Oxford*, 1724

4529 ——— Peter Langtoft's Chronicle, 2 vol. LARGE PAPER, *russia*, - - *Oxford*, 1725

4530 Liber Niger Scaccarii, 2 vol. LARGE PAPER, UNCUT, *Londini*, 1774

4531 Herbolario Volgare della virtu delle Herbe, *wood cuts*, *green morocco*, *senza anno*.

4532 Memoires de Brantome, 2 vol. *Venetian morocco*, *Leide*, 1666

4533 Les Characters des Passions par Sr. de la Chambre, *Venetian morocco*, - - *Amst*. 1658

4534 Il Cardinalismo di Santa Chiesa, 3 vol. *blue morocco*, 1668

4535 Lettres Choisies du Balzac, *blue morocco*, *Elzev*. 1652

4536 Virgilio Eneide, del Annibal Caro, *Venetian morocco*, *Padova*, 1609

4537 A Bundle of Odd Volumes of Magazines, &c. ———

4538 Æschines, et Demosthenes, - - *Oxon*. 1695

4539 Æschyli Tragœdiæ, - - 1809

4540 Agricultural Reports of Eighteen Counties, 18 vol. 1798

5541 Andrews's Anecdotes, - - - 1790

4542 Barry's Sermons, Finch's Bampton Lectures, Bryant on the Scriptures, and 10 more.

4543 Bath Guide, (The New), - - 1807

4544 Another Copy, and Heroick Epistle to Sir W. Chambers, 1805

4545 Bastille Remarques sur la, 1789. Bourn's Gazetteer, 1807, and 4 more.

4546 British Martial, 2 vol. 1806. Encyclopædia of Wit, and 3 more.

4547 Cavallo on Balloons, 1785. Catalogue of the Leverian Museum.

4548 Classical Journal, 7 numbers, - - 1810, &c.

£	s.	d.	Lot	Description	Buyer
	4	-	4549	Dictionary of Quotations, Chapman on Education, Gregory's Legacy, and 4 more.	Triphook
	2	-	4550	Farmer's Guide, 2 vol. 1770. Lee on Botany, 1788. ——	John
	6	-	4551	Faublas par Louvet de Couvray, 8 vol. - 1790	Triphook
	1	-	4552	Ferguson's Lectures, 1776. Ferguson on Electricity, 1778	John
	8	-	4553	Florian, Œuvres de, 8 vol. - *Leipsic*, 1796	Triphook
	7	-	4554	Goldsmith's History of England, 3 vol. - 1790	Barclay
	1	-	4555	Histoire de France sous Louis XI. 2 vol. and 5 more. ——	John
	8	-	4556	Homeri Ilias a Clarke, 2 vol. - - 1774	Evans
	1	-	4557	Horace, translated by Francis, 4 vol. - 1778	Triphook
	1	-	4558	Jenyn's Disquisitions and Evidence of the Christian Religion, 2 vol. - - - 1782	Do.
	8	-	4559	Johnson's Rambler, 4 vol. 1784. Johnson's Table Talk, 1798. Remarks on Johnson's Life of Milton, 1780.	Do.
	1	-	4560	Junius's Letters, 2 vol. - - 1783	Michael
	1	-	4561	Lymington and Margate Guides, and 2 more. ——	Triphook
	1	-	4562	Maclaurin's Algebra, 1772. Maskelyne's Answer to Mudge, 1792. Pinkerton's Medals.	John
	2	-	4563	Melville's Trial, and 2 more. ——	Michael
	3	-	4564	Miseries of Human Life, and 3 more. ——	Triphook
	1	-	4565	More's Sacred Dramas, 1782. Mason on Self Knowledge, 1797.	Michael
1	17	-	4566	Nouvelles et Romans par Madame Cottin, Genlis, &c. 36 vol. *sewed.*	Freeling
	5	-	4567	—————— Betsi, 2 vol. Camille, 2 vol. Clementine. La Campagne, 2 vol. Le Jeune Sauvage. Together 8 vol. *half bound.*	Triphook
	5	-	4568	—————— Lettres de Sophie, 2 vol. La Laideur Aimable, 2 vol. Malheurs de l'Inconstance, 2 vol. Rosalie, 2 vol. Victorine, 2 vol. 10 vol. *half bound.*	Do.
	10	-	4569	Novels and Romances. Angelo Guicciardini, 4 vol. Castle Rackrent. Epics of the Ton. James the Fatalist, 3 vol. 9 vol.	Do.
	10	-	4570	—————— Destination, 3 vols. Raymond, 2 vol. Three Monks, 2 vol. Infidel Father, 3 vol. Castle of Dunbayne, 11 vol.	Do.
	17	-	4571	—————— The Nun, 2 vol. Rimualdo, 3 vol, Infernal Quixote, 4 vol. Wife and Mistress, 4 vol. 13 vol.	Do.
	19	-	4572	—————— Arthur Fitz Albini, 2 vol. Columella, 2 vol. Days of Chivalry, 2 vol. Bravo of Venice. Mystery of the Black Tower. 8 vol.	Natton
1	10	-	4573	—————— Ellinor, 4 vol. Gondez the Monk, 4 vol. Zofloya, or the Moor, 3 vol. 11 vol.	Triphook
	15	-	4574	—————— Farmer of Inglewood Forest, 4 vol. The Genius. Inquisition. Philosophical Quixote, 2 vol. 8 vol.	Do.
1	10	-	4575	—————— Ferney Castle, 4 vol. Laura, 4 vol. The Libertine, 2 vol. Santa Maria, 3 vol. 13 vol.	Do.
	14	-	4576	Oulton's Traveller's Guide, 2 vol. - 1805	Christie

£	s.	d.	Lot	Description	Buyer
	5	-	4577	Pizarro, and 4 vols. of Plays.	John
	2	-	4578	Prior's Poems, 2 vol 1779 Rannie's Poems, 1791.	Triphook
	2	-	4579	Regimental Companion, 3 vol. and 6 more.	Dickenson
	7	-	4580	Watts on the Improvement of the Mind, 2 vol. and 3 more.	Christie
	1	-	4581	Williams's (H. M.) Letters, 3 vol. and 4 more.	Do.
11	11	-	113	Anderson's House of Yvery, 2 vol. *red morocco, wants one portrait,* (that of Sir J. Percival) - - 1742	Triphook
	1	-	171	Archy's Dream, *imperfect,* - 1641	Do.

Quarto.

£	s.	d.	Lot	Description	Buyer
	16	-	4582	Vega Carpio, (Lope de), La Filomena con otras diversas Rimas, Prosas y Versas, - *Madrid,* 1621	Rodd
3	13	6	4583	Vera (Juan Antonio de) El Fernando o Sevilla Restaurada, Poema Heroico, *plates, fine copy, elegantly bound in Venetian morocco, by Roger Payne, Milan,* 1632	Triphook
1	1	-	4584	Verdizotti, Cento Favole Morali, *cuts after Titian's designs, Venetia,* 1570	Do.
1	15	-	4585	Verstegan's Restitution of Decayed Intelligence, *russia, Antwerp,* 1605	Boyce
	11	-	4586	Vicars's England's Parliamentary Chronicle, *russia,* 1644	Triphook
1	16	-	4587	Vicars's Mischeefes Mysterie, or Treason's Master-piece, the Powder Plot, *first edition, scarce,* - 1617	Freeling
	1	-	4588	Victoris de Larben Propugnaculum Fidei Christiane, *sine ulla nota.*	Payne
2	15	-	4589	Vienna, wherein is storied the valorous Atchievements, Famous Triumphs, constant Love, &c. of the Valiant Knight Sir Paris of Vienna, and of the Faire Vienna, *frontispiece, London, no date.*	Freeling
1	10	-	4590	Vigne (De la), Sensuyvent les Epitaphes et complaintes du dict seigneur pour lors faictes et composez par le dict de la Vigne, *black letter, wood cuts, yellow morocco, sans date.*	Heber
1	2	-	4591	Villa nova, Regimen Sanitatis Salernitatum, *green morocco, with joints,* - *Impressus Bisantie,* 1487	Gaskoin
4	4	-	4592	Villani. Le Storie di Matteo e Giovanni Villani, 2 vol. *red morocco,* - *Fiorenza Giunta,* 1581-87	Clarke
2	-	-	4593	Virgil's Bucolicks and Georgicks, with an English Translation and Notes by Martyn, 2 vol. *plates,* 1749	Barclay
4	4	-	4594	Virgille. Les Faitz merveilleux de Virgille, *black letter, red morocco,* - *Paris, J. Trepperel, sans date.*	Triphook
29	8	-	4595	Virgilius. This Boke treath of the Lyfe of Virgilius, and of his Deth, and many Marvayles that he dyd in his Lyfe Tyme by Whychcraft and Nygramansy throwgh the helpe of the Devyls of Hell, *black letter, wood cuts,* EXTREMELY RARE, ANWARPE BY ME JOHN DOESBORCKE, *no date.*	Do.
1	7	-	4596	Vives' Instruction of a Christen Women, tourned out of Latyne by R. Hyrde, *black letter,* *H. Wykes,*	Rodd

4597 Voilleret, Le Preau des Fleurs Meslées, *red morocc, Londres, chez W. S. sans date*

4598 Volckman Philosophia Peripatetica Austriacorum Cæsarum Symbolis adumbrata, *blue morocco, with joints, Pragæ*, 1673

4599 Voorhof der Ziele, Hoogstratens, *fine impressions of the plates*, - - - - *Rotterdam*, 1668

4600 Vox Borealis, or the Northern Discoverie, *Printed by Margery Mar-Prelat*, 1641

4601 Vox Populi, or Newes from Spayne, translated according to the Spanish Coppie, both Parts, the Second with Plates, - - - 1620-24

4602 Wakfeldi (Roberti) Oratio de Laudibus et utilitate trium Linguarum Arabicæ, Chaldaicæ et Hebraicæ, *inlaid, red morocco, with joints*, RARE, *Londini apud Winandum de Worde, sine anno.*

4603 Walton's Lives, edited by Zouch, *large paper, blue morocco, with joints*, - - *York*, 1796

4604 Warner's Syrinx, or a Seavenfold Historie, handled with varietie of pleasant and profitable Arguments, *black letter*, RARE, - - *T. Purfoot*, 1597

4605 Warre, The Free Schoole of, or a Treatise whether it be lawful to beare Armes for the Service of a Prince that is of a Divers Religion, - *J. Bill*, 1625
R. Twysden's Copy, with his Manuscript Notes.

4606 Warren's Pleasant New Fancie of a Fondling's Device, entitled and cald the Nurcerie of Names, VERY RARE, *Richard Jhones*, 1581

4607 Warton's History of English Poetry, 3 vol. - 1775

4608 WEBBE'S DISCOURSE OF ENGLISH POETRIE, together with the Author's Judgment, touching the Reformation of our English Verse, EXTREMELY RARE, *from the Roxburghe Collection, russia, John Charlewood*, 1586

4609 Western Wonder, or O Brazeel, an Inchanted Island Discovered, *green morocco*, - - 1674

4610 Whitney's Choice Emblemes and other Devises, *fine copy, russia, with joints*, RARE, *Leyden, Plantyn*, 1586

4611 Wickliffe's Two short Treatises against the Orders of the Begging Friars. An Apology for John Wickliffe, by Thomas James, Keeper of the Bodleian Library, 2 vol. in 1, *blue morocco, with joints*, - *Oxford*, 1608

4612 Wilkinson's General Atlas, coloured, - 1794

4613 Willis's Time's Whirligig, or the Blue-new-made Gentleman mounted, - - - 1647

4614 Wilson's Arte of Rhetorike, *black letter*, *J. Kingston*, 1567

4615 Wilson's History of the British Expedition to Egypt, 1803

4616 Wine, a Satyr against, with a Poem in Praise of Small Beer. Sylvia's Revenge, or a Satyr against Man, 1707

4617 Wit's Miserie and the World's Madnesse, *black letter*, *Adam Islip*, 1596

4618 Witchcraft. The Wonderful Discoverie of the Witchcrafts of Margaret and Phillip Flower, executed at Lincolne, March 11, 1618, *inlaid, blue morocco*, - 1618

4619 Women, an Apologie for, by W. Heale, *Oxford*, 1609

4620 Women. This Boke is named the Beaulte of Women, translated out of Frenche in to Englysshe, *wood cuts, fine copy, morocco*, VERY RARE, *Robert Wyer, no date.*

4621 Wood's Athenæ Oxonienses, by Bliss, vol. 1, LARGE PAPER, - - - - 1813

4622 Woodville's Medical Botany, 4 vol. *coloured plates*, 1790

4623 World (The) Turn'd Upside Down, - 1647

4624 Woyten's Emblemata *blue morocco, with joints, Aug.* 1727

4625 Wright's Detection of Errors in Navigation, *blue morocco*, *V. Sims*, 1599

4626 Wyrley's True Use of Armorie, to which is added a Poem, entitled the Glorious Life and Honorable Death of Sir John Chandos, &c. *scarce*, *J. Cawood*, 1592

4627 Xenophontis de Cyri Institutione Libri octo cura Hutchinson, *russia*, - - *Oxon.* 1727

4628 Yarranton's England's Improvement by Sea and Land, *maps*, - - - - - 1677

4629 Yarington's Two Lamentable Tragedies—one, The Murther of Maister Beech, a Chaundler in Thames Street—the other, of a Young Child Murthered in a Wood by two Ruffins, *morocco, scarce*, - 1601

4630 Yorke's Royall Tribes of Wales, *blue morocco*, *Wrexham*, 1799

4631 Ysidorus de Summo Bono, *Lovanii J. de Westph.* 1486

4632 Zayas y Sotomayor, Novelas Amorosas de, *Madrid*, 1659

4633 Zettre, Emblemes Nouveaux, *fine impressions, green morocco*, - - - *Francof.* 1617

4634 Zincgrefii Emblematum Ethico-Politicorum Centuria, *green morocco, with joints*, - *Francfurti*, 1624

4635 Zouch's Life of Sir Philip Sidney, *boards*, 1808

4636 Camden's Remains concerning Britain, *portrait*, 1637

4637 Campbell's Pleasures of Hope, - 1803

4638 Communications to the Board of Agriculture, 2 vol. in 3, 1797. &c.

4639 Geraldson's Addition to the Sea Journal of the Hollanders unto Java, *plates*. - *John Wolfe*, 1598

4640 Le Miserie de li Amanti di Messer Nobile Socio, *splendidly bound in Venetian morocco*, *Vinegia*, 1533

4641 Fennor's Descriptions, or a True Relation of Speeches, &c. in verse, *red morocco*, - - 1616

4642 La Faulcete Trayson, et les Tours de ceulx qui suivent le Train d'Amours, *black letter, russia, scarce*, *sans date.*

4643 The Female Advocate, or an Answer to a late Satyr against Woman, - - - - 1686

4644 De Historie van Doctor Faustus, *cuts*, - - 1764

4645 Tales and Quicke Answeres, very mery and pleasant to rede, EXTREMELY RARE, *morocco*, *no date.*

This volume was re-printed under the Title of Shakspeare's Jest Book.

4646 Vattel Le Droit des Gens ou Principes de la Loi Naturelle, 2 vol. in 1, - - - - *Neufchatel*, 1777

Folio.

4647 Voragine (Jacobi de) Liber de Vitis Sanctorum, *Venet. per Ch. Arnoldum*, 1477

4648 Voyage Pittoresque de la Suisse, par La Borde, 4 vol. *first impressions of the plates, elegantly bound in blue morocco, with joints*, - - *Paris*, 1780

4649 Walpole's Catalogue of Royal and Noble Authors, 2 vol. 12mo. inlaid in large folio, ILLUSTRATED WITH NUMEROUS PORTRAITS, *elegantly bound in red morocco.*

4650 Weigelii Habitus Præcipuorum Populorum tam Virorum quam Fœminarum, - - *Ulm.* 1639

Two hundred and nineteen Prints, very fine impressions, mounted on large writing paper, *bound in red morocco, with joints.*

4651 WIERIX. A Collection of Engravings by John Jerome and Anthony Wierix, in 3 vol. with Title Pages and Indexes beautifully written, the Prints mounted on fine Drawing Paper, and superbly bound in green morocco, with joints.

The Three Volumes contain FOUR HUNDRTD AND THIRTY-NINE ENGRAVINGS, VERY FINE IMPRESSIONS, of the Works of these celebrated Masters.

4652 Willdenow, Historia Amaranthorum, *coloured plates*, *Turici*, 1798

4653 Wood's Athenæ Oxonienses, 2 vol. in 1, - 1721

4654 Xenophontis, Cyri Expeditio in Latinum traducta a Poggio Florentino. A Manuscript of the Fifteenth Century, upon vellum, with illuminated capitals, *red morocco.*

4655 York, Minutes of Evidence on the Conduct of the Duke of, 1809

4656 Ysaie le Triste, fils de Tristan de Leonnois, et de la royne Izeut de Cornouaille, *black letter, red morocco*, RARE, *Paris, pour Galliot du Pré*, 1522

£	s.	d.	Lot	Description	Buyer
3	13	6	4657	Zamorensis, (Roderici Episc.) Speculum Vitæ humanæ, *first edition, Sweynheym et Pannartz, Romæ, in domo Petri de Maximis* - - 1468	Triphook
1	4	-	4658	Alia Editio, - *Zainer de Reutlingen*, 1471	Do.
2	3	-	4659	Zoega De Origine et usu Obeliscorum, *russia, Romæ*, 1797	Cochran
4	4	-	4660	Zompini. Le Arti che vanno per via nella Citta di Venezia, inventate ed incise da Gaetano Zompini, *plates, russia,* with English description . . *Venezia*, 1785	Calkin
1	1	-	4661	Ordonnances Royaulx de la Jurisdicion, etc. de la Ville de Paris, *wood cuts, morocco,* - *Paris*, 1528	Triphook
3	3	-	4662	The Chroniclis of St. Alban, VERY RARE, *but imperfect*, 1483	Do.
34	13	-	4663	LUCRETII CARMINA, JOHANNES RAINALDUS MENNIUS EXSCRIPSIT. A very beautiful Italian Manuscript of the Fifteenth Century, upon vellum. The Initial Letters and Capitals are exquisitely illuminated in gold and colours. Manuscripts of this Author are of VERY RARE OCCURRENCE.	Payne
17	-	-	4663*	Catalogus Librorum ante 1500 impress. in Bibliotheca Marlburiensi, MS.	Triphook

Music.

£	s.	d.	Lot	Description	Buyer
-	-	-	4664	The Life, Death, and Burial of Cock Robin, set to Music by the Marquess of Blandford, *red morocco.*	withdrawn
			4665	XII. Divertimenti per Cembalo con Accompagnamento di Violino, Corni e Tympani, Composti dal Marchese di Blandford, 1790 (Violino Primo e Basso), *blue morocco,*	
1	11	6	4666	The same (Violino Secondo), *blue morocco.*	Triphook
			4667	The same (Corno Primo e Secondo), *blue morocco.*	
			4668	The same (Tympani), *blue morocco.*	
	14	-	4669	Twelve Glees, Ten for three Voices, and Two for four Voices, composed by the Marquis of Blandford, 1798, *green morocco.*	Do
1	3	-	4670	Another copy, *red morocco.*	Do.
	6	-	4671	"Say Myra why is gentle Love," set to Music by the Marquis of Blandford.	Do.
	6	-	4672	Another copy.	Do
	6	-	4673	Another copy.	Laing
	6	-	4674	Another copy.	Freeling
	5	-	4675	Another copy.	Triphook
	10	-	4676	Two copies.	Natton
	9	-	4677	Two copies.	West
	7	-	4678	Fanny Glendore, a celebrated Welsh Beauty of the Thirteenth Century. The Words and Music composed by the Marquis of Blandford, 1815.	Wyatt
	6	-	4679	Another copy.	Triphook

£	s.	d.	Lot	Description	Buyer
	7	-	4680	Fanny Glendore, - - - 1815	Edwards
	13	-	4681	Two copies.	Freeling
	5	-	4682	Two copies.	Heber
2	7	-	4683	Eighteen Sonatine per il Cembalo, composte dal Signor Marchese di Blandford, *half bound in morocco.*	Payne
	5	-	4684	Twelve Valtzers composed by the Marquis of Blandford, Two Series.	Freeling
	5	-	4685	Another set.	Laing
	5	-	4686	Another set.	Natton
	6	-	4687	Another set.	Prest
	7	-	4688	Two of the same.	Triphook
	6	-	4689	Two do.	Do.
	6	-	4690	Two do.	Dunbar
	1	-	4691	Six Valtzers, First Series.	Prest
8		-	4692	The Gipsey's Song,—La plus Jolie.—If then to Love thee be offence,—Three Songs set to Music, by the Marquis of Blandford, with THREE PRINTS, engraved by Agar, from Drawings by Cosway. La Plus Jolie, with the Portrait sold in Dr Callcott's Sale for 12.12.-	Booth
7	7	-	4693	Another copy, with the same prints.	Triphook for W. T. Esq
23	12	6	4694	A Volume of Manuscript French Songs, with the Music, with flourished borders representing persons playing on different sorts of Instruments, Grotesques, &c. the whole executed in a very superior style of Penmanship, *bound in russia, with joints.*	Do. Do.
1	10	-	4695	"Happy Isle," composed by the Marquis of Blandford, *green morocco.*	Do.
-	-	-	4696	Sei Arie, composte dal Marchese di Blandford, *red morocco,* 1791	Withdrawn

£	s.	d.	Lot	Description	Buyer
	4	-	4697	Franklin's Annals of King James and Charles I. folio, 1681	Booth
11	-	-	4698	History of Wales translated by Lloyd, 4to. *fine copy, red velvet,* - - R. Newberie.	Higgs
	11	-	4699	Catalogue of the Paris Library, 8vo. *priced,* - 1791	Booth
	11	-	4700	Salustio per Carani tradotto, 12mo. *morocco, Fiorenz.* 1550	Triphook
	4	-	4701	Juvenal's Satyres, by Stapylton, fol. - 1660	Wyatt

£	s.	d.	Lot	Description	Buyer
	6	-	101	Amoureux Repos de Guillaume des Autelz, *imperfect,* 1553	Dunbar
4	-	-	285	Old Ballads, 3 vol. vol. 2 *imperfect,* - 1723	Edwards

London: Printed by W. Bulmer and Co.
Cleveland-row, St. James's.